THOMAS BARNES
OF FARNWORTH
AND THE QUINTA

Thomas Barnes
of Farnworth and The Quinta

A Chronicle of a Life

1812–1897

JENNIFER BARNES

Quinta Press

Quinta Press, Meadow View, Weston Rhyn,
Oswestry, Shropshire, England, SY10 7RN

www.quintapress.com

ISBN   978–1–897856–34–5 (paperback)
         978–1–897856–35–2 (hardback)

Acknowledgements

I would like to thank all the people who have helped me to produce this book, patiently accompanying me on my many excursions in search of information, and reading through and checking the typed work. In particular, I am very grateful to Brian Roberts of Oswestry who over the years has shared so much of his material about Thomas Barnes at The Quinta and Weston Rhyn and encouraged my research, and to Dr Digby James, not only for giving me a guided tour of the Quinta Church and the Quinta Schools when my book was in its very early stage of development, but also for offering to publish it for me.

I also want to thank the descendants of James Freeland Barnes and Dennis Wilberfosse Barnes who supplied so much information about the family and cheerfully agreed to my delving into their family history.

Thanks also to Caroline Furey and the Staff at Bolton Archives and Local Studies, to the Staff at the Lancashire Record Office in Preston, and to the Librarians in Farnworth and Oswestry Libraries, all of whom have made my search for information so much easier.

Bolton Archives has given permission to use the material from their archive collection together with the copies of the photographs of Thomas Barnes and his wife, his son James Richardson Barnes and his wife, the early drawing of Farnworth Mills, and the picture of the Opening of Farnworth Park, all of which are Copyright of Bolton Council from the Bolton Museum and Archive Collection.

I have permission from the Lancashire Record Office to use the letters from the Barnes Family and material from the records of Queen Street Seminary in Farnworth, from Manchester Archives to use the letter from Thomas Barnes accepting the invitation to the Opening of Manchester Town Hall and from West Sussex Record Office for the material from their collection of Cobden's letters. Through Cengage Learning I have been given permission to use the material from Gale's online collection of 19th Century newspapers from the British Library which I have been able to access through my local library's online archives.

CONTENTS

Photographs and Illustrations

The Family Tree of
Thomas Barnes born in Farnworth in 1812

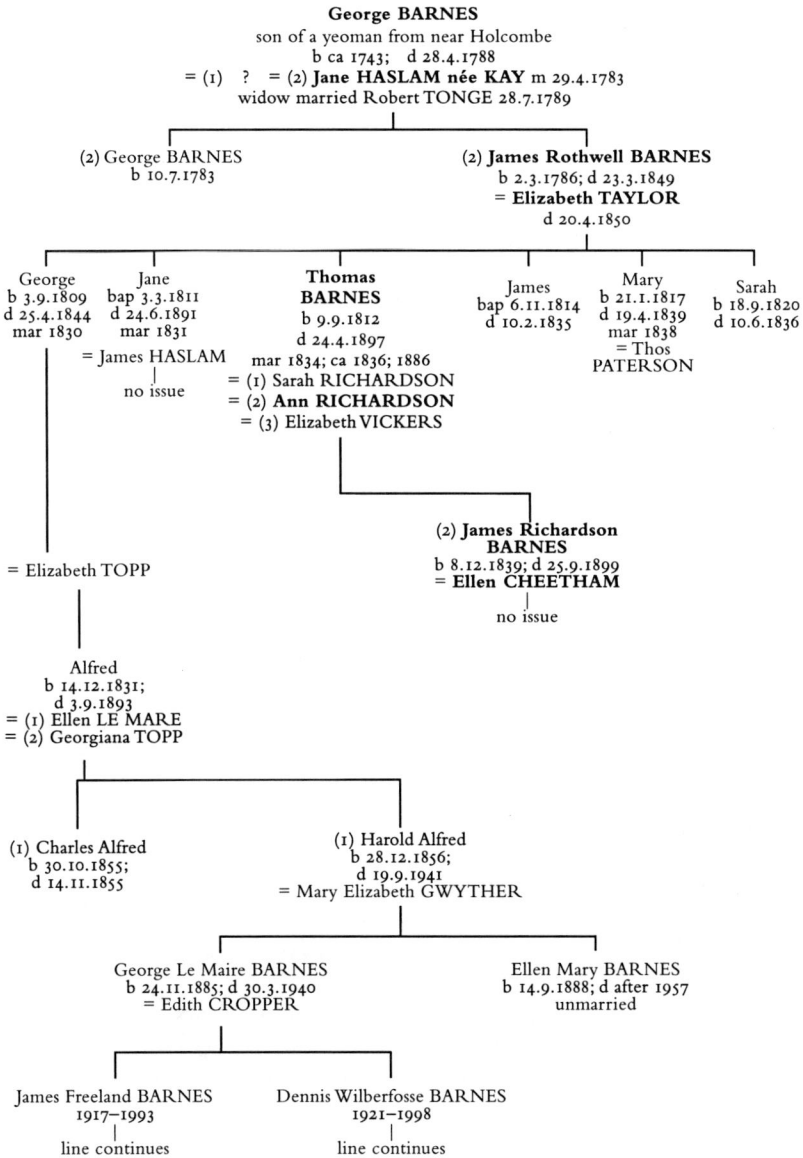

George BARNES
son of a yeoman from near Holcombe
b ca 1743;   d 28.4.1788
= (1)   ?   = (2) **Jane HASLAM née KAY** m 29.4.1783
widow married Robert TONGE 28.7.1789

(2) George BARNES
b 10.7.1783

(2) **James Rothwell BARNES**
b 2.3.1786; d 23.3.1849
= **Elizabeth TAYLOR**
d 20.4.1850

George
b 3.9.1809
d 25.4.1844
mar 1830

Jane
bap 3.3.1811
d 24.6.1891
mar 1831
= James HASLAM
|
no issue

**Thomas
BARNES**
b 9.9.1812
d 24.4.1897
mar 1834; ca 1836; 1886
= (1) Sarah RICHARDSON
= (2) **Ann RICHARDSON**
= (3) Elizabeth VICKERS

James
bap 6.11.1814
d 10.2.1835

Mary
b 21.1.1817
d 19.4.1839
mar 1838
= Thos
PATERSON

Sarah
b 18.9.1820
d 10.6.1836

(2) **James Richardson
BARNES**
b 8.12.1839; d 25.9.1899
= **Ellen CHEETHAM**
|
no issue

= Elizabeth TOPP
|

Alfred
b 14.12.1831;
d 3.9.1893
= (1) Ellen LE MARE
= (2) Georgiana TOPP

(1) Charles Alfred
b 30.10.1855;
d 14.11.1855

(1) Harold Alfred
b 28.12.1856;
d 19.9.1941
= Mary Elizabeth GWYTHER

George Le Maire BARNES
b 24.11.1885; d 30.3.1940
= Edith CROPPER

Ellen Mary BARNES
b 14.9.1888; d after 1957
unmarried

James Freeland BARNES
1917–1993
|
line continues

Dennis Wilberfosse BARNES
1921–1998
|
line continues

Thomas Barnes as a young man

Foreword

This book is the result of being sidetracked whilst researching my own family history in Lancashire in the Bolton and Farnworth area. My father's mother began her working life in 1891 at the age of ten as a half-timer at a cotton mill in Farnworth and attended Queen Street Seminary on school days. The mill was Barnes's Glynne Street Mill and the school, I discovered, had originally been founded by the Barnes family and others. Twenty years later my grandmother married into a local Barnes family. I had to discover whether my working-class Barnes family was related in any way to this prosperous middle-class Barnes family who had brought the cotton industry to Farnworth at the beginning of the nineteenth century. I soon discovered a fascinating story of a family whose life was closely linked to many of the most significant people and events over two and a half centuries, not only in Lancashire but also across the world. The story of Thomas Barnes covers the period when the family was, perhaps, at the peak of its success. It is a story set against the background of Regency and Victorian Britain amongst the grime and bustle of the Lancashire cotton mills, the world of Gladstone and Liberal politicians in Manchester and Westminster, the fervour of Nonconformist chapels, the tranquillity of country life on a large estate straddling the Welsh border between Shropshire and Denbighshire, a world which included railway companies, insurance companies, banks and coal mines. For a short time it even encompassed a cotton plantation in Jamaica.

I collected so much information that it was difficult to know how to present it. Most of my sources have been secondary sources such as newspaper reports and printed books. Early writers about Farnworth acknowledged the importance of the family to Farnworth, sometimes even dedicating their book to Thomas Barnes. They summed up his achievements but rarely gave details. His great-nephew, Harold Alfred Barnes, wrote about his role in the Congregational Church and added a few comments about him as a man but I have only a handful of letters written by Thomas himself, and only two of these are private letters to family members. Because the actual running of the mills in Farnworth had to be put into the hands of the mill managers, Thomas does not appear to spend as much time running his business as he undoubtedly did. I have not found much material about what went on in the mills but have included snippets throughout the story as a reminder that this was his main source of income and was where his roots remained. The same is also true but to a lesser extent of the Quinta estate where Thomas employed an estate agent and various other managers but I have found more references in the local papers to what went on there. His political life was well-documented in the press and many of his public speeches were reported in local and national newspapers. Where I have used these I have either quoted directly from the newspaper report (slightly modernizing some punctuation and a few spellings) or have incorporated the style into my own writing to give a flavour of Thomas's own style. The result is that the picture which emerges is dominated by the public formal side of the man but I hope that the private man can be glimpsed between the lines. It is through what he did that the true picture emerges.

I have decided to set the book out as a chronicle and have left it to the reader to follow the interweaving strands of his life except for six topics where I have found it easier to group the information over a span of years. So many dates and even days of the week have been included intentionally to indicate how hectic his life was, especially in the years when he was a member of Parliament. This was the age of the railway—Thomas not only ran a railway, he also used it.

One thing must be kept in mind whilst following his daily activities. Thomas did all this despite having lost one foot in an accident before even starting out on his career. I have recorded the details of the accident but have not mentioned it again because Thomas never did, either. Only once when speaking about quite a different topic did he say: "People don't know what they can do until they try. As long as people walk upon crutches, they never will walk without them."[1] That certainly was one of the guiding principles of his life.

I know that this is an incomplete study but even so, it represents only a fraction of the material that I have amassed. I hope that the reader, like me, will want to find out more. I have discovered so much including one thing that I should have known all along—that my Barnes family is not related in any way to the mill-owning Barnes family of Farnworth. My grandmother never mentioned anyone without giving a potted history of their antecedents. She would have known if she had married into the family of her former employer!

Jennifer Barnes
2012

Note

[1] *Bolton Chronicle* 23.1.1868 [Bolton Archives and Social Studies]

Introduction

Thomas Barnes was born into an age of social and political change. Many wars began and ended during his lifetime. On the one hand, England at the time of his birth was the world of Regency elegance but on the other hand, it was also the world of the Industrial Revolution which was drawing impoverished agricultural workers to the factories in towns like Bolton. 1812 was still in the canal age, still part of the age of sailing boats and three years before the first steamer crossed the Atlantic, still in the age of stage coaches, horses and carriages, of illiteracy amongst the working classes. It was a world of turnpike roads, apprenticeships, disputes over parish responsibilities for paupers without settlement orders. In 1811 George III's mental state had deteriorated to such an extent that, in the 52nd year of his reign, he had had to hand over to his son George to rule as Prince Regent. Social unrest was all too evident. People were afraid of an invasion by the French at any moment, and the cost of equipping the army and the loss of trade with the Continent were having an effect, not only on the wealthy who had to pay higher taxes, but also on the poor who had to pay more for their food. The Luddites rebelled in 1811 and 1812, fearing the threat to their jobs from increasing mechanization.

All this was bringing moves to change society. When the French Revolution began in 1789 it had been welcomed by many but feared by others as a possible incentive to the working people in Britain, too, to rebel. After the French Revolution allowed Napoleon to take over as a dictator, public opinion in Britain, especially amongst the upper classes, turned against the original aims of the revolutionaries and the Combination Acts imposed strict restrictions on working people congregating. However, society was changing. In 1807 William Wilberforce had managed to end the British involvement in the slave trade and it became an offence for British subjects to take part in the capture and transport of slaves. In 1812 Elizabeth Fry began her campaign for prison reform. Demands for Parliamentary Reform were already being heard. Dissenting voices were being raised in religion. Already

Wesleyan Methodism had found many followers, particularly amongst the working classes.

At the other end of the social scale, this was also a world where the Marchioness of Salisbury was planning an extravagant birthday party at Hatfield, Vauxhall Gardens were about to close for the season with a Grand Fête and fireworks, and the Theatre Royal at Covent Garden was preparing to stage The Beggar's Opera. This was the Regency Age in which Jane Austen had just completed her "Sense and Sensibility" and Byron his "Childe Harold". Sir Walter Scott was writing his novels, Coleridge, Keats, Shelley and Wordsworth their poetry.

This was the situation at the time of Thomas's birth in 1812. A snapshot from the daily papers on 9 September, the day he was born, shows Napoleon Bonaparte's troops in Russia just about to enter Moscow, news from the Peninsular Wars about Wellington fighting in Spain and Joseph Bonaparte, the King of Spain, fighting in Portugal, skirmishes in the English Channel resulting from the blockade set up by Napoleon from Boulogne to destroy British trade, and on the other side of the world, partly as a result of the British counter-action for this blockade, fighting on the American-Canadian frontier along the St Lawrence river.[1] Three years earlier, in 1809, Abraham Lincoln, Charles Darwin and William Ewart Gladstone had been born. Both Thomas Barnes and Gladstone were born in the rapidly expanding areas of Lancashire, Thomas in Farnworth close to the cotton-producing town of Bolton and Gladstone in Liverpool, the port which imported the raw cotton. Both were sons of fathers involved in the cotton industry. However, Gladstone's father was already prosperous and able to have his son educated at Eton and then at Oxford University, so that he could enter politics as a Tory MP when he was only 23 years old. Thomas Barnes did not come from a privileged background. With no family to support him and with no inherited wealth or property, his father was still struggling to support his family when Thomas, his third child, was born. He had only recently managed to build a small cottage next to the public house where he had been brought up. He now also had a small shed where he had just started to employ some of the handloom weavers who until then had been working for him in their own homes. In 1812 he was still running the business practically single-handed and life was a struggle for the family. Nevertheless, Thomas did receive some early education from the Congregational minister's wife at Halshaw Moor. He then walked to school in Bolton until he was 14 years old when he had to leave school to help his older brother and father in the family business. Thomas's working life in these early days must have followed the same pattern as his father's except that when the business began to prosper a little he was based in the warehouse in Manchester. However, he managed, like Gladstone, to enter politics as an MP but not until 1852 when he was already 40 years old. Gladstone soon left his Tory politics behind and switched his allegiance to the Liberals who were demanding reform of the Parliamentary system. Thomas Barnes never had to make this switch. From the start he supported the Liberal cause and even before becoming a Liberal MP had been an active member of the group which included men like Richard Cobden and John Bright and which came to be known as The Manchester Men.

In Thomas Barnes's early life there were few, if any, of the luxuries of the Regency upper classes. His middle class world was much closer to the working classes with their roots in agricultural life. His aunts visited to do the spring cleaning or to bottle the fruit from the garden. His brother was happy to share soup in the soup kitchen with the poor. When the family acquired a carriage it was not a grand affair and was only used to ferry travellers to the finger post in the village before they transferred to a stage coach in the early days or in later years to the railway station.[2] There was never any suggestion of going to the theatre or the opera or even of reading novels. Thomas, unlike his brother and his nephew, does not appear to have even read poetry. Charles Dickens was also born in 1812 but in his many speeches Thomas never made any reference to his novels. His reading matter was the factual matter found in the newspapers and political and economic documents. When forced to have two months confined to the house through illness he worked his way through Macaulay's histories.[3] And, of course, his other main source of reading matter was the Bible. Nor did light music play much part in his life. Brass bands and cornet quartets did accompany some celebrations and he attended song recitals at church and Sunday School events. He also was involved later in life with psalmody competitions and the Welsh eisteddfod but music did not play the important part in his life that it did in his son's and nephew's.

Thomas grew up in a family which was literate, mainly self-educated, and increasingly able to provide the trappings of middle-class life as they built new mills and the business expanded. His father moved from the small cottage to a larger house, Summerfield, and in the early 1850s Thomas copied his older brother George and built himself a house in Farnworth, Limefield. Eventually his father retired to Darley Hall in Farnworth where he spent his last few years leading the life of a gentleman. In the mid 1850s Thomas also acquired a large estate, The

Quinta, near Chirk on the Welsh Borders, whilst continuing to run Limefield in Farnworth. Even before train travel made journeys easier, the family began to travel further and further afield, to North Wales, the Lake District, to the South Coast, to Ireland, to Scotland, to the Rhineland and Paris. Soon Thomas was regularly travelling by train even as far as London on business trips. His son was educated in Birmingham and then at London University, following in the footsteps of his cousin Alfred who had been the first in this Barnes family to have a university education. Mainly through his links with Liberal politics, but also through his father's connections and then through his own business connections, Thomas came into contact with a wide range of influential people. By the mid 1860s he was managing to combine the life of a busy cotton manufacturer in Farnworth with the life of a country squire in Shropshire, spending long periods in Westminster as an MP, fulfilling all sorts of roles in church matters, championing the cause of popular education and dealing with the day-to-day affairs of his own school, Queen Street Seminary in Farnworth. Through his links with various cotton supply companies he had even acquired an estate in Jamaica where he was growing cotton in response to the need to find new sources of cotton. He had responsibilities as a Director of many companies—railway companies, banks, insurance companies. He was President of many associations ranging from horticultural societies to missionary societies, and made regular appearances at Liberal meetings.

Coupled with this were his strong Nonconformist beliefs and the world of Halshaw Moor Chapel which gave him an awareness of the working classes, a concern for the poor and a desire to improve their conditions, both at work and at home. He never lost his belief in the importance of education, but not an education determined by the state or any particular religious doctrine. Spreading the message of the Gospel was his creed and for this he supported the work of missionaries all his life. As his wealth increased he found more and more ways of using it to benefit others.

There was little time in the early days for anything but work. It was only when the mills were "stopped" for an annual overhaul that the family went on one of their short holidays. Even his holidays were often "busmen's holidays". He took his young nephew Alfred to Ireland to show him prisons, mental hospitals and the conditions of the poor as well as the scenery and the pleasures of fashionable spas.[4] Having grown up in the smoke and grime of Farnworth, Thomas did appreciate the beauty of Nature which was one of the main attractions of the area around The Quinta and was one of the reasons he donated the Park to Farnworth. Sunday was a day off work but was dominated by services at Chapel. When he was young, Sunday mornings in the unheated chapel must have been uncomfortable affairs. The women were said to have hidden heated bricks under their skirts to survive the chill.[5] The only festivities he attended were linked to the Chapel and the Sunday School. They were usually "teas" or sometimes fêtes. In the 1840s Thomas provided entertainment for his workers during the Christmas break—slides shown on a magic lantern, pep talks, music played on cornets and recitals of songs. But the evening did end with dancing which seemed to have been greatly enjoyed. Local dinners in Farnworth were to mark anniversaries of various kinds and were always all-men affairs, complete with after-dinner speeches. There were no Grand Balls of the sort described by Jane Austen. It was only after he moved to The Quinta and became accepted as one of the local gentry that Thomas began to attend dinners in grand houses and celebrations on a grand scale. When he celebrated his son's coming-of-age and when he laid on the lavish celebrations for the opening of Farnworth Park he was doing something new in Farnworth. Normally Thomas did not indulge in excesses. He was ready, however, to spend money when it was needed. For example, he gave generously to good causes and subscribed to many funds, especially funds for building chapels. He spent a large amount of money at The Quinta, not only on the new Hall, but also on improvements to the tenants' housing. He built a chapel there and maintained it to the day he died. He paid a large proportion of the cost of building the Quinta Schools. His only weaknesses seem to have been the money he spent on his hobby of horticulture. At The Quinta he employed at least two gardeners whose main job was looking after his exotic plants in the greenhouse and hot house and growing flowers, fruit and vegetables for him to show at local and national horticultural shows. He also seems to have enjoyed dabbling in farming and by the end of his life had made a name for himself as a cattle breeder.

Thomas was a "serious" man who associated with "serious" people. He kept his emotions firmly under control and refused to be roused to anger. He was a non-smoker and a very moderate drinker but was not a bigot. He was willing to let others smoke and drink but regretted the effect it might have on them. Even though he supported the temperance movement, he was not against all alcohol and did drink an occasional glass of wine and did have a brewery at The Quinta for his workmen and did entertain with beer, wine and spirits on special occasions. He was a strict father but rare glimpses of his compassion showed him to be a man of tender feelings.

Although his Liberal views placed him in a position where he was fighting for change, he was no revolutionary. Disputes were to be won through the strength of argument supported by detailed fact. Serious points were made more palatable by the use of humour, often down-to-earth and sometimes related in Lancashire dialect. He was a man of peace and always encouraged the Government to steer clear of war and to remain neutral if possible. He was a man of principle and to the end of his life remained true to the political causes he believed in when he entered politics. He believed in basic honesty and was shocked when there was a suggestion of a government policy to annul certain types of debt. To Thomas a debt was a debt and had to be repaid.

He was 84 years old when he died and the world was a very different place. While he was still a very young child the first steamer had crossed the Atlantic and twenty years after that, steamers were making the journey to India. The Suez Canal was opened in 1869. In 1815 before he was three years old the Napoleonic Wars came to an end with Napoleon's defeat by Wellington at the Battle of Waterloo. He lived through Napoleon's death in 1821 and became an MP a few months before Wellington's death in 1852. In his lifetime he saw the Prince Regent being crowned George IV in 1820, his death ten years later in 1830 after an unpopular reign, and the Coronation of the next King, William IV, whose reign was also short, lasting just seven years. Thomas lived through Queen Victoria's coronation in 1837, her marriage, and Prince Albert's death in 1861. When Thomas died in April 1897, the country was about to celebrate the Queen's Diamond Jubilee. He was born just as the Regency period began, and died in the late Victorian period when the British Empire was still expanding.

He saw slavery abolished throughout the British Empire in 1833 and in 1862 the freeing of slaves in America. He saw the birth of the railway age with the first railway between Stockton and Darlington in 1825, followed by the rapid expansion of the railway system. When the Napoleonic Wars ended in 1815 the price of bread was kept high by the passing of the Corn Laws and when the Anti-Corn Law League was founded in Manchester in 1838, he was one of its founding members. He was seven years old when the Peterloo Massacre took place in Manchester and seventeen when Peel formed the first Metropolitan Police force in 1829. He was thirteen when the University of London was founded, allowing Nonconformists to study for a degree. He saw a revolution in communications. In 1812 newspapers had to rely on official bulletins, letters and written reports for news of the various wars. Some of these from across the Channel were already a month out-of-date when they were reported in the newspapers, having had to travel overland and by sea. In 1837 Morse perfected the electric telegraph system, the telephone was invented in 1876 and in 1895 shortly before Thomas's death Marconi had invented wireless telegraphy.

He was alive when gold was found in California in 1847, in Australia in 1850 and on the Witwatersrand in the Transvaal in 1886. He saw the end of the East India Company in 1858. He experienced the Crimean War from 1854 to 1856, the outbreak of the American Civil War in 1861, the Franco-Prussian War in 1870 and the Congress of Berlin which ended it in 1878. Foreign leaders rose and fell—Kaiser Wilhelm I was in Prussia with Bismarck as his Chancellor, Lincoln in America. He saw the Boers in the Transvaal declare independence in 1879 and the First Boer War from 1880 to 1881. At the time of his death in 1897 the tension in the Transvaal and the Orange Free State was a warning of the approaching Second Boer War. He experienced the effects of the Cotton Famine in Lancashire at the time of the American Civil War. He became a member of the Jamaica Committee after the Morant Bay revolt in Jamaica in 1865 not far from his cotton plantation. He saw the development of India as the railways spread and more cotton was grown there. He was alive when Africa opened up and when Livingstone made his first journey in 1849. He saw the gradual improvement in the education of the masses and the introduction of compulsory education in 1870. He saw improved conditions in the factories as various Factory Acts became law. In his time Reform Bills opened up the franchise to a wider section of society, leading to a uniform county and borough franchise in 1884 which gave the vote to many more householders, lodgers and occupiers of houses. However, he did not live to see the extension of the vote to all men over the age of 21. That did not happen until 1918.

He witnessed the effects of Darwin's theory of the Origin of the Species, the political doctrines of Marx and Engels. He was born into a world where the home was lit by candlelight, saw this replaced by gaslights and then by electric lighting. He used iron to construct his railways and admired iron buildings like the Crystal Palace and Bolton's Market Hall. He saw huge developments in manufacturing processes such as Bessemer's and then Siemens' new steel processes and the great burst of inventions and manufactured items which were shown off at the 1851 Great Exhibition. He shared in the new movements in architecture led by men such as Pugin when he built his own new hall, church and Sunday School on the Quinta estate. If his early life was the Regency world of Jane Austen, his adult life was the world depicted by Charles Dickens. When he died in 1897 the first popular newspaper, *The Daily Mail*, was still in its first year. It was now the world of Tchaikovsky, Zola, Thomas Hardy, Ibsen, Kipling and Bernard Shaw. The Greco-Turkish War had just been declared and on the day he died, Saturday 24 April 1897, the town of Larissa had just been completely evacuated before falling to the Turks three days later.

Reading the advertisement section of *The Liverpool Mercury* published on the day he died gives a flavour of this new Lancashire just before Queen Victoria's Diamond Jubilee. From a flourishing commercial centre passenger ships were sailing to all parts of the world, to America, the West Indies, Canada, South America, India, China, Australia, the Mediterranean, as well as to ports around the British Isles. A wide range of goods was coming into Liverpool and being shipped out from there; there were reports on the cotton trade in Liverpool and Manchester, the dividends of public companies, railway traffic returns; telegrams reported on the whereabouts of a huge number of ships all around the world; column after column listed property auctions and sales, items for sale and wanted, jobs vacant and jobs wanted. In one man's lifetime, what changes had occurred!

Notes

1   *Liverpool Mercury;Morning Chronicle* [19th Century Newspapers online]
2   Lancashire Record Office (LRO) The British Records Association DDX 75/120
3   *Bolton Chronicle op. cit.* 31.1.1867 [Bolton Archives and Social Studies]
4   LRO DDX 75/124
5   B.T. Barton *History of Farnworth and Kersley* (pub. 1887, Bolton)

CHAPTER 1

1812–1845

The early years—the ups and downs and the start of everything

Farnworth at the beginning of the nineteenth century was a very different place from the highly industrialised town it was soon to become. In 1811 fewer than 2,000 people were living there, for the most part in small cottages spread across a largely rural area with five or six square miles of moorland. Some of these cottages lined the main street, Market Street, and others were alongside the road from Bolton

Thomas Barnes as a young man

to Manchester. Many, however, were along country lanes or set in fields and some even had their own small plots of land. This was Farnworth before the arrival of steam power. Any industry that did exist was mainly cottage-based hand spinning and hand weaving. Thomas Barnes was born here in the area called Halshaw Moor on 9 September 1812 in a small cottage on the Manchester road at the junction near Moses Gate. His father, James Rothwell Barnes, was the first person to bring the cotton industry to Farnworth but had not yet built up his huge spinning and weaving business. Soon after his marriage in January 1809 James Rothwell Barnes had begun by buying warp and weft and "putting them out" to handloom weavers in the Halshaw Moor area. By the time Thomas was born his father was still no more than a manufacturer of coarse goods but he had managed to build himself a cottage next door to the Golden Lion Inn where his mother, widowed three times, had brought him up. He prepared warps on a warping loom in this cottage but continued to work as a "putter-out". He soon managed to build a weaving shed near the cottage and was able to employ some weavers to work at the eleven handlooms in the shed. However, he was still employing many more in their own homes. The building of this first weaving shed around 1810 marked the start of the business but it was still on a very small scale. Money was short and he had to run the whole business with the help of just one assistant.

Thomas was baptised on 29 November 1812 at the newly-formed Halshaw Moor Independent Chapel in Farnworth, the third child and second son of James Rothwell Barnes and his wife Elizabeth, the daughter of Roger Taylor, a butcher and farmer from nearby Ringley. As a young child Thomas attended a so-called "dame school" for a short time, probably the one run by Mrs Dyson, the wife of the minister at Halshaw Moor Chapel. She did teach all three of James Rothwell Barnes's sons. He then went with his older brother, George, to Mr Wilson's commercial school in Bolton. Another pupil at the school was Rev. Dyson's son Simeon who described how the three of them would plod on foot to school in Bolton, hoping to be able to walk alongside Miss Lucy Todd, a girl from a well-to-do family who rode there on her pretty white pony.[1] On Saturday 3 July 1823, Mr Wilson announced in the Bolton Express that his school in Moor Lane would be open for the inspection of the pupils on Tuesday 15 July. Thomas would have been nearly eleven at the time. When Mr Wilson died, Thomas was transferred to a private school in Bolton taught by Mr Cover, an Independent minister who later became one of the first missionaries to the South Sea Islands. He was probably the same J. T.

Cover of Bolton who was one of the people invited to a Sunday service at Halshaw Moor Chapel in May 1834. Simeon Dyson also described the three boys' excitement when the Bishop of Chester came to consecrate the new St John's Church on Halshaw Moor in September 1826. They went to the entrance lodge at the gatehouse entrance to Darley Park to see the Bishop returning to Darley Hall, the home of Mr Rawson, his host. (These three young boys could not have guessed that James Rothwell Barnes would one day become so rich that he could buy Darley Hall and its Park for his retirement home.) In 1826 or 1827 when Thomas was 14 years old he had to leave school to help his brother George to manage their father's manufacturing business because their father was ill at the time. Many years later in July 1852, Thomas referred to his school days when he attended a meeting to discuss the setting-up of a public library in Bolton in rooms above the Exchange which had housed a reading room and library until seventeen years before. He said that he had quite decided on supporting the new public library. He had always regarded it as a kind of disgrace to Bolton that the library formerly kept in those rooms was broken up. It existed at the time he went to school, when he used to call for books and read them; and he had since considered it a very great loss that there was not some such library for the use of the public.

Halshaw Moor Chapel was an Independent chapel set up in 1808 by Thomas's father and several other families in the Farnworth area. It played a very important part in the life of the whole family. When Thomas was only 14 years old he and his older brother George were at a meeting held at the Chapel on 21 August 1827 at which a Juvenile Branch Missionary Society was formed "in aid of the London Missionary Society for sending the Gospel into the heathen world". George took the Minutes at this meeting and Thomas seconded one of the five Motions. This document in George's spindly handwriting is preserved in the Lancashire Record Office and marks the first reference I have found to this side of Thomas's life.[2] George became a member of the chapel on 28 October 1827, one month after his eighteenth birthday. Thomas was 19 years old when he joined the chapel on 27 May 1832.[3]

His brother George married in 1830 and his sister Jane in 1831. George's son Alfred was born in December that year. Life appeared to be on an even keel and the business was expanding. In Farnworth his father now had a spinning and a weaving mill, both powered by steam. However, there was a major disaster on New Year's Eve 1833 when a high chimney at the mill was blown down in a gale killing four young women in a power-loom weaving shed and badly injuring three others. In January 1834 Thomas married and James Rothwell made plans for his sons' future. In that year he built another mill at nearby Dixon Green. His eldest son, George, was to take on the management of this mill. Thomas who was now 22 years old was to take charge of the warehouse in Manchester which, like the Farnworth mills, was much larger than it had been in 1811. His third son, the youngest, James, was now 20 years old and was to stay at the old mill and work together with his father. James Rothwell thought he had provided a secure future for his three sons. However, disaster struck again. On 10 February 1835 James accidentally fell down the hoist from the cotton room in the third storey of the Lower Mill, the "Old Mill", and was killed. After the death of their younger brother the remaining two brothers, George and Thomas, went into partnership with their father. *Pigot & Dean's Trade Directory* for 1836 records: "James Rothwell Barnes & Sons, Farnworth, spinners and manufacturers by power". Thomas continued to be based at the Manchester end of the business in the warehouse at 3 McDonald's Lane while George worked with his father managing the business in Farnworth.

On 29 January 1834 Thomas had married Sarah Richardson at St Mary the Virgin, Prestwich. They were married by licence and two of their three witnesses were John Richardson and John Grundy. The third witness, James Sheldrick, appears to have been connected with the church.[4] Sarah was the daughter of William Richardson, a cotton manufacturer of Lilly Hill, Stand, Whitefield, and his wife Alice, and was baptised at the same church on 3 October 1802.[5] She was, therefore, ten years older than Thomas. In May 1834, shortly after Thomas and Sarah married, three members of the Richardson Family were invited to attend a Sunday service at Halshaw Moor Chapel. They were James Richardson of Lower Lilly Hill, and James and Edward Richardson of Lilly Hill, two of Sarah's brothers.[6] In 1841 Sarah's father, William Richardson, a cotton manufacturer, was still alive, aged around 70, living at Lilly Hill with two other sons, John who had been a witness at the wedding and William, one year younger than his sister. In the Parish Church at Whitefield is a plaque erected by his friends and workpeople in memory of William Richardson's son James. In 1841 this James Richardson, aged about 40, was married and living in a separate household with his wife and family at Lilly Hill. All three men, James, John and William, were cotton manufacturers like their father. An undated letter from George Barnes, Thomas's brother, probably written in 1843, mentions that a Miss Richardson from Manchester was visiting their mother. She could well have been another of William's daughters. According to a chronicle of All Saints Church, the Parish Church of Stand, Sarah's brother Edward married Jane and in 1884 their sons George and Herbert Richardson donated a stained glass window on the north side of the church in their memory.7 A daughter of either George or Herbert Richardson married a Dr McMillan. The members of this branch of the Richardson family were great benefactors to Stand Parish Church. However, in the early 1800s there was an Independent Chapel at Stand which might have been the link between the Barnes and Richardson families.

The year 1835 continued to bring tragedies for the Barnes family. In September Thomas and Sarah had their first child, a daughter called Emily. In October the baby died, aged just five weeks, and not long after that, on 3 December 1835 at Spring Cottage, their home in Farnworth, Thomas's wife Sarah also died. She was only 34 years old and they had not reached their second wedding anniversary. Sarah and her baby were buried together in the burial ground of Halshaw Moor Chapel. Family tragedies continued—Thomas's youngest sister, Sarah, died on 10 June 1836, aged only 15. She had probably been suffering from consumption as she had been taken to the South Coast shortly before this in an attempt to improve her health. She was very ill on the journey and had a bad cough.

On 4 January 1837 Thomas married again. His second wife was Ann Richardson, Sarah's sister. They married by licence at St Mary the Virgin in Prestwich where Thomas and Sarah had married almost exactly three years earlier. Their two witnesses were James and William Richardson. Ann was about two years younger than her sister, but still older than Thomas. His brother George referred to the two of them in a letter written on the 31 May 1837. "Brother Thomas and Ann are going to Liverpool to sail on *The Conway Castle* for Conway. Mr Burdon recommends Wales rather than Cumberland for Ann. Miss Gaskell is going with them for a day or two." A week later he was able to report that Thomas and Ann were seasick going to Bangor and added: "Ann is much better, she is often hungry and can eat as much at one meal as in a day at home."8 This suggests that Ann, like her sister, was not strong. However, she lived until 1880 in spite of her poor health. In 1862 her husband wrote about her: "Ann excited herself more than was necessary, but she is apt to do that, as are all people who have got livers out of order. Livers and nerves are sometimes very troublesome."9 In March 1839 Ann was one of the Directors' wives on a committee set up to oversee the knitting and sewing at Queen Street Seminary. Thomas's third sister, Mary, married a much older

man, Thomas Paterson, in the summer of 1838. He worked for the
Barnes family and was later a partner in the business. Not long after
their marriage, on 19 April 1839 Mary died. I do not know the cause
of death but she could very well have died while pregnant. All this
badly affected Thomas's father's health. Thomas and Ann's son, James
Richardson Barnes, was born on 8 December 1839 at Summerfield,
his grandfather's house in Great Lever. His birth was registered in
Bolton in the December quarter of 1839 and he was baptised on 23
February 1840 at Halshaw Moor Independent Chapel. The baptism
registers record that he was born in Middleton parish. Great Lever was
part of Middleton parish. According to Barton in his *History of Farnworth
and Kearsley* Thomas and Ann had several children but James Richardson
was the only one who survived.

In Thomas's Obituary in *The Bolton Evening News* on 26 April 1897
no mention is made of either of his two wives, Sarah and Ann Richardson.
Instead it states that in 1850 Thomas was married at Bolton Parish
Church by Rev. Canon Slade to Miss Elizabeth Howard Knowles of
Little Bolton. This appears to be a factual error but a strange one for
a paper to make about a man who had been an MP for Bolton and
very much in the public eye for much of his life. In an attempt to clear
up this mystery I sent for the marriage certificate of Thomas Barnes
and Elizabeth Howard Knowles. The marriage took place in Bolton
Parish Church as stated and the ceremony was performed by Canon
Slade but it was on 31 March 1847, not in 1850. This Thomas Barnes
was a bachelor, of full age, a manufacturer of Little Bolton, and he
was described as the son of John Barnes, a farmer. Elizabeth Knowles
was a spinster, also of Little Bolton. No father's name was given. The
witnesses were a Thomas and Mary Wood and William and John
Barnes. All were able to sign their own names. He was probably the
Thomas Barnes, manufacturer of cotton goods of Little Bolton, listed
in the 1843 *Slater's Trade Directory* with addresses at 9 Barn Street,
Bolton and Water Street, Little Bolton. I have searched the 1841 Census
to see if there was any sign of a Thomas Barnes in Water Street, Little
Bolton, or in Barn Street, Bolton. There wasn't. Nor was there anything
in the 1851 Census, although it was very hard to read—a very faint
impression on a black page. I am assuming that the information in
Thomas's Obituary was wrong about this marriage and I now think
that *The Bolton Evening News* had confused Thomas Barnes, MP for
Bolton, with a Thomas Barnes, also a manufacturer of cotton goods,
who was a Councillor in Bolton at least between 1849 and 1853. This
Thomas Barnes, a cotton manufacturer from Bolton, attended the

Manchester Exchange on Tuesdays and Thursdays. He probably had a business address at 20 Bury Street, Little Bolton, and a home address at Tipping Place where he was living when he was sworn in on the Grand Jury in Bolton on 26 June 1847.[10] On Tuesday 19 November 1850 it was probably this other Thomas Barnes who was with a group of Bolton councillors at an evening meeting held in the Temperance Hall in Little Bolton to protest against what was described as "the recent papal aggressions, by the introduction of Cardinal Wiseman as head of Roman Catholicity in this country, and the ordination of bishops". This "select, although multitudinous" meeting had been called anonymously by placard, but Peter Ainsworth took the Chair and the meeting was supported by a large group of influential men from the neighbourhood.[11] The subject of the meeting was certainly not one which would have appealed to Thomas Barnes of Farnworth.

The main argument to support the theory that *The Bolton Evening News* had got its facts wrong is, however, that in both the 1841 and 1851 Censuses Thomas was living with his wife Ann. In 1841 their one-year old son James was with them. Although they had married, in fact, after the 1835 Marriage Act, marriage to a deceased wife's sister was illegal and was only made legal in 1907. At around the time of his father's death the whole question of this type of marriage was under discussion in the area. A large meeting of the clergy of the rural deanery was held in Bolton parish church Sunday School in mid March 1849 to discuss proposed alterations to the Marriage Laws relating to marriage to a deceased wife's sister. It was agreed to oppose the measure and a petition was subsequently drawn up with many signatures on it.[12] I noticed in an article about Thomas that during one of his periods as MP he was an advocate for a Bill entitled "The Deceased Wife's Sister Bill". However, I have not yet found any references to his involvement with this in the many political speeches he made in Bolton during the time he was Bolton's MP.

In 1837 Thomas became one of the four deacons of the Chapel at Halshaw Moor. His diaries showed how Thomas tried to reconcile being a business man with being a Christian. Rev. Hewgill, the pastor at Market Street Congregational Church in Farnworth, quoting from them at the time of Thomas's death said they showed "the development of a fine, strong, healthy, sincere Christian character". Thomas had become a member of the Congregational Church in 1832 and when he was 25 and already a deacon of the Church, he wanted to enter the ministry. However, his father dissuaded him, and he settled for the life of a businessman. For the whole of his life he showed how important he considered a Christian minister's role to be. In his diaries he discussed a deacon's character and the services he performed. Rev. J. F. Munro, the pastor at Francis Street Church, recalled in his memorial service for Thomas that the first speech he ever heard him make was on the same subject. Thomas said then about the Christian minister, "I know no office so sacred in the sight of God and so fraught with good to mankind." Thomas worked as a deacon at the chapel in Farnworth for 35 years, until he had to resign after moving to The Quinta. Market Street Church then elected him Honorary Life Deacon. When he died at the age of 84 he was the senior member on the roll of the Old Independent Chapel. For the whole of his life he supported the Congregational Church in every way he could. In 1841 he was elected onto the committee of the Bible Society. He gave annual £100 contributions to the London Missionary Society, built the Quinta Congregational Church and Sunday School, provided a manse and a living for the pastor at The Quinta, gave land for the building of Francis Street Church in Farnworth, and supported many struggling chapels. When the Quinta Church was opened in 1858 he said at the luncheon after the ceremony that one of his reasons for coming to The Quinta was "that he might be able to give his ministerial friends an opportunity of pleasant and profitable relaxation when, by overwork, they had become exhausted, and needed rest". He certainly did that, and his son and daughter-in-law continued to offer the same hospitality after his death. There were not many of the leading Independent ministers of the time who did not spend some time at The Quinta, enjoying the rest and hospitality it offered, and who did not preach at Quinta Church. Rev. Monro said of Thomas, "He retained his great reverence for the ministry to the last, and in a thousand ways made that felt by those who were engaged in it."

In 1838 the Barnes family together with half a dozen other mill-owners in the Halshaw Moor and Moses Gate area set up a school in Queen Street to provide a basic education for the children of their workers.[13] Thomas's brother George was the driving force behind this school, Queen Street Seminary, and remained its Treasurer until his death. The firm's account book shows that James Rothwell Barnes paid £900 out of the firm's money for the new school.[14] From the start the Secretary was Thomas Paterson, the man who had just married Thomas's sister Mary. The first meeting of the eighteen or so Directors was held in December 1838 and soon after that, on 26 December 1838, the school opened as an Infant School with two teachers recruited from the Normal Seminary in Glasgow, a married couple, Mr and Mrs

Wallace. Soon there was also a Juvenile School with Mr McIntyre as the teacher. School fees were 2d a week for infants and 3d for the older children, to be paid in advance. The school depended on subscriptions, mainly from the Directors who were allowed to inspect what was going on at any time. When it first opened twenty-two subscriptions had been pledged amounting to just under £300 and over £200 of this had already been paid up. Thomas and George had each paid £40 and their father £60 which allowed them to recommend up to a total of 140 free scholars, one for each pound subscribed. In the years before George's death the collection of subscriptions became very lax and when Thomas took over in 1844 as Treasurer the first thing he had to do was to clear the accumulated debt. A committee decided to ask friends of the school for the money. The men decided that their wives and daughters could do the begging. As they put it, "female collection is the best answer". By September that year the school had so many free scholars that it decided it could not admit any more. The children had to provide their own slates but the school provided pens and ink. The Directors eventually settled on two books which the pupils also had to buy—Leitch's Monitorial Class Book, Part 3, which was to be sold for 4d, and Leitch's Juvenile Reader which cost 1s 6d. The school relied on the use of monitors. H. A. Barnes described the teaching method used: "The headmaster, out of school hours, coached the monitors in the coming day's lessons, then when school assembled each monitor gathered his class round him and taught them the appointed subjects. When teaching was over the headmaster held a sort of review or little examination to assure himself the work was properly done." A public examination took place annually, usually on Christmas Day.

After the death of their brother James in 1835 George and Thomas received equal shares of the annual profits in the family business. At the end of the financial year on 30 June 1836 their father kept two-thirds of the annual profit of £8,350 and George and Thomas shared the remainder. However, in that year, Thomas who was based at the warehouse in Manchester only appeared to have £304 invested in the business compared with his brother's £2,011 and his father's £38,889. It was clear that George was playing the major role in assisting his father. This was still the situation in the following year, 1836/37, but from then on until 30 June 1840 Thomas received a much smaller proportion of the annual profits than George. It was George who represented the firm in October 1838 when the firm appeared before the Magistrates at Bolton Petty Sessions accused (and convicted) of three breaches of the 1833 Factory Act.[15] This was probably the time when Thomas was seriously considering entering the ministry before his father persuaded him to become a businessman. In the years 1836/37 and 1839/40 a mill at Worsley was mentioned in the stock accounts where there were 19 bags of cotton in the first year and 260 in the second year. In addition, a mill at Bolton had 284 bags of cotton in 1839/40. I have no other information about these two mills but it could have been that Thomas was intending to set up a separate business.

The inventory in the stock accounts for 1835/36 gives an indication of what was going on at Farnworth Mills at the time. Seven or eight types of material were being produced—grey twills, grey swandown, yellow swandown, satteens, "velveteens" such as beaverteen, hessians and cords. Some of the goods were already priced off and ready for sale in the Manchester warehouse but the bulk of the stock was still unpriced and not ready for sale in the "Home House" in Farnworth. There were 877 items in Manchester and 1,657 in Farnworth together with some stock away at other firms such as Egerton Dye Works, Pollitt's, Hall's and Crompton's Croft. The total value of these goods was well over £7,000.

The valuation of the raw material and yarn either in the process of being used or still unused adds information about the weaving process itself. Warps were sent out to two firms, Blomerley's and Turner's, for sizing. In one room, called the Gaiting Room, the twist thread was on the dressed beams. More twist was either on the looms or on the beams in the dressing machines. The weft yarn was either already woven on the looms or in tins at the side of the looms or stored in the warehouse in skips or tins. Other rooms mentioned were the Scutcher Room and the Carding Room, the Spinning Room and the Throstle Room. Everything had a valuation—dressing flannel, roller cloth, heald yarn, reeds, roller leather, gaskins and brushes, even the rovings, slubbings, waste cotton, "flies" and "strils", droppings, sweeps and cop bottoms.

The most valuable items were the bales of cotton. Three types of cotton were mentioned, all from America: Mobiles, Orleans and Boweds. Before the American Civil War most Alabama cotton went through New Orleans and Mobile. Bowed cotton was originally called Bowed Georgia cotton because it was cleaned from the seed by snapping it with a bow-string. This method was later replaced by a saw gin. At Farnworth 62 bales were already mixed and in tins and another 54 were unopened. The Mobiles cotton was the most valuable at £19 10s per bale; the Orleans cotton was worth £14 10s per bale and the

Boweds slightly less—£14. Altogether nearly £4,000 was invested in these raw materials.

A final section in the stocktaking accounts lists all the other items needed in the mill—16 lb of flour for the dressing process (£28 16s), 1½ casks of clay at £1 6s per cask, 28 lb of Prussian blue at 4s a lb, and a very costly item—sperm oil at £70. An oil cistern was worth £5, the nails in the warehouse £7, an iron safe and a desk in the counting house £10, a desk, drums and a cupboard in the warehouse £10, and tables and beams £5. Thirty-two scraping frames were worth £16, a set of "weighs" in the Manchester warehouse £5, and 8 weigh beams and mounts in the Farnworth warehouse £14. In addition there were blocks, ropes, a screw jack and 60 dozen tubs and buckets, all of which added another £17 10s to the value of the assets. A weighing machine was valued at £31 and the factory bell at £4. A wrought iron water cistern was valued at £42. Two horses and their "furniture" were also included in the inventory. The horses were valuable—worth £45— and the "furniture" added another £5. There was also a gig with its harness, worth £20. Two years later two new carriages joined the gig—two phaetons, one smaller than the other.

The buildings and engines were valued at £10,508 and the machinery at £9,688. These were listed in a separate book which is not with the material deposited in Bolton archives.

Some accounts for Dixon Green Mill, the mill originally built for George, are included in the stock account. It had 18 bales of Mobiles and Orleans and some cotton in bins and as waste. It appears to have been a spinning mill only. Some sums of money had been paid out for the mill in 1835/36 and in 1836/37 even more had been spent on the building work going on there. One document in Bolton archives describes the lengthening of a sough (a drainage tunnel) in front of Dixon Green Mill near Bowker cottages, Mr Tonge's house and the Smithy.

After his second marriage Thomas lived at Summerfield, his father's house in Great Lever. When his son James was baptised in February 1840 Thomas was described as a manufacturer from Farnworth. In the 1841 Census his was one of the five households listed as living at Summerfield. With him were his wife Ann and their son James, aged 1. They had a young female servant, Margaret Banks, living with them. In the household were also Ann Taylor, aged about 15, and Watson Smith, aged about 25. As Taylor was the maiden name of Thomas's mother, Ann might have been a relative.

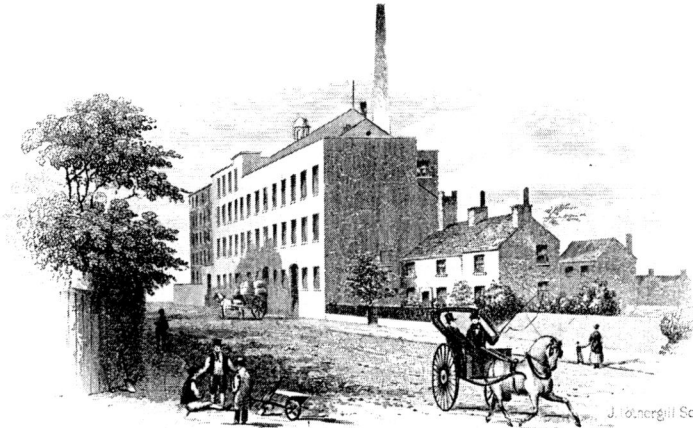

MANCHESTER WAREHOUSE, 20, CANNON STREET,

Farnworth Mills

From a very early age Thomas had been concerned with the conditions of the poor and sick and in 1840 he was appointed on the committee for the relief of the distressed poor of Bolton. It was the time of the great trade depression and in Bolton in 1841 mills were either standing still or working a four-day week. It was estimated that there were 10,000 people in the district who could not pay rates, and hundreds who were said to be living on 2d per day, owing to the depressed condition of the cotton industry. However, profits for Farnworth Mills in the year 1840/41 were £9,081 and in the following year only dipped to £7,860. On 30 June 1841 400 looms were operating in the Lower Mill and 302 in the Higher Mill and in the following year even more— a total of 724. In 1840 the firm had even bought an expensive new four-wheel carriage, a britzka worth £110. The picture of the mill at the top of the firm's invoice shows two men driving in what I think is a gig.[16] At the time the firm was called James R. Barnes & Son. Occasionally newspaper reports before 1844 refer to the firm as this. I have not found any other reference to the warehouse at 20 Cannon Street except on this invoice which was found between the pages of a Commonplace Book belonging to George Barnes now in Bolton archives. I think this could be another indication that Thomas was intending at this stage to set up independently. In 1841 the Manchester warehouse was still in McDonalds Lane. Pigot's 1841 *Directory of Manchester and Salford* reads: "James Rothwell Barnes, fustian, pillow etc., manufacturer, Farnworth, 3 McDonalds Lane, Tuesday, Thursday, Saturday."

However, after the birth of his son at the beginning of 1840 Thomas did start to take on an equal share of the work at the Farnworth Mills again and from July 1840 until the death of his brother in 1844 they each received one quarter of the annual profit. Profits remained good—in 1842/43 they were back up to over £9,000 in spite of various building projects. A report in *The Manchester Times* on 7 May 1842 certainly named the firm as J. R. Barnes & Sons. In the following year, 1843/44, a profit of £8,340 was declared only a few weeks after George's sudden death in April. His share was allocated as usual but no names were added to the share-out of profits.

Some time between the 1841 Census in June and August 1842 Thomas moved to Limefield, his new house on Manchester Road at Moses Gate, even though it was probably still unfinished. The accounts for the year 1842/43 include cash paid out on various unfinished buildings, one of which was Thomas's house. In August 1842 Farnworth set up a Watch Committee, called the Bowling Green Committee because it met in the Bowling Green Inn, as a safety measure in case the "Plug Rioters" made a second visit to the town. Strikes protesting at the wage cuts following the General Strike of 1842 had broken out, first in Ashton, then in Manchester. The rioters went from place to place turning out the workers. No-one worked without a permit from the strike committees. A dangerous mob visited Farnworth and "drew the plugs" out of the boilers, bringing the main factories in the town to a standstill. On 22 August 1842 Thomas Barnes's name was added to the list of special constables who were armed with truncheons in case of attack. His father who lived in Great Lever was not involved (but was on the jury when the Plug Rioters were tried in Lancaster in 1843).[17] There was a list in *The Manchester Times & Gazette* on Tuesday, 31 January 1843, headed "Deputies arrived up to the time of Meeting". In it, Thomas Barnes was named as the only deputy from Halshaw Moor. I have not yet found information to clarify just what this referred to. *Slater's Trade Directory* for 1843 still listed the firm as James Rothwell Barnes & Sons, cotton spinners and manufacturers of Farnworth Mills, but there was a separate entry for Thomas at his address in Farnworth.

The first reference I have found to Thomas's interest in politics was on the evening of Wednesday 17 May 1843 when he chaired a meeting, originally in Queen Street Training Seminary, and gave a speech on the subject of Sir James Graham's amendments to the Factory Education Bill, something closely linked to the work of the school. Other speakers were the Rev. J. W. Massie and the Rev. E. H. Nolan. Because so many people attended, the huge assembly moved to the Independent

Chapel.[18] His brother George seconded one of the Motions and kept a cutting of the newspaper report in his Commonplace Book now preserved in Bolton Archives. Thomas never lost his interest in education throughout the whole of his life.

Two months later on Monday 17 July 1843, Farnworth Floral Exhibition was held in Queen Street Seminary. Pinks, geraniums, fuchsias, fruit and vegetables were shown—the display of pinks was especially good and was said to be even better than the display at either the Bolton show or the Botanical Gardens in Manchester. Thomas Barnes was amongst the prizewinners, winning a First Prize in the class for black and white pinks with his variety "Margaret" and Fifth Prize for a variety called "Faithful". He won another Fifth Prize in the class for purple-laced seedlings with a variety "Greensides". He also had the best pan of roses and the best cauliflowers. The report on the flower show in *The Manchester Times* mentioned the political repercussions of the meeting at Halshaw Moor in May: "This society bids fair for being one of considerable eminence, notwithstanding the coldness with which it is treated by some of the gentry of the neighbourhood, some of whom supported it last year, but in consequence of Sir James Graham's 'Olive branch', having extended its *benign* influence amongst them, have withdrawn their patronage from the society, though we cannot see what floriculture has to do with either politics or religion."

I am assuming that it was Thomas Barnes of Farnworth who won these prizes. His brother, George, referred to the family's interest in flower shows in a letter on 26 September 1840.[19] There were, however, many references at the time to a Thomas Barnes and his gardener Peter Mottershead winning prizes at the Botanical Gardens in Manchester. I think this man was the brother of Robert Barnes, later Mayor of Manchester. There is, however, no question that Thomas Barnes of Farnworth was interested in horticulture. Once he moved to his estate on the Welsh Borders he was able to really indulge in his passion for horticulture.

On 27 December 1843 Thomas was in Manchester at a public meeting in Grosvenor Street Chapel in Piccadilly. He was described in the list of Manchester gentlemen who had subscribed at the meeting as Mr Thomas Barnes of Halshaw Moor.[20] He gave a generous subscription of £500 as did also George Hadfield. George Hadfield was a man whose Liberal politics and views on religion and education were very much in line with Thomas's ideas. He became MP for Sheffield and moved in the same circles as Thomas over many years. The meeting in Piccadilly was in support of popular education and had been called to hear the report of a deputation who had recently attended a conference in London. It had also been called to discuss how to increase the number of day schools in Manchester and the surrounding area. The Rev. Dr Vaughan moved the first resolution and other speakers were the Rev. James Gwyther and the Rev. J. W. Massie.

A week or so later there was a meeting on 3 January 1844 in the Temperance Hall in Bolton in aid of the Great League Fund. Thomas's involvement with the Anti-Corn Law League must have begun around this time. A donation of £100 was made by the family firm called at this time Messrs J. R. Barnes & Son.[21] George was still alive at this time. This is yet another suggestion that until George's death in April that year Thomas had been intending setting up in business on his own behalf. Maybe he did not find the work in the warehouse in Manchester fulfilling enough.

Notes

1. "Recollections of Halshaw Moor" on *Farnworth blogspot*
2. LRO *op. cit.* DDX 75/119
3. Uncatalogued material on Barnes family [Bolton Archives and Social Studies]
4. Records of St Mary the Virgin, Prestwich (transcribed) [Lancashire Parish Clerk online]
5. Ibid.
6. Harold A. Barnes *The Story of Halshaw Moor Chapel* (pub. 1908)
7. Frederick Ernest Lowe *Scraps of Information on the Parish Church of All Saints, Stand, Manchester* (pub. 1910, Whitefield) [LRO]
8. LRO *op. cit.* DDX 75/120
9. LRO *op. cit.* DDX 75/129
10. *Manchester Times* [19th Century Newspapers online]
11. Ibid.
12. *Bolton Chronicle* [Bolton Archives and Social Studies]
13. LRO SMFa Farnworth, Queen Street Training Seminary 1838–56
14. Uncatalogued material *op. cit.* [Bolton Archives and Social Studies] From this point on, all references to the firm's stock accounts are based on this material.
15. Bolton Free Press 6.10.1838 [Bolton Archives and Social Studies]
16. Uncatalogued material *op. cit.* [Bolton Archives and Social Studies]
17. B.T. Barton *op. cit. History of Farnworth and Kersley* (pub. 1887, Bolton)
18. *Manchester Times* [19th Century Newspapers online]
19. LRO *op. cit.* DDX 75/120
20. *Manchester Times* [19th Century Newspapers online]
21. Ibid.

CHAPTER 2

June 1845–1852

Taking on the family business, buying The Quinta and going to Westminster

Whatever Thomas had been planning had to change after George's death in April 1844 which left Thomas as his father's sole partner. Judging from the annual stocktaking accounts for the year 1844/45 James Rothwell Barnes was so badly affected by his son's death that Thomas must have taken over the running of the business almost immediately. For the first time he had £15,458 invested in the business and his father only £3,559. Thomas also received a half-share of the year's huge profit of £18,764. A new type of cloth called "Imperials" was being produced and the balance in the Bank of Bolton had been reduced from nearly £6,000 to just over £1,500. Profits were also high in 1845/46—£16,992—made on a capital of only £36,768. This 46% profit was not quite the highest in the firm's history, but nearly.

Thomas now began to play a more prominent part in the family business. He gave a New Year's Party for the workpeople in January 1845 and invited several of the wealthier families in the neighbourhood to join in the celebrations. Around 700 people were treated to a sit-down tea in one of the store rooms at the Higher Mill which had been cleared out and decorated for the occasion. Thomas lent a magic lantern complete with "astronomical, microscopic, scenic and humorous" slides and gave a commentary on them as they were shown. There were other delights in the form of an electrifying machine and a demonstration of laughing gas. A cornet band, Mr Fisher's Cornopean Band, and some glee singers provided music. Some of the workpeople recited and sang. They rounded off the evening with waltzes and quadrilles and danced until late into the night. The newspaper report of this event concluded with the wish that there should be more of these social events to bring employers and employees together. During the evening Thomas gave "an affectionate address" to his workpeople, reminding them of the difficult time they had at Christmas in 1842 and contrasting it with the present. He wanted them "to make hay while the sun of prosperity was shining upon them", and encouraged the young single men to start saving to buy a house before they married. He estimated they could manage that in two or three years. To encourage them even more he advised the girls not to consider as a potential husband any young man who was wasting his money.[1] Thomas's ability to mix easily with his workforce was something he later carried over to his relationship with the tenants and workers on his Quinta estate. It was also something remembered about him after he died.

When a breakaway group of Congregational Dissenters in Bolton who had been holding their meetings in the Temperance Hall founded a new chapel, it was Thomas who laid the foundation stone on Wednesday 13 August 1845 with a silver trowel presented to him on behalf of the ladies of the congregation. Afterwards he chaired a tea-party in the Temperance Hall. Laying foundation stones and chairing tea parties became a regular feature of his life from now on.

Thomas's name began to appear more often in the paper around this time. On Saturday 29 August 1845 *The Manchester Times* reported that he was one of the people who signed a letter to the Mayor of Manchester asking him to call a public meeting to discuss the possibility of setting up a direct railway link between Manchester and Southampton. Thomas had good reason to be interested in the spread of railways at this time. By 1844 his father was connected with the proposed Bolton, Wigan and Liverpool Railway and was already well-established as a proprietor of the Manchester, Bolton and Bury Canal Navigation and Railway, and later of the Manchester and Leeds Railway. By the time he died in 1849 this company was the new Lancashire and Yorkshire Railway Company. I have no evidence that Thomas became a shareholder in the company until after his father's death but his links with the Lancashire and Yorkshire Railway led to him becoming Chairman of its Board of Directors for many years.

He continued to support the idea that owning a house was a good basis for a secure marriage. On Monday 15 December 1845 he lent a room at the Seminary in Farnworth for a meeting of a deputation from the Freeholders' Building Society.

On 13 December 1845 there was a large meeting in Manchester at the League Rooms of subscribers to the fund set up to promote the Anti-Corn Law League. This meeting was called because the Prime Minister, Peel, had been so scared by news of the Irish potato blight that year and the poor wheat crop in England that he believed famine was imminent and decided to suspend the Corn Laws. Russell, the leader of the Whigs, had called for the total repeal of the Laws, encouraging Peel to make a move. But his Cabinet refused to support him and he resigned. This meeting must have been called during the two-week period when Peel was out of office. They wanted to discuss what kind of fund should be provided "should the excited expectations of an early abolition of the Corn Laws be disappointed". They agreed unanimously to raise £250,000, the so-called Quarter of a Million League Fund, and to petition Parliament. They decided to convene a meeting on the morning of Tuesday 23 December 1845 by sending a circular with the names of the supporters. Cobden and Bright were the first names on the list. Also on it were J. R. Barnes, and under it— Barnes, junior, presumably Thomas. By the time the typesetting was completed, news had reached them of Lord John Russell's accession to office—but the fight was to continue.

The success of the 1845 New Year party encouraged Thomas to repeat the event the following year. This description of the decorations captures the scene: "The room was hung with pink and white drapery, gracefully festooned, interspersed with mottoes and evergreens". This time the workpeople themselves took more part in the organisation and several of them made speeches. One of them acted as Chairman for the evening and this year he was the one to give the pep talk "upon the necessity of cultivating their intellectual faculties and improving their moral and social conditions by an earnest pursuit of knowledge, without which they could not even properly discharge their duties as servants". Thomas restricted his speech to urging upon their attention the necessity of sobriety, cleanliness, industry, and economy, whilst they were in possession of health and strength, and to expressing an earnest wish for their moral, as well as physical, welfare. All this took about an hour and a half but then the fun began. Again the magic lantern came out and three of the workpeople sang comic and sentimental songs. This time at ten o'clock there was a firework display and a balloon was sent off. Again, the evening ended with dancing, accompanied by the Farnworth amateur band.

Newspaper reports in January and March 1846 talk about workpeople employed by Thomas Barnes, not by Messrs J. R. Barnes & Son as in the previous year. This arrangement continued after James Rothwell's retirement in 1846 and until his death.

On Wednesday 4 February 1846 Thomas was at an evening meeting in the large school room at Halshaw Moor to consider the measures about to be introduced into Parliament by Sir Robert Peel. He proposed that the Chairman should be Rev. Woodward, a Buckinghamshire man, who spoke about the evils of the Corn Laws. Other speakers were Thomas himself, Mr A. Prentice from *The Manchester Times*, Mr J. J. Finnigan, and Mr Dyson. The meeting resolved unanimously never to relinquish their efforts until total and unconditional repeal of the Corn Laws was accomplished.

Another interesting episode was reported in *The Bolton Free Press*. On Saturday 8 March 1846 a deputation of his managers and overlookers met Thomas to ask for a cut in their hours of work. Thomas agreed without hesitation to reduce their hours from twelve a day to eleven without reducing their wages. He again took the opportunity to try to persuade them to use some of their extra free time to "cultivate and improve their moral and intellectual facilities". Apparently in making this cut in working hours Thomas led the way as other firms in the area followed his example. The newspaper reported that this was one of the first benefits of free trade as it would not have taken place "had it not been for the prospect that the restrictions on commerce will be totally and for ever removed". When Thomas decided to stand for Parliament, free trade was one of the issues he promoted.

It was around this time that he became an active worker in connection with the establishment of an Athenaeum in Bolton. This was an idea sponsored by Robert Heywood and John Hick, a leading conservative and chairman of the engineering firm of Benjamin Hick & Son. It was intended to replace the Mechanics' Institution as a cultural centre for working men. Apparently it was a well meant idea which failed. Robert Heywood was a man who was to play an important part in Thomas's life. He was born in 1786, the same year as James Rothwell Barnes, but outlived him by twenty years, dying in 1868 just before Thomas's career as a politician ended. He was a Nonconformist, a cotton manufacturer and one of the leading Liberals in Bolton, promoting Thomas's candidature as MP for Bolton from the very beginning. W. E. Brown in his study of Robert Heywood's life, *Robert Heywood of Bolton 1786–1868*, gives a very detailed account of his many interests, business, private and political. Reading this made me realize the many parallels between his life and Thomas's even though there are no references to the relationship between the two men in the book. After the death of his own father Thomas must have looked on Robert Heywood as a role model. He certainly followed in his footsteps wherever he could.

On Monday 6 April 1846, Thomas was summoned at the County Sessions Rooms in the Town Hall, Little Bolton, by Mr David Jones, Sub-inspector of Factories, for an alleged breach of the Factory Act.

Mr Jones conducted his own case, and Mr J. Gaskell appeared for the defendant. The information charged that on 8 January Mr Barnes had received a notice from Joseph Ewings, Sub-inspector of Factories, to the effect that the cog wheels at the end of every throstle frame in his factory, not then securely fenced, appeared to Joseph Ewings to be dangerous, and likely to cause bodily injury to the workers employed in the factory, and that on 17 March 1846 John Smethurst, a person employed in the factory, suffered a certain bodily injury, in consequence of Thomas Barnes, the occupier of the factory, having neglected to fence the cog wheels at the end of the throstle frames in the factory, whereby Thomas Barnes had forfeited a penalty of not less than £10 or more than £100. It appeared that on receiving the notice from Mr Ewings on 8 January the manager of the mill communicated with Mr Barnes and received instructions to procure tin casing to cover the whole of the throstle frames on a plan mentioned by Mr Ewings. Mr Bury, a tinman, was sent for but the job was so difficult that it took a fortnight before he could get the pattern to fit properly. Both Mr Barnes and the manager urged him forward with the work, and on 17 March, when the accident happened, all the frames had been covered but two. John Smethurst, the boy who was injured, was playing with the roller of the frame, when his elbow was caught by the small wheels which inflicted a flesh wound. The case was dismissed as the magistrates were satisfied that Thomas had done all he could to fit the tin covers after receiving Mr Ewing's notice on 8 January.[2]

An interesting advertisement appeared in *The Manchester Times* on 17 July 1846.

> "On sale: 3 pairs of hand mules, two of 456 spindles, and one of 480, each 1⅒" distance. May be seen at work at Thomas Barnes' Farnworth cotton mills. Apply at the mill, or 18 New Brown Street."

This is the first reference I have come across to the address in New Brown Street. The stocktaking records for 1843/44 mention that goods were stored in the "New and Old Warehouses". It is possible that was when the move was made. The address of the Manchester warehouse on the etching of the Farnworth mill belonging to J. R. Barnes & Son, possibly drawn after George's death in 1844, was at 20 Cannon Street. On 13 November 1846 T. R. Barnes of New Brown Street was a new subscriber of one guinea to the Manchester and Salford Asylum for Female Penitents. Was this yet another typesetting error for J. R. Barnes, or was this something to do with Thomas and Robert Barnes?

Robert Barnes who was later to become Mayor of Manchester was certainly a supporter of this asylum.

In June the following year, 1847, two boys called Hadfield and Butterworth appeared in court charged with stealing a handcart from Mr Barnes's door in New Brown Street. They claimed they thought nobody owned it and were dismissed with a caution. In *Slater's 1852 Manchester Directory* it is clear that by then Thomas did have premises in New Brown Street. The entry reads: "Thomas Barnes, spinner and fustian manufacturer, 18 New Brown Street, Manchester, with a house near Bolton." I have not found any evidence that his father, James Rothwell Barnes, was ever in New Brown Street. Perhaps Thomas had moved to New Brown Street after his father's retirement. When the Manchester Eye Hospital appealed for money on 28 October 1848 it was the firm of Messrs Barnes & Son, Farnworth, which donated £5.

On 27 January 1847 a violent thunderstorm at nine o'clock in the evening damaged one of the chimneys at the works at Moses Gate. This accident was not as serious as the collapse of the mill chimney on New Year's Eve 1833 and the mill was only put out of action for two and a half hours, even though some of the cotton in the scutching room was set alight. The report in *The Bolton Chronicle* filled in the details:

"On Tuesday evening last a violent thunderstorm took place in this town and neighbourhood. About nine o' clock rain and hail fell very heavily, and continued to do so for some time. About a quarter past nine there was a vivid flash of lightning, followed by tremendous roaring of thunder, which shook the buildings. The clap was more violent than any which has occurred in this town for many years. The lightning seems to have spread for a considerable extent. Some damage was done by it to a chimney at the works of Messrs Barnes, at Moses Gate, Farnworth. The chimney in question is octagonal and perhaps about 40 yards high. The lightning struck it at the top and shattered some of the stone work, pared a quantity of bricks from one of the angles at about 12 or 15 yards from the top, and from another angle at the bottom. A strong brick flue, extending from the furnace to the chimney, which, at the end next the chimney, runs horizontally on the ground for about 20 yards, was rifted open from the chimney so far as it extended on the ground, but the portion underground was not damaged. In the scutching room, which is near the chimney, some cotton was set on fire, and the lights about the mill were put out. Fortunately the fire was discovered by a watchman who gave the alarm, and caused it to be immediately extinguished. There being another chimney in connection with the mill, only about two and a half hours' delay was caused in the working by the accident."

Although the annual stocktaking accounts for the year 1836/37 record that the firm had just bought a new fire engine and pipes for £140 there was no fire engine at the mill in 1847. However, by 1852 Thomas had invested in another fire engine, the *Fire Fly*. It was called to Bolton in July 1852 when the Star Concert Room burnt down. Again, on 12 August 1853, the firm of N. & J. B. Hacking publicly thanked Messrs Thomas Barnes & Co. and two of the Cromptons "for the promptitude with which they sent their Engines, and the valuable service rendered at the recent fire on their premises (Lark Mills)".

By 30 June 1847 it was clear that Thomas was in charge of the business. In 1846 his father had bought Darley Hall in Farnworth where he intended spending his retirement. During the year Thomas had £39,170 invested in the firm and his father only £9,689. Profits were down to a more normal level of £6,504 and the only innovations noted in the stocktaking accounts were new safes and furniture for the Counting House and the introduction of yet another type of cloth, this one called "Reformers".

During the 1840s the celebrated Shapcott Family Brass Band had come to Farnworth to give a series of concerts at Queen Street School. The employees of Barnes's Mill who attended the concerts were so impressed that they asked Simeon Dyson who was at the time the manager at Barnes's Mill to act on their behalf and ask Thomas about starting a brass band. The band was formed in 1848 and practised twice weekly at night in the breakfast room at the mill. In 1896 it was still called Barnes's Band. By 1910 it was Farnworth Old (Barnes's) Band.

Something odd happened in the financial year 1847/48. A later member of the family, Harold Alfred Barnes, who had made a detailed study of the firm's books, added a note: "October 1847. Commercial Panic due to Railway Mania." He worked out that the firm had made a loss of £3,096 during the year. There is no hint in the stocktaking accounts as to the cause of this. The firm was still producing satteens but had added yet another type of cloth, "Royals" to join the previous years' "Imperials" and "Reformers".

Thomas was now becoming more involved in politics. On Monday 22 November 1847 there was a meeting of South Lancashire electors at Newall's Buildings, Manchester. A resolution moved by John Bright MP expressed disappointment that Mr Villiers was unable to accept the representation of South Lancashire. Richard Cobden MP put forward another name—Alexander Henry—and it was agreed to send a deputation to him. Thomas Barnes of Farnworth was one of the members of the large committee.

On 20 January 1848 Thomas lent a room in the Queen Street Training Seminary to a newly-formed society, the Farnworth and Kersley Mutual Improvement Society, where the Rev. T. H. Smithson of Manchester gave the first of the Society's lectures: "The uses and advantages of knowledge, and the value of literary institutions as a means of acquiring it".

In 1848/49 the firm continued to produce a wide range of cloth with its twills, grey nankeens, grey satteens, its "Royals" and "Imperials" and a new one called "Diagonals". It made a profit this year of £5,895 but James Rothwell Barnes was not at the annual stocktaking on 30 June to receive his share. He had not enjoyed his retirement for long and had died on 23 March 1849. Thomas was left in sole charge of the business. There is no specific mention of the business in Farnworth in his father's Will. Thomas was made Trustee of a sum of £50,000 to be invested in two equal halves on behalf of his mother and sister, Jane Haslam. They were each to receive the annual profits from the investment. His mother inherited all the household furniture, plate, linen, china, wine, books, paintings, horses and carriages. Until his death James Rothwell Barnes had been the guardian of George's son, Alfred. Provision was made for Alfred to receive his grandmother's share of the annual profit after her death for his "maintenance, education and advancement in life". Alfred's mother had just died at Christmas 1848 when James Rothwell Barnes wrote this his last Will. Alfred had already started as a student at university and probably inherited wealth from his parents but his grandfather obviously wanted to make some provision for him. Thomas inherited the remaining portion of his father's wealth which must have been around £30,000, and all the rest of his father's real and personal estate. James Rothwell's widow only survived her husband by one year. She died just a year later on 20 April 1850. Thomas continued to live at Limefield. He had now lost his parents and two brothers and two sisters. His family now consisted of his wife Ann, his son James Richardson, his sister Jane and his nephew Alfred. Darley Hall where his father had lived for the three years up to his death was let to various tenants from then on.

On 24 November 1849 *The Bolton Chronicle* contained a notice of a sale of "very valuable furniture, oil paintings and engravings" to be held at Summerfield "in consequence of the owner changing his residence". I do not know if the contents of Summerfield House still belonged to the Barnes family or not but they might have been left behind when James Rothwell moved to Darley Hall. The notice of the sale of "the remaining portion of valuable household furniture for which the owner has no further use" lists items in the various rooms and gives a hint of what sort of house Summerfield was. It had a drawing room and a breakfast room and outside there were stables, a garden, a yard and outhouses. Three paintings were for sale: "*Arahonish Castle*" by Templeton, "*Caerlaverock*" by W. Mackenzie and "*Scenes on the Wye*" by Pether. Perhaps the family had brought these back as holiday souvenirs. The engravings for sale in their gilt frames were "*Una*", "*Raffaele and Formarina*" and "*Despatch of La Fleur*". The family had left behind all sorts of odds and ends including a pony harness, a lawn roller, a wheel barrow and a hot bed frame. Summerfield itself probably continued to be owned by the Barnes family as members of the family lived in it at various times over the next forty years.

Two months after his father's death Thomas made a public appearance on 3 May 1849 in the Temperance Hall in Bolton when he chaired a meeting to consider the case of the Rev. J. Shore who had been imprisoned for preaching in opposition to the canons of the Established Church. They agreed to send a petition to protest against this "tyranny consequent upon a union of Church and State", and a collection was made towards defraying the expenses.

Thomas now became involved in public life as a Lancashire county magistrate. His father had been a county magistrate from 1838 until his death on 23 March 1849. On 27 August 1849 Thomas also qualified as a magistrate. His appointment was not without some controversy. An exchange of letters between Joshua Walmsley at the House of Commons in London and Robert Heywood in Bolton in May 1849 shows that party politics were involved even here. Mr Heywood wrote:

"With regard to additional magistrates I have to observe that about ten days ago two gentlemen from Farnworth, a very populous district in this neighbourhood, called upon the magistrates with a petition in favor of appointing W. Harrison Blair brother of the Member. No answer was then returned as it was considered doubtful how far it was proper to interfere in the matter but a meeting has since been held declaring that there appeared no necessity for a further increase excepting filling up the vacancy occasioned by the death of Mr Barnes who lived in that neighbourhood by appointing his son. This was not satisfactory to one of the magistrates who deemed it necessary to have one from each party and it was at length agreed to recommend both as suitable persons and forward such opinion to Mr Lomax our senior magistrate now in London."[3]

Thomas was amongst the 110 magistrates who assembled for the adjourned Annual Sessions for the County of Lancaster at the Court House, Preston, on Thursday 6 September 1849, ten days after he qualified as a magistrate. In 1850 he was again at the Annual General Sessions held at the Court House in Preston on Thursday 27 June. The number of magistrates attending this time was very much smaller than on the previous occasion. In August 1850 he was at the County Licensing Meeting for the Division held at the Town Hall in Little Bolton. After he became MP for Bolton he managed to sit again as a magistrate during the Christmas recess on 4 January 1855 in the Town Hall, Little Bolton, when he and Harrison Blair heard a case of theft from a railway carriage. Many years later, on 25 October 1878, he was on the Grand Jury at the Assize Courts, Strangeways, at the Winter Assizes for County No. 1, comprising the Northern and Salford Divisions of the County of Lancashire.

At the time of his death Thomas was the senior County Justice of the Peace for Bolton Petty Session Division but had not sat on the Bench for many years. At the County Sessions in Haulgh on the morning after he died the Presiding Magistrate, Mr Walton Ainsworth, paid tribute to Thomas's work as a magistrate which had begun 48 years before. He said he knew him personally to be a genial man, and an excellent magistrate, who did his duty well.

On 16 March 1850 Thomas had received a handwritten balance sheet which had been amended from April 1849, shortly after his father's death, to include the sale on 20 August 1849 of what could have been shares in two railway companies. The details are difficult to make out in the document but seem to refer to the Midland Railway (which began in 1844) and the M. S. & L. (Manchester, Sheffield and Lincolnshire Railway, which became the Great Central Railway in 1897) which had been formed by amalgamation in 1847. These shares could have been the remnants of the "Railway Mania of October 1847" referred to by Harold Alfred Barnes. This balance sheet was for another source of Thomas's income. With interest of £74 10s 5d from October on £2,000 the final balance in March was £2,064 18s 4d. In August 1853 when interest was one farthing in the pound he was still making a note of the amount of interest he was to receive on this account.[4] He also had income from his shares in other companies. For example, he received £973 3s 9d as half-yearly dividend from the Lancashire and Yorkshire Railway Company for the half-year ending 31 December 1854.

During the year 1849/50 Thomas was joined by two partners, Simeon Dyson, the son of the minister at Halshaw Moor Chapel, and Thomas Paterson, his widowed brother-in-law, and the firm became known as Thomas Barnes & Co. Simeon Dyson had started work as a cotton finisher and in 1843 had built his own house, Rose Cottage—now 41 Church Street. In October 1849 Thomas Paterson was working as Thomas's cashier at 18 New Brown Street in Manchester when Thomas wrote to John Gouldsborough to ask for payment of £56 14s 8d interest and the return of some money loaned to him.[5] When the annual profits of £6,229 were shared out at the end of June 1850 his two partners received their share in proportion to the amount of capital they had invested. Simeon Dyson received a twelfth and Thomas Paterson a tenth. In Bolton archives there is an undated document in Thomas's handwriting on good quality paper which appears to be the terms of some sort of partnership agreement:

"Rent to be £2,000 per annum for 2 Mills, Foundry, Public House, Walsh's Smithy, all the cottages Yardleys House, Johnsons House (Mr P [= Mr Paterson's] House is not included), Steam engines and Mill gearing and shafting, steam and gas pipes, gas apparatus.

All repairs, inside and out, to the buildings, lodges, to be done by the firm. The ground rents to be paid by Thomas Barnes as landlord. Insurance paid by the firm. All the capital to be charged 5 per cent before any profits are reckoned.

Upon the machinery 10 per cent to be allowed every year upon the previous year's valuation. No notice to be taken of the small repairs of machinery, nor anything reckoned for them. But machines that are thoroughly repaired in the Mechanics shop to be valued higher—say 15 per cent below the cost of new machines.

Cotton and raw material to be valued at cost price except that be above the price of the day, and then it must be valued at the price of the day. Cloth in the rough and yarn to be valued at a minimum price, that is, the lowest price at which they were ever valued and always at the same price until the cost or selling price becomes lower, then to be valued at that cost or selling price, and that to become the standard of value. Finished goods to be valued at what they will sell for as near as can be ascertained.

The size of the concern may be increased out of the profits and each person to furnish capital in proportion to his share.

Interest at 5 per cent to be allowed upon all capital."[6]

The structure of the company did not change for the next ten years. From 30 June 1850 until 30 June 1860 Thomas and his two partners shared the profits on a pro-rata basis.

Thomas was amongst the main supporters when Sir Joshua Walmsley, MP for Bolton, was paid a public tribute by his constituents on Thursday evening 10 January 1850 in the Temperance Hall in Bolton. About 700 people assembled in the hall and later another 300 were admitted to the gallery. After tea, Sir Joshua Walmsley made a speech at a meeting chaired by Robert Heywood, a man who would soon be promoting Thomas's political career.[7]

Thomas would have been unable to attend an important meeting of spinners, manufacturers, and others interested in the cotton trade, which should have taken place on 25 June 1850 but which was postponed to Tuesday 30 July. He was still on a two-week tour of Ireland with his nephew Alfred. This meeting was held in the Clarence Hotel, Spring Gardens, Manchester, to discuss proposals to grow cotton in the East and West Indies. He must have expressed an interest in this as he was one of the men appointed at the end of the meeting on a provisional committee "to advise as to the most practical means of promoting the growth of cotton generally". The others on the committee were Sir Elkanah Armitage, Henry and Edmund Ashworth, Mr R. Gardner, Mr T. Chappell, and Mr Houldsworth. Christopher Cross and J. B. Hacking had called the meeting and several influential people were showing an interest in the scheme. John Bright had written a letter which was read out—some years ago he had written to "an intelligent gentleman in Jamaica, who was making some experiments there". They planned to form a joint-stock company with a capital of £50,000 in shares, and to apply to the government under an Act of Parliament for a patent limiting the liability of shareholders to the amount of their own calls. Half the capital was to be used immediately in the cultivation of cotton in Jamaica. The American Civil War was still eleven years away and the dreadful Cotton Famine which caused so much hardship in places like Farnworth and Bolton was also still a long way off but even in these early days Thomas was interested in finding a new source of cotton which did not rely on American slave labour.

Three weeks later, on 21 August 1850, Thomas chaired a meeting of spinners in the lecture room of the Mechanics' Institution at Farnworth where the same plan for increasing the supply of cotton was again discussed. Mr Cross proposed the formation of a British Colonial Cotton Company with capital of £50,000 in 5,000 shares at £10 each. Thomas immediately said he would put his name down for 100 shares, provided the liability was limited. Mr Cross and Mr Hacking were to see the Committee appointed at the meeting at the Clarence Hotel on

30 July and other influential spinners, to find out how far they approved of the proposed plan and whether they were willing to cooperate in carrying it out. The meeting was adjourned to Tuesday 3 September.

The whole family played important parts in the life of the Chapel and the Sunday School at Halshaw Moor. Thomas became a teacher in the Sunday School when he was 18 years old and its Deputy Superintendent in 1835, then its Superintendent until he retired in 1851. His diaries show that he took his work at the Sunday School very seriously. When he taught a class, or was Superintendent, he was there twice a day. A Sunday's work for him was: morning—Sunday school, service; afternoon—school and service; evening—Little Lever, service and prayer meeting.

As a Sunday School Superintendent he must have been a frightening figure. His great-nephew wrote: "I don't know that he ever rewarded success in examination [... ...] but his punishments were condign and, I hope, unique. Any boy who displeased him was called out from his class and made to stand in front of the whole school bearing round his neck a black board about the size of a folio sheet of music, upon which was painted in large white letters 'Naughty Boy'.[8] Such was Thomas Barnes's discipline." However, there was no doubting his Christian faith. After his father's death he took Alfred, now his ward, on a tour of Ireland where he combined pleasure with business and visits to see the social conditions of the Irish people—visits to a prison, a poor house, a lunatic asylum and the run-down parts of Limerick. Thomas's diaries show that he had always been concerned with the question of how best to help the sick and the poor but as a newly-appointed magistrate he would have been especially interested in all of this. On one of the two Sundays, 28 July 1850, they attended a rather special service: Alfred wrote: "Archbishop Whately and some other dignitaries of the Established Church are here. His Grace came last Thursday on a 'visitation'. We went to hear him preach in the Church in Killarney— the sermon was for a society to afford curates in destitute parts of Ireland. He held up as an example the way in which the Dissenters support their ministers by voluntary efforts. In the evening we had a private prayer meeting among ourselves for Ireland, especially that it might have the light of the Gospel. Mr F.[*Fletcher*], Dr M.[*Massie*] and Uncle engaged in reading and prayer." They prayed: "The prayer of a righteous man availeth much." "Wheresoever two or three assembled in my name there will I be in the midst of them".[9] This private prayer meeting was nothing unusual for Thomas. At home in Farnworth he often attended the cottage prayer meetings, "taking his part in them with manifest delight", or so Rev. Hewgill commented. He also said of him, "His delight in public worship was always great." In this respect he was unlike his brother George who was sometimes very critical of the services he attended. However, both he and George had something in common—they were both anxious about their ability to live up to the demands made by a Christian life. Rev. Hewgill said that Thomas thought very seriously about how his life on earth might affect his eternal life. "He was conscious of the perils which beset him, and the strong temptations rising out of a successful business career."

On Wednesday 10 July 1850, shortly before the trip to Ireland from 18 to 31 July, Thomas had played an important part in the opening of the new Independent Chapel in Farnworth. Just before his death his father had contributed £1,000 of the £4,000 needed to build it. This new chapel, replacing the old chapel at Halshaw Moor, and big enough to hold 1,200 people, was a stone building in the Gothic style of architecture. It had stained panelling and the inside walls looked like marble. In the morning the sermon was preached by the Rev. Dr Thomas Raffles and a collection made amounting to £32. After the service there was a dinner at Queen Street Seminary and once the table cloth had been removed Thomas took the chair. Chairing meetings was also to play a large part in his life from now on. Rev. John Angell James from Birmingham, Rev. Dr Raffles from Liverpool, Rev. Dyson and Rev. McMichael from the new Farnworth chapel and other men gave after-dinner speeches. In the evening Rev. James preached to a large congregation, after which a collection was made which brought the total amount from the two services to £82.

On 5 October 1850 Thomas took the chair at the Farnworth and Kearsley Agricultural Society at the Society's Fourth Annual Show. This must have been a highlight in the life of the town as many of the works shut down to give their employees a day off to attend the show. Apparently agricultural shows of this type were a fairly new phenomenon and judging by the addresses of some of the prize-winners this one in Farnworth attracted farmers and cottagers from a fairly wide area. They brought their horses, bulls, cows, pigs, turkeys, geese and ducks to be admired and judged. There were also classes for vegetables but this October show only attracted entries in the classes for potatoes, swedes and mangelwurzels. A local firm had brought a display of its range of patented tiles and bricks. Thomas presided at the meal in the afternoon at the Vitriol Makers' Arms. He admitted to being no agriculturalist as he had no land of his own. Presumably he meant no farming land as he did by now own the Birch Hall and Darley Hall estate with its parkland. It was not until two years later, in 1852, that he bought his vast estate at The Quinta with its farms. However, even in 1850 he was very interested in agriculture, especially because of its importance to the prosperity of society in general. Thomas proposed the first two of the many toasts at the meal—to the Queen, and then to Prince Albert, Alfred Prince of Wales, and the rest of the Royal Family. In both cases the qualities he praised in the royal family were qualities which he also worked towards throughout his life. Queen Victoria, he said, was "one who has swayed the sceptre with mercy and moderation; one in whose reign many wholesome laws had been enacted, peace maintained and art and science productive to a vast extent. They often had heard of the good times of Queen Bess, but now they lived under the reign of good Queen Vic." Of Prince Albert he said that even though when he came amongst them he was a stranger, he had, "by his prudent bearing, cultivated mind, and philanthropic sympathies, enlisted the respect of all, independent of party". When a toast was proposed to Thomas, the Society's President, and his "worthy character and ability" praised, he thanked them and re-emphasized his concern for the interests of the society, and of agriculture.[10] It is clear that by 1850, even before he decided to stand as MP for Bolton, he was a respected and influential figure in the local community. The two Patrons of this Society of which he was President, were the two local Earls—the Earl of Ellesmere and the Earl of Bradford.

On Thursday 23 January 1851 Thomas attended an important political gathering of Reformers at the Albion Hotel, Manchester. It was advertised as a social soirée to meet the members of South Lancashire, the member for the West Riding of Yorkshire, members of the Borough of Manchester and other politicians, and as an opportunity for them to give their views and allow Reformers "to ascertain how far the active politicians of this district were in unison with themselves on those great points of our future policy which are likely to be insisted on by the more advanced sections of liberals in the House of Commons". The five MPs present were: T. M. Gibson, John Bright, Alexander Henry, Richard Cobden, and Joseph Brotherton.[11]

On 10 February 1851 Thomas had a serious accident. His Obituary in *The Bolton Evening News* in 1897 gave a graphic account of what happened. "In the following year (1851) he met with a sad accident whilst driving in Moor Lane, Bolton. The horse took fright and collided with a coal cart. The groom was thrown out and Mr Barnes, who was pitched forwards, attempted to regain the reins, when the vehicle collided with a lamp-post, and he was violently ejected. His right leg became entangled in the spokes of the wheel, and he was dragged along for a short distance. The leg and foot were so lacerated that amputation (of one foot) was necessary, the unfortunate gentleman submitting to the operation with great fortitude and composure." *The Christian World* also reported this incident: "Years ago, when riding or driving through the streets of Bolton, his horse took fright at the sudden glare issuing from a large foundry, and he was thrown. It was found that his leg was fractured, and required an immediate amputation to preserve his life. He was carried straightway to a surgeon's, to whom, with the greatest calmness, he gave his instructions respecting the severance of his limb. That practitioner subsequently declared that never was he so deeply impressed with the reality and power of religion as when witnessing its influence on his patient during that painful operation".

Two days after the actual accident a report appeared in *The Manchester Times*, giving the facts less dramatically: "On Monday forenoon last, an accident occurred by which Thomas Barnes, Esq., of Farnworth, met with a most serious accident and two men were also much hurt and bruised. It appears that about half past eleven o'clock, Mr Barnes was proceeding up Deansgate, with his servant man, in a gig; and when at the top of White Lion Brow, the horse suddenly became restive, and reared and plunged most violently, becoming quite unmanageable; and having knocked down two men in the street, ran against the shop of Mr James Yates, general dealer, and was completely thrown over, and Mr Barnes and his servant were dashed to the ground, but the latter was not much hurt. One of the men knocked down had his forehead severely cut, and the other was wounded in the legs, and Mr Barnes received a most serious fracture in the leg. He was immediately conveyed to Mr Mallett's, surgeon, and from thence home, followed by Mr Mallett, Mr Snape and other surgeons, who found it necessary to amputate the leg above the ankle joint. After the horse had recovered its legs, it dashed off at a furious rate up Brinks Brow to the top, where it stopped, no other accident occurring on the road. From inquiries made by our correspondent yesterday, Mr Barnes appears to have somewhat recovered from the shock, and is considered to be in a favourable state." The Saturday paper gave an up-date: "On Wednesday last we noticed a melancholy accident, by which Thomas Barnes, Esq., of Farnworth had lost one foot. It appears from the report of the surgeon, that there has not been the slightest unfavourable symptom, and he may be said to be in the most favourable state." If the date of the following extract from his private diaries, quoted at his memorial service by Rev. Hewgill, is correct, what he wrote on 9 February 1851, the day before his accident, is very poignant. "I think sometimes that in the eternal world I shall look upon the affairs of time in a very different way from what I do now. I shall esteem them very differently. It will appear a wonder to me that I could let the things of earth occupy so large a place in my thoughts."

On 30 March 1851 at the time of the Census Thomas and Ann were living in their new house, Limefield, with two female servants both born in Cumberland: Mary Banks, aged 35, from Crossthwaite, and Mary Crossthwaite, aged 25, from Keswick. Their son James was not with them. Presumably he had been sent away to school.

Only two months after his accident Thomas and eight other Farnworth cotton spinners were listed as members of a committee which had agreed to lend money to Mr Walkinshaw to set up a model farm in Trinidad as an experiment in growing cotton there. In the same year, 1851, the firm of Thomas Barnes, Farnworth Cotton Mills, Bolton, exhibited at the Great Exhibition in London. In the *Official Descriptive and Illustrated Catalogue of the Great Exhibition* produced by Thomas Ellis the firm is listed in Section III, Class II, as Number 40 out of the 65 cotton exhibitors. It had three pieces of work on display:

White Polynesian swansdown, combining fineness of back with considerable thickness of substance.

A piece of moleskin in different stages, illustrating the progressive method of raising, dyeing, printing and finishing a substitute for low woollen cloths.

A piece of printed moleskin, pattern designed and registered by the exhibitor, printed by John Jackson & Co., Manchester, and finished by John Whitehead's (of Eton) patent process of raising and finishing after dyeing and printing.

I am assuming it was Thomas's firm who also exhibited at the 1855 Paris Universal Exhibition and at the 1859 Paris Exhibition. When the report of the Lancashire manufacturers at the Paris Exhibition appeared in the press on 29 March 1859 the firm T. Barnes & Co. was one of the two firms who had exhibited their fustian products. The press commented: "The fustian exhibition turned out creditable. Moleskins of various qualities were contributed by both French and German manufacturers, but especially on the French side their number was very small, and their samples could scarcely be compared with the excellent assortment of different qualities, dyes and finishes, contributed by Messrs T. Barnes & Co. and by S. & T. Ashton. The printed fustians, especially printed moles, contributed by T. Barnes & Co. and Kershaw,

Leese & Sidebottom were likewise highly appreciated by jury and merchants."

The annual stocktaking on 30 June 1851 was only a few months after Thomas's accident. During the year the firm's profits had dropped to £2,350. Simeon Dyson now received one-eleventh of the profits and Thomas Paterson one-tenth. At the back of the stock book Thomas again began to keep a separate account which had lapsed after 1844 when George died. In 1851 he recorded that he was receiving interest on just under £71,000, presumably the amount of capital he had invested in the business. At the time of the 1851 Census Simeon Dyson and his wife Alice (née Walker) were living in Rose Cottage with three young children, Juliana, 8, Ada, 6, and Walter, 4. Simeon who was now a partner in the business described his occupation as 'clerk to cotton manufactory'.

On the very evening of his accident Thomas had been expected to attend a public meeting of the friends of a national system of education in the Town Hall, Little Bolton. Robert Heywood who took the chair announced that Thomas Barnes had met with an accident, or else he would have been present. After Thomas became an MP he addressed the House on more than one occasion before 1864 to set out the advantages of a voluntary system of education. One of his first appearances after the accident was at a meeting of the Congregational Board of Education in Manchester on 20 September 1851. He was listed as one of the laymen present when the Congregational plan of popular education was discussed. Another subject under discussion at this meeting was how to raise money for the Congregational teacher-training college, Homerton College. The college needed £3,000 to pay off its debt, £2,000 per annum to cover the running costs, and £500 for publications. In a matter of minutes £3,000 was raised: Thomas gave £500, as did Mr Watts the Chairman, and George Hadfield.

By Monday 20 October 1851 Thomas had resumed his duties as a magistrate and attended the Salford Hundred Michaelmas Quarter Sessions at the New Bailey Court. His name started to appear in reports on political meetings. For example, he was on a list of Committee members who received a notice from George Wilson at Newall's Buildings in Manchester about a meeting to be held in the Free Trade Hall on the evening of Tuesday 11 November 1851 to meet Louis Kossuth, the former Governor of Hungary, who was being received throughout the country by large enthusiastic meetings of supporters. In 1851 a committee was set up in Manchester with George Wilson, formerly chairman of the Anti-Corn Law League, as its chairman, to support the aims of what eventually became known as the National Parliamentary Reform Association. Joshua Walmsley, one of Bolton's MPs since 1849 and a very radical reformer, had been a driving force behind this movement set up after the collapse of Chartism. When the Manchester committee of the Parliamentary Reform Association held a conference for its northern supporters in December 1851 Cobden and Bright attended and Robert Heywood was the representative from Bolton. The aims of the Association which had begun as a demand for manhood suffrage, vote by ballot, equal electoral districts, triennial parliaments and the abolition of property qualifications for MPs were toned down at this conference to two main demands—for household suffrage and some redistribution of seats.

By February 1852 Thomas appears to have returned to normal life. Soon after the defeat of Lord Russell's Whig ministry he was amongst the 108 men, former Council members of the Anti-Corn Law League, who met on Tuesday 24 February 1852 at the rooms of the Manchester Financial and Parliamentary Reform Association in Newall's Buildings to decide what to do now that the Earl of Derby was to head a new Tory government intent on restoring the duty on corn. P. R. Arrowsmith was one of the speakers who debated the proposed revival of the League. This meeting was described in *The Manchester Times* as "one of the most influential and numerous gatherings we have witnessed of the old Council of the League since the old and palmy days of its power". Amongst the subscriptions to the fund to support the re-establishment of the League, Thomas's subscription of £500 was only matched by one other person. The League was formally re-launched on 2 March 1852 at a meeting of the Council and Friends of the late League in the large room at Newall's Buildings, with George Wilson in the Chair. Although the fund already had £72,402 7s 0d and £763 11s 5d from the subscriptions of working people, another call for subscriptions was made. A second instalment (of 2s 8d) came from the workpeople at Thomas's mills in Farnworth. On the day before this Thomas was one of the magistrates when the Salford Hundred Bench sat at the New Bailey on Monday 1 March 1852.

On 10 March the Reform Registration Association in Bolton held a meeting chaired by Joseph Crook to hear of the retirement of Sir Joshua Walmsley. Even at this early stage they intended to select two candidates "pledged to carry out free trade in its fullest extent" to contest the election and appointed a committee to do this. A deputation then approached Thomas and on the following day, 11 March, he met the Reformers at the News Room in Fold Street, Bolton, to introduce himself and set out his views. He "addressed them as a candidate for their suffrages upon the broad basis of parliamentary and financial reform". *The Manchester Times* commented, "He satisfied all grades of reformers in his views upon public matters, and may now be safely termed the popular candidate." On 12 March in a letter addressed to the Electors of the Borough of Bolton Thomas set out his political views:

To the Electors of the Borough of Bolton

Gentlemen—Having been solicited by an influential Deputation, representing a numerous and important section of your body, to offer myself as a Candidate for your suffrages at the approaching election, I am induced to do so, and beg to state briefly my political opinions.

I am most decidedly of opinion that a resolute perseverance in the application of Free Trade principles to every branch of commerce is imperatively required, to promote and secure the welfare and contentment of all classes of the community; and shall resist to the utmost, every attempt, by whomsoever made, to impose the unjust and mischievous restrictions which the Legislature has wisely abolished.

I am of opinion that further Reform of Parliament is necessary, and shall support such proposals to effect this object as receive the sanction of the well-known body of earnest Reformers in the House of Commons, and especially the principles embodied in Mr. Hume's Annual Motion.

I shall consider it to be my duty to endeavour to secure wise and strict economy in every department of the Government, and feel persuaded that the National expenditure may be considerably reduced without impairing the efficiency of the public service.

Our warlike establishments I believe to be strong enough under judicious direction, to maintain inviolate our national security.

The Local Business of the Borough shall, at all times, command my prompt attention.

I shall take an early opportunity of addressing you publicly, when I shall be able to enter more into detail on various subjects of general interest.

I have the honour to be, Gentlemen,

Your obedient servant,

Thomas Barnes

Limefield, March 12 1852

On the following Tuesday, 16 March 1852, Thomas appeared at a public meeting in the Temperance Hall in Bolton convened by the

Reform Association to introduce himself to the electors. This meeting was also chaired by Joseph Crook who was nominated as Chairman by P. R. Arrowsmith and seconded by T. Thomasson. Thomas began his first ever public political speech:

"Gentlemen, electors, and non-electors,—for the first time in my life I stand before you at what may be termed an electioneering meeting. Having been solicited by an influential deputation to become a candidate at the next general election, I have, as stated in my address, consented to do so, and now appear before you to give some explanation of my opinions upon various subjects of interest. I do not conceal from you that I esteem it a high honour to be thus solicited to become a candidate for your suffrages. I appear before you as a plain man of business, sprung from amongst yourselves, and wish to make a plain statement of my views and opinions. I desire to stand before you with the clearest transparency; I have nothing to conceal; what I am in reality, such I wish to appear before you."

He began with the subject of free trade: "The first, and, as I consider, the most absorbing topic is that of free trade; and, as a free trader, in the fullest sense of the term, I stand before you. But it is an easy matter, gentlemen, for a man to declare himself a free trader: the supply will always be suited to the demand. When constituencies call for free traders, all candidates will be such; and you may reasonably ask what evidence I can give of my sincerity. I like the question that was used frequently by Napoleon in reference to his generals and officers who were seeking employment and promotion,—What has he done? And by this testing question I am willing to be tried. What evidence have I given of my being a free trader? I became a member of the Anti-Corn Law League when it was first formed, and continued to be so until it was dissolved; I contributed to its funds; I have done so also since its revival; and it is an old saying that if a man parts with his money you may be sure he is sincere and earnest. I was one of the Council of the League; I am so again: which I submit is pretty strong evidence that I am not a free trader of to-day, but of some standing."

He then explained why he believed there should be no change to the Corn Laws. "In reference to the alteration of the Corn Laws, I would ask who is it that seeks their alteration? Who wants them altered? Who is it that is tired of cheap bread? Who gets too big a loaf for his money, or pays too little for his loaf? Who has too many meals in a day? Are there any of the working classes so situated? If not, I presume they do not want a bread tax. Then, do the commercial classes want it altered? Are the merchants tired of having such free commerce? Do they desire again to be lost in the mazes of sliding-scale calculations—to be plunged into lottery, gambling speculations, inseparable from it? I have never heard of any complaints from that quarter. Do the shopkeepers of the country desire a change? Do the tailors sell too many clothes? The advertisements of Hyam & Moses & Son indicate nothing of the kind. Who, then, wants the change? The answer lies between the farmer and the landowner. 'I cannot pay my rent', says the one, 'with produce at such a low price'. 'I cannot maintain my establishment, pay my mortgage interest, marriage portions, settlements, such like, with a less rent'. So these two are at a dead lock. What is to be done? 'Oh, just put on a 5s fixed duty. There are 20,000,000 of people. It will raise £5,000,000 for them—that's all—they will never feel it, and it will relieve us.' All that I have to say to these gentlemen is, that as their difficulty arises out of a mere question of rent, 'just settle it between yourselves, we have nothing to do with your affairs'.

We have imported during the last five years an amount of human food equal to 50,000,000 quarters of wheat; and if that had not been the case, would the people have had enough? I should, if in Parliament, and shall even out of it, do all I can to prevent the free-trade policy from being reversed. It is the great humaniser of mankind; it is the best bond of peace; it is the preventative of war, that great destroyer of the human race. I shall consider it my duty to use all the means within my power to prevent even the thin end of the wedge of protection from being again inserted."

The next topic was his views on the present Reform Bill. "I will now pass to another subject, which I consider to be next, if not equal, in importance, namely that of parliamentary reform. The present Reform Bill is about twenty years old, and requires amending to a considerable extent. It is about as well suited now to the people of this country as a suit of clothes would be for a man who had been measured for them twenty years ago, when he was a boy of about twelve years of age: the coat barely covering the elbows, the legs of the trousers reaching no lower than the knees, and presenting altogether a very threadbare appearance. The Reform Bill now fits the country no better; the body politic has outgrown it; and the easiest and most rational plan to remedy this state of things, is to get a new measure. And if we cannot succeed in obtaining a new Reform Bill satisfactory to us on every point, and most adapted to the wants of the people,—if we cannot do the best we would, we must endeavour to secure the next best. All who pay the rates ought to have the franchise, and also every person who is the owner of property, whether freehold, leasehold, or copyhold, of the value of 40s per annum. I think, gentlemen, this is the least we ought to expect. I am prepared myself to go a little further— but here I would stand, and say, this, and nothing less. If obtained, it will make way for something more, and when the time comes, we shall get it. This, I think, is the least that can be asked or offered. I know not what may be obtained but it appears to me that for this the country is quite prepared. Judging from my own experiences of the labouring classes, I should say that they are ready and able now to exercise a free and independent vote—to give it intelligently and honestly."

His belief in the value of the ballot was something which remained unchanged throughout the whole of his time in Parliament: "But, gentlemen, there is one more thing that must accompany the new Reform Bill, and without which no Reform Bill can, in my opinion, be at all perfect, or worth much. I allude to the ballot. The ballot must be given. I cannot conceive why any man can for a moment raise his voice against it. What is there in this measure that is un-English or improper? We use it in our clubs; and there it is considered a very fair, English, honest, and excellent plan; and why should it not be considered so in this case? Not only does it carry fairness upon its very face, but we say, in the present state of society, it is a taunting mockery to give the working man the franchise and not give him the ballot. If I were myself in the place of either a working man or a small shopkeeper, I should fervently pray the legislature to keep the franchise to itself, unless I might have the ballot along with it. The ballot, I think, gentlemen, must be a part of any Reform Bill."

The way in which he tackled the subject of the unequal distribution of parliamentary seats was typical of the way he approached similar topics in future speeches—using selected statistics to reinforce a point: "The next thing, gentlemen, I would allude to, is the distribution of members; and if you will allow me, I will just read to you what I have taken from a late number of *The Times*. It is not long, but I think it clearly makes out a case, and will obviate the necessity of saying anything else upon the subject. The writer takes the counties of Middlesex, Dorset, and Cornwall. In Middlesex, the annual value of the property for 1847 was £7,584,668; in Cornwall, £976,209; and in Dorset, £789,342. Yet each sends 14 members to Parliament. The number of inhabited houses in Middlesex is 242,798; in Dorset, 34,771; in Cornwall, 68,214. Yet each sends 14 members to Parliament. The population of Middlesex is 1,895,710; Cornwall 356,662; and Dorset 177,597. Yet each sends 14 members to Parliament. I wonder if there ever was a greater anomaly than that; to my mind it is one of the greatest that could be presented in any nation. Again, take another anomaly. Let us compare six counties whose united property and population nearly equals that of Middlesex, and how does the case stand? It stands thus. The population of Middlesex is 1,895,710 and the population of these united counties is not much different. The property of Middlesex is £7,584,668 whilst that of these six united counties is £7,533,335. Now, then, let us see about the representatives. Middlesex sends 14 members to Parliament, and these six counties, the population and property of which are very nearly the same, send 102 members."

Another point in his manifesto was the call for shorter parliaments: "The next question upon which I deem it necessary to give you my views is the duration of parliaments. I think seven years is too long a time for anyone to have matter of such great importance placed in his hands, without being called to account for it, and I think we should shorten the duration of parliaments. I should go down to three years; I would say that in any new Reform Bill, parliaments should not be allowed to continue more than three years together without being dissolved."

To illustrate his point that the Government needed to make financial cut-backs he drew on illustrations from wastage in the navy: "Having thus made some observations, and stated very briefly my views upon these subjects, I will now speak in the same short way with respect to financial reform. Here is a subject that demands reform as well as a change in the representation of the country. Taxes we do and must pay, and always shall have to pay, so long as we have a government. Then it is an important thing that all the taxes we pay should be properly applied. Unfortunately we cannot say quite so much of them. The necessity that there should be a reform upon this subject is seen if we go to the naval departments and see how out taxes go. There, by the monstrous way things are carried on, we shall have illustrations how the money is spent. Ships built that cannot sail; some that turn up like a dead fish, on one side; some that float in the dock for a very short time, and then are pronounced unseaworthy; and so the thing goes on. And this they call building ships. If they want a fast sailing vessel, they have to go to Mr Whyte, of Cowes; they cannot build a vessel that can sail along with Mr Whyte's; and Mr Green, of London, tells us that he can build our men-of-war for very much less than they cost. I cannot do more than just hint at these, to let you see that there is necessity for reformation."

He set out his views on the merits of direct taxation: "Upon my general views of taxation, I may remark that I think taxes should be so laid that we take as little as possible out of the pockets of the people; and that it should all go into the exchequer. The expensive apparatus that is in existence at the present time, in the shape of excise officers and servants of one kind or another, that are said to be necessary in order to collect the taxes, is so great as to eat up a very large proportion of what we pay. I for one am a friend to direct taxation—that I know is a very favourite subject in this town. There are many truths said in joke. I once heard a man say, 'I like direct taxation; I like the income-tax for everybody but myself. I don't like the excise man taking money out of my pocket without receiving an equivalent'. Now it is the excellence of direct taxation to take money out of our pockets; and it would make the whole country wide awake to know what has become of the money. But if we take the taxes out of bread, sugar and such like things, we pay the money to the shopkeeper, and in time we quite forget that we are paying taxes; and thus we feel easy upon the subject, and never ask any questions of the government respecting the money we are paying. We shall never have a cheap and economical mode of government except we have direct taxation along with the other, if not entirely, and carry out the principle so as to take something direct out of the pockets of the people."

He then examined various forms of taxes: "All taxation upon the produce of industry I look upon as prejudicial in the highest degree to the general welfare of all. I consider the taxes upon knowledge the worst that can exist. What is to elevate the people but knowledge? And why should the fountain-head be taxed? We had better tax the water that comes from heaven, than tax knowledge. We should be thankful that ours is a wet climate, or, perhaps, water would have been taxed ere this! What are those taxes on knowledge? We have an annual revenue from the duty on paper of £800,000. Then there is received for advertisements the sum of £155,000. There is also the penny stamp on newspapers, and a duty on foreign books; and from this source, according to a return for 1850, was derived to the revenue an aggregate sum of £1,380,668, extracted from the knowledge of the people, and acting as an obstacle to their being instructed and informed. Taxes on what you may call cleanliness are also objectionable. Take the article of soap. We look upon it as a very great evil; and anything that will prevent the health, comfort, and happiness of the people, must be prejudicial to the well-being of society. I therefore think that the tax on soap is one which ought at a very early period to be removed."

Unnecessary expenditure on the army was the next topic: "Then, gentlemen, next of all comes the army. What is to be done with that? Well, gentlemen, I think that the army is large enough; and I do not feel disposed myself to increase it, either by augmenting the number of our regular soldiers, or by forming a militia. I feel confident that the forces that we have at the present time are sufficient for us. It seems to be acknowledged on all hands that it is very improper for us to interfere with foreign lands. I think we have no right to meddle with the business of other people. If France chooses to elect a president, let her do so; if she wants an emperor, let her have one; or if she desires neither one nor the other, still let her have her own way; we have no right to meddle; it is the business of the French people, and not ours."

He did not believe that the colonies should rely on the British army for protection. "Then if we do not interfere in the affairs of foreign nations, I want to know what the army is for? A great number of the troops are in the colonies. What are they doing there? There is not a finer race of men in the world than those in the colonies. The colonies can protect themselves, and that very well, as they ought to be made to do; and I am sure, if we put it to them whether they would not rather protect themselves than pay for the protection we give, we should very soon find what they would do. Under the present arrangements, and while maintained at such an enormous cost, I do not see what advantage the colonies are to us; it would be better for us, as well as for them, that they should be made self-governing and independent nations. I should deplore any step being taken that would make the colonies our enemies. Our friends and relatives—some of them—go to those places and they there lay the foundation of their future fortunes. They are allied to us by kindred, by sympathy, and by all their early associations; and I think if we just let them form governments for themselves, and manage their own business,—if we do with them as we do with our own sons when they get into young men, say to them, you must turn out and live by your own exertions, work your own way, we have done all we can to help you, now you must help yourself; and if we do so, we shall find our colonies rising into the greatest prosperity, and every one of them, as young nations, will be bound to Old England by the strongest ties that can bind one nation to another. Then we may very safely bring our soldiers from the colonies, and thus all necessity for increasing the army on that account will be done away with."

He continued to discuss "the foolish talk of French invasion". Even if the French did invade, 30,000 men could be assembled in a few hours. The fear of the French was "a thing got up for the sake of getting up an increased army, and expenditure of public money, and to find places for a number of people who do not like to take their coats off and work with their hands or heads".

He maintained that Britain's natural defence should anyway be, not soldiers, but sailors. He had details of where all the British naval ships were at that moment, and not one was in an area which needed defending. They were on the South American coast, the African coast (where they were "interfering with that most inhuman of all traffic, the traffic in human flesh"), in North America, the Eastern Ocean, the Pacific, Lisbon (where there was no danger of invasion), the Mediterranean (where there was "nothing to do but bask in a bright sun").

In the second half of his speech he set out his views on religious liberty, a subject which played an important part in both his political and personal life. "My views are simply these: that religion is a thing that concerns every man's conscience in the sight of his maker. It is a matter that we have to do with Him, and not with any human being. No human being has any business to interfere betwixt me and my maker. I carry this principle out, and I say that all governments should know no distinction betwixt one religious denomination and another. I say that governments should leave this thing alone. If religion is a thing of truth, it will exist without their aid; if it a thing of error, they ought not to attempt to prop it up. And I say that governments have no business whatever to favour one or to persecute another; they are equal, and every man's conscience is equal, and no Government should step in betwixt one man and another. I am, therefore, as you will perceive, for religious equality; and I say the government should not touch it in any form whatever, neither help nor hinder, nor in any way interfere in any of the forms, the discipline, or in anything that concerns any one of them."

The question of grants of public money to religious bodies was another repeated theme in his political life. "And you will, of course, expect from me that I should condemn the appropriation of any part of the public funds to any denomination whatever. I should oppose all grants of public money to every denomination alike. There is only this and another course that is just: if you pay one, you must pay all. You have the choice of the two, and I should decidedly prefer to keep my money in my pocket, and pay it to none. I do this, gentlemen, upon moral grounds; I do it also upon religious grounds, and looking upon it as a religious man, I say there is nothing that has damaged religion more than grants of public money made to it. If the state grant money to a church of any denomination, it will reserve to itself the right of dictation, and it would be unreasonable to expect otherwise. If we give money to any particular object, we have a right to see that the money is properly applied: so the state, if it grants money to any particular church, it must of necessity, and in justice to the persons who contribute with them, interfere with the management of it, to see how the money is expended and applied, also, forced exactions for the support of religion are opposed to the spirit of it. What is the spirit of it? It is simply this, that religion should be supported by the followers of it, of every denomination, from a feeling of love. Whatsoever a man gives to his religion, should be given as an expression of gratitude, as a free, willing, and voluntary contribution."

He finished with a summing-up of how he hoped to conduct himself: "I should esteem it a very high privilege, if I should, by your suffrages and independent votes, be elected. But I say this, gentlemen, that I would a thousand times rather stay at home, and never be placed in that position, unless I am carried by free, moral, and pure votes. It is the purpose of my life, and I hope ever will be, to do everything that I can, in every possible way, to elevate myself and all around me in the scale of morality; and I should deeply deplore the use of any means, during the election, that would, in the slightest degree, injure the morals of any man. It is righteousness that exalts a nation, and sin is a reproach to any people."

Before the meeting ended he answered a question on national education, saying that he did not think there was a need for a state-run education system. The problem was getting parents to send their children to the schools which already existed. He was against any move to make attendance compulsory.[12]

His first-ever political speech was very well received, the audience reacting with cries of "Hear, hear" or "Shame", cheers or laughter. The views he expressed now changed very little throughout the years he was in Parliament. After the speech was over, Henry Ashworth, an old acquaintance of Thomas's father, proposed that Thomas Barnes was a fit and proper person to represent the Liberal public of the Borough of Bolton. Robert Heywood, one of the deputation who had invited Thomas to stand, seconded the motion which was then carried by the meeting.

On 2 April 1852 Thomas attended another meeting at Newall's Buildings, this time to choose a free-trade representative for South Lancashire. As Thomas lived in Farnworth, he would have been a

South Lancashire elector. Alexander Henry, their present MP, was
retiring on health grounds and John Cheetham of Stalybridge was put
forward as his successor. In the report of this meeting Thomas was
referred to as Mr Thomas Barnes of Bolton. It would be unlikely that
a Bolton elector would have attended the meeting and it was certainly
Thomas Barnes of Farnworth who was at the follow-up meeting on
Tuesday 6 April, when John Cheetham was formally nominated. John
Bright seconded the nomination. Thomas was one of the very large
Brown and Cheetham Committee with George Wilson as its Chairman.
Thomas had many links with John Cheetham whose daughter, Ellen,
later married his son James Richardson. Both men were cotton spinners
and Independent Dissidents. Both were elected at the 1852 election
and lost their seats at the same time in 1857. John Cheetham was
President of the Cotton Supply Association and Thomas was on its
Committee.

On 8 April 1852 at the Anniversary of the Lancashire Congregational
Union in Liverpool a report was read about the progress of the Chapel
Building Society, a scheme to build fifty Congregational chapels within
five years, which had been proposed the previous year by George
Hadfield. A Committee had been appointed then but now more money
as needed. As the old system of begging for funds was now proving
more and more unproductive a new annual subscription scheme of £2
and upwards was suggested. Every subscriber of £1,000 or more was
to be a Trustee of the funds raised and deposited in the bank. George
Hadfield wanted to make things move even faster. He promised to
give £5,000—£100 for each of the fifty chapels if built within seven
years. Thomas Barnes and Mr Walls had also promised to give £1,000
in five years.

By 10 April Thomas's prospects in Bolton seemed assured. A second
candidate had been selected, Joseph Crook, who had chaired both the
meetings at which Thomas had been put forward. *The Manchester Times*,
a pro-Reform paper, described the situation: "There are four candidates
in the field: the Conservative member Mr Blair; Mr Ainsworth who
does not appear to be acknowledged on either side; Mr Barnes of
Farnworth, cotton spinner; and Mr Crook of Bolton, cotton spinner.
The latter gentleman has been canvassing during the week, and, if
report be correct, entertains, from the reception he met with, every
prospect of success. With regard to Mr Barnes few doubts are entertained,
as he is decidedly the popular candidate."

Thomas did not play a very active part in the build-up to the election
for the next two months. He was involved in important business in

London which prevented him from attending the meeting in the Temperance Hall on Thursday 15 April when Joseph Crook made his introductory speech to the electors. He had, however, written on 13 April from an address in London, Castle Falcon Hotel, Aldersgate, to explain the reason for his absence. This letter was read out by H. M. Richardson, a solicitor who was to play a decisive role in Thomas's political career. The letter explained that Thomas was engaged in business he could not leave until completed. It was written in most encouraging terms and Thomas said he hoped he and Joseph Crook would be placed side by side at the election and that the friends of one would be found to be the friends of the other. The letter was received with much applause.

Thomas did, however, manage to fit in a meeting at the Reform Association Newsroom in Fold Street on Monday evening, 3 May, before rushing back to London the following day. The meeting, scheduled for the Wednesday, had had to be rearranged to fit in with his busy timetable. Mr Thomasson was in the chair, and Thomas made a short speech, assuring them of his full agreement with the plan to have a single committee for the two candidates. After the applause had subsided, Mr Crook also delivered a short address, and Mr Richardson, Mr Parkinson and two or three others spoke on the success of the present canvass, assuring the meeting that if the same feeling continued there could be no doubt of triumphant success.

Thomas's business in London was probably concerned with the Lancashire and Yorkshire Railway Company. He was now the Chairman of the Board of Directors and had to call a Special General Meeting of the Company on Tuesday 25 May 1852 to confirm, or not confirm, two bills which were before Parliament at the time. Presumably he was in London to see these two bills through Parliament.

Although he spent a great deal of time in London in the three months after he had agreed to stand as a candidate at the 1852 election, he was in Bolton on 24 May 1852 when the town celebrated the Queen's birthday. The festivities were very similar to those in Farnworth in 1864 when Thomas celebrated his son's coming-of-age. "At an early hour a number of flags were seen floating from the different buildings, and the bells of the Parish Church poured forth many a lovely peal." Had there been any military in the town a *feu-de-joie* would have been fired, too. Thomas and Joseph Crook were at the public dinner in the evening at the Swan Hotel with another hundred men, including some of the principal members of the Corporation.

Thomas was at another public meeting to promote the Anti-Corn Law League on 27 May 1852 in the Temperance Hall in Little Bolton when Mr R. R. R. Moore spoke on the subject of free trade. As Chairman, Thomas introduced the meeting saying that "a ministry was in office that was pledged to a restoration of protection, notwithstanding the great blessings consequent upon free trade". He said of Lord Derby that if he "refused to attempt to restore protection, he ought to be turned out for inconsistency; if he attempted to restore it, he would be turned out for the attempt; and if he said he would stand still, he must go out for that".

On Thursday 10 June 1852 there was a large meeting of non-electors in Bolton to support the candidature of Thomas Barnes and Joseph Crook. By the 26 June Thomas had arrived back from London, "having", as *The Manchester Times* commented, "been engaged in London upon Parliamentary business nearly the whole of the time since he became a candidate for Parliamentary honours; he has therefore had but little opportunity of making a canvass in person, but the committee, acting on behalf of that gentleman and Mr Crook, have been most energetic in their exertions." On Saturday 26 June Thomas's letter to the electors of the Borough of Bolton was printed in *The Bolton Chronicle* and an open-air meeting was then held on Monday on a plot of land in Blackburn Street, again in support of the two Reform candidates. The build-up to the 1852 General Election on 8 July was about to begin.

Election preparations reached fever-pitch in the couple of weeks after Parliament was dissolved. A series of at least five open-air meetings on behalf of Thomas and Joseph Crook was held in the evenings, starting on the Thursday two weeks before election-week. It was clear that the two men were supported by the working men, very few of whom had the vote. These "non-electors" by using the "indirect influences at their command" were to play an important part in this election. In election week itself committee rooms were organized and placards appeared on walls, mainly issued by the Reform Association and mainly on the subject of free trade versus protection. A huge crowd of between 16,000 and 18,000 assembled on the Market Place in front of the hustings on Nomination Day and for the three hours of speeches jostled for position. Crush barriers had started to be used in other places, but not yet in Bolton. People were pushed and crushed and there was some actual fighting and kicking. *The Bolton Chronicle* reported: "To give a description of the proceedings at the Bolton nomination on Wednesday would be impossible; and it may be sufficient here to state that they were of a most uproarious character, cheering, groaning, hissing, or singing, being indulged in in the case of every speaker, so as to defy the vast multitude hearing any considerable portion of what was advanced, and therefore to prevent the forming any opinion of the candidates or their principles from what they said." Nevertheless, all the speeches were given and must have been audible, judging by the responses of the crowd who cheered or groaned, depending on their political allegiance. Each candidate was nominated and seconded and then made a speech on his own behalf. Thomas was nominated by P. R. Arrowsmith who paid tribute to his many moral qualities— he was a good master, a true friend, and "one who fills that situation in life in which he has been placed with honour to himself and benefit to his fellow-creatures". He was "an unflinching friend of free trade, and a friend of the rights and liberties of his fellow men". His nomination was seconded by Robert Heywood who described him as a "man of the strictest integrity, a staunch friend of civil and religious liberty, a free trader, a friend to the ballot, to extended suffrage and shorter parliaments. He would attempt to remove all abuses—in the army, navy, church or state."

When the Mayor asked the crowd for a show of hands two-thirds were in favour of Barnes and Crook. Therefore a poll was demanded on behalf of the other two candidates to take place on the following day. To everyone's surprise both Liberal candidates headed the poll after the first hour's voting and maintained the lead until the polls closed at four o'clock. The Liberals had really only expected to send one Liberal to Parliament—Thomas Barnes. However, Joseph Crook had beaten the Conservative Stephen Blair by just 10 votes. The Liberal victory was summed up as a victory for free trade and a defeat for protection. The defeated Conservatives were disappointed that a number of their supporters had failed to vote and they were already suggesting bribery and corruption on the part of their Liberal opponents. Once the election was over, Thomas and Joseph Crook published a letter of thanks addressed this time, not just to the electors, but to the electors and non-electors who had played such an important part in their success:

To the Electors and Non-electors of the Borough of Bolton

Gentlemen, we most sincerely thank you for the hearty support which you have afforded in the noble struggle for the cause of a wise commercial policy, and in vindication of a comprehensive and salutary Reform.

We are, gentlemen, your obedient servants

Thomas Barnes and Joseph Crook

Twelve years later *The Christian World* wrote an article about Thomas and commented that immediately after all the excitement of the week Thomas was back doing his work at the Sunday School in Farnworth on Sunday morning, "delighting as much in his seat at the school as in his seat at St Stephen's".

View of Quinta Hall across the lake

Quinta Congregational Chapel

Thomas expanded his business in Lancashire but also used his wealth to buy an estate on the Welsh Borders, The Quinta in the parish of St Martin's. Its address was sometimes given as Shropshire and sometimes as Denbighshire. In the early days the nearest village was referred to as The Lodge. This later became part of present-day Weston Rhyn. The Quinta's address varied from being near Chirk, to near Craignant, and sometimes to near Oswestry. "Quinta" is a Portuguese word indicating a country estate and The Quinta which Thomas bought was indeed a vast country estate originally owned by the Myddleton family of Chirk Castle. By 1838 the occupier and owner of the 17th century house was Frederick West of Gulham Court in Berkshire. The estate had been in the West family for many years. It was set in 72 acres of pasture, meadows, lawns and pleasure gardens and by the mid 1840s Frederick West had erected a limestone folly on a hill facing the house on the edge of what became known as Temple Wood, a half-scale Stonehenge, reputedly a copy of some Druidical ruins in either Jersey or Guernsey. In a letter dated 20 January 1965 James Freeland Barnes, a descendant of Thomas's brother George, wrote an account of what the family knew about the ruins which he referred to as the Temple in Temple Field close to Templegarth, Bronygarth. "The Temple is a Victorian folly, a fact which is only too apparent from the iron cramps which held pieces of it together and from the machine-made drill holes visible down some of the edges which were made for the insertion of wedges or even small blasting charges. [... ...] William Cathrall's *History of Oswestry* published by George Lewis in 1855 is however silent on the subject of the Temple which leads me to suppose that the family story (confirmed by my Aunt Dr Ellen Barnes) is correct. This is to the effect that great-great uncle Thomas, while holidaying in the Isle of Wight was so enraptured with an alleged druidic temple he saw there (and which was probably also spurious) that he came home and caused a similar one to be put up in the Temple Field. Anyhow, my grandfather [Harold Alfred Barnes] always said that it was a fake and a not very good one either."

In the 1850s the estate was leased to Rowland Jones Venables before Thomas Barnes bought it. Amongst documents in the Shropshire Archives in the Venables Collection is a note dated 18 October 1852 signed by Rowland Jones Venables to the effect that some enclosed deeds were held by him on the part of Mr Edward Lewis and himself as executors and that they were covenanted to produce them to Mr Thomas Barnes, the purchaser of the Quinta estate. (Many years later Thomas attended Rowland Jones Venables' funeral at Selattyn on 21

May 1868. It was not a public funeral as no invitations had been sent out but up to twenty of the local gentry sent their private carriages as a mark of respect. Thomas's carriage was the second in the procession after the family members, following immediately behind Sir Watkin Williams Wynn.) Thomas's first move after buying The Quinta was to knock down the old hall and rebuild it in a stone and a style which did not seem to please the locals. One said that with its dull grey limestone it was even for those times a remarkably unattractive house whose only saving grace was that it lay within a park established by Frederick West. Niklaus Pevsner's comments on The Quinta were: "A fantastical though not large house in the Gothic style completed in 1858 for Thomas Barnes, railway magnate and Liberal MP for Bolton. Thoroughly asymmetrical, the walls are rock-faced. Large windows with flame-like tracery. Plenty of foliage carving and many improving texts." James Freeland Barnes was not impressed with the house, either. In the same letter written on 20 January 1965 in which he described the Temple folly he added, "At that time there was a considerable craze for antiquities—genuine or spurious—as witness that neo-gothic monstrosity The Quinta itself—and which I can remember when the hall was lined with pitch-pine panelling with suitable gothic 'texts' by way of decoration." All that now remains of the original 17th century house is the old stabling block. New stables were being built in August 1860 when a party from Farnworth visited The Quinta. In 1925 there was also still a lodge known as "The Castle" which has now vanished. It was possibly the smaller house, Tŷ Newydd, which once lay to the east of the old hall.

Thomas's taste for "exuberant" Victorian Gothic architecture was not appreciated in Denbighshire and even now a local historian (C. Neville Hurdsman) describes the house as being in the style of Thomas's native Lancashire but very much Victorian, with a leaning towards the better styled railway buildings. In 1925 a local group visited the house—which they described as an "elegant new mansion"—and had a guided tour of the beautiful gardens and grounds with grand conifers planted by Thomas when he first bought the estate. When I visited Quinta Hall and park in March 2006 the ornamental lake and wide expanses of lawn with large conifers are still the first things you see as you drive up the curving drive to the house at the top of the hill. It is still possible to imagine how the house would have looked in its heyday with its turret and huge conservatory, before it was boxed in by the assortment of unattractive school buildings and 20th century outbuildings, remnants of its life as a Dr Barnado's Approved School for Boys from 1940 to

1980. As a result of this, it is not a Grade 2 Listed building like the Quinta Church and the Quinta Sunday School. Nevertheless, it is an impressive example of Victorian Gothic architecture and the quality of the craftsmanship with which it was built is still very obvious. The décor was put in the hands of Mr Chase, a famous London decorator. The carved stone window frames, the solid oak doors, the beautiful parquet floors, the baronial hall with its carved fireplace and polished wood staircase sweeping up to the first floor are just some of the examples of the work which went into the house.

The ceilings must have been impressive. Now they are painted white but one of the original red and green Tudor roses which used to cover each of the plaster squares has been left as an indication of how things were. Similarly, a small ceiling in a tower room still has its intricate Victorian design. As late as 1925 the walls were covered with painted inscriptions such as the Welsh proverb "Heb Dduw, heb ddim. Duw a digon" ["Without God, without anything. God is enough."]. A carved inscription over the fireplace in Gothic lettering still greets you: "Warm ye in friendship". Before 1865, the writer of an article in *The Christian World* was also impressed by these inscriptions: "We were delighted to observe, during a recent visit, that he has revived the good old custom, traces of which we meet with in old houses in Edinburgh, and on the Continent—viz., inscribing sentences from the good old Book amongst the external and internal carvings of his dwelling. [... ...] It was pleasant to see this rim of a Divine sentence running through the oaken carvings of the splendid staircase: 'Seest thou a man diligent in his business, he shall stand before kings; he shall not stand before mean men', and among the frescoes of the ceilings in the sumptuous dining room, these stimulants to harmony and temperance: 'Better is a dinner of herbs where peace is, than a stalled ox and contention therewith', 'Wine is a mocker; strong drink is raging, and he that is deceived thereby is not wise'."[13] James Freeland Barnes wrote about the house in a letter dated 26 May 1966: "I have a very dim recollection of visiting the house in the 1920s when my step great grandmother [Georgiana] was alive and it remains in my memory as a very formal and somewhat forbidding Victorian house of the last century."

Thomas bought the Quinta estate in 1852. However, I wonder whether he had already started to invest in the area before this. In his *History of St Martin's and Weston Rhyn* C. Neville Hurdsman gives an account of the rectorial and lay tithes at the time of the Commutation of Tithes in 1838. The rectorial tithes amounted to £962 and the bulk of them were bought by two men, Lord A. E. Hill Trevor (£330), and Mr Dickens of Ty'ndŵr (£270). Rev. J. C. Phillips of Ty'n-y-Rhos bought £56–worth and Thomas Barnes the remaining £36–worth. He must have paid a considerable sum for them—for his £330–worth Lord Trevor paid £10,500, which represents a 3% return on his capital. On this basis Thomas must have paid about £1,500 for them. However, he also bought what appears to be the whole of the lay tithes—all £170–worth of them. If he paid on the same scale as he did for the rectorial tithes, he must have paid another £5,000 for these. It is not clear from Mr Hurdsman's book just when these tithes were bought but it illustrates how big an investment Thomas made when he bought The Quinta. It is possible that these tithes were linked in some way with the two properties Trehowell and Preesgweene which both were part of the Quinta estate at the time of the final sale in 1929–30. Before the sale in 1928 the Quinta estate had paid £6 2s into the St Martin and Weston Rhyn Charities. After the sale in 1931 the new owners of the Trehowell and Preesgweene estates had each continued to pay their share of the Charity.

Back in Farnworth the mills still demanded Thomas's attention. The annual stocktaking on 30 June 1852 just before he was elected as an MP for the first time showed a good profit for the previous year of £10,533. Simeon Dyson's share rose again, this time to one-tenth, equalling Thomas Paterson's share. From now on, signatures were added to confirm the share-out.

At one time during these early years Thomas was also in partnership with two brothers called Cross. His own brother, George, had been on holiday several times with members of the Cross family, but I have not found in George's diaries any reference to C. and J. Cross, only to Mr Cross, T. Cross and some sisters. The partnership with the two Cross brothers is not recorded in the annual stocktaking accounts. Unlike other partners, they did not receive their share of the annual profits. A notice appeared in *The Manchester Times* on Wednesday 20 December 1854 dissolving Thomas's partnership with J. Cross who had died, still leaving as a partner another brother, Christopher Cross.

Partnership dissolved

C. Cross, T. Barnes & J. Cross (deceased), Farnworth, Lancashire, manufacturers of textile fabrics; as far as regards J. Cross.

Christopher Cross also left the partnership some time during the next few years. Unfortunately things did not go well for him after that. He appeared in the Manchester Bankruptcy Court on 9 March 1858 when a brief summary of his career was given. "The bankrupt was formerly in business at Bolton, connected with Mr Barnes MP, and subsequently carried on business with Mr Snape at Habergham Eaves near Burnley, under the title of D. Snape & Co. Mr Snape retired and then Cross carried on business on his own account, but got into difficulties."[14]

Another aspect of Thomas's life which took up much of his time was his involvement with Queen Street Seminary, the private school which had been set up by his father and other Farnworth industrialists to provide an education for the children of their workforce. It was totally non-denominational and supported mainly by subscriptions and by the children's fees. James Rothwell Barnes was the chief subscriber and the school was referred to as his private seminary. Both George and Thomas also contributed from the start and until his death in 1844 George was the Treasurer. Thomas took over this position after George's death at a time when finances were beginning to be strained. He often had to preside at meetings where teachers were given very little choice about taking on more work for no additional pay. For example on Christmas Day 1845 an offer was made to Mr Fyfe, the teacher in charge of the Juvenile School, either to accept an additional salary of £5, making his current salary £90 per annum, or £100 provided he started a Girls' Night School on two nights a week. Mr Fyfe obviously was overworked and his main teaching was suffering. When the Directors wanted to examine his School he refused to allow it. Thomas Barnes sent him a very high-handed note saying that he had the right to examine the school and fully intended doing so.[15] On two occasions, both before he became a Member of Parliament, Thomas found new recruits for the staff while he was in London, the first one in June 1847, and the second one in January 1851. He did have personal reasons for visiting London at the time. After the death of his mother in 1848 his nephew Alfred was at University College, London. A few years later his own son, James Richardson, went to a school at Denmark Hill in London before going on to take a BA degree at London University.

Alfred became one of the directors of Queen Street Seminary in Farnworth in 1854 when he was about 22 years old. From then on, he played a leading role and was eventually the school's Principal Manager, making regular visits until his death in September 1893. In the years immediately following George's and his father's deaths until he became an MP in 1852 Thomas was concerned with the everyday running of the school. For example, tenders for building jobs were approved by him like this one from William Seddon:

21 October 1851

William Seddon agrees to build a wall in front of the Queen Street Seminary to the height required, supplying all materials and labour to the satisfaction of Thomas Barnes of Farnworth, Esq., for £5.5.0.

Thomas regularly had to interview new teachers and deal with staffing problems. For example, in 1850 he interviewed Miss Elizabeth Handley in London for a post in the Juvenile Girls' School on a twelve-month trial basis at a salary of £24 per annum plus half the School fees. This was then raised to £30. A letter shows how fair Thomas could be when dealing with problems. When Miss Dalling was appointed as Mistress of the Juvenile Girls' School at the Seminary in May 1854 her salary was £28 per annum plus half the School fees. Actually, her salary was really only £20, £10 less than her predecessor, Miss Handley, had been receiving, as she was expected to use £8 to pay her own assistant. Presumably this is the £8 referred to in the letter.

Limefield, 15 February 1855

To Mr Joseph Ditchfield

Miss Dalling has been this evening to explain what she does with the £8 and I quite approve of her mode of expending it. I think it is judicious and proper. We must repose confidence in her and leave it to her. I may not have time to speak to you tomorrow morn before I go off and so I write now that you may know how I feel upon it.

Yours, T. Barnes[16]

He regularly chaired the annual public examination of the schools in December, even after becoming an MP. In 1856 the Minutes' book contained a description of the event: "The school was tastefully decorated with evergreens. The Exhibition of Needle and Nitted [sic] work was very good. And the children on the whole showed themselves to be as well up as could be expected with their Geography—and their reading and ciphering was as well as could be expected, also their Scripture History. The attendance of Visitors was very good, many having to stand during the examinations, and seemed very pleased with the progress which the children have made." By now his nephew Alfred was involved and seconded the vote of thanks.

As a young man Thomas kept private diaries for fourteen years between 1838 and 1852, that is, from the age of 25 to 39, or more revealingly, from around the time of his son's birth to the buying of The Quinta. Harold Alfred Barnes quoted from them in his book about Halshaw Moor Chapel, and Rev. W. Hewgill used them as the basis of a eulogy at Thomas's memorial service at Market Street Chapel on the Sunday after his death. Where the diaries are now, I do not know, but I am sure they have been carefully preserved somewhere. Amongst many other things, they revealed his attitude towards money—like his father, he tried to be thrifty, but unlike his father, there was a side to him which saw that sometimes money had to be spent: "Went to Manchester at 8 o'clock, found a hole in my pocket which had let out all my gold. I have lost one or two pounds. Money will go. I thought of saving something by wearing out my clothes. I might as well have had a new pair of trousers as have lost my money." The diaries showed how this attitude developed. He once wrote: "Money is a difficult thing to manage, it is hard to get and hard to keep, and troublesome to have the direction of." During his lifetime he had had experience of this in the heavy financial losses he had sometimes incurred, and where he blamed himself for having had a too easy-going trustfulness in other men. He reflected on this in his diary: "While I ought not to be covetous or filled with the cares of this world, I ought as a matter of duty to look after and take care of such property as God gives me. I ought to look upon it as an instrument of usefulness." Another extract showed his thoughts on the stewardship of wealth. A man only gave him a £5 subscription for the Lancashire College. Thomas wrote: "Felt sorry that a man with so much more than he spends should not see it his duty to give more to such an important object."

Notes

1   *Bolton Free Press* [Bolton Archives and Social Studies]
2   *Manchester Times* [19th Century Newspapers online]
3   ZHE/45/37 [Bolton Archives and Social Studies]
4   Uncatalogued material *op. cit.* [Bolton Archives and Social Studies]
5   Ibid.
6   Ibid.
7   *Manchester Times* [19th Century Newspapers online]
8   Harold A. Barnes *op. cit. The Story of Halshaw Moor Chapel* (pub. 1908)
9   LRO DDX 75 124
10 *Bolton Chronicle* 5.11.1850 [Bolton Archives and Social Studies]
11 *Manchester Times* [19th Century Newspapers online]
12 Ibid.
13. The quotation which is still on the stairs actually reads: "The hand of the diligent maketh rich and addeth no sorrow. Seest thou a man diligent in business, he shall stand before kings." The final phrase added by the writer in 1865 is not there now.
14 *Manchester Times.*
15 LRO *op. cit.* SMFa Farnworth, Queen Street Training Seminary 1838–56
16 Ibid.

CHAPTER 3

1852–1857

The first years in Parliament—politician, cotton master and country squire

On 9 July 1852 Thomas and Joseph Crook had been elected as Bolton's two Reform members of Parliament. Thomas was unable to attend celebratory dinners given in their honour at the end of August and the beginning of September in Bradford Ward, Church Ward and Derby Ward, but was at the opening on Friday 24 September of a week-long bazaar, the Factory Operatives' Bazaar, in the Temperance Hall in celebration of the Ten Hours' Act. 1,800 workpeople from firms in and around Bolton had produced over 6,000 articles which were displayed on stalls set out like those at the Great Exhibition.[1]

Two days before this on Wednesday 22 September he had been at a meeting held in the Royal Hotel in Manchester after a public breakfast to discuss the foundation of the Milton Hall and Club, a meeting place in London for Nonconformists. The aim of the association was "to unite different sections of Nonconformists in more harmonious action for strengthening their cause and increasing their influence and to promote amongst them a more intimate social and friendly intercourse". It was intended to raise £50,000 for this by selling 1,000 debentures at £50 each bearing interest of 4%. Thomas proposed the motion: "That this meeting, having heard the statements of the deputation from the Committee, and anticipating great advantages in strengthening and increasing the influence of Nonconformist principles by the establishment of a Milton Hall and Club, highly approves of the design disclosed by the prospectus, and pledges itself to support the institution, and recommend it to the Evangelical Nonconformists of the United Kingdom."

By now Thomas was playing an increasingly important part in the life of the community. By February 1851 he was one of about one hundred people listed as "persons of whom the Bank of Bolton consists". He was then simply described as Thomas Barnes of Farnworth, spinner.

Although Thomas was connected with the Bank of Bolton, he did invest his money with other banks. In September 1852 he had £15,000 deposited with the Huddersfield Banking Company. His annual statement of interest dated 25 December 1863 is now in Bolton archives. (His £15,000 had made a total of £282 3s 2d.)

By Wednesday 13 October he was in London where he was amongst the 200 guests in the Egyptian Hall for the banquet and entertainment given by the Lord Mayor to distinguished Dissenting ministers. Thomas was one of the nine members of Parliament present together with a large number of Nonconformist Church ministers and other guests.[2]

Three days later on 16 October he was again in Bolton to attend a tea party on Saturday afternoon for the large number of people who had been involved in the Factory Operatives' Bazaar the previous month. Over 1,900 people, mainly women, sat down to tea together in the Temperance Hall. Thomas, Joseph Crook and the Lord Bishop of Manchester were on the platform and a letter from the Earl of Shaftesbury congratulating the participants was read out. He had been one of the driving forces behind the whole idea. When Thomas made his speech he said "he believed that these were the good old times, for they had never before been in such a state of prosperity; he was an advocate for, and strongly supported the parks, the libraries, mechanics' institutions, etc.; they were most excellent auxiliaries to the happiness and well-being of society; but there was one other thing he considered of paramount importance, and he hoped to see the day when every working man would live in his own house. The young women present he would recommend to adopt a custom followed in another part of the country. It is usual in that part when a young man came to "pop the question", for the young woman to put this question in return, "Have you got a cow?", and if the females of this part would adopt the question, "Have you got a house?" he thought it would have its beneficial result. He advised the working classes to take the matter of a park into their own hands, and he was sure they would succeed. There was in the town a population of 60,000, out of which there would be 20,000 workers, which, if the park cost £10,000, would only amount to 10s each, or 5s a year for two years, a little more than one penny per week."[3]

A Great Free Trade Banquet had been advertised in the press since 9 October. It took place on 2 November in the Free Trade Hall in Manchester immediately before the opening of Parliament. Circulars of invitation sent out from their offices in Newall's Buildings at the beginning of October by the Council of the Anti-Corn Law League stated that already nearly thirty members of the new Parliament had promised to attend, such as Cobden for the West Riding, Brown, Heywood, and Cheetham for Lancashire, Bright and Gibson for Manchester, and Barnes and Crook for Bolton. In addition there would be 160 other prominent people from various parts of the country. In the published list of guests intending to attend, Thomas's name was the fourth on the list, following Milner Gibson, Cobden and Bright. His Parliamentary colleague, Joseph Crook, was much further down the list. The banquet was a monumental affair: at eight tables on the platform were the 250 invited guests and Vice-Presidents; in the body of the hall 2,050 guests sat at 16 tables; another 530 dined in the gallery and room had been found for thirty reporters. John Cheetham, one of the newly-elected MPs was one of the speakers.[4]

Almost as soon as they began their term of office, Thomas and his colleague Joseph Crook faced a set-back when a petition against their return to Parliament was presented on 25 November by H. P. Gipps, MP for Canterbury, on behalf of George Greenhalgh, a Tory elector from Bolton. *The Manchester Times* described George Greenhalgh as the "objector-general for the Tories". The petition accused Thomas Barnes and Joseph Crook of being guilty of extensive bribery and corruption at the previous election, which, if proved, would have invalidated their election. This petition was just one of many presented at the time. *The Bolton Chronicle* on Saturday 4 December contained a list of 120 members of Parliament who had been petitioned against. Of these, 74 were members of the Opposition, and 46 members of the Government party. The large number of petitions was explained by one of the Bolton Liberals as a last-ditch attempt by Lord Derby to save his government by reducing the majority of Reformers in the House of Commons. However, all these petitions did not prevent the fall of Lord Derby's government and his replacement by Lord Aberdeen.

The next few months until the hearing in the House of Commons on 30 April 1853 were to be dominated by this petition. The legally worded petition set out three main complaints: "the two Liberal members of Parliament and their agents, managers, friends and supporters were guilty of bribery and corruption, treating and personation, at the last election. They had given or offered gifts, presents, money or rewards, or they had used threats, intimidation, or undue influence to induce people to vote for the Liberals, and not for the Conservative candidate, Stephen Blair. They had provided food, drink, entertainment, and provisions for the same purpose. Before, at and during the election, if not the two Liberal members themselves, then others on their behalf had given or offered money, food, drink, entertainment, provision, presents or rewards, offices or places, again to influence the voters."

Thomas Thomasson called a meeting in the Temperance Hall on 6 December to discuss their position. He had the following circular printed:

BOLTON ELECTIONS

Sir,

I have to inform you that a petition was presented in the House of Commons, on the 25th November, against the return of THOMAS BARNES, Esq., and JOSEPH CROOK, Esq., alleging that Mr Barnes and Mr Crook, and their agents, were guilty of Bribery and Treating at the last election for this Borough; that Gross, Extensive, and Systematic Corruption, Bribery and Treating, were practised at such Election; and that the return of the members was procured by these means.

I, therefore, beg to request your attendance at a meeting to be held at the Temperance Hall, on Monday Evening Next, the 6th inst., at Half-past Seven prompt, to adopt such steps as may be thought proper with reference to the Petition.

Yours, faithfully,

THOS. THOMASSON.

Dec. 3, 1852

N.B.—This Circular will be your Ticket of Admission

Kenyon & Abbatt, Printers, Market-Street, Bolton

A large number of Liberal supporters attended the meeting. Among them was the solicitor, Henry Marriott Richardson, who was later to prove a stumbling block for Thomas's prospects in the 1857 election. He was already a strong supporter of Joseph Crook. Thomas and Joseph Crook had decided not to attend the Monday evening meeting but to let the electors sort the matter out. They continued with their Parliamentary work—Joseph Crook had returned to Westminster on Monday afternoon and Thomas was to return on Wednesday. The Liberals were confident that the allegations in the petition were unfounded. They firmly believed that the last election had been fought upon purer grounds than on any previous occasion. P. R. Arrowsmith confirmed that no alcohol had been used to secure votes. They had spent very little, less than £400, on the election itself. Thomas had even refused to let Mr Thomasson and Mr Arrowsmith pay his expenses, as they had wanted to do. At the end of this meeting a "fighting fund" was set up which eventually raised £8,000.

In Parliament Thomas soon found himself in the minority on the two occasions he voted on free-trade questions. The voting was reported in *The Manchester Times* on Wednesday 1 December and on Saturday 4 December when Thomas voted for Mr Villiers' motion.

On 8 February 1853 Thomas became, as a shareholder and policy holder, a director of the London Board of the Industrial & General Life Assurance & Deposit Company which had its main office at 2 Waterloo Place, Pall Mall, and branch offices in Manchester, Stockport, Birmingham, and Mile End Road. The company had begun in February 1850 and was offering policies to people between the ages of 10 and 70. Its aims were set out in *The Manchester Times*: "For enabling all classes to participate in the advantages of life assurance by granting policies as low as £5; by accepting premiums in quarterly, monthly, or weekly payments; by making beneficial provision where circumstances prevent the assured from paying all the premiums, and affording other advantages hitherto unattainable by means of assurance companies." On 2 August 1854 he was still listed as one of its seventeen directors when the Industrial Life Assurance Company advertised for agents in London. By then, John Cheetham was also a director.

At a meeting of Bolton Town Council on 16 February 1853 it was agreed to send a petition from the town to Parliament in favour of a reduction of the duty on soap, tea, and other excise duties and to ask Thomas to present it for them.

At the end of February 1853 Thomas was reported as having voted in the majority on an amendment to the wording of the bill about the Maynooth Grant but he was absent on 3 March when a vote was taken on Joseph Hume's motion "That this House will, at an early period, take into consideration the duties that are strictly protective in the existing tariff on articles of import into this country, both of manufactures and agricultural produce, with the view of speedily repealing the same, as affecting unfairly every interest in the country". The main free-traders such as Bright, Cobden, and George Hadfield voted for the motion but John Cheetham voted against it, and was severely criticised for doing so in the Liberal press.

On Friday 15 April 1853 Thomas was one of a large deputation including Bright, Hadfield and Miall from the mercantile associations of Manchester, Liverpool, Bristol, Leeds, Bradford, Preston and other manufacturing towns, interested in promoting the development of the resources of India, who were received at the Board of Control by its President.

He was also together with Cobden and Miall one of the seven MPs amongst the patrons of a Grand Fancy Bazaar, the Ocean Penny Postage Bazaar, held in the Exchange in Manchester from Tuesday to Thursday, 26 to 28 April 1853 to raise money to promote an idea developed around 1849 by the League of Brotherhood to extend the penny postage rate to overseas mail. A notice announcing the bazaar explained why they wanted to make this appeal to Parliament: "An ocean penny post is already felt by the large masses of the people to be one of the great necessities of the age, and that necessity becomes daily more evident and urgent as the tide of emigration bears off, in quick succession, such large drafts of our people from the homes of Old England to the gold fields of Australia, and the corn fields of Canada and the United States. Much effort is still needed to diffuse information on this important subject, to demonstrate, not only its value, but its practicality, and to secure the co-operation of all classes in pressing the demand earnestly upon Parliament and the government." Manufacturers, merchants and tradesmen were asked to contribute items to the bazaar, and the three female Secretaries also asked for gifts of flowers and refreshments.

Eventually the charge of bribery and corruption brought against Thomas and Joseph Crook was settled. H. M. Richardson had been engaged as a solicitor in the defence of the two MPs. Sixty witnesses were called to the hearing in London on 30 April, including Mr Richardson himself who was accused of paying two mill managers to travel to Bolton from Preston on Voting Day. According to H. M. Richardson's account of the hearing in his *Reminiscences of Forty Years in Bolton* published in 1885 the evidence provided by witnesses for the prosecution was "of a most amusing and laughable character". One illustration he gave was that of Joseph Keough, a confectioner, "a very singular character indeed. This worthy kept a confectioner's stall, and stated that a contract had been made with him to buy up the whole of his stock-in-trade, consisting of gingerbread, Eccles cakes, nuts, and pop, on condition that he voted 'straight'. This man was anything but straight when he arrived at the Committee room. His articulation was of that order that arises from a defective utterance, and he told such a rambling and absurd story that not a single member of the Parliamentary Committee could understand a word he said." After a hearing which lasted two days, on 2 May 1853 a Select Committee of the House of Commons dismissed the petition against the two Bolton MPs as "frivolous and vexatious" and their many supporters celebrated in the evening with a dinner at the Burlington Hotel in Piccadilly. H. M. Richardson was given a victor's welcome when he arrived back in

Bolton the next day. He was met by a large crowd and band playing 'See the Conquering Hero Comes'.

On 3 May the Bolton Reformers held a meeting in the Reform Newsroom to hear an account of the proceedings from Thomas Thomasson and Henry Marriott Richardson. At this meeting H. M. Richardson had still not developed the antipathy against Thomas which was soon to become apparent. In fact, at a meeting of Bolton Town Council on 11 May, it was Mr Richardson who proposed that the Council should ask Thomas Barnes and Joseph Crook to support the Municipal Corporations Act 1853 in Parliament. It was nearly a month before the excitement caused by the defeat of the petition died down in Bolton. A great political festival was arranged by the Reformers in Bolton, starting with a tea party in the Temperance Hall to honour their two members of Parliament on Wednesday 8 June and followed by a public meeting the next evening. The idea of a procession for Friday was abandoned at the last minute.

H. M. Richardson's dispute with Thomas and his supporters seems to have arisen as a result of something that happened when he put in a claim for his expenses. In his *Reminiscences* he was clearly still feeling aggrieved over thirty years later. He never referred to Thomas by name, but I think he must have been the "gentleman" referred to when he wrote:

"It may be useful and interesting, at this stage, to remind my readers that, upon *paper*, some £8,000 was put down as a fund to defend the seats with the utmost firmness and vigour, "regardless of expense". The seats were successfully defended at a cost of less than *hundreds* of pounds, as compared with the *thousands* of pounds just referred to. [... ...] The expenses of successfully defending the seats were considerably under £800, and at least one half of this sum was out of pocket—costs for agency, counsels' fees, clerks' wages, and travelling and hotel charges. I was underpaid by a substantial amount, and I insisted upon being generously dealt with, as I had devoted all my energies to the cause I had undertaken, sustained much anxiety, and had rendered an amount of physical labour which could not very well be compensated in itemed charges. One excuse for refusing to pay me in full was that personally I had in some degree contributed to the petition being brought, by the payments I had made to the two voters who came from Preston, and therefore I ought to be *considerate* in my charges on that account. This was a mean method to adopt, and it stung me to the quick, coming as it did from the very last person in the world who ought to have entertained such an illiberal and shabby view of the matter. I resented it with scorn and contempt; nor would I listen to any apology which over and over again was tendered to me by way of explanation. Like the 'Great Duke' (he of Waterloo), I said:—'No, it was no mistake; it could be no mistake, and it shall be no mistake.' I bided my time and I had my revenge. An offer was made by a very prominent Liberal to head a subscription for the purpose of making a 'presentation' to me. This, too, I declined, and, shortly afterwards my relationship with the Liberal party became strained. I had been honourably acquitted by the Election Committee of the House of Commons, as was well known to the gentleman who had so meanly reminded me of the Preston incident; but even had the contrary been the case, I gave him to understand that he, of all other persons in the world, should have been the last to have taken me to task about it. I don't care to go into further details, and only mention it now to show that I was justified in detaching myself from the Liberal party of that period."5

At the Farnworth Mills' annual stocktaking on 30 June 1853 the year's profits were declared as £6,874 17s 11d and the two minor partners, Thomas Paterson and Simeon Dyson each received an increased share of one-ninth.

At a meeting of Bolton Town Council on 27 July 1853 it was agreed to ask Thomas to present another petition from Bolton Corporation to Parliament. This petition, in support of the Juvenile Offenders' Bill which was then before Parliament, was proposed by P. R. Arrowsmith and seconded by H. M. Richardson.

On 20 September 1853 the Rev. J. C. McMichael who had been the co-pastor at the chapel in Farnworth for the past six years resigned from the position to become pastor at Stalybridge chapel. Thomas chaired the meeting of the church deacons and proposed a resolution regretting their loss. On 25 September Rev. McMichael preached his farewell sermon to a crowded chapel.

On 12 October 1853 the Liberal Reformers held a huge meeting in Edinburgh, the so-called Peace Conference. As well as the main figures such as the MPs Cobden, Bright, Hadfield, Miall, Heywood and Crook, other important figures including Thomas Thomasson of Bolton were present. Thomas had had to send a letter of apology for absence as he had a clash of engagements—he was at the opening of Bolton Public Library and Museum.

Eighteen months earlier, on the day before the first evening open-air meeting was held to launch his electoral campaign in July 1852, Thomas had been one of several men who had been invited to a special meeting of a newly-formed committee to discuss the setting-up of a

Public Library and Museum in Bolton. Thomas subscribed 100 guineas but was unable to donate any books as he had just given his spare books to a similar scheme in the Farnworth area. He could not have missed this opening of the Public Library on 12 October 1853. After the Mayor, William Gray, had performed the official ceremony in the Reading Room he treated his guests to refreshments in the Exchange Newsroom below, "a cold collation" set out in a most sumptuous style, provided by Mr Cork of the Swan Hotel. At the end of the meal P. R. Arrowsmith proposed a toast to their two MPs and Thomas returned thanks on behalf of himself and Joseph Crook who was at the Peace Conference. He paid a tribute to his colleague: "He must say he never met with a more zealous, earnest, straightforward, and honest man in his life". His own policy would always be "to legislate for the benefit of the country at large, without respect to any party politics". "He felt delighted at being present at this day's proceedings; he believed it would be a bright day in the annals of the borough. It had frequently been said that day, that it was desirable that all men of the borough should also avail themselves of the advantages of the public library; he was also anxious that all women of the borough should avail themselves of it. He was glad that Bolton was one of the first towns to open a free public library." Thomas's support for the Library Movement was one of the many contributions he made to public life remembered in tributes paid to him after his death.

On 17 October 1853 Thomas accepted the office of President of the Bolton Mechanics' Institution for the coming year at the Institution's annual meeting. He also made an excellent speech, one of whose themes was the recent opening of the new library. Robert Heywood, the Chairman, had said that "many timid people, including himself, were afraid that the Free Public Library would injure the Mechanics' Institution, but the report had happily destroyed those fears, and he heartily rejoiced to find that such was the case."

In the following week a number of events connected with the Congregational Union took place, one of which was a Public Breakfast Meeting in Cavendish Street Lecture Hall in Manchester, to promote the interests of the Congregational Board of Education. Thomas presided at the meeting where the main subject of discussion was how the Congregationalists should take up the challenge of educating the masses. Several of the speakers were convinced that the Congregational Board should now "take leave of mere controversy, and attend chiefly to the practical work of providing educational means; but they did, especially Mr Morley and Dr Massie, profess their undiminished adherence to the principle of voluntaryism as sufficient for the need of the people". Thomas alleged that it "was impossible for 'Government' to reach that class who really needed schools—that is, the class who were sunk lowest in the social scale". The meeting also reported on the new Training College at Homerton.

As President of the Mechanics' Institution Thomas chaired another meeting on 17 November 1853 in the Temperance Hall, Little Bolton, when Dr Bowring, the British Consul in China, gave a very interesting talk on China. Thomas, Joseph Crook and Thomas Thomasson were in a group of ten men who had been invited by Robert Heywood to a dinner party beforehand to meet Dr Bowring.

On Tuesday 24 January 1854 Thomas was amongst the 300 people invited to meet at the Albion Hotel in Manchester for a political get-together. The aims of this event as set out in *The Manchester Times* would appear to have been a blue-print for Thomas's own annual addresses to his constituents. "For some years it has been the custom of our representatives in Parliament to visit Manchester at some time during the winter recess, and usually in immediate anticipation of the opening of the session, and to meet in social reunion as many of the more prominent free traders and members of the Liberal party as could conveniently be assembled at the Albion Hotel, or in the Town Hall, or elsewhere. On such occasions past policy and the history of the bygone session of Parliament have usually been reviewed, the present position of parties has been animadverted upon, and the probable business of the ensuing session has received more or less of anticipatory criticism and elucidation." George Wilson, Chairman of the late Anti-Corn Law League presided. All the Reform MPs attended—Thomas Barnes and Joseph Crook for Bolton, Milner Gibson and John Bright for Manchester, Richard Cobden for the West Riding, John Cheetham for South Lancashire, J. Heywood for North Lancashire, E. Miall for Rochdale, George Hadfield for Sheffield, and James Kershaw for Stockport.

Once Parliament had re-assembled after the Christmas recess, it was reported that Thomas was amongst the MPs who supported a deputation from the Protestant Dissenting deputies of the three denominations who had an interview on 3 February 1854 with Palmerston, the Secretary of State for the Home Department, on the abolition of church rates, the Dissenting Marriage Acts Amendment Bill, and the Places of Religious Worship Registration Bill.[6] On Saturday 18 February 1854 Thomas was at a meeting of the Parliamentary Committee on Ecclesiastical Matters which had been formed ten days earlier at a meeting of MPs at Fendall's Hotel "for the advancement of religious liberty, with especial reference to the rights of Protestant Dissenters". His name headed the list of Committee members.

On Wednesday afternoon 15 February 1854 Thomas was with friends and supporters of the London Training Institution, also called the Reformatory for Adult Male Criminals, at a meeting in the lecture theatre of the House in Great Smith Street, Westminster. The Chairman was the Earl of Shaftesbury and the purpose of the meeting was to say farewell to twenty-six of the inmates of the institution who had completed the twelve-month industrial training provided there and were now about to emigrate to the colonies at the expense of the charity.

On Tuesday 21 February 1854 both Thomas and Joseph Crook were at a large and influential meeting of the friends of Reform, convened by Mr Hume in Committee Room No. 12 to consider what line of policy should be adopted with reference to the bill now before Parliament for amending the representation of the country.

It was probably Thomas who went with Mr Whitehurst as part of a deputation from London to Cheltenham to a "spirited and successful meeting" of the Vote by Ballot Society which was reported as having taken place a few days before Saturday 25 February 1854.

Thomas was one of about twenty-five MPs who offered to act as Stewards at a public dinner to be chaired by Lord John Russell at the London Tavern, Bishopgate Street, on Saturday 25 March 1854. This dinner was given by the friends and supporters of the Philanthropic Society's Farm School at Redhill, Surrey, a school for the reformation of juvenile offenders and for the protection of destitute children of convicts.

During his first term in Parliament Thomas played an important part in Farnworth's efforts to establish their own supply of gas for lighting. Bolton already had a Gas Company which was planning to supply Farnworth as well. However, Farnworth ratepayers were afraid that this would be against the interests of Farnworth and in the mid 1850s decided to oppose the Bolton Gas Company's application to Parliament by getting a proviso inserted in the Bill that protected the interests of Farnworth and Kersley. A deputation was sent to appear before the Committee of the House of Commons. Thomas and Harrison Blair lent their support to the Farnworth deputation. However, before the deputation appeared before the Committee an agreement was reached that Farnworth and Kersley should be struck out of the proposed Bill. The Bolton Gas Company agreed to supply the districts in bulk by putting a meter at Moses Gate Station until the townships could supply themselves. Thomas and Harrison Blair agreed to act as guarantors to the Bolton Gas Company for the plant and mains they supplied, and also for the payment of the gas. Parliament agreed to rush through a Bill to allow Farnworth to set up a separate Gas Company. Thomas and Joseph Crook, as the local members of Parliament, were added to the select committee appointed to investigate the bill for the extension of the powers of the Bolton Gas Company. This select committee met on Thursday 13 March 1854. The Act received Royal Assent on 10 July 1854. Thomas Barnes was one of the first twelve Directors of the new Farnworth and Kersley Gas Company and was appointed Chairman at its first meeting on 17 July 1854. A month later he chaired the first General Meeting of Shareholders.

He had intended to attend a tea-party in the Temperance Hall in Bolton during the Easter recess on Monday 17th April 1854 but both he and Joseph Crook, his fellow MP, were unavoidably absent. This tea-party, attended by over 700 people, was to raise funds for the Widow and Orphans' Fund of the United Oddfellows whose 1,800 members in that district alone had over the past four or five years paid out over £700 a year for funerals and double that amount for sickness. At this meeting reference was made to the Friendly Societies' Bill currently before Parliament as being "a very unfriendly Bill". In fact, on 10 May it was agreed at a meeting of Bolton Town Council to forward a petition from the Board of Guardians against the Friendly Societies' Bill for Thomas to present to Parliament.

At the beginning of May Thomas was one of the MPs who voted against Mr Heywood's motion for referring the Oxford University Bill to a select committee. He was Chairman of a public meeting on the evening of 24 May 1854 organised by the friends of voluntary and religious education at Bloomsbury Chapel to hear a lecture by Mr E. Baines of Leeds on "the present state of the educational question". Thomas said he disagreed with the opinion, often expressed, that all the crime and misery of the country arose from ignorance, contending that these were to be attributed to the depravity of human nature and the operation of physical evils. If the physical condition of the mass of the people were improved, education would, he said, come of itself.

Immediately before the week of the Whitsun recess Thomas was at the second reading of Lord John Russell's Oaths Bill and in the week ending 15 July he voted (in the minority) when it was proposed to send an address to the Queen to ask her to appoint a Commission to go to India to inquire into the tenure of land in Madras.

One of the laws which were passed during this session had repercussions on the Mechanics' Institutions with which Thomas was involved in Bolton. This new law affected the way in which all literary and scientific institutions in the country were regulated and included public libraries, reading rooms, museums, schools of art and design, and art galleries, placing them all under government control. Because one particular clause would have affected the Mechanics' Institutions, the Manchester Athenæum and the Manchester Mechanics' Institution had sent a deputation to London to lobby seven MPs, including Thomas, who had all agreed to oppose it. Led by Milner Gibson, these MPs managed to get the clauses which gave power of reference to the charity commissioners rejected at the third reading of the bill, a long session which went on until two o'clock in the morning. The Bill then went to the House of Lords and again representatives were sent from Manchester to London where they met Lord John Russell and the group of MPs which included Thomas. With their help they ensured an organised opposition in the House of Lords to the amendments then proposed by the Lords.

Profits for the Farnworth Mills were declared on 30 June 1854 and had risen to £13,979. Again, the share received by Thomas's two partners went up, this time to one-eighth each. During the year improvements had been made to the mills. A new building had been erected in the Gas Yard at a cost of £210 and there had been a new floor in the Gaiting Room. A new boiler and its fittings had cost another £340.

At the beginning of August 1854 Thomas, together with John Bright and George Hadfield, voted against the Public Health Renewal and Amendment Bill. On nearly every occasion when Thomas's vote was recorded, he was in the company of other Liberals such as John Bright and John Cheetham. Only rarely does Joseph Crook's name appear in the reports. In fact, when a summary of the number of attendances of the 26 Lancashire MPs at the 240 Divisions in the House of Commons that session was published in August, Thomas was the third highest attender. He had been present 137 times and absent 103. John Cheetham was thirteenth in the list and Joseph Crook third from the bottom with only 77 attendances and 163 absences.

In November 1854 Thomas was one of a group of manufacturers and two other MPs, Mr Oliveira and Mr McGregor, who went to France as a trade delegation to investigate the state of the wine trade there—the current stock of wines in the various districts, the yield of last vintage, and the prospects for future production. They also wanted to consult the main manufacturers whose products were at the time protected by high import duties and try to persuade them to put pressure on the French government to modify those duties as regarded British fabrics, a concession that would have resulted in a large increase in trade between the two countries, and speeded up the adjustment of the wine duty question. I have not yet found any report on whether or not they succeeded in these aims.

In the autumn of 1854 a National Patriotic Fund was launched to support the widows and orphans of the men killed in the Crimean War. The subscription scheme in Manchester was already well under way when the Mayor of Bolton called a meeting on 13 November to set up a similar scheme in Bolton. Although opinions at the meeting differed as to the necessity or the cause of the war, Thomas seconded Canon Slade's resolution that Bolton would contribute towards the fund. He said: "It was their duty to support the bereaved of those who fell in the country's battles. If, as was said by some, it was a great crime to go to war, it must then be said the country is the criminal; and therefore they were bound to support those whom the country had called out on their behalf". He and one other firm subscribed £100. Other contributions were much lower. His support for these widows and orphans was remembered over forty years later when tributes were paid to him at the time of his death. He also presided at a public meeting on Wednesday 29 November 1854 in the Mechanics' Institution, Farnworth, to promote the National Patriotic Fund for the Farnworth and Kersley district.

Around this time dissenting voices began to be heard amongst the Bolton Liberal supporters, one group clearly more in favour of Joseph Crook than of Thomas Barnes. One example of this was on 18 November 1854 when a group of bleachers, dyers and finishers held a public tea meeting in the Temperance Hall chaired by Joseph Crook in connection with the Ten Hours' Bill. Members of a committee appointed to promote the bill were also present. They moved a vote of thanks to the members of Parliament who had been supporting their cause and read out a long list of men in both Houses, including the names of Thomas Barnes and Joseph Crook. At this point a man called Richard Partington said that "Mr Barnes's name had no right amongst the other worthy members, he having caused the deputation in London the greatest inconvenience, and solemnly declared to them that he was opposed to legislative interference. He therefore begged to move, as an amendment, that Mr Barnes's name be expunged from that list". He added that "Mr Barnes was not a Ten Hours' man but the masters' friend, and he received the deputation of masters, when in London, with the greatest cordiality". However, this view was contradicted by Mr Waring, one of the deputation who had met Thomas in London. He said that "whenever they had waited upon Mr Barnes in London, he always gave them his best attention, and said he would give their bill his best consideration; and when they applied to him for a subscription to their funds in support of their proceedings, he freely gave them £5 towards the attainment of their object". In fact, Thomas would have been at the tea meeting that evening if he had not had to attend another engagement. Eventually Mr Partington withdrew his amendment.

On 27 November 1854 there was another foretaste of troubles to come. At a Committee Meeting of the Licensed Victuallers' Association in Bolton another delegation who had been to London to lobby their MPs on the new Sunday Beer Act and related matters reported on their results. Mr Crook had received them most courteously, but declined to give any definite opinion. He said he would consult with a colleague. Mr Barnes said "he was of opinion that it was harsh to attempt to prevent people having refreshments on Sunday. The legislature could not make people sober by acts of Parliament; there were pleasure seekers and always would be. He, however, seemed opposed to throwing the trade open, but he would not be tied down to any particular line of conduct". The committee agreed to send a petition to Parliament. Questions concerning the sale of alcohol were to cause Thomas many problems whilst he was an MP.

He was being kept busy at Westminster. Just before Christmas 1854 he and John Cheetham voted with the majority at the Second Reading of the Enlistment of Foreigners Bill. Most of the other prominent Liberal MPs voted with the minority. At the beginning of February 1855 he was amongst the principal Liberals who voted against the motion "That a select committee is appointed to inquire into the condition of our army before Sebastopol, and into the conduct of those departments of the Government whose duty it has been to minister to the wants of that army". The motion was carried overwhelmingly by 807 votes to 150. At the end of March the leading Liberals, including Thomas and Joseph Crook, voted in the majority at the Second Reading of the Newspaper Stamp Bill.

On many occasions he was asked to present petitions to Parliament on behalf of his constituents. One of these petitions was the result of the weekly meeting of Bolton Guardians on 28 February 1855. The Board of Guardians at Nottingham had sent a copy of a petition they had prepared which they were asking other unions to support. They objected to the very stringent and sometimes cruel rules which the Poor Law Board was forcing them to apply as Guardians when giving out-door relief. They hoped that the Bolton Board of Guardians would be allowed to exercise a greater degree of independence in the distribution of relief in their area. The Bolton Guardians agreed to ask Thomas to present a similar petition to Parliament on their behalf. Two weeks later at the meeting of the Bolton Guardians on 14 March a letter from Thomas on a different topic was read out. He had spoken to Mr Baines about the additional Guardians, and Mr Baines had informed him that the subject was still under consideration, but would soon be decided. Thomas believed, however, that the required increase in the number of Guardians would be granted. He was probably right because there was an item in *The Manchester Times* on 4 August 1855 that an additional Guardian was to be elected for the township of Farnworth. Amongst the three nominations was Thomas's 23–year old nephew Alfred who had been proposed by Mr T. Cross. I don't know whether or not Alfred was elected on this occasion.

Even while he was at Westminster Thomas continued to be involved in his church activities. On the evening of 10 May 1855 he was one of the platform party at the annual meeting of the Sunday Schools Union at Exeter Hall. F. Crossley, another MP, was the Chairman and amongst the others present were John Cheetham, Rev. Dr Campbell and Rev. Dr Massie. At the meeting it was reported that a site in the Old Bailey had been bought for the new Jubilee Building.

On 24 May he and Joseph Crook were in a large delegation of members of Parliament, the Mayors of Manchester and Bolton, the Town Clerk of Salford, and representatives from other organisations, who met the President and Vice-President of the Board of Trade, the Right Hon. Lord Stanley of Alderley and the Hon. E. P. Bouverie, to discuss the recommendations of the shipping dues commission, and especially in relation to the local bills before Parliament relating to dock accommodation in the port of Mersey, and the necessity of preventing the present position of the Liverpool town dues being in any way thereby affected. The deputation met Lord Stanley again on 22 February 1856 to discuss the Local Dues in Shipping Bill. On this occasion Viscount Palmerston was also involved in the discussions.

Profits for the Farnworth Mills had dropped slightly in 1854/55 to £6,821 but Simeon Dyson and Thomas Paterson still each received their one-eighth share. During the year another type of cloth called "Flotillas" was produced.

Thomas was one of the main opponents of state education. When, in July 1855, Sir George Grey was congratulating the Government on the improvements in the provision of state education, a question was raised in the Editorial in *The Manchester Times* as to the quality of the work being done in the 5,575 general schools, the ragged schools, and the 65 industrial schools. "Sir George Grey says it is excellent. On the other hand, Mr Barnes, Mr Miall, and Mr Hadfield declare that its bad character is such as whets their antagonism to state education." Sir George Grey was referring to a speech Thomas made in the House of Commons on 26 July 1855 when MPs were discussing the amount of annual grant to be paid by the State towards public education. Thomas pointed out that the children who were benefiting were not poor children but middle class children. Money was being wasted on pupil teachers and over-educating certificated teachers. He was quoting from an Inspector's Report when he said, "During the twelve months previous to the time of the Report, the attempt to improve the education of the labouring classes has been attended with little success, and little progress has been made by the scholars".

Thomas, John Cheetham and George Hadfield were also among the MPs who met a delegation from members of building societies who feared that if Clause Six in the State Carriage Duties Bill were passed, building societies would have to pay stamp duty on their mortgages, something from which they had been exempt up to then. Through the pressure of the opposition, the clause was withdrawn.

After the 1855 summer recess and before the re-opening of Parliament, Thomas was in Bolton on 16 October to attend a soirée at the Temperance Hall when the Mechanics' Institution celebrated the opening of their new larger premises in Oxford Street. The Chairman was Lord Stanley MP, and Thomas was there as President of the Institution. The room was decorated for the occasion and music was provided by the Gilnow saxhorn band. In front of the orchestra was a banner displaying in large letters the words "Knowledge is Power". After tea, the gallery of the hall was thrown open to the public upon payment of 6d each for admission and in a short time it was crowded. Thomas gave a long speech in support of general education, and was repeatedly applauded. He proposed the following sentiment: "The Bolton Mechanics' Institution, presenting as it does a good supply of standard literature in its library, of current literature in its reading and newsroom, of efficient *viva voce* teaching in its classes; forms a centre from which radiate influences of an elevating character throughout the entire borough; and is therefore deserving of the countenance and co-operation of all parties interested in the prosperity of the town." A week or so later Thomas was back in Oxford Street to chair the annual meeting of the Bolton Mechanics' Institution in the Reading Room of their new premises. P. R. Arrowsmith, the Mayor, thanked Thomas for his valuable services in connection with the institution. He said he was a man "always found in the van for social progress, and a friend to education". Thomas returned thanks and said that "he regretted that although they now possessed a far superior building to what they had done hitherto, they had not succeeded in the erection of a building suitable to the wants of a population like Bolton, consisting of 70,000 inhabitants. He expressed his hearty concurrence with the objects of the institution, and would be always ready to render every assistance in his power to promote its welfare". He proposed that Joseph Crook should take over from him as President for the coming year. He and P. R. Arrowsmith were elected vice-presidents. In December 1859 he did express some doubt as to the success of the Institution. He was speaking in Wrexham at the First Anniversary of the local branch of the Young Men's Christian Association. He said the Young Men's Christian Association had taken the place of the Mechanics' Institutions formed thirty to forty years earlier which had failed to take hold of the masses to that extent to which they were intended. The Mechanics' Institutions had no politics, and, unlike the Young Men's Christian Association, no religion.

Although Thomas was still fulfilling his public duties in Farnworth, by September 1855 he and his wife Ann and son James had moved to The Quinta. Thomas and his wife were first mentioned in the local paper, *The Wrexham and Denbigh Advertiser*, on 14 September 1855 when they and their party from The Quinta were at the very first Chirk Horticultural Meeting, an event which had just been inaugurated by Colonel Biddulph of Chirk Castle. Because of his commitments as MP for Bolton, Thomas's social appearances in Wales could only be in the summer recess before Parliament reassembled in November. Even in these Parliamentary recesses he was constantly on the move between Wales and Farnworth.

In autumn 1855 the new mansion at The Quinta was in the process of being built. Thomas and his family were living in temporary accommodation in a cottage in the grounds but the park and gardens which had surrounded the old Hall were not affected by the building work. He began to introduce the local people to the same sort of events he had been used to in Farnworth. On Friday 19 October 1855 he treated the children at the National School at The Lodge village to a "substantial" tea. Samuel Winter, Thomas's bailiff at The Quinta, led the long procession of children from the village to the park to have a look at the still unfinished mansion. There, outside, in front of Thomas and Ann, they sang a hymn before they returned for their tea. Then Thomas made a speech and presented a copy of Dr Watts' hymns to all those who could read. He promised to give the rest of them a similar hymn book as soon as they learnt to read.[7] Already the newspaper was referring to Thomas as a "kind gentleman" especially as it had learned that he intended repeating the treat on 2 November for the local Nonconformist Sunday Schools. This event followed the same pattern. Friends, teachers and scholars of the Wesleyan Reform School and the Welsh Calvinistic Methodist School were also treated to a "sumptuous" tea. They visited the park and gardens before singing outside the cottage where the Barnes family was living. Then they gave "three cheers for Mr Barnes, three for Mrs Barnes, and three times three for Master Barnes". They returned in procession to The Lodge where Thomas and Ann joined them for their tea and plum cake in the beautifully decorated Wesleyan Reform Chapel. One of the boys from the Wesleyan Reform Sunday School welcomed Thomas into the neighbourhood and thanked him for his kindness. After tea they held a meeting in the Welsh Methodist Chapel where Thomas made a speech and left a large package of books to be distributed amongst the children.

On 19 December 1855 Thomas spoke as one of the Borough Members at the grand opening of Bolton's new Market Hall and the déjeuner afterwards at St George's School. James Clegg gave an account of the event in his *Annals of Bolton*, published in 1888. Thomas Barnes "said with pardonable pride they might challenge any borough in England, or even in the world, to come and look at it, he looked upon it with as much admiration as he looked upon the Crystal Palace when he first beheld it". The event itself was said "to have had no parallel in the town since the Coronation of Queen Victoria."

Once Thomas returned to Westminster after the Christmas recess he was soon involved in lobbying again. On 21 February 1856 he was part of a deputation including Mr Wickham (now Chairman of the Lancashire and Yorkshire Railway Company), Mr Oliveira, Mr Hadfield, Mr Crook and the mayors of most of the large towns of England, who met Sir George Grey at the Home Office to protest about the Counties and Boroughs Bill which, if passed, would transfer to the Government in London so much of the power which ought to belong, and had hitherto belonged, to the local authorities in the matter of police control. Because the deputation did not receive a satisfactory answer from Sir George Grey, they agreed to make an appeal to all Independent members of Parliament to uphold local government against centralisation.

During the next weeks Thomas spoke in the House of Commons on three occasions on the subject of education. On 6 March 1856 he spoke in a debate in the House on the proposed system of national education. He made very similar points to the ones in the previous year's speech but added another point which was to feature in future speeches—the parents' responsibility for educating their own children. His conclusion was that "if the Resolutions were agreed to, he hoped that any enactment founded upon them would provide for a considerable modification of the present system, so as to provide a system more adapted to meet the wants of those classes most requiring State aid". A month later on 4 April 1856, he spoke to object to a State grant being paid for public education in Ireland. Six days after this he attended a continuation of the debate in the House on national education. At quarter past midnight it was Thomas who called for an adjournment of the debate, provoking Disraeli to say in astonishment that "the motion had been made before the House and Country had been afforded the means of ascertaining the views of the Government on a question of such importance. The hour was not so late". At the adjourned debate the following night the situation was the same. After several long speeches and after Palmerston had said that the Committee had been debating for two nights without arriving at any result whatever, Thomas again intervened to say he would now move that the Chairman report progress, and ask leave to sit again. This proposal was not accepted but another one "That the Chairman do now leave the chair" was, and the debate was adjourned at half past one in the morning until the following Monday.[8]

At the beginning of March 1856 Thomas supported Sir William Clay's bill for the abolition of church rates and on 14 March he was part of a deputation from the London and Manchester Peace Conference Committee who had an interview with Viscount Palmerston. On Wednesday evening 2 April, he was Chairman at a large meeting at Crosby Hall in London of the supporters of voluntary education to discuss how to proceed in view of Lord John Russell's education resolution. Thomas challenged the supporters of state education to show that any of the measures now before Parliament would really promote the cause of education among the people. He characterised Lord John Russell's resolutions as ignoring altogether the duty of parents to educate their own children. The meeting agreed to send a petition to Parliament. He and the "small but faithful band" of other

MPs who advocated voluntary education as opposed to state education were formally thanked for their support.

On 9 April 1856 Thomas and other leading Liberals voted in the majority of 230 for the second reading of the Oath of Abjuration Bill and a week later he voted for Mr Spooner's motion on the Maynooth Bill. Then, at the end of April, he voted in the majority against Mr Whiteside's motion on the Fall of Kars (restored to Turkey by the Russians after the peace of Paris).

On 18 April 1856 he spoke again at a Committee of Supply when it was proposed to give a grant to pay the expenses of Nonconforming, Seceding and Protestant Dissenting ministers in Ireland. He proposed an amendment (which was not accepted) to reduce the amount by about £350—the allowance for five new Presbyterian ministers. He said the Presbyterians of Ireland were the only body of Dissenters who claimed aid of this kind. He thought it most unjust to the poor handloom weavers of Bolton and other places that their money should be spent for the establishment of new congregations in the North of Ireland. He protested against the vote as unjust and unchristian.[9]

A public meeting was held in Finsbury Chapel, London, on the evening of Wednesday 7 May 1856 as part of the Religious Liberty Society's conference. Thomas was one of the members of Parliament there and when he spoke he said "as a member of Parliament he came to beg the people of England to free him, for one, from the distress, annoyance, and difficulty of discussing ecclesiastical questions in the House of Commons—as a political man, to free public questions from the odium consequent on the mingling of religious questions with them—and as a religious man, to liberate the consciences of men from the shackles of state control; for such a connection was equally hurtful to politics and religion. It was no more the place of the Government to provide for the health of the soul than for that of the body—faith than physic. Religious men should say to the Government what Government often said to religious men, namely, mind your own affairs. It belonged to men that sincerely held a faith themselves to support and promote it. It was no duty of Government. Not that he had any enmity to the Church of England. If they must have a state church, he preferred that church; but he would still more desire none at all. Both politics and the church would be relieved by their severance."

In the records held at the Lancashire Record Office there is a letter written by Thomas before the next election in 1857 to his nephew Alfred and his new wife Ellen:

Farnworth near Manchester May 10/56

Dear Alfred,

Yours of the 7/5 I rec^d yesterday just as I was leaving William Street for the train, to come home. I have left your Aunt behind in London, as she did not think it was worth while coming home for so short a time as 2 or 3 days. I have unfortunately to return to London on Tues. mor^g on Lady Hewleys business.

It is very unfortunate just to have the meetings of the Trustees in our holiday week—the last of the session, and to break into the middle of it in this way. But so it is and I must make the best of it. But to your note, I was one of the unfortunates in the Perseverance, and I had many "mischances" that day, which I must tell you about when I see you, for I have not time now, yet I fared better than some for I got home by ½ p 12 p.m. and saw as much as any body else did on board that ship. We were certainly badly used, but you do not hear the real cause of our mishaps and disappointments. It would not be "loyal" to talk about it. Privately and secretly—the real cause is said to be the "Queen"—so we must swallow the pill and say nothing, only resolve, as I have done, never to go again. I believe the chief reason was "her whim". She did not want us to go to Portsmouth for fear of crowding her, and so we were sent to Southampton. We ought to have gone to the same port as her "Majesty", and followed in her wake, but as she has told us to go another way, for the future I mean to go my own way and not always "follow her Queenship". We are very angry, but we "nurse our wrath and keep it warm". The direct and immediate cause of delay was no doubt an "accident", but the arrangements were not good, and no provision made for any contingency or accident, every thing rigid and exact—all well if all goes right, but nobody having discretionary power, all ill if anything goes wrong.

9 a.m. here. I find Jos. Ditchfield's wife, poor Sarah, is dead and was buried on Thursday. Jos. is in a very declining state. I fear a few days will see him near his beloved wife again. Think of their dear little orphan Girl! How mysterious to us are the dealings of God with his own true children! [... ...]

I expect to be in Town on Tuesday and the House meets on Friday next (Whit Friday) but I expect no interesting business. What there may be at the end of this month I cannot tell, nor anyone. No doubt we shall have field days, but when they will come off in the House, I do not know.

Are you not disposed to go to Devonshire? It would well repay you. There are many pleasant places. Go to see Torquay. Weymouth and Sidmouth are very pretty. The ride from Exeter to Torquay is most lovely at this season. Go and look at it. You will not repent. I hope Ellen is very well and will return home as strong as an Elephant.

Give my love to her, and accept the same yourself.

Your aff. Thos. Barnes[10]

The event to which Thomas was referring was Queen Victoria's Review of the Fleet which took place in the Solent on Wednesday 23 April 1856. Many members of Parliament had arrived in Southampton the evening before and were waiting on the quay early on Wednesday morning ready to be taken out to the two steamers allocated to them, the *Transit* for the members of the House of Lords and the *Perseverance* for the members of the House of Commons. They sat and waited on the boats which were to ferry them out to the steamers and watched the efficient way the private shipping companies dealt with their passengers and with flags flying and bands playing sailed out of the harbour. The politicians continued to wait for a train which should have left London at six o'clock but still had not arrived three hours later. A rumour reached them that the train had broken down and so they all, peers and commoners, got into one of the ferryboats, leaving the other for the train passengers when they arrived. From then on what should have been a glorious day out turned into nothing but one of confusion and frustration. Getting them out of the ferry boat on to the two separate steamers took a long time and the members of Parliament were just about to get back into another ferry boat to take them to join the peers on the *Transit* when news came that the train had arrived an hour late and its passengers were finally on their way having had to wait another three-quarters of an hour for a ferryboat. After another long delay the peers from the train were put on the *Transit* and two to three hundred angry members of Parliament arrived on the *Perseverance*. The Queen had arrived at Spithead at noon and it was now half past one. The two steamers still had several miles to sail before reaching the Review and when they did get there they had missed the main event and had to be satisfied with seeing the Queen leading the Fleet towards the Nab Light. Alfred had probably read the detailed report in *The Bolton Chronicle* on the following Saturday which pointed out "the incomplete arrangements and want of punctuality which denoted the 'charmed circle' of official management" and contrasted it with the "order and regularity", "comfort and convenience" provided by the private shipping companies. It, too, criticised the decision to send the politicians to Southampton instead of to Portsmouth.

Thomas appears to have been making a political point in his comments in the letter when he writes that in future he would not always "follow her Queenship". Many years later in 1908 his great nephew Harold A. Barnes wrote about Thomas and said: "He was a past master in the Socratic method of education, education by enquiry. I myself have suffered from his plaguey investigations, and I used to fancy he devoted his leisure to inventing craddles to vex unwary youth." I think this letter may contain one of his "craddles".

The compassion shown in this letter for the plight of Joseph Ditchfield's orphaned daughter is a side of Thomas's character which could be overlooked in the mass of information about his public life. It is seen again nearly ten years later in a letter he wrote to Richard Cobden, not long after the opening of Farnworth Park. The greater part of the letter is an account of a "gun accident", possibly on the Quinta estate. Thomas's concern for the family and Dod, the unfortunate father, is evident:

"We have all had a gloom thrown over us by the melancholy result of the gun accident. It is affecting, very affecting, in its incidences. Poor Dod was not in good health at the time. He had lost three little children, all his family within a short time of each other and had been unstrung by their loss, especially by that of the eldest, a little Boy of about three years old, who was drowned in a small pool of water in the Garden. He had not got up his spirits and was not in full, good health. He was attacked by fever and died of that. His wound was nearly well. His poor widow returns to her father's house after a happy married life of less than six years, leaving her husband and all her children behind her. She is young and good looking and fortunately strong minded. I hope she will be able to bear her heavy losses with resignation. She has acted heroically during all her afflictions and bereavements."[11]

The other interesting reference in the letter written to his nephew Alfred is to Lady Hewley's business. I presume that this is linked to Halshaw Moor Chapel. The minister of the Chapel in the early days was Rev. Joseph Dyson who was invited by the congregation to move from Yorkshire to become their Pastor. He was to receive whatever the pew-rents produced, clear of all deductions, for the first two years of his ministry, during which time any incidental expenses would be covered by subscriptions from the congregation. In one of these early years he was receiving a very meagre salary from the pew-rents—only £38 4s. To help matters his wife opened a school which James Rothwell Barnes's three sons attended. A house was built for him in the chapel yard where he lived until his death fifty years later. The Barnes family did what they could to support the minister and his family. Harold Alfred Barnes described one way they helped: "Every year in October old Mrs Barnes gave a new silk gown to Mrs Dyson which served as a party frock that winter and a best dress the following summer. In later years Mrs Thomas Barnes kept up the custom, even in Mrs

MacGregor's time, explaining that it was a family tradition and she did not care to allow it to lapse. The Lords and Barneses also saw to it that Mrs Dyson was never without calico." At the end of Rev. Dyson's first two years application was made to the Trustees of Lady Hewley's Charity for some assistance towards the minister's support. They did receive an annual grant of £5 but for a few years only, as the Unitarian body tried to appropriate the Trust and threw it into the Court of Chancery. For many years the Trust dragged its slow course of litigation along, and all recipients of its bounty were deprived of its benefits from the day it entered that tedious and expensive court of law. Presumably the matter had not been sorted out by 1856 if that was what Thomas was referring to in his letter. He was still one of the six Trustees of the charity in February 1862 when it was referred to as Dame Sarah Hewley's Charity. The other Trustees at that time were Sir Samuel Morton Peto, James Ross, Alexander Gillespie, Robert Barbour and John Remington Mills.

On 12 June 1856 Thomas spoke again at a Committee of Supply to protest against the annual state grant to public education. This long speech was the longest he was ever to make in Parliament. He covered the same ground he had covered in his previous speeches on the subject and proposed keeping the grant at the amount given the previous year. However, his amendment was not accepted and the grant was raised to the amount originally proposed.[12]

During this session of Parliament from July 1855 to June 1856 Thomas had made half of the speeches he was to make in the twelve years he spent at Westminster. After this, his speeches were few and far between. Perhaps he was discouraged by the little effect they had. Apart from his success at getting the debate on national education adjourned, all his other attempts at amendments were overruled.

The year 1855/56 was a poor one for profits at Farnworth Mills. Only £3,568 was declared on 30 June 1856 but the two minor partners were given an increased share of this and each received one-seventh, leaving Thomas with just £2,549. Harold Alfred Barnes had added another comment here: "1856–57: Commercial disturbance due to American failures".

In 1856 Thomas was gazetted Deputy Lieutenant of Lancashire. The Commission was signed by the Lord Lieutenant of Lancashire on 18 July 1856.

Thomas's son, James Richardson, was mentioned in *The Wrexham Advertiser* in 1856 when he attended a Fancy Fair and Bazaar in Llangollen at the end of August to raise funds to build a chapel on Ruthin Road.

He was referred to as T. Barnes, junior, of The Quinta. Presumably he was now home from his school in London for the summer holidays.

Thomas does not appear to have been at The Quinta on Wednesday 5 November 1856 when a "plentiful repast" was provided in the "quiet village of Lodge", this time for the proprietors of the Quinta Coal Company to celebrate the finding of a first-rate bed of coal on the Quinta estate. Eighty workmen, their wives and sweethearts, all dressed in their holiday clothes, sat down in the afternoon to tea, plum cake, roast beef, ham and other luxuries in a public building loaned for the occasion. It had been tastefully decorated with evergreens, flowers and mottoes. They, too, then went to view Quinta park and pleasure grounds and the "splendid new mansion". They spent the time amusing themselves in the park until evening when they returned to hear speeches by several of the proprietors who spoke about the duties of masters and men, the importance of temperance, industry, frugality, and mental improvement among the working classes. In spite of this, the guests went home feeling they had had a good time, "far superior to anything they had ever seen at public houses on similar occasions".

Thomas was involved in a scheme to build a new Independent Chapel at Ruabon. He had put his name down to subscribe £100 of the £500 promised. His contribution was considerably more than that of the other subscribers, except for Sir W. W. Wynn's contribution. This local landowner had not only bought the old chapel for £140 but had also given a plot of land near the railway station in Ruabon for the proposed new building.

In the autumn of 1856 before Parliament re-assembled after the summer break Thomas was busy in Bolton. He presided at the first of the lectures on the subject of the Protestant Reformation in England given by Mr Henry Vincent in the Temperance Hall in the second week of October. Joseph Crook chaired the second lecture. In the same week on the evening of Wednesday 8 October 1856, he and Joseph Crook were two of the platform party at a very grand event in Manchester, the inauguration of the new Trade Hall when 2,500 ladies and gentlemen were entertained by the proprietors. John Cheetham made a speech and at the end of the evening Thomas proposed the vote of thanks to the Chairman, George Wilson. The following Wednesday, 15 October, he attended the annual meeting of the Bolton Mechanics' Institution and like Robert Heywood and P. R. Arrowsmith was appointed Vice-President for the coming year. Joseph Crook continued as President.

Later in the year, and presumably after returning to Westminster, he still managed to be in Bolton when Monsieur Louis Kossuth returned to Lancashire to give two lectures on 17 and 18 November 1856, the first entitled "The Austrian Concordat, a complement to the political system of Continental despotism, its effects on Hungary and bearings on the interests of Protestantism", and the second "Italy in general, nature and character of the Italian movement, its vitality and prospects". Monsieur Kossuth's host in Bolton was P. R. Arrowsmith. Thomas was present at the second lecture which Mr Arrowsmith chaired. At the end of the evening Thomas moved a resolution "expressing the cordial sympathy of the meeting with Monsieur Kossuth in his present position, regarding him as the true representative of Hungarian nationality, and deploring the position of his unhappy country, also reprobating any alliance on the part of this country with treacherous Austria, or any other power having for its object the suppression of liberty, etc., and pledging the meeting to use every legitimate influence to prevent such a course".

On 13 December 1856 an advertisement appeared in *The Times* naming Thomas as one of the thirteen directors of a finance company, the London Discount Company with offices in Finch Lane. Three other MPs were amongst the directors: John Cheetham, H. W. Wickham and the Chairman, William Scholefield. With capital of one million pounds, the company offered to discount approved bills and receive money on deposit at the current rate, starting on 18 December. It was clearly a new venture as the company's offices on the ground floor of the building were not yet ready and the business was still using temporary premises on the first floor.

After the Christmas recess he was at a soirée given by the Bolton Mechanics' Institution on 29 January 1857 when over 200 people attended. He proposed a toast to The Bolton Mechanics' Institution, and the progress of literary taste and culture in the borough, and later gave a speech, principally addressed to young men.

Once back at Westminster, he was soon involved in his usual activities. He attended an evening dinner at the London Tavern, Bishopgate Street, on Wednesday 18 February when the Milton Club met in public to mark the start of its parliamentary operations for the session. Thomas had been at the meeting in Manchester in September 1852 when this Club had been founded as a meeting place for Nonconformists pledged to fight for the liberation of religion from state patronage and control. Now, in 1857, two hundred supporters of civil and religious liberty met to enjoy a sumptuous meal. The Chairman was John Remington

Mills and amongst those present was John Cheetham. When Thomas made a short speech in response to the toast he spoke passionately in favour of religious liberty: "What! Are we here yet? Have we got no further than this? Are we still debating about civil and religious advantages to every class of the community? Have we been talking all these years on that subject?" He continued to say the first newspaper debate that he read after leaving school, was that on the Catholic Disabilities Bill. Then the talk was about equal civil and religious rights; and here we were at the latter half of the nineteenth century, still harping on the same string. It was enough to make us ask, "After all, does the earth move?" True, we had made some progress. A man would not now say that the sun went round the earth. A man might believe, or not believe, in the atomic theory of Dr Dalton. No man discussed another's views in astronomy, in chemistry, in mechanics. What he wanted to know was, why they should not put religious opinions in the same category? David Hume, the philosopher and historian, was found by an old woman up to the middle in a bog and unable to extricate himself; and he stretched out his hand and implored assistance. The old woman made it a condition that he should say the Lord's Prayer. And our Government were like the old woman: they were still exacting a test. This he strenuously protested against; he objected to his civil privileges being made dependent on anything religious, and he wished to see Government lay down a rule that civil privileges should have no more connection with religious opinions than they had with opinions on matters of science.

Six days later on 24 February 1857 he spoke at a Select Committee on Railway Accidents who were to inquire into the causes of railway accidents and to look into the possibility of removing these causes by further legislation. He said he supported the Committee but observed that it used to be the House of Parliament itself that interfered to prevent many beneficial restrictions upon companies being carried out—restrictions imposed when the Marquis of Dalhousie was the Head of the Board of Trade.

In early March 1857 Richard Cobden asked the House of Commons to vote on his motion censoring the Government for the bombardment of Canton, an incident in the second war with China which had begun in the previous year. To Cobden's own surprise his motion was passed by 265 votes to 249. Whether he intended it or not, the result of this defeat of the Government by 16 votes was that the Prime Minister, Lord Palmerston, was forced to ask for dissolution of Parliament. A General Election was called for 28 March 1857.

In the days before the 1857 election, meetings were held in many towns to debate the China question. At one of these meetings, in Ashton-under-Lyne on 12 March, a meeting which was very anti-Cobden in tone and very pro-Palmerston, one of the speakers, Alderman Mason, referred to Thomas's views when he said he believed what had been said to him by Mr Barnes MP for Bolton, that if the country only let Lord Palmerston unmistakeably know what was wished, he was a man who possessed the moral courage to carry these wishes out. Thomas's influence was obviously felt beyond his own constituency. What Thomas said was that the country had been at war throughout the whole time of Palmerston's Government so that it had not been given the chance to show what it would do in peace time. To upset the Government at this time appeared to him to be unwise

Thomas had been in a dilemma when faced with the vote on Cobden's motion. He was one of a few Lancashire MPs who failed to register any vote. He was recorded as being "absent without good or sufficient reason", and without being "paired". Even *The Manchester Guardian* expressed its disapproval: "We shall look with some interest to the explanations of those absentees who ought to have been present, and kept away." Joseph Crook, Thomas's fellow Liberal MP was one of thirty-five Liberals who formed a coalition with Conservatives to vote for the motion, and thus for the defeat of Palmerston's Government. Most Liberals voted against the motion. The fact that on this crucial vote the two Bolton Liberals, both pledged to promote the aims of the Reform Party, had gone their separate ways, was Thomas's downfall. He realized this but, being a man of principle, could not vote either for or against the motion. He did his best to justify why he had not voted but really all he could say was, that "he did it from a conscientious conviction, that as far as he could judge, it was the right thing for him to do. He did not mean to say it was a satisfactory thing, and he did not mean to say he was satisfied with himself. It was anything but satisfactory on a great and important question like this, not to record a vote." His supporters in the Reform Association did their best to back him but it was obvious that they nearly all disagreed with the decision he had made on this occasion.

At a two and a half hour meeting on 18 March in the Reform Rooms in Fold Street in front of eighty to ninety people Thomas and Joseph Crook gave an account of the five years they had spent in Parliament, justifying their actions. One of Thomas's supporters in earlier years, Henry Marriott Richardson, seemed to have developed a personal animosity against him and prevented the meeting from passing a resolution to support both candidates at the coming election. They therefore had to face a public meeting two days later in the Temperance Hall when Mr Richardson again successfully proposed an amendment that the vote of support for the two men should be taken separately. The result was that Joseph Crook was given a unanimous vote of approval together with loud applause but Thomas was not received with anything like as much enthusiasm. However, the original resolution to support both men was also passed and both men were adopted as candidates to campaign against a third man, William Gray. He had been the Mayor at the 1852 election and now put himself forward as a Liberal-Conservative who would go to Westminster as an Independent. He was a good and obviously a popular choice.

The Manchester Times, a paper which supported Reform, had been confident of the Liberals' success in Bolton when it reported in its Saturday edition on 14 March: "We believe that Messrs Crook and Barnes will be returned without opposition. The address of the present members, Thomas Barnes and Joseph Crook, is expected to be out this day. At present there is no probability of any opposition, as the register is greatly in favour of the Reformers, considerably more so than on any former occasion. Rumour, however, says that the Conservatives intend endeavouring to prevail on Captain Gray to contest the election, but that party being disorganised, and having neglected the register, there is little hope of their success in a contest."

Thomas's address to the electors did not appear in *The Bolton Chronicle* until 21 March, the same day on which a notice in *The Times* announced that Thomas had agreed to act as one of the Stewards at the Anniversary Festival of the Haverstock Hill Orphan Working School Charity which was to be held on 25 March. As this now turned out to be the day before Nomination Day, it is unlikely that Thomas was in London at the London Tavern in Bishopgate Street for the Festival. His election address ran:

TO THE ELECTORS OF THE BOROUGH OF BOLTON

Gentlemen,

A dissolution of Parliament is determined upon, and you will soon be called to exercise the important duty of electing your Representatives.

It is nearly five years since you invested me with this important trust, and during that time I have endeavoured faithfully to discharge the duties of the office, and have at all times acted, to the best of my judgement, in strict consistency with the principles and opinions I professed.

My public conduct is before you, and while I can hardly venture to hope it will be esteemed by all as free from error, I can safely say it has never been guided by factions or interested feelings, but at all times by a desire to do the best for my country. I have never given a Vote of importance without anxious consideration, nor abstained from voting without sufficient cause.

In again presenting myself before you as a Candidate, I have only to say that I still hold the opinions I expressed at the last Election.

On all occasions I have Voted for the Ballot, and for all proposals made to effect an improvement in our representative system. I have given a cordial support to efforts made for the extension of civil and religious liberty,—for legal reform, and for the improvement of the social condition of the people. These objects will still have my sympathy and support.

I deem it necessary now, and think the present time favourable, to direct special attention to the Public Expenditure;—to put a check on the spirit of extravagance which has been created by the large expenditure of the late War, and which now pervades every department of the state; and to effect reductions where they can be *safely* and *wisely* made. By these means only can we secure any mitigation of the pressure of taxation.

Hoping I shall be favoured with a renewal of your confidence, I beg to assure you it will be my ambition to merit a continuation of your approbation by a faithful and zealous discharge of the duties devolving upon me as one of your representatives.

I have the honour to be, Gentlemen, your faithful Servant,

THOMAS BARNES.

London, March 14 1857

Robert Kenyon, General Printer, Market-Street, Bolton

The run-up to this election was a very low-key affair compared with the 1852 election. The Reform Association did not hold any of their open-air meetings, perhaps because this election was in March, and not in July as in 1852. Instead, on the Monday evening, 23 March, eighty to a hundred Liberal supporters, both electors and non-electors, met in the Temperance Progression Room at the Old Waterworks Office in Moor Lane. The various speakers did support both candidates in their speeches but the emphasis was very clearly on Joseph Crook. The Chairman, R. Hadfield, referred to the tensions in the Reform Association which H. M. Richardson's attitude at the earlier meetings had mirrored. He commented that it was a source of sorrow to him to find the Reformers not working harmoniously together on such an occasion as this.

Nomination Day was Friday 26 March. As usual it was held in the Market Place in front of more than sixteen thousand people, all cheering, clapping, hissing or hooting. Thomas was nominated by Robert Heywood who had seconded his nomination at the previous election. He admitted now that he had not known Thomas very well on the last occasion: "At that time, I did not know much of the gentleman, but I knew his father, and had a very high opinion of him; and I naturally supposed that the son would have been in good training." Although Mr Heywood had not always agreed with the way Thomas had voted, he was able to put him forward as a supporter of all the principles of the Reform Movement. He attributed his failure to vote to his character: "If a gentleman takes all matters into consideration, and gives them his best attention, and, besides, votes conscientiously and honestly, I think he is entitled to our respect and to our future support."

Joseph Crook was nominated in much more enthusiastic terms by P. R. Arrowsmith who had nominated Thomas in 1852. H. M. Richardson continued his campaign against Thomas by publicly announcing what had been clear from the first meeting of this campaign, namely that he was trying to remove Thomas by splitting the vote. Waving his hat he called out, "Crook and Gray for ever".

Thomas made a most statesmanlike speech, trying to persuade the voters not to vote solely on the China question. "Now, you will not forget, I am sure, that you want something besides China. You don't live upon China, and you want something beside that. You want a Parliament, and a Government. You want a Government that will look to the interests of people at home as well as abroad. You want—people in this country want—home legislation. They want protection. They want laws making for them as well as for China. Gentlemen, I know very well that you have too much sense to be drawn off the scent of a real fox by the trail of a red herring. No red herring for you. You will follow the real game,—Reform, reform of Parliament, extension of the suffrage." He expanded upon the need for Government reducing expenditure to allow for lower taxes. "Now, gentlemen, we think there is no way of getting this but giving to the people themselves more power to control the public expenditure of the country. Therefore, gentlemen, we desire, we have voted, we shall vote, for an increase and extension of the suffrage. Gentlemen, we are no new Reformers. We are not chickens just hatched and come out of the shell. We are old Reformers. We have been at it for twenty years. We are not new converts. We have advocated Reform, Economy, and Retrenchment for above twenty years. Gentlemen, believe practice and not promises; look to principles and not professions. Look to those that have done something; and as one bird in the hand is worth two in the bush, so one man that has been tried is worth two new ones; believe old men, those that have been tried, those that you know; trust them, and not new converts. Why have not these new converts advocated these principles for twenty or thirty years? Why, because they did not believe in them, and now that they are wanting your suffrages they are putting on the garment of Reform. Gentlemen, don't be deluded by chaff. You are not to be caught by chaff. I am sure you know the difference between real, good wheat, and chaff."

Only when the speeches were over was the crowd quiet for the first time. The Mayor asked for a show of hands in the market-place. The non-electors were, therefore, able to have some say in the election of their representative, up to a point. In order to prevent people voting for the wrong candidate, this time the candidates' names were posted up on large placards which were held up above the heads of the crowd. The result of the show of hands was two-fifths for Thomas Barnes, one-half for Joseph Crook, and three-fifths for William Gray. How such accuracy could be reached in a crowd of that size, I do not know, but the Mayor declared the winners to be William Gray and Joseph Crook. Mr Heywood demanded a poll on behalf of Thomas Barnes to take place the following morning. A poster was issued that morning encouraging all the voters to split their vote between the two Liberal candidates:

Reformers

be true to the two Reform candidates

No Plumpers!

but vote

Barnes and Crook

and the result will be their

Triumphant Return!

Central Committee Room, Fold Street

Friday Morning

D. Knott, Secretary

Robert Kenyon, General Printer, Market-Street, Bolton[13]

There were a possible 1,933 voters, each able to vote for two candidates. The nine polling booths opened at eight in the morning. For the first two hours Barnes and Crook took the lead and then Gray moved ahead and stayed there until the poll closed at four o'clock. William Gray's committee issued regular statements as to the state of the poll, sometimes as often as four times an hour. By noon the Reform committee had lost track of the voting "in consequence of some disarrangement in their sheets" and had to rely on the numbers given by the opposition. Their final numbers were very close to the official count declared by the Mayor on Monday morning: 930 for Gray, 895 for Crook, and 832 for Barnes. Although William Gray's victory was expected, his huge 98 vote lead over Thomas Barnes surprised everybody.

In spite of the request that there should be no "plumpers", many people did plump. Perhaps if fewer had decided not to split their vote, Thomas might have beaten Joseph Crook. I found a list of results showing this "plumping". Although the figures do not seem to tally with the official count, the breakdown is interesting.

> Plumped for Grey 652
>
> Plumped for Crook 13
>
> Plumped for Barnes 26
>
> Voted for Gray & Barnes 102
>
> Voted for Gray & Crook 177
>
> Voted for Barnes & Crook 704

Thomas's next letter dated 30 March 1857, the day after polling day, was also produced as a poster. In it, he thanked his supporters despite his defeat at the polls.

BOLTON ELECTION

TO THE
ELECTORS
AND
NON-ELECTORS
OF THE
BOROUGH OF BOLTON.

Gentlemen,

The Poll is over, and it has not been favourable to myself. I am no longer one of your Representatives. I can not, however, take leave of you, without thanking most heartily, the 832 Electors who honored me with their suffrages on this occasion.

The position I formerly held as your Representative, and the great number who have now honored me with their support, have, I think, justified me in demanding a Poll, and asking you to record your votes. I have great satisfaction in believing that they have been the honest, unbiased expression of your attachment to the great principles of *Reform, Retrenchment* and *Civil Religious Liberty.*

I regret that they have not been more successful, and have the honor to remain,

Gentlemen,

Yours very respectfully

Thomas Barnes.

Farnworth, March 30, 1857

John Burrell, Printer, Fold Street, Bolton[14]

On Monday 1 April after the Mayor had declared the official result, Thomas as the defeated candidate was certainly not expected to make a speech but he did. His relief at being freed from his public duties certainly sounds genuine. He said: "Mr Mayor and gentlemen, the state of the poll has deprived me of the high honour of being your representative, and also relieved me from the onerous and arduous duties which devolve upon that man who conscientiously and assiduously attempts to discharge those duties. I appear before you, as you are all aware, as the unsuccessful candidate. I am not ashamed to look you in the face. I am not ashamed to appear before you, even unsuccessfully, because I come before you with a clear conscience and with clean hands. In no one case have I ever used, in any manner whatsoever, the slightest influence to draw aside from the gallant gentleman who is returned, any one pledge of vote that has been promised to him; and, gentlemen, I appear before you with the proud satisfaction—with the consciousness, the honest consciousness—of having, during the time that I filled the office which in 1852 you elected me to, discharged the duties that devolved upon me. My conscience does not reproach me with having in any one case neglected them. I appear before you and can say I have broken no pledges. I have forsaken no principles, I have neglected no duties. The principles and opinions which I expressed in 1852 I hold this day. I am not changed, but the state of the poll shows that a majority of the electors of Bolton have changed. They no longer desire—a majority of them no longer desire—to see those principles carried out; and they have, as I suppose—I know no reason why I should not say it—I suppose they have honestly elected the honourable and gallant gentleman to represent the Conservative principles which the majority of electors of Bolton now profess. Gentlemen, in 1852 I came forth, solicited and earnestly entreated, to stand as a candidate before you. I was dragged from a privacy I was not very willing to leave, but felt compelled by a sense of public duty. I now retire again to that privacy, with the full satisfaction that I have done my duty. If the electors of Bolton do not desire to have my services, I have no fault to find with them. I earnestly, in taking farewell of you, earnestly, sincerely, and from the bottom of my heart thank those 832 who have recorded their votes in my favour. I beg, in this public manner—the most public I can make—to present to them my best thanks, especially to those who have assiduously and earnestly canvassed, and worked in the committee, to secure my election. It has on this occasion failed. It is no fault of theirs if a hundred of those who once professed Liberal opinions have changed those opinions and gone over to the side of my honourable and gallant opponent. As long as a man lives, I suppose he has a right to change his opinion. I hope the day is not far distant when it will be shown to have changed again, and changed for the better. Gentlemen, I leave you without any feeling of acrimony. I have no complaint to make of my honourable and gallant friend. I have no accusation to bring against him. I indulge no ill-will towards him or you. With best wishes for you and for him, for his health and the efficient discharge of his duties, I have now the pleasure, in again thanking those who have laboured for my return, of bidding you farewell, and going back to the privacy which I much delight in, waiting and ready, should you ever think proper to call me forth, to come at your bidding. Gentlemen, I have one more remark to make, and it is this. I am not the only defeated candidate. Much greater, much better men—men with much more talent than myself—have been rejected at contested elections; and I can say, with one remarkably distinguished for his eloquence in speech and for the beauty of his writing—Here I stand before you, defeated, but not dishonoured, nor disheartened."

He had heard on Saturday afternoon after the result was known in Bolton that Cobden himself had lost his seat, together with the two Manchester Reformists Bright and Gibson. In fact, John Bright, like Thomas, had absented himself from the vote on the Canton affair without good or sufficient reason. Thomas Milner Gibson, like Joseph Crook, had voted for the motion, but unlike Crook, lost his seat too. John Cheetham, Liberal MP for South Lancashire, had absented himself from the vote but was re-elected.

And that was the end of Thomas's first period as an MP. He was not well at the time and was unable to return from The Quinta to chair the Tenth Conference of the Sunday School Unions of Lancashire and Cheshire held on 10 April 1857 in Mawdsley Street Independent Chapel because of a severe cold. He was also unable to chair another conference, this one of Sunday School Unions at Exeter Hall. Maybe the strain of the election had been too much for him. Around this time, 1857 or 1858, he offered Queen Street Seminary, his private Day School, which had up to this time been non-denominational, to Halshaw Moor Chapel for the Church and congregation to manage as they thought best. The Church did not take up the offer.

For more than six months after his defeat in the Bolton elections there were no more references to Thomas in *The Manchester Times* apart from one just two weeks after the election when a painting which he had loaned, *Sisters of Mercy Preventing Boys Illtreating a Jew* by W. J. Grant, was listed in the catalogue of the huge Art Treasures Exhibition at Old Trafford. Paintings and other art exhibits had been assembled from many sources, including some from the Royal Collection. On Wednesday 14 May 1857 he was one of the members of the Society of Arts who attended a meeting at their rooms at the Adelphi to hear J. B. Smith, MP for Stockport, read a paper on the question of how to obtain more supplies of cotton. The Chairman was Thomas Bazley of Manchester.

When the firm's profits of £6,803 were declared on 30 June 1857 the share given to each of the two minor partners was again one-seventh. In his separate account at the back of the stock book Thomas recorded that in 1858 he paid off the previous year's loss. I cannot find evidence of this loss unless it was the £1,896 15s deducted from the next year's balance before profits were declared. On 17 October 1857 the firm advertised the sale of a single-lap machine, 36" on the lap, made by Mason, and in excellent condition. In June 1858 the deduction of nearly £1,900 from the profits left £6,529 8s 3d to be divided between the three partners. The two minor partners each received one-sixth of this. The firm's name did not appear again in *The Manchester Times* until 4 September 1858 when it was in a list of subscribers to the Cotton Supply Association. The donation by Thomas's firm of £100 was not the largest in the list—some firms had given £250.

Notes

1   *Bolton Chronicle* [Bolton Archives and Social Studies] All accounts of Thomas's elections in Bolton between 1852 and 1868 are based on articles from *The Bolton Chronicle*, unless indicated otherwise.

2   *Manchester Times* [19th Century Newspapers online]

3   Ibid.

4   *Bolton Chronicle* [Bolton Archives and Social Studies]

5   H. M. Richardson *Reminiscences of Forty Years in Bolton* (pub. 1885)

6   *Manchester Times* [19th Century Newspapers online] Most accounts from now on of Thomas's political activities in Westminster and London are based on *The Manchester Times*, unless indicated otherwise.

7   *Wrexham and Denbigh Advertiser* [19th Century Newspapers online] From 1855 onwards, most references to events at The Quinta are based on *The Wrexham Advertiser*, unless indicated otherwise.

8   Speeches in Hansard (hansard.millbanksystems.com)

9   Ibid.

10   LRO DDX 75/126

11   Cobden Papers Ms 8 f21 West Sussex Record Office

12   Speeches in Hansard *op. cit.*

13   ZZ/130/6/13 Bolton Archives and Social Studies

14   ZZ/130/5/8 Bolton Archives and Social Studies

CHAPTER 4

1857–1860

The gap years—failed elections and politics at a lull

It was August 1857 when Thomas's name appeared in the local paper for the Border Counties again. On 18 August Thomas as Branch Treasurer was one of the speakers at the annual meeting of the Lodge Branch of the British and Foreign Bible Society held in a tent specially erected in the village.[1]

On 7 September 1857 he provided another of his tea and plum cake parties, this time for over five hundred scholars and teachers from seven different chapels in the area around The Lodge and some from Oswestry. They began with the usual procession to The Quinta, led this time by Thomas Minshall from Oswestry. By now the mansion was finished and Thomas and his family were no longer living in the cottage in the grounds. The party gathered to sing hymns outside the newly-finished mansion. Then they gave three cheers for Mr and Mrs Barnes, and three cheers for Master James Barnes (who were all present), and the group from the local schools marched back to a field in the village for their tea and games. The children and friends from Oswestry spent the rest of the afternoon in the Quinta Park. In the evening there was a public meeting in a tent in which the ministers of all the churches took part. At nine o'clock the meeting was brought to a close with a prayer led by Mr Porter, the gardener at The Quinta, but not before a resolution had been passed: "That a Sunday School Union be established in the neighbourhood and that the anniversary be celebrated in a manner similar to the meeting of that day."[2]

Thomas was now becoming part of the social scene in the area around Chirk. For example, on 2 October 1857, A. Mackintosh, the chief engineer on the Great Western Railway line from Chester to Wolverhampton, gave a great festive banquet to all the people employed on the building of the track. The marquee in which they dined was in a field adjoining the Chirk Castle Arms and was decorated with flags and the coats of arms of the local gentry—including Thomas's own coat of arms. Thomas was also one of the guests at another grand banquet, this one held in Chirk Castle itself in March 1858 to celebrate the coming of age of Colonel Biddulph's son and heir. Thomas probably remembered this occasion when he put on a similar celebration for his own son's coming of age two years later. In August 1858 his 18–year-old son James was also becoming part of the local social scene, appearing as a guest at a local wedding. When Miss Bellysk, the daughter of Colonel Biddulph's agent at Chirk Castle, married on 15 October 1858 the guests drank a health to Colonel Biddulph, "the greatest landed proprietor in the parish", followed by a health to Mr Barnes of The Quinta, who was not one of the guests. The same thing happened a month later in Glyn Trian at a supper in the Castle Mills Inn when the landlord, Mr Williams, married Mrs Ann Hughes. The first toast was again to Colonel Biddulph, the second to Mr and Mrs Barnes of The Quinta, and the third to Mr and Mrs Stubbs of Brookside. There was no indication that any of these were at the supper. Nearly five years later Thomas's health was still being drunk at dinners which he did not attend. On 20 June 1863 the Chirk Union Friendly Society held its Anniversary Dinner in the Schoolroom at Chirk. Dr J. Edmunds, the local doctor, gave the toast to Thomas, the fourth in the list of toasts: "To a gentleman who had not long come to reside amongst them—one who was doing a vast deal of good. He gave employment to a great number of people and did much good in many other ways besides." This was repeated three years later in June 1866 when the Chirk Union Friendly Society held its Anniversary Dinner at the Hand Hotel in Chirk. The order of the toasts was again: Colonel Biddulph, Mrs Biddulph, Lord Hill Trevor, Sir Watkin, Mr Barnes of The Quinta (proposed by Dr Edmunds), and Mr Bellyse. On 22 June 1869 the Society celebrated its 44th anniversary in the usual way and again Thomas was included in the toasts, this time coming third: first came a toast to the Patron, Colonel Myddelton Biddulph, then one to Sir Watkin Wynn and his Foxhounds, and then one to Mr Barnes of The Quinta, followed by toasts to Mr E. Bellyse, the Colliery Proprietors of the District, and the officials of the Society. The Friendly Society at The Lodge showed their respect in a different way. After their annual Festival on 16 May 1863 they formed a procession and went to three houses: Thomas's at The Quinta, Rev. J. C. Philips' house at Tyn-y-rhos, and to Brookside House, the home of J. S. Stubbs. Thomas continued to be included in the toasts at formal dinners. When the St Martins Trevor Lodge of Oddfellows held their Annual Dinner on 20

June 1873 Mr Ravenshaw proposed the health of Lord A. E. Hill Trevor and of Mr Barnes of The Quinta, as two of the neighbouring landlords.

When the Parliamentary Reform Committee based at 15 King Street, Cheapside, London, published a draft of their five demands for reform in *The Times* on 5 January 1858 Thomas's name was in the long list of private individuals and thirty MPs who had signed in support.

In September 1858 Thomas attended the 19th autumnal meeting of the Congregational Union of England and Wales at Halifax. On the second morning, 19 September, he proposed that they should print the Minutes of the meeting together with a paper outlining the origin, development and striking peculiarities of Congregationalism in the two countries. His suggestion that the next meeting should be held in Aberdare in Wales was agreed to.3

As soon as Quinta Hall was finished Thomas began building an Independent Congregational Chapel at The Lodge opposite the entrance to the park. He chose as his architect Thomas D. Barry of 47 Bedford Street North, Liverpool, who designed a building in the Gothic revival style, unusual for a Nonconformist building of this period, and exceptional in being a private benefaction. The Quinta Chapel (called at the time the Quinta Congregational Church) was completed in just four months by the builders Messrs Hugh Yates and Edward Hughes of Liverpool. It could seat 250. It opened for worship on Thursday, 14 October 1858.

A long report was printed in the local paper, *The Oswestry Advertiser and Montgomeryshire Mercury*, a few days after the event: "The day appointed for the opening services was Thursday last, and the weather on that day was, fortunately, propitious, with the exception of a little rain which fell in the afternoon. During the morning large numbers of people arrived in the village from Oswestry, Shrewsbury, Chirk, Wrexham, and other places, many of whom had been invited to partake of Mr and Mrs Barnes's hospitality, and by eleven o'clock, the time fixed for commencing service, the chapel was quite full. Many others arrived afterwards, so that the building was densely crowded, and several were unable to gain admittance. The Oswestry Old Chapel Choir had kindly given their services for the occasion, and the excellence of their singing, combined with the admirable manner in which the accompaniment on the fine-toned harmonium was played, added not a little to the happiness of the day."

Rev. Dr Raffles of Liverpool preached in the morning. A summary of the sermon was printed in the newspaper article: "The sermon was preached by the Rev. Dr Raffles, who delivered a very eloquent discourse from a part of the 12th verse of the 19th chapter of Revelation— 'And on His head were many crowns'. Want of room prevents our reporting the sermon fully, and we give a brief outline of it. The reverend doctor said:—The Book of Revelation is confessedly a mysterious book, and it behoves us to be content with ascertaining the general scope of its contents, and the outline of its occurrences, while we draw from it those doctrinal principles and practical lessons with which it is so richly fraught. We have in the chapter before us a figurative representation of Christ, in which He is represented as having on His head many crowns, and, as the crown is an emblem of empire, we are led to conclude that many empires are subject to Him. To number them all were beyond a mortal's, perhaps an angel's power, for when we have done our utmost to grasp the grand total, it may be said, 'Lo, these are a part of His works'. There are four sceptres, however, which we are certain the Redeemer holds, and these may suffice for an illustration of my text:—the sceptres of Creation, Providence, Grace, and Glory. First, the sceptre of Creation. This belongs to Him by right, as the maker and proprietor, for 'by Him were all things made', and who has so just a right to possess and govern all things as He who created all? Wherever we turn, whatever our eye rests upon,—the animalculæ which find their world in a drop of water, and the countless morning stars which stud the sky, the flower which blooms unseen in the sequestered valley, and the stately cedar which crowns the hallowed brow of Lebanon,—the atom on which we tread, and the Alps whose lofty summits seem to bid defiance to man,—each and every one is a department of the Redeemer's empire, and the crown that indicates possession of all adorns His brow. Not less does the sceptre of Providence belong to Christ. What but the possession and administration of this empire is implied in such words as these: 'Beholding all things by the word of His power, and by Him do all things consist'? All things being beheld by Him, and consisting by Him, can denote nothing else than His providence over all things, by which they are made to subserve the grand ends for which they were brought into existence. Thirdly, the Kingdom of Grace belongs to Christ. This empire He has purchased with this blood. He possesses by virtue of His mediatorial intercession. He performs its high functions in His character as mediator. And how great a work does He accomplish in this kingdom. He accomplishes the redemption of His people. This He has effected by the offering up of Himself as a sacrifice and propitiation for their sins. Lastly, I spoke of the Kingdom of Glory as belonging to

Christ. But of that empire how can I speak, who am still in the body, when 'eye hath not seen, nor ear heard, neither hath it entered into the heart of man to conceive what God hath prepared for those that love Him'; who with a mortal tongue can presume to speak of that world where sin exists not, where death never smites, where friends never separate, where sabbaths never end, where the sun shall no more go down, but all shall be the peace, and the purity, the rapture, and the blessedness of an uninterrupted, perfect, perpetual Sabbath, and on the head of Him who shall be the light of that perennial Sabbath, there are many crowns.

After service, those who had been invited to be the guests of Mr Barnes proceeded to The Quinta, and amused themselves, till luncheon was ready, by looking over the magnificent rooms of the mansion, and the tastefully laid out grounds belonging to it, the spacious greenhouses, which contain many specimens of choice and rare plants, being especial objects of attraction. About two o'clock the company sat down to a most bountiful repast in the very beautiful dining saloon."

Dr Raffles made an after-lunch speech "filled with humour and feeling". This speech was also reported in full in the paper: "When luncheon was finished, the Rev. Dr Raffles rose and said—I would not for a moment interrupt the pleasant conversation which is going on in coteries in different parts of the room, but I feel that you will sympathise with me in the motive for which I rise. It would ill become us, after the fashion of the world, to propose toasts and with loud and jubilant noise to give expression to our feelings, but as Christians there are sentiments of gratitude which it would ill become us to ignore. I feel that we are all under a deep debt of gratitude to our worthy host for his princely hospitality; to-day we are greatly honoured—I feel myself so, and I am sure you all do—in being guests on this occasion. I feel a weight of obligation in connection with bygone days, and in connection with the interests of the kingdom of Christ in that populous county (Lancashire) with which our host is partially connected. I know that the neighbourhood of Farnworth, where he formerly resided, owes a deep debt of gratitude to him—how deep I cannot tell; nobody will know it but He who sees in secret, and who has reserved his reward till another day. But I do know that they cherish the memory of his living amongst them, and I hope they will not lose him altogether; he will be present by his acts of kindness, by his warm wishes and fervent prayers. I would tender to him the thanks of this assembly, and especially of his tenants. I do most heartily tender to him their grateful acknowledgements for all he has done for them in conjunction with the Word of God, in the erection of that neat, that commodious, that simply elegant structure, in which we worshipped this morning. I know I am only expressing the feelings of the whole neighbourhood, the sense they cannot but entertain of the service which he has rendered to them in the dearest interests of themselves, their children, and their children's children. I know that only the pure Gospel will be preached there—the true word, by which sinners may be saved and God glorified. I know he will secure that. And may the Gospel and its ordinances, introduced there this day, be handed down to the remotest portions of time. Mr and Mrs Barnes, may God bless you, and may we all meet you in Heaven!"

Thomas replied "in an able address which will for ever place him in the front rank of Nonconformists". He said: "I do not know whether I shall be able, with any degree of propriety, to acknowledge the very kind manner in which my highly esteemed friend has brought my name, and the names of my wife and son, before you, and in which you have responded. He has expressed more than I know how to reply to, and I can only say that I feel extremely obliged to him, and that we are all glad to see him here. We have been enabled to open this house, and the other house in which we worshipped this morning. I am glad that the first party here has been one of Christian friends, assembled to [*illegible*] upon a building dedicated to the service of God. It is my wish that this should be a house entirely devoted to the service of God and the promotion of true religion. I wish it to be the home of Christian principle. I can aspire to a higher state of things than I can ever hope to reach; I should like to make it the home of intelligence and piety. We are not our own, and all we do should show that we think of this, and that we are endeavouring to make all things converge to this one point—God's glory on earth and man's good. I am very glad that my esteemed friend Dr Raffles has introduced the conversation as he has, for it relieves us from proposing toasts and then calling upon persons to respond. I must offer to you our thanks for honouring us with your presence to-day; and there are some to whom I am under special obligation for their services in connection with the church. I must mention Dr Raffles, Mr McGregor, Mr Thomas, and Mr Martin, of Westminster, who all responded instantaneously and cordially to my request that they would preach at the opening; the architect, Mr Barry, and the builders, Mr Hughes and Mr Yates, to whom I am obliged for the very rapid manner in which the work has been accomplished, for the beauty of the design, and the excellence of the workmanship; and the Oswestry Old Chapel Choir—who, though I name them last, are by no means least;—by the readiness and heartiness with which they have rendered services, I feel exceedingly gratified: concerning the goodness of their singing I need not say one word.

We have erected a building for the worship of God, and have called it a church. This, I know, will be looked upon as an invasion of an old custom, which designates all places of worship not exactly connected with the Church of England, as chapels. I mean to break through that rule. I do not understand why the name of 'Church' in England should be confined to one denomination. In other countries it is not so; in Scotland and America, and also in those parts of the Continent where more than one denomination exists, every place of worship is called a church, and why England should be an exception to this rule I do not know. It can only be a relic of those bygone times when oppression and persecution existed, and I see no reason why we should not break through it. And we have called the building a Congregational Church. I need not say why I have done so, because all who know me know, that if I did build a church, I should build for that form of worship which I practise. I have called it a Congregational Church because I think the congregational style of worship the simplest and most in accordance with that practised by the early Christians. I call it so because I like the congregational form of worship and government best. I do not say it must be the most scriptural; I know there are various opinions on that point, and all we can do is to have our own opinions and go on in peace. I hope the pure gospel will be preached in the church as long as it stands, and I desire that it shall not be shut to any other denomination. It must have a name that we may be known who and what we are, but I do hope it will be open to preachers of any denomination whatsoever who preach the gospel. I should like to see a clergyman of the Church of England there. One reason I can mention why I call it a Congregational Church, if it were an Episcopal Church, its doors would be closed against every other denomination. I would leave it to any man, whether my plan is not the best—to have as broad a platform as possible. Unfortunately it has been the opinion in this country, but I hope it is now dying out, that the building of any other church is an attack on the Church of England. I think that a great error. I look upon all the orthodox denominations as strong buttresses outside the Church. We feed the Church, we sustain it, and I believe it has, for the last hundred and fifty years, been greatly indebted to other churches. I believe it is better than it would have been if there had been no dissent. I consider the Church of England as an integral and very important part of the Protestant Church we cannot dispense with; we must, as Christians, try to purify it, and make it more valuable. I believe there is not one denomination of true Christians which can be dispensed with without doing harm to Protestantism.

I will say no more, but merely again thank you for being our guests, and thank Dr Raffles for the service which he has rendered; it would be out of place for me to say anything concerning the sermon, but I feel thankful that the first discourse in the church has been one so calculated to exalt our Saviour, before whom I hope that all of us may cast our crowns. I will depart from our rule by giving one sentiment, and will leave you to drink it in water or wine, sitting or standing— Health, long life, and a successful reign to the Queen, and health and long life to the rest of the Royal Family." The toast was drunk, accompanied by applause and Thomas then introduced Rev. J. Denham Smith from Kingston, Ireland, who gave an excellent humorous after-dinner speech.

In the afternoon the visitors strolled round the Quinta grounds before tea at five o'clock and returned to the new chapel in the evening to hear Rev. G. D. McGregor from the chapel in Farnworth preach on a text from Romans 8:32: "He that spared not his own son, but delivered him up for us all, how shall he not with him give us all things". The church was again crowded to overflowing.

On the following Sunday, the opening services were continued. "On each occasion the church was crowded to overflowing, every available standing, as well as sitting space, being occupied, and many remaining outside, or going away, quite unable to gain admittance. In the evening, the congregation had begun to assemble as early as half past five, and at the commencement of the service there could not have been fewer than 500 congregated in the church." Rev. Samuel Martin of Westminster preached in the morning at eleven o'clock and in the evening at half past six, taking as his subject in the morning the text from Acts 4:12: "Neither is there salvation in any other, for there is none other name under heaven given amongst men whereby we must be saved", and in the evening from John 12:27 and part of 28: "Now my soul is troubled. And what shall I say? 'Father, save me from this hour'? No, for this purpose I have come to this hour. Father, glorify thy name." He was a very impressive and eloquent speaker and his evening sermon held the attention of the congregation from beginning to end. They were "riveted by the lucidity of his exposition, and the simple power, force, and eloquence with which he illustrated and applied the truths of his text." Between these two sermons in the afternoon at three o'clock Rev. Robert Thomas of Bangor preached in Welsh from

Romans 5:6: "While we were yet helpless, at the right time Christ died for the ungodly."

In 1898 Ernest Elliot wrote in his book *Congregationalism in Shropshire*:

"The Rev. T. Davison who served the Quinta Church as pastor for 20 years has said that the residence of Mr Barnes at The Quinta will be chiefly memorable for the erection of the Congregational Church—a beautiful Gothic structure, covered with ivy and roses, and internally decorated with great taste, constituting it one of the chief attractions of the district." John Newman in his book *Shropshire* wrote that "the chapel with its Decorated tracery, steep slated roofs and a spirelet beside the porch, could easily be mistaken for an Anglican church. Even less is the short, separately expressed chancel in the Nonconformist tradition". Niklaus Pevsner's comments were: "Built by T. D. Barry at Barnes's expense in 1858 for Congregationalists. Quite a disciplined design, though demonstrative by Nonconformist standards, and early in its use of a [Decorated] style. Five-bay nave, [south] porch and short chancel all of coursed rock-faced stone. Steep roofs with banded slates. The small but elaborate SW steeple has an open bell-stage and ashlar spire."

The report in *The Oswestry Advertiser and Montgomeryshire Mercury* of the opening of the chapel in October 1858 gives a detailed account of the newly-completed building: "In the design of the church, the aim of the architect has been to combine a simple but tasteful architectural effect, with moderate outlay, yet with a due regard to complete stability, and employment of the very best materials and workmanship. The design is 'Flowing Middle Pointed', or the decorated style prevalent in the 14th century, and consists of a nave, 56ft by 24ft; choir, 15ft by 10ft; vestry, at north-east of nave, 9ft 6in by 8ft; south porch, 9ft by 5ft 6in. At the south-west angle is an engaged turret, with ringing chamber below, recessed into an effective octagonal stone belfry and spire, the whole height being 60ft.

The church forms an agreeable group from the road, and there are several nice points of view from the Quinta park and terraces. Internally, the effect is harmonious and substantial; the roof is of the description called 'waggon headed', that is, instead of being open to the apex, it is ceiled at the intersection of its diagonal braces, the void space above being used for the purposes of ventilation. The principal trusses are supported by arched ribs footing upon moulded stone corbels. The sittings, which accommodate 231 persons, are entirely finished in pitch pine, having cut and moulded stall ends of suitable design, the most prominent having carved poppy heads and elbow bosses. An effective ornamental screen separates the choir from the nave; the open panels of this and the pulpit being lined with crimson damask. The aisle floors are laid with Minton's octagonal red, buff and black tiles, in patterns.

The ornamental locks, hinges, pulpit lights, etc., were supplied by Messrs Hart & Son, London. The church is warmed by a circulation of warm air in fire clay tubes, on a simple, effectual, and most inexpensive system."

For the next three years until they had a regular minister Thomas led the service at the church himself if necessary. Ernest Elliott continued his account of Thomas Barnes's involvement in the church by saying that he contributed not only financially, "but also personally, in conjunction with his late excellent wife, co-operating in all the varied activities of church and Sunday school work. The relations between Mr Barnes and the minister were the most cordial and hearty. There was not the remotest approach to authority and dictation on the part of Mr Barnes towards the minister who entirely depended on him for pecuniary support, but invariably the greatest respect and affection." The church is still considered of such architectural merit that it is listed as a Grade II building. It is still an independent church. It does not belong to any denomination and controls its own destiny. It receives no financial support apart from that provided by its members and visitors. This was always the case. Thomas Barnes gave all the financial support, providing a lovely manse and a liberal salary. After his death it became a registered charity. The Shropshire archives contain Charity Commission accounts for the Quinta Chapel from 1909–1915, and from 1918–1940.

I visited the Quinta Church in Weston Rhyn in March 2006 and was shown round by the minister, Dr Digby James. It stands close to the red-brick Quinta School, in sharp contrast with its stone and much more restrained architecture. The churchyard is a lawn with just one grave, that of Thomas's son, James Richardson, and his wife Ellen, a simple square stone outline laid out on the grass with no headstone. The lych-gate was erected in 1933 in their memory. As in the Quinta School building, everything about the church is of the highest quality of craftsmanship. All the windows are now protected against vandals by plastic shields but the care once taken in their construction is evident. A rose window with plain glass like a wheel with its spokes formed by leaves is the focal point of the church. All the original box pews have now been replaced by traditionally positioned pews. There is one original Victorian stained glass window. On the walls are several plaques, almost all in memory of the Barnes family. In the vestry are two rooms, both with photographs and busts of the Barnes family, together with portraits of all ministers of the church. Although it is clear that the church is struggling financially, it is obviously still very much in use as a centre of worship.

Thomas's decision to build the church was said to have been all very much to the annoyance of his Tory and aristocratic neighbours. The first indication I have found of this tension is an article printed in *The Wrexham Advertiser* just before a report of the opening of the new Church. Someone using the pen name "Amicus" (a friend) who had happened as a visitor to attend the opening had been very impressed by what he saw. He concluded that others should follow the good example set by Thomas Barnes: "Go thou and do thou likewise." There appeared to be no need to include an article like this in the paper except to emphasize that there was support for this Dissenting chapel.

Only a few weeks after the opening of the church a series of letters published in the Correspondence Column of *The Wrexham Weekly Advertiser* on Saturday 11 December 1858 illustrated the ill-feeling that did exist in the area. Richard Stokes had been the Master at the National School in Selattyn, a position to which he had been appointed by the Vicar of Selattyn, Rev. John Husband. On 15 November John Husband wrote to Richard Stokes to say that when he had given Richard Stokes the job he had been assured that he was a member of the Church of England. "I now find you are a dissenter, and in the habit of attending dissenting places of worship. I cannot continue to employ you as a schoolmaster beyond the end of the present quarter." Apparently Richard Stokes and his wife had attended the opening of the Quinta Chapel and had also been to some services. Richard Stokes gave a spirited reply, setting out his religious beliefs and including the remark: "I am not ashamed to confess that I have on several occasions attended the Congregational Church at the Quinta, and I unhesitatingly affirm, I have never heard anything contrary to the pure and unbiased Gospel of our blessed Saviour, such as I believe to be the rule and faith of the Evangelical section of the Church of England." His reply infuriated the Vicar. On 17 November he wrote back: "I do not take the Oswestry paper, or I should have warned you immediately on seeing that you and your wife had taken a prominent part at the opening of a Sandimanian meeting house". The Vicar slipped up here. Mr Stokes's name had not been included in the article. Someone had informed on him. (Robert Sandeman was an 18th century Scotsman who inspired the Scottish Baptists in some of the Welsh-speaking churches.) On 19 November Richard Stokes had the final say: "One final word regarding dissent. I believe that *if* there be any *sin* in dissent, it rests entirely on the head of the clergy of the Church of England, who by their apathy and indifference to the flock over which they have been made overseers, have compelled the people to seek out more faithful pastors." And his parting shot was to say that he had had legal advice and now claimed a full quarter's pay from the date he was given notice. He then wrote to the paper to ask them to publish the exchange of letters. It was clear that Thomas would have to work hard to counteract the ill feeling of the established Church.

Back in Lancashire Thomas presided at a Public Tea Meeting at the Temperance Hall in Bolton on 8 November 1858 when Dukes Alley Chapel celebrated its Centenary.

Early in the following year Thomas appeared more regularly on the political stage. On 1 February 1859 he was one of a deputation of Reformers from Bolton in the Assembly Room of Manchester Free Trade Hall at a Conference of Lancashire Reformers in support of the general principles of John Bright's Bill. The delegation from Bolton consisted of R. Heywood, T. Thomasson, P. R. Arrowsmith, Mr Satterthwaite, H. Ashworth from The Oaks, William Aspinwall, H. Moss, I. Wright, S. Jackson, J. Hodgkinson, James Haslam, A. Lawson, A. Riding, Thomas Broomley and Fred Jones. Several of these men were to be Thomas's supporters when he returned to politics in April. During his speech John Bright paid tribute to Thomas when he said, "I go into this partly in reference to what my friend Mr Barnes has said".

Bolton held its own meeting to consider Parliamentary reform a week or so later. When Thomas spoke he paid his own tribute to John Bright, moving, "That this meeting gratefully recognizes Mr Bright's eminent services in the protracted contest for the repeal of the Corn Laws; and remembering the severe illness which has recently withdrawn him for a time from public life, offers him its hearty congratulations upon his restoration to health, and expresses its earnest hope that he may long be spared to devote his rare abilities to the promotion of those objects which he has at heart, and which are closely identified with the political and social wellbeing of all classes of the community." He went on to say that he believed that there was not one man in this country that had a warmer place in the hearts of the people than John Bright. There was not a man who had laboured more sincerely for the welfare and advantage of the public generally; and there was not a man who had deeper sympathies with the working classes, both in times of commercial depression and in political struggles for freedom.

A Great Reform Meeting was held in the Music Room in Wrexham on 9 March 1859 to give people the opportunity of expressing their opinions on the Government Reform Bill. The Chairman, the Mayor of Wrexham, read out letters of apology for absence, the first from Colonel Biddulph MP, and the second from Thomas:

The Quinta, 8 March 1859

My Dear Sir,

I feel much obliged to you for the invitation to attend a public meeting in Wrexham, on the proposed Reform Bill of the Government, and regret that I am unable to do so. I am prevented by an engagement in Bolton at the same time, which it is not possible to postpone, or I would have done so for the purpose of attending your meeting on Wednesday, and uniting with the earnest reformers of Wrexham and the surrounding districts in protesting against and opposing the deceitful sham which the Government have had the temerity to propose. I see only one good thing that can result from it, and that is, the hopelessness of looking to the present Government and the party that support them, for any satisfactory measure of reform. The failing which has ever characterised them still adheres to them, they cannot make reasonable and moderate concessions in due and seasonable time. We must turn from them to those who know the wants of the country better. We have an unfailing and able advocate in John Bright, and to him and his measure we must turn. I am glad to see that one of your resolutions recognises his services. That, and the other resolutions also, have my hearty approval, and will, I hope, meet with the unanimous approval of your meeting.

Regretting that I cannot be with you,

I am yours very truly,

Thomas Barnes

After Thomas's defeat in the 1857 election Bolton had been represented by William Gray, a Conservative, and the Liberal, Joseph Crook. At the beginning of April 1859 the two Bolton MPs had each made controversial decisions about the vote on Disraeli's Reform Bill. This Reform Bill was Radical enough to displease many Tories, but too conservative to win over many Radicals. Lord Derby's second Government lost the vote on this Bill. It was forced to dissolve and call an election for the beginning of May. William Gray, now Captain Gray, had voted as an Independent against the Bill, but Joseph Crook had voted for it, a vote which displeased most of Bolton's Liberal Reformers. Joseph Crook was aware that even his most faithful supporters disapproved of the way he had voted. Nevertheless, he was still considered the best choice of the working man and a public meeting was arranged for the evening of 8 April in the Temperance Hall in Bolton to give him a chance to explain his vote. When the placard announcing this meeting went up, a group of Liberals who had supported Thomas in the past felt that Joseph Crook was being given an unfair advantage. They went to Robert Heywood to suggest that Thomas should be invited to stand again. Robert Heywood immediately wrote to James Winder to arrange a meeting for the following day:

The Pike, 8 April 1859

Dear Sir,

I have had several of Mr Barnes's friends who are desirous to retain your services in the forthcoming election.

Enclosed is a sketch of a proposed requisition for your consideration and I will call tomorrow morning a little before ten.

Yours truly

R.H.

James Winder, Esq.[4]

The plan was that after this meeting they would approach Thomas. However, his supporters could not wait for the meeting. In the evening after visiting Robert Heywood they went to Limefield and persuaded Thomas to write his address to the electors there and then so that it could appear in *The Bolton Chronicle* on the following evening.

TO THE ELECTORS OF THE BOROUGH OF BOLTON

Gentlemen—Having been solicited by an influential deputation to offer myself as a CANDIDATE at the coming election for the honour of representing you in the next Parliament, I do so with confidence, and beg to assure you that my best services will be devoted to your interests.

My political opinions, which are well known to you, are unchanged.

Her Majesty's Ministers have advised an appeal to the country on the question of reform. A Reform of our representative system is indeed needed, and an honest proposal for this object, which will give a comprehensive extension of the suffrage, with the protection of the Ballot and a re-distribution of seats, will have my earnest support.

Should I have the honour to be elected as your representative, your local affairs will also be watched over with my utmost solicitude.

I am, gentlemen,

Your faithful servant,

Thomas Barnes

Limefield, 8 April 1859

From this point onwards there was a series of meetings which revealed the serious split in the Bolton Liberals with one group campaigning for Joseph Crook, the choice of the non-electors, and the other group calling themselves the Friends of Mr Barnes. The way in which Thomas Barnes had been invited and the so-called "hole and corner" meetings of his Committee enraged the opposing camp. After the meeting on Friday evening Joseph Crook himself was rumoured to be unwilling to stand again unless he was given a written invitation signed by a large proportion of electors. The first meeting of the provisional committee of Thomas Barnes's supporters was held on the afternoon of Saturday 9 April, as planned, with Robert Heywood in the Chair. Reporters were not admitted as "matters of a confidential nature" were to be discussed. However, like several of these private meetings, this meeting was fully reported in *The Bolton Chronicle*. There was obviously a "mole" supplying the reporter with the information. Thomas Thomasson who had arranged the public meeting for Joseph Crook on the previous evening was very annoyed by the reaction of Thomas Barnes's committee and feelings ran so high that the meeting had to be adjourned to the evening. This meeting was attended by supporters of both camps and the mood was no better. Joseph Crook's supporters talked of "treachery and trickery in the camp" and even people who did not actively object to Thomas wanted him to address a public meeting before being invited to stand as one of their Liberal MPs. Again, the meeting had to be adjourned until Monday evening. Here, at a much calmer meeting, Thomas made a speech expressing his sorrow at the differences that had arisen among the Reformers, and hoping that something would be done to remove them. He left it to his committee to decide whether to fight a joint campaign with Joseph Crook or to work as a separate committee. The view of the meeting was that they did not want to support Joseph Crook but they decided to wait until Wednesday evening before coming to any final decision when the state of affairs, nationally and locally, might be clearer.

Whilst this meeting was taking place on Monday evening five hundred non-electors were holding their own open-air meeting in the market place in support of Joseph Crook who had not yet announced his willingness to stand again. The working men agreed to do all they could to ensure Joseph Crook's re-election. Thomas's supporters were described as the "clique" of "half-a-dozen ragamuffins" who took it upon themselves to invite Thomas to stand as a representative for Bolton. One speaker was not quite as disrespectful to Thomas, who, he said, was "an honourable and noble man whose only fault was being caught by claptrap". However, when he reported that Thomas appeared to be reluctant to fight a joint campaign with Joseph Crook a voice from the crowd was heard to call out, "We can do without him then, he does not belong to Bolton".

On the following afternoon, Tuesday 12 April, Thomas was in Manchester in the Assembly Room of the Free Trade Hall as one of the platform party at a conference of leading Lancashire Reformers. One of the speakers was John Bright.

On Friday Thomas and his supporters met again in the Reform Newsroom. Thomas set out his political views which had not changed much over the last seven years. He was in favour of John Bright's proposed Bill on the question of Reform. He still opposed state grants in aid of religion but he had changed his attitude to the question of the grant to the seminary at Maynooth. Until all similar grants had been abolished, he would regard the Maynooth grant as an exception, and would not vote for its abolition. The meeting could not decide whether or not to arrange a public meeting for Thomas to face the electors. They decided to wait a few more days, and to avoid doing any canvassing which would further incense Joseph Crook's promoters.

On Saturday evening a letter appeared in *The Bolton Chronicle* which was very hostile to Thomas. On that same evening Thomas wrote to Robert Heywood, the Chairman of his Committee, offering to resign for the sake of unity. He actually wrote two letters—an official one and another marked "Private". The official one ran:

Farnworth, 16 April 1859

My dear Mr Heywood

In thinking over the complicated state of affairs in Bolton at the present time, it appears to me that a proper course for me to take, under existing circumstances, is to place myself in your hands, as one of the oldest and best friends of the Reform Party in Bolton, and to inform you that I am quite willing to retire and make the way clear for united action, if you think my present position is an obstacle in the way of this, and if you advise me so to do.

Waiting your reply,

I remain yours truly

Thomas Barnes[5]

The private one reveals more about the difficulties which had arisen:

Farnworth, 16 April 1859

Dear Mr Heywood

In sending the enclosed I wish to say to you without reserve that it will be quite agreeable to me to retire. Things are in such a condition with our party in Bolton that I should prefer it. Therefore do not suppose I shall have any objection to such a course. I look upon you as a sort of Peace maker. I am not free to act for myself and without some sanction and authority. If I do the Gentlemen who form my Committee may think I have not acted honourably towards them. I desire to avoid doing anything that would not be fair and honourable towards them and for the real interests of the Reform party.

I am, dear Sir, yours truly

Thomas Barnes[6]

On Monday 18 April Thomas and his supporters met again and Thomas offered to resign. Reporters were once more refused admission but *The Bolton Chronicle* managed to get a clear report of what went on. "Thomas Barnes begged that under existing circumstances, they would act without reference to him personally. Looking at the present somewhat unfavourable aspect of affairs, he was quite ready to retire, if that should be deemed the better course. In regard to the public meeting of electors convened for the following night, he counselled that they should accept it, attend it, and abide the result." The Committee decided to attend the meeting on Tuesday evening. Whilst the Monday meeting was taking place a parallel meeting was being held in the Temperance Hall in support of Joseph Crook. The first resolution was against Thomas: "This meeting protests against the unprecedented manner in which Mr Thomas Barnes has been brought forward as a candidate to represent this borough in Parliament, and deeply sympathises with Mr Joseph Crook on account of the ungentlemanly manner in which he has been treated by them". The meeting then pledged itself to use all legal and constitutional means to return Joseph Crook to Parliament as a representative for the borough.

On Tuesday afternoon the two groups of Liberals came together to plan the agenda for the large public meeting to be held in the evening in the Temperance Hall. As one of the leading Liberals of the borough P. R. Arrowsmith was chosen to propose in his role of peace-maker the following resolution: "At the present crisis it is the bounden duty of the Liberal electors of this borough to nominate and to use every exertion to return two Liberal members at the coming election." Thomas Thomasson was to propose a two-pronged resolution: "That this meeting offers to Joseph Crook Esq. the expression of its thanks for his valuable services as one of the representatives of this borough in the late Parliament, assures him of its continued confidence, and hereby requests him to allow himself to be put in nomination at the ensuing election; and that Thomas Barnes Esq. having offered himself as a candidate, this meeting considers him eminently fitted by his spotless public and private character, and by his expressed opinions on the great questions of the day, efficiently to represent the Liberals of this borough in the House of Commons, and hereby offers him its earnest and zealous support." Between seven and eight hundred Liberal electors met that evening in the Temperance Hall. Despite Mr Arrowsmith's appeal for harmony there was a great deal of dissent from Joseph Crook's supporters who were unwilling to vote for any resolution which linked the two men. Before reading out Thomas's letter offering to resign Robert Heywood inflamed the argument by defending him: "That a gentleman of his talents and disposition, called forth from his delightful retreat to devote his time and abilities to the public service, should meet with such treatment, and from those he supposed to be his friends, was truly mortifying, and in no way creditable to the cause they all professed to espouse." The mention of The Quinta as "his delightful retreat" was seized upon by Thomas's enemies to fuel their jealousy. Thomas Thomasson's resolution was put to the vote in two parts. Support for Joseph Crook was almost unanimous but only about half the meeting voted in favour of the part referring to Thomas Barnes. However, it was decided that from now on a general committee would continue with a joint campaign. On the following day Thomas and his committee met to discuss the outcome of the previous evening's meeting. Half the committee recommended that he should withdraw but the other half wanted to wait until they had canvassed the voters before making any decision. Thomas left the decision to his committee which was then formally dissolved as a separate committee. That evening a joint committee made arrangements for joint canvassing. However, if the leaders of the Reform Association had agreed to support both candidates, the non-electors had not. On the same evening they held another open-air meeting in the Market Place to hear that Joseph Crook had agreed to stand again and was about to publish his electoral address in the newspaper. It was clear that Thomas Barnes had little or no support amongst this group of Radicals. This meeting was adjourned to the following evening when it was held in the Temperance Hall, ostensibly to support the great principles of Radical Reform but really to form a committee to secure Joseph Crook's return. A motion that they should try to secure the return of both candidates failed even to find a seconder. Thomas must have been well aware of all this because on this same evening he wrote another address to the Bolton electors announcing his retirement from the contest.

TO THE ELECTORS OF THE BOROUGH OF BOLTON

Gentlemen—A short time ago I was induced by the solicitation of a number of gentlemen of your body to appear before you as a Candidate for your suffrages in the coming Parliamentary Election.

I was led to believe that my appearance in that capacity would be generally acceptable to the Liberal Electors of Bolton, and serviceable to their cause.

For this purpose and with no object in view but the extension of sound political opinions and rights, I consented to become a candidate. I regret to learn that this act has been misapprehended by some among you, and by that misrepresentation and many erroneous statements (weapons commonly used at Elections), a division of feeling has been created among the Liberal Electors.

I am desirous to remove any cause of division which my present position may have been used by the opponents of Reform to produce in your ranks, and, if possible, to restore harmony and good feeling among Reformers at this great crisis. Hoping that by my Retiring this may be effected, I respectfully do so; and with sincere wishes that there may be greater unanimity among you in all future time,

I remain,

Yours respectfully,

Thomas Barnes

Limefield, April 21 1859

Although this letter did not appear in *The Bolton Chronicle* until Saturday 23 April, news of it somehow leaked out and H. M. Richardson broke into the meeting in the Temperance Hall on Thursday evening and announced "amid enthusiastic cheering" that Thomas had retired. He was almost gleeful as he addressed the meeting, saying that "by their united influence as non-electors they had read a most salutary lesson,—first, to the clique at whose door Mr Barnes may lay his present unfortunate position, then to the borough at large, and finally to all cabals who took upon themselves the right to dictate without consulting the masses and the intellectual body amongst whom they came to discuss topics well understood. It was well this lesson had been read, and he ventured to prophesy no half dozen men in this borough would ever attempt such dictation again." He tried, rather unsuccessfully, to be fair to Thomas, saying "it would be wrong for the people, as conquerors, to crow over a fallen enemy, because they had by virtue of their intelligence inflicted a blow at dictation which had fallen, perhaps, upon the shoulders of a man who was more to be pitied than condemned, and who would have met with the sympathies of the masses if he had had the common sense to say to that clique, 'Who are you? I must go before those who return me to Parliament. I cannot listen to you, but must have the reflex of their will'. If Mr Barnes had done that, he would have stood a chance of being in the honourable position of one of the representatives of this borough." He finished with spiteful remarks about The Quinta and about a disputed vote during Thomas's last period in Parliament: "As to Mr Barnes, the working men would have been traitors to their order if they had not set their faces against his seeking to be returned for this important borough with the long muster-roll of offences against him, or at all events until he had come before the public and explained them to their satisfaction; and therefore when Mr Heywood spoke of Mr Barnes's 'delightful retreat', he (Mr Richardson) asked, if by virtue of fortune and success in business,—if in consequence of his having been able to amass wealth until it had reached probably a fabulous amount from the blood, bones, and sinews of the working classes,—he asked was it common honesty on the part of Mr Barnes to vote against measures which had for their object the amelioration of that very class which had enabled him to buy his 'delightful retreat'?"

After the news of Thomas's resignation there was a failed attempt to persuade Thomas Thomasson to stand in his place. With no-one else contesting the seats there was no need for election fever. According to *The Bolton Chronicle*, "there probably never was an election in this borough since its enfranchisement in 1832, when there was more apathy as to its issue." Thomas returned to The Quinta and Captain Gray and Joseph Crook were returned unopposed on Election Day, 3 May 1859.

Thomas's attempt to re-enter Parliament in 1859 did not end here, however. At the very last minute he was called back from The Quinta to stand as a Liberal candidate in Bury. Barton in his *History of Bury* published in 1874 gives an account of this election. In the previous Parliament the Liberal candidate, R. N. Philips who later became High Sheriff of Lancaster, had been elected and was intending to contest the seat against the Liberal Conservative, the Right Honourable F. Peel. However, on 25 April Mr Philips retired from the contest because an anonymous placard had been posted up and his name associated with it. He said that if he was to be made the object of attacks in his private life he did not want public honour at such a price. It was then thought that the election would be a walk-over for Peel. However, two days later Thomas arrived in Bury at four o'clock in the afternoon. In the evening he addressed a public meeting in Union Square and shortly afterwards issued an address to the electors. He was proposed as prospective Liberal candidate by Thomas Wrigley and seconded by Scholes Walker. After the candidates had both addressed the crowd in the Square a show of hands was taken and it was declared that the majority were in favour of Mr Peel. A poll was demanded on Thomas's behalf and at eight o'clock the following morning the election contest began. A declaration was made at the hustings at quarter to five. 633 votes were cast for Peel, 477 for Thomas. After the declaration a riot broke out. Stones and brickbats were thrown and the police had to restore order. So, Thomas's attempt to become MP for Bury began and ended within just over twenty-four hours. Considering the suddenness of it all, and the fact that he had been brought post haste from The Quinta, the number of votes cast for him was quite remarkable.

On 19 May 1859 Thomas agreed with the Trustees of the Dixon Green School Charity in Farnworth to exchange a 326 square yard plot of land he owned on the west side of Smale Hill for a 163 square yard plot of land on the north-west side of Smale Hill alongside the main road at Dixon Green. On this plot was the old Farnworth endowed school now in such a ruined condition that it could no longer be used. Thomas also paid £10 to cover the value of the materials of the old school building. The larger plot adjoined the land on which the schoolmaster's house stood. This, too, was now a ruin.7 Thomas's offer was made so that a new school and schoolhouse could be built together on one plot in Albert Road. The Board of Charity Commissioners had agreed that the exchange could be made as it was to the advantage of the Dixon Green School Charity. In October 1864 the Grammar School, with Mr Whittan's house next door, together with some cottages belonging to Messrs T. Barnes & Co., formed the western boundary of the new park.

Thomas's Liberal politics could have alienated him from many of the local aristocracy and gentry in the area around The Quinta. However, he was not shunned by all. Sir W. W. Wynn, a local landowner, was happy to use the Quinta Estate for hunting with his fox hounds. The first record I have found for this regular event was on Saturday 26 March 1859. In fact, a new important chapter in Thomas's life was about to begin.

A report in *The North Wales Chronicle* on 18 June 1859 (based on an article in the previous week's *Wrexham Advertiser*) mentioned that

Thomas Barnes Esq. of Farnworth near Manchester and of The Quinta, Salop (late MP for Bolton) was one of the influential names added to the list of office bearers of the Provincial Welsh Insurance Company. It added: "Mr Barnes, we understand, is to be the Chairman of the Company and will, no doubt, bring a large accession of business and connections to the office". He was Chairman of the Board of the Company by the end of 1859 and his first important public occasion as Chairman was on 3 January 1860 at the laying of the foundation stone for the Company's grand new offices in the High Street in Wrexham. His name and Ann's headed the impressive list of important guests and he escorted Lady Williams Wynn who had laid the foundation stone to the Wynnstay Arms in Wrexham for lunch after the ceremony. It was her husband Sir Watkin Wynn, one of the Trustees of the company, who proposed the toast to Thomas. Thomas replied that his connection with the company was only of recent date. He took no credit to himself for the prosperous condition of the Institution. For that they were indebted to the Board of Directors. Thomas's election as Chairman of the Board was confirmed by the shareholders at the Annual General Meeting of the Proprietors at the Wynnstay Arms on 29 February 1860. Mr T. T. Griffith said: "I believe I may say without offending him (the Chairman) that few gentlemen are better able to come to a proper judgement as to whether business is properly conducted than is Mr Barnes."

After the election in Bury there was a presentation ceremony at Mr Philips' house at Park between Besses o'th-Barn and Prestwich on Friday 17 June 1859 when testimonials were presented to Thomas as the unsuccessful Reform candidate and to Mr Philips as their former MP. Thomas was presented with a pierced silver vase, richly chased and bearing his coat of arms. He was accompanied by his son, James Richardson.

In the year 1858/59 profits at the Farnworth Mills rose to £13,436 and Simeon Dyson and Thomas Paterson each received their one-sixth shares on 30 June. A new type of cloth, "Alliances" was being produced together with soft raised twills, bleached soft swandown and raised and shorn swandown.

A few weeks later, on 22 August 1859, there was another event to mark the Bury election. The Liberals in Bury wanted to pay Thomas another token of esteem and respect and asked if they could visit him at The Quinta "where they could express perhaps more warmly and heartily their feeling of gratitude and thankfulness for the interest he had taken in them, than by merely inviting him over to them to receive their thanks". They therefore arranged a cheap railway excursion to Chirk station. The train with up to 1,000 people from Bury, Bolton and Farnworth left Bury at six o'clock on the Lancashire and Yorkshire Railway, and arrived at Chirk station soon after eleven. Some people went straight to The Quinta but most of them walked in procession, waving flags and accompanied by a brass band. Thomas had provided two large tents near the mansion with seats and tables in them. Refreshments included ginger beer, milk, beer, bread and cheese. He had also provided food in the dining room for guests who sat down in parties of around thirty at a time. There were several toasts and speeches. Thomas expressed his delight in his new home: "You say you like this place. Well, I liked it when I bought it, but I never liked it better than now. I never saw so many bright and cheerful faces here. I never saw so many persons who seemed to be enjoying themselves so much, and it will always give me pleasure to see people enjoying themselves, for if we can make it our great object to contribute to the good and comfort of others, then we shall ourselves be happy, whilst we are administering happiness." In reply to one of the speeches he said: "As to the late contest, I must say that I am not very much disappointed at the result, for I am more inclined to have a seat in the country than in Parliament." "I do not think it likely that I shall ever be in Parliament again." Mr Rollinson replied that they still hoped to have him as the member for Bury one day. Thomas summed up the problem: "I am not radical enough for Bolton, and too radical for Bury, so between two stools I fall."

Court cases linked with the Bury election went on for several months. There were several accusations of "bottling" of voters (on both sides) and an inquiry into whether or not Peel's victory was the result of bribery and coercion. Eventually it was decided that it was not. On 28 September 1859 a dinner was given in the Assembly Room of the Albion Hotel in Bury to present testimonials to R. N. Philips and Thomas for standing as candidates in the last election.

In summer 1859 Ann seems to have been on her own and twice was reported as attending social events by herself. On 4 August 1859 she was on her own at a bazaar at Chirk Castle attended by 1,000 people and on 9 September that year only her name, not Thomas's, appeared in the list of people at the Chirk Flower Show.

Thomas continued to take an interest in and to support local Dissenting churches. On 20 and 21 November 1859 Pen-y-bryn Church celebrated its Anniversary. Thomas had been expected to take the Chair at the public meeting on the second evening but was prevented from attending.

At the annual rent audit for the Quinta estate on 2 December 1859 Thomas was given an opportunity to describe what he had done so far to improve the estate. Mr J. S. Stubbs (who lived at Brookside) proposed Thomas's health. He said he had known "their worthy landlord" long before anyone present, and could testify to the high esteem in which he was held in Lancashire before he came to dwell in that neighbourhood. Since he had come to the Quinta estate he had spared nothing in making improvements and rendering his tenants comfortable. Thomas responded: "When he first came into possession of the Quinta estate he found it in a very neglected condition. At once he set about to put it in order, and make it, if possible, a model estate. He first repaired the cottages, and had since been constantly engaged in repairing old buildings and erecting new ones, and he was resolved to go on until he made the estate a pattern to all around." The sort of work that had to be done was illustrated by an advertisement in *The Wrexham Weekly Advertiser* on 20 November 1858. Samuel Winter, Thomas's bailiff at the Quinta Office, urgently needed twenty to thirty drainers to work on the Quinta estate.

Another of Thomas's interests at the time was the newly established Young Men's Christian Association. He chaired a public meeting in the evening of 27 December 1859 in the Music Hall in Wrexham when the Wrexham Branch of the Association held their first anniversary tea party and public meeting. It was at this meeting that Thomas contrasted the Young Men's Christian Association with the Mechanics' Institutions which, he said, had failed during their thirty to forty years to capture the interest of the masses. They had no politics, and unlike the YMCA, no religion.

In Farnworth on 10 January 1860 the stable structure of the business was shaken after ten years when it was announced in *The London Gazette* that the partnership of T. Barnes, T. Paterson and S. Dyson, Farnworth, Lancashire, cotton spinners, was dissolved. Only Simeon Dyson resigned as a partner and when the profit of £11,780 was declared on 30 June Thomas Paterson received an increased share of one-fifth. Two new names appeared in the stock accounts—that of James Newhouse who was to receive a salary of £150 and that of a long-standing employee of the firm, Joseph Winter, who was to receive a present of £150.

On 31 January 1860 Thomas was one of around one hundred men at a meeting in Manchester of the Council of the Lancashire Reformers' Union who agreed to send a deputation to Lord John Russell to press Lancashire's claim to a larger number of representatives in Parliament.

When the Denbighshire Assizes were held in Ruthin on 26 to 28 March 1860, Thomas was one of the Grand Jury. On 19 April 1860 he went to witness the cutting of the first sod of a new road from Chirk to Glyn, which had recently been granted permission in a bill passed in Parliament. With him was one of his main tenants at The Quinta, Mr J. S. Stubbs of Brookside. (After Thomas's son James married in 1864, he and his new wife eventually moved into Brookside.) Mr Stubbs had been at the dinner in the Britannia Inn on 2 December 1859 which Thomas gave to the principal tenants on the estate. He had sat immediately to the left of Thomas and was obviously a man of some social standing.

Thomas had become involved with another branch of education at his home at The Quinta. On Friday 3 August 1860 a public meeting and concert were held at Brymbo and Broughton British Schools to commemorate the completion of the new building. There was a luncheon in the schoolroom where "there was the fruit of the vine in abundance, but none of the juice of the grape in its fermented state". Both Thomas and his wife Ann were present. Thomas took the Chair at seven o'clock for the public meeting before the concert. In his speech he said: "British Schools had conferred great blessings upon the country generally, but time was when these schools had to struggle against existing prejudices and fairly fight their way to favour. They had to fight their way not only against the ignorance of the times, but against a class of educated persons, who held that it was dangerous to educate the working classes—a class of persons he was glad to say that was dying out fast."

He was still at The Quinta on 12 August 1860 when he attended an arbitration hearing at the Wynnstay Arms in Ruabon. The plaintiff was Mr Whalley of Plasmadoc, and the defendants the directors of the Vale of Llangollen Railway. Mr Whalley wanted compensation from the Company because the railway passed through the grounds of Plasmadoc near the mansion. Thomas was amongst those giving evidence on behalf of the plaintiff. He said: "I have seen the mansion of Plasmadoc, and the direction the railway crosses through the park. In my estimation Plasmadoc will be very much deteriorated as a residence by the railway passing through the grounds. I certainly should rather not have a line of railway running through my park."

On 18 August 1860 Thomas showed off his new estate and mansion to his employees in Farnworth. He had given a day's holiday to all the people employed in his mills and had invited them to spend the day at The Quinta. An extract from an article in *The Oswestry Advertiser* describes the event: "Four to five hundred people travelled on a special train with low fares to Chirk station. Unfortunately it rained all day. They arrived at eleven o'clock, accompanied by the band of Farnworth Rifle Corps, which, as well as the Corps itself, is composed of the employés from Mr Barnes's mills. There were also many visitors from the neighbourhood, making a total of up to one thousand people present. A large shed, covered with canvas, had been erected among the new stables now in course of erection at The Quinta. There was an unlimited supply of refreshments—bread, meat, ale, ginger beer, etc. The band, under the direction of Mr James Barnes played a number of popular pieces in capital style for dancing before they set off home from Chirk at seven o'clock."

In September 1860 Thomas became involved with another cotton company. At a meeting on 14 September 1860 in the Mayor's Parlour in Manchester Town Hall a new company, the Manchester Cotton Company, was proposed. It was to be considered formed as soon as one half of the capital of £100,000 was subscribed. Thomas was named as one of the provisional Directors. The aim of this company was to establish a cotton-purchasing company and to encourage the cultivation of cotton in various parts of the world, particularly India and Australia. John Cheetham, President of the Cotton Supply Association, had written to say he was in favour of the proposed company.

On 8 November 1860 Thomas attended a soirée in the new Ragged School in Bark Street, Bolton. This school had been founded by Luke Boardman around 1855 and the soirée was to mark the opening of a new school for 800 children. Thomas Bazley MP presided, supported by Thomas, Captain Bridson, Councillor Harwood, and other supporters of Ragged Schools. The Ragged Schools relied on charity to give destitute children, many of them orphans, teaching in the evenings and other forms of help such as food and clothing and the means to enable them to earn a little money. In one of Thomas's Obituaries it was mentioned that he had been a supporter of the Lostock Industrial School. I have not found any references to him in connection with this school. However, he was a Friend of Bark Street Ragged School. On 26 December 1863 this Ragged School held its Eighth Annual Tea Meeting. Amongst letters of apology were three from the Barnes family: from Thomas, his son James Richardson, and his nephew Alfred. It is possible that they were spending Christmas together at The Quinta. At this meeting the officers for the coming year were elected. In their absence, Thomas was elected as President and Alfred and James Richardson as members of the Acting Committee. The Vice Chairman was the Mayor, R. Harwood, and the Bank of Bolton (with which Thomas was connected) was the Treasurer. Originally Lostock Industrial School was called Bolton Ragged Industrial School and was founded as a Ragged School in 1854. I am assuming that Bolton Ragged Industrial School was originally Bark Street Ragged School which was certified for 180 Boys on 30 November 1863. At that time it was in Commission Street, Bolton. It then moved to a 35–acre site at Lostock Junction and was re-certified on 13 June 1870 for 200 boys. I have not yet found any evidence of Thomas's involvement with the school after it became Lostock Industrial School. However, Luke Boardman's Ragged School formed a large section of the procession through Farnworth when the Park was opened in 1864.

   Although Thomas was always ready to help the Independent churches he was not a narrow-minded sectarian and made many generous donations to other denominations. He promoted many Christian and philanthropic movements. Even as early as June 1859 Sunday services were being held at Quinta Church in connection with the London Missionary Society. On 27 October 1860 he presided at the Forty-sixth Annual Meeting of the Chester Auxiliary to the London Missionary Society in the Music Hall in Chester. One of the platform party was Rev. G. Gill, a missionary from the South Seas. By this time the Society had 23 missionaries in the South Seas, 20 in the West Indies, 39 in South Africa, 19 in China and 51 in India. The large audience consisted of people from all classes of society. The meeting opened with praise and prayer after which Thomas made his introductory speech. He said "they ought to thank God that missionary meetings had become an essential part of Christian exertion of all Christian denominations. They were no longer novelties, common they certainly were, but by no means small and insignificant. He thought that no person had fully realised the importance of a society that had been established for the spread of the gospel in heathen lands. Every society of that kind had claims on the support of the Christians, but there was no society, according to his notion, that had so strong a claim on the sympathies of Christians as the one whose claims they had met to advocate that night. It had strong claims on account of the catholicity of basis upon which it was formed, and which had characterised its operations to the present time. It was a noble and Christian-like idea that prevailed in the minds of those men that founded this society when they called it the London Missionary Society, not a society of any one sect, not a society to send out missionaries in connexion with any particular body, the idea was to spread the gospel, and to evangelize the nations of the earth by giving the people that knowledge of Jesus Christ that he came to save sinners, and the way they might be redeemed. The whole absorbing idea with the originators was to send the pure gospel of Christ to the ends of the earth, and its catholicity, as he had said before, had been maintained to the present time. The directors were ready, and they always had been ready, to send out Christian men of any denomination, and they left it to the converts which missionaries might be successful in making such denominations in their own country, that they might think best suited to the place in which they lived. Therefore, on that broad basis, the London Missionary Society had strong claims on the support of Christians of all denominations. A still stronger claim arose from the success it met with in every part of the world. God had poured down blessings on the efforts of the missionaries in the South Sea Islands, a story of which the Rev. Mr Gill, who was present, would give them. In China, and the places which intervened between the Cape of Good Hope and India, in fact, in almost every part of the world, the blessing of God had rested upon their labours to an extent that far exceeded the expectations of the most sanguine of the founders of the society. He trusted that the effort of the meeting would be to send them to their homes anxious to do more for the spread of the gospel of Christ amongst the heathen than they had hitherto done. They ought to remember that they could not compromise their exertions by anything they could give; no gift of money could atone for personal effort for the spread of religion, not only at home, but abroad. He sometimes thought that if every Christian, man and woman, would put this question to themselves, "If it is the duty of Christians to send religion to the heathen, and to carry out the divine command, 'Go ye into all the world and preach the gospel to every creature', there would be less apathy to assist these institutions. If that injunction was given to every Christian, it must be their duty either to go themselves or to render efficient help to those who were willing to go. If they felt the force of that, there would not be any lack of men and means to spread the gospel of Christ." Throughout the speech the audience cheered.[8] In June 1861 Rev. R. Best travelled from Bolton one weekend to preach two sermons at Quinta Church on behalf of the Society. In 1864 Thomas was a director of the London Missionary Society, and one of the largest contributors to its funds. For the twenty-five years or so before this he had presided regularly at the Society's annual meetings in Bolton and Farnworth. On Sunday 11 September 1864, two prominent ministers, Rev. Samuel Martin of Westminster and Rev. James Parsons of York, were at Quinta Church to preach sermons in aid of the Society. The Missionary meeting held on Friday 23 July 1868 when Rev. W. Jones, a missionary from India, spoke, was presumably linked to the London Missionary Society.

Notes

1. *Wrexham Weekly Advertiser* [19th Century Newspapers online]
2. Ibid.
3. *Manchester Times* [19th Century Newspapers online]
4. ZHE/55/17 [Bolton Archives and Social Studies]
5. ZHE/55/2 (& ZHE/55/3) [Bolton Archives and Social Studies]
6. Ibid.
7. Farnworth Grammar School Archives 1859 [Bolton Archives and Social Studies] SLFA/2/11/19
8. *Cheshire Observer* [19th Century Newspapers online]

CHAPTER 5

1857–1887

Thirty years of gardening at The Quinta

It is clear that after moving to The Quinta Thomas took his interest in horticulture very seriously. He very soon became joint Patron of the Chirk Horticultural Show whose Third Annual Show was held on September 4 1857 in a field opposite the Chirk Castle Arms adjoining the Hand Hotel in Chirk. The other Patron was Colonel Biddulph of Chirk Castle. Both men's wives were also involved as the two Lady-Patronesses. *The Wrexham Advertiser* paid them a tribute saying they took "a warm interest in the success of the society, as indeed they did in every other scheme calculated to be of practical utility to their poorer neighbours". A tribute was paid to Thomas, too. He was described as "a gentleman who has recently settled in the neighbourhood but whose philanthropic endeavour to better the condition of the working classes is already well known and appreciated here as in Lancashire". Thomas's bailiff, Mr Winter, was also on the Committee and judged the Cottages and Gardens Competitions. Another member of the Quinta staff, Mr W. Porter the Head Gardener, also played a large part in the show. He exhibited a dozen and a half balsams and won First Prize for a melon in the Gardeners' Competition, Second Prize for a collection of vegetables and an extra prize for a model of the Quinta gardens based on the design by Mr Henderson, a landscape garden designer from Birkenhead. Lavish arrangements had been made for the day. The band of the Royal Denbigh Rifles played in the afternoon and cheap trains had been arranged from Shrewsbury and Chester to Chirk station. In the evening Thomas and Ann attended the society ball. The editorial in the paper concluded: "We hope this society will continue to be well supported, as its object is to foster a spirit of emulative industry amongst the cottagers of the two parishes, St Martins and Chirk, and to incite, by competition, a better cultivation of the cottage gardens, the effects of which cannot fail of being extremely beneficial to all parties concerned."

The show was held again the following September and Thomas and Ann were still Patron and Lady-Patroness. The show had now been renamed "The Chirk Cottagers' Horticultural Show" and yet another parish had been invited to join—Llangollen. Plants from Chirk Castle and The Quinta formed the centrepiece in the exhibition tent. Mr Porter, the gardener at The Quinta, had sent "an exquisite device, a kind of floral obelisk, worked in flowers of every variety of hue, tastefully intertwined and judiciously blended". As an indication of the interest that was taken in the growing of plants at The Quinta, I have copied the names of the flowers included in the exhibit from The Quinta: "Silver Swan, Duchess of Lancaster, Tartar, Grass, Wonderfull, Venus de Medici, Dr Smyth, Globosa, Major, Favourite, Gloucus, Bank's Glory, Dr Geranna, Psyche, Little Bopeep, Prince Albert, and so on." Thomas does not appear to have attended the show but his wife and family did. Both Mr Porter, the Quinta gardener and Mr Winter, Thomas's bailiff, were also amongst the visitors.

The show took place as usual on 9 September 1859 in tents in a field opposite the Hand Inn at the corner of the road leading to Chirk railway station. This time Mr Porter's offering took the form of a pagoda made mainly from bedding plants. Most of the prizes were won by Colonel Biddulph of Chirk Castle, but Thomas's gardener took home five First Prizes for two bunches of white grapes, six roses of distinct varieties, twelve varieties of cut flowers, a collection of six varieties of vegetables, six stove or greenhouse plants, and a Second Prize for four fuchsias. Again, it was only Thomas's wife, Ann, who was mentioned in the list of visitors.

In that year, 1859, a second Flower Show was set up in the area— the newly resurrected Wrexham Floral and Horticultural Society. It had once been a flourishing society but had lost its popularity and had been discontinued. On 14 June 1859 it held its first show since its re-establishment on the race ground in Wrexham. Unlike the Chirk Flower show, this show did not have separate classes for Cottagers, and appears to have been an opportunity for the gentry and middle classes to show off their gardening skills. Thomas, through his gardener, Mr Porter, was one of the main exhibitors with a first-class collection of fuchsias, geraniums, calceolarias, and a stand of twelve cut flowers. He won four First Prizes, each worth 5s, for the best greenhouse plant, two fuchsias, one light and one dark, three calceolarias of distinct varieties, and a specimen geranium. He also won one Second Prize, worth 3s 6d for two heaths.

This society was to hold two flower shows each year. The second one took place in Grove Park on Tuesday, 13 September 1859, (or, according to *The Cheshire Observer*, on 20 September,) shortly after the Chirk Show. Although neither Thomas nor his wife was there to see it, his plants won three First Prizes for twelve cut flowers, a collection of variegated leaved plants, six stove or greenhouse plants and seven Second Prizes for the best stove plants, two scarlet geraniums, three achimenes, four heads of celery, a dish of peas, and eight varieties of vegetables. The report in *The Cheshire Observer* stated: "Thomas Barnes of The Quinta stood by far the first in the list as a general competitor, and the articles produced did infinite credit to his excellent gardener, Mr Porter." Sadly, not long after his success at the 1859 Chirk and Wrexham shows, Mr Porter's wife died at their home in Quinta Hall Gardens on 3 October.

Nevertheless, Mr Porter continued to produce flowers for Thomas to exhibit. The first of the Wrexham Floral and Horticultural Society's two shows in 1860 was held at Grove Park on Tuesday 12 June in the schoolroom and in a large tent. This time he won five First Prizes for the most ornamental plants in bloom, the best stove plant, two heaths, four exotic ferns, two bunches of white grapes, five Second Prizes for two bunches of black grapes, a collection of six stove or greenhouse plants, three fuchsias, three calceolarias, twelve cut flowers, and two Third Prizes, one for a stove plant and the other for a greenhouse plant. His exotic ferns were awarded a special prize. Like the Chirk Show, this one, too, was dominated by the entries from Colonel Biddulph at Chirk Castle and Thomas at The Quinta. There were complaints that so few other local gentry had sent entries. Neither Thomas nor Ann attended the show.

The next Wrexham Flower Show, its fourth, was held on Tuesday 11 September 1860 at Grove Park. The complaint in June had had an effect. There were many more exhibitors and the show was said to be "looking up". Mr Porter won six First Prizes, six Second Prizes and two Third Prizes. The First Prizes were for six greenhouse plants, three fuchsias, twelve roses, six phloxes, two bunches of white grapes, and thirty-six pods of peas. His Second Prizes were for a stove plant, a collection of variegated-leaved plants for bedding, exotic ferns, twelve cut flowers, three cauliflowers and eight varieties of vegetables. He won Third Prizes for another stove plant and a greenhouse plant.

Mr Porter was not the only gardener at The Quinta. At the time of the 1861 Census three gardeners lived separately in Gardener's Cottage: Edward Davies, aged 50, and two younger gardeners who were boarding with him. (Edward Davies died on 24 June 1869 at the Rhos, Bronygarth. He was 58 years old and described as "late of the Quinta Gardens".)

Mr Porter entered for the show held on Tuesday 11 June 1861 in the rope-walk field and came second in the over-all list of prizewinners. This time he won five First Prizes, four Second Prizes and one Third Prize. The First Prizes were for three geraniums (distinct varieties), four exotic ferns, three gloxinias, a stand of twelve cut flowers, and a brace of cucumbers. He won Second Prizes for greenhouse plants, a collection of six stove or greenhouse plants, two heaths, and a herbaceous plant in a pot. The Third Prize was for a stove plant. Again, neither Thomas nor Ann attended. The second show in 1861 was held on Tuesday 10th September on the race course. It was described as "the best ever" show and now needed three interconnected tents to house the display. Mr Porter took First Prize in the four main classes with his stove and greenhouse plants and received special mention for one of his entries in the stove plant category—some particularly fine plants of Gesneria Nova Species. The eight First Prizes he won were worth 5s each, except for the collection of six stove or greenhouse plants for which he received 15s. The First Prizes were for the most ornamental plant in full bloom, a single stove plant, a greenhouse plant, a collection of six stove or greenhouse plants, twelve hollyhocks, six culinary apples, three heads of cauliflower, and a collection of eight varieties of vegetables. The Second Prizes were for a collection of six stove or greenhouse plants, three achimenes, a brace of cucumbers, six roots of carrots, and thirty-six peas in pods. In spite of the show's success the local paper, *The Wrexham Weekly Advertiser*, criticized the poor response from many of the local gentry: "There are several gentlemen's houses whose gardeners have contributed nothing to the exhibition of late—some, we believe, having sent nothing since the re-establishment of the society." One of the houses mentioned was Wynnstay, the residence of Sir W. W. Wynn.

Chirk Flower Show had been held a few days earlier on Friday 6 September 1861. Mr Winter from The Quinta was one of the judges but there were no entries from The Quinta mentioned in the report.

I have not traced any records of the flower shows in 1862 and did not find any report in 1863 until Tuesday 22 September when the Chirk and St Martins Horticultural Society Annual Exhibition was held in the "delectable grounds of The Quinta by the kind permission of Thomas Barnes". It had been moved at short notice from its usual venue in Chirk because of the sudden death of R. Myddelton Biddulph's second son a few days before. As the Chirk Show was normally held on a Friday and the Wrexham show on the following Tuesday, it would appear that the two shows had been combined on this occasion. The editorial in *The Wrexham Weekly Advertiser* complained: "Flowers from gentlemen's residences in the district which formed such attractive objects in former shows were missing from the present one." However, Mr Porter made up for this with plants from The Quinta. He "excelled in his geraniums, his Tom Thumbs were regular giants." As in the previous year the show was held in three interconnected tents. "In the centre tent was a row of Mr Porter's magnificent geraniums and fuchsias displayed in vases—and we certainly never saw their equals." He also had on display several varieties of ornamental foliage plants—coleus verdiafolia, caladium pictum and caladium maculata—as well as grapes and apples. Two cottagers living at The Quinta won prizes—Edward Jones a Third Prize for the best-kept cottage garden in St Martin's parish, and Eleanor Arthur a Second Prize for three heads of parsley. Both Mr Winter and Mr Porter were on the Managing Committee and Mr Porter was one of the judges. The weather was poor but in spite of the rain there was dancing from half past four. "Sets were formed and damp though the grass was, some scores indulged in the excitement of the merry dance." Although Thomas was not mentioned, his son, James, was one of the "numerous and respectable visitors".

I have not found any reports of the two shows in 1864 but a new Flower Show held its first meeting in September 1864 when new assembly rooms, the Victoria Rooms, were opened in Oswestry by the Earl of Powis. The aristocracy of Shropshire and the neighbouring counties attended and part of the programme of events was a Flower Show. The President of the Show was Sir W. W. Wynn of Wynnstay. *The Wrexham Weekly Advertiser* reported curtly: "Mr Barnes of The Quinta sent only grapes." During the year Mr Porter, the Head Gardener at The Quinta, had been replaced by Mr Louden who had already established himself so much that he was reported as assisting the Subcommittee to award the prizes. The only prize he took home himself was one First Prize for black grapes. By the end of August 1866 he was a judge himself, judging the classes for professional gardeners and amateurs at the Third Annual Meeting of the Ellesmere Floral and Horticultural Society's show at Ellesmere. (The term "amateur" referred to people who did not regularly employ a gardener.)

A week or so after this event Mr Louden was competing at the Chirk Flower Show on Friday 7 September 1866, a show which was held "under somewhat more favourable circumstances than for one or two preceding years". James Richardson and his new wife, Ellen, were present. The Quinta and two other houses, Brynkinalt and Halston, had sent "a more than usually dazzling display of plants and flowers". Mr Louden won twelve First Prizes, the greatest number ever won by The Quinta, for two bunches of white grapes, two bunches of black grapes, six nectarines, a collection of cut flowers, three fuchsias, a single fuchsia, three geraniums in pots, six stove or greenhouse plants, a single stove or greenhouse plant, six ornamental foliage plants, lycopodiums, and six different dishes of fruit. His Second Prizes were for six peaches, six culinary apples, six dessert plums, three fuchsias, six ornamental foliage plants, and he came second in the sweepstakes for twelve dahlias of distinct varieties. Two Third Prizes were for six peaches and six fine foliage plants.

The Oswestry Floral and Horticultural Show was held for the third time in the Victoria Rooms on 1 and 2 September 1868. No member of the Barnes family or their gardener, Mr Louden, was mentioned in the report but The Quinta had sent "a rich and choice selection of fruit, including pine apples, peaches, grapes, plums, etc., not for competition". The following year when the Oswestry Fruit and Flower Show was held on Friday 3 September 1869 Mr Louden was one of the three judges in the classes for Gardeners. On the previous day, Thursday, 2 September, he had been a judge at another show, the Ellesmere Floral and Horticultural Society's Sixth Annual Meeting, again judging the classes for professional gardeners and amateurs.

In May 1872 the National Flower Show was held at the Botanical Gardens, Old Trafford, and Thomas Barnes of Farnworth won a First Prize of £4 for a display of ten herbaceous calceolarias. In spite of all the references to Thomas's interest in horticulture at The Quinta, this is the first time I have found any reports of entries from him at Flower Shows outside the Quinta area. Some time after Thomas finally lost his seat in Parliament, his gardener at The Quinta, James Louden, won Third Prize at the Royal Caledonian Horticultural Society Show for "the two best bunches of Alexandria Grapes". (This information was included in "*The Gardener V2*" by William Thomson. First Prize on this occasion went to the Earl of Strathmore's gardener, and Second Prize to Sir William Wallace's gardener.)

When the Oswestry Annual Floral and Horticultural Show was held in Sweeny Hall Park on Thursday 27 August 1874 Mr Louden was again one of the judges for the produce of professional gardeners and amateurs.

In August 1876 there was a show on a much grander scale, the Oswestry and West Midland Agricultural Show which was spread over three days from 1 to 3 August in Lord Harlech's Brogyntyn Park. In the previous year the Oswestry District Society and the Shropshire and West Midland Agricultural Society had combined for the first of these Agricultural Shows. In 1876 Lady Williams Wynn was one of the two patronesses of the Flower Show, now a part of the joint agricultural show. One of the "choicest contributions" sent to this show was one from the Quinta conservatory.

On Thursday 30 August 1877 Mr Louden was again a judge for the Professional Classes at the Fourteenth Annual Ellesmere Floral and Horticultural Show in the grounds of Ellesmere House.

A very interesting article appeared in *The Wrexham Weekly Advertiser* on 17 August 1878 which gives a good idea of the scale of gardening at The Quinta. "The Fruit Crops are not quite as unfavourable as those of the two preceding seasons, but are by no means encouraging. In the reports from *The Gardeners' Chronicle* Mr Louden, The Quinta, Chirk, writes as follows: Apples with us are a miserable failure, the only exceptions are Lord Suffield, Hawthornden, Cellini, Cox's Pomona and Tower of Glamis; the trees in spring were very promising but owing to the bad autumn of last year and the cold wet April of the present, they failed to set properly. Pears, as a rule, flowered sparingly, most sorts are a blank; the exceptions are Beurrè [sic] Diel, Belle de Noel, Beurrè d'Amanlis, Louis Bonne of Jersey, Beurrè de Capiaumont and Dunmore. Peaches on open walls are thin, but fine in quality; under glass they are very good in every way. Plums are a very heavy crop, and fine in quality. Damsons the same. Walnuts thin, but good in quality; other Nuts a very heavy crop."

In the second week of June 1880 Mr Louden showed Thomas's collection of grapes at the Royal Horticultural Society Summer Show in London. In the collection of black Hamburgh grapes, Mr Thomas Barnes of The Quinta was placed first. He was also first in the other class for black grapes. *The Gardeners' Chronicle* says that the Black Hamburghs for which Mr Barnes obtained First Prize were "large handsome even bunches, the berries black and well finished. This lot was well ahead of all the others in the class." The class for any other black grape brought fewer entries, the best lot being the three fine and superbly coloured bunches of Burchardt's Prince, shown by Mr Louden (Mr Barnes's gardener). "These were of the true Prince form, and were most meritorious examples of a grape not generally known." For Muscats of Alexandria Mr Louden took Second Prize.

On 8 August 1881 Mr Louden was one of the judges for garden produce at the Ruabon and Rhos Horticultural and Industrial Society annual exhibition in Wynnstay Park.

Although Thomas was still one of the Patrons of the Oswestry District Agricultural Society Show, he was not mentioned amongst the visitors when it held its Twentieth Annual Exhibition at Oswestry on 24 September 1881.

By August 1883 another show was in the calendar—the Lodge and Bronygarth Cottagers' Flower Show which was held at The Quinta on Tuesday 21 August. This was their second annual show and was not on as grand a scale as some of the earlier local shows. Miss Julia Chapman was the Honorary Secretary of the Committee and was James Richardson Barnes's main competitor. James, referred to now as Major Barnes, entered in the classes for Amateurs and won two first prizes for six kidney beans and six turnips, and five second prizes for six varieties of vegetables, six spring onions, six carrots, a hand bouquet composed exclusively of greenhouse flowers, and for six distinct varieties of cut flowers. Ellen gave the prizes. She and Mr E. Parry-Jones had also donated a special prize for woodcarving.

On the previous day, Monday 20 August, Mr Louden had again acted as a judge for garden produce at the Ruabon and Rhos Horticultural and Industrial Society annual meeting in the grounds of Wynnstay Park. He did this again the next year on Monday 18 August 1884, when the Society had changed its name to the Ruabon and Rhos Cottagers' Horticultural and Industrial Society.

The following week on Thursday 28 August 1884 the third show of Lodge and Bronygarth Horticultural Society was held in the grounds of The Quinta. On a central table in the large tent was an exquisite display of exotics from the Quinta gardens sent by Mr Louden. (In the report of this show there was also a reference to a Mr Meldrum who showed a very well carved ecclesiastical panel. He later played a significant part in Thomas Barnes's story.) James Richardson, now Colonel Barnes, was still competing mainly against Miss J. Chapman. This time he won four First Prizes for eight varieties of vegetables, six kidney or round potatoes, six carrots, and six turnips, and three Second Prizes for six spring onions, two vegetable marrows, a collection of flowers, one truss of each of six varieties. Mrs Jones, the wife of the local vicar, and not Ellen, gave the prizes this year. Colonel Barnes and the Vicar, Rev. D. R. Jones, were the judges for the sports. A vote of thanks was given by the Vicar to Thomas for letting them use the Quinta Park for a third time. It was not reported that Thomas was there. On a motion of Colonel Barnes, a vote of thanks was given to Mrs D. R. Jones. At the call of the Vicar three cheers were given for Colonel Barnes.

On Friday 5 September 1884 Mr Louden was a judge for garden produce at another show, the Wrexham Floral and Industrial Society's Ninth Show which was held on its usual site in Grosvenor Road.

When the First Annual Exhibition for a newly established Horticultural Society at Marchwiel took place in the grounds of Marchwiel Hall, the home of Mr Benjamin Piercy, in September 1887, Mr Louden was one of the judges there, too. By this time Thomas had taken a back seat and it was James Richardson and his wife Ellen who were to carry on the horticultural tradition.

James Richardson Barnes

CHAPTER 6

December 1860

James Richardson's coming of age.
The gift of the Park

On Saturday 8 December 1860 Thomas's son, James Richardson, came of age. On that day the family was still at home at The Quinta where the first celebration was held. Another celebration, a feast for Thomas's workers in Farnworth, had been arranged for the Monday after this, not only to mark James's birthday, but also to celebrate the fiftieth anniversary of the founding of the business. Apparently James had been put in charge of superintending the arrangements for the feast, something which had kept him so busy for several weeks that he had not had time to prepare speeches for the birthday celebrations at The Quinta.

This celebration was covered in great detail in *The Wrexham and Denbighshire Weekly Advertiser* on 15 December but it had already managed to give a forecast of what was to happen on the actual day, Saturday 8 December. "We beg to call the attention of our readers to the demonstration which takes place this day to celebrate the majority of James Richardson Barnes, Esq. A procession of the tenants and friends will be formed at The Britannia Inn at eleven o'clock, and will be headed by the Llangollen Brass Band, and two oxen and eight sheep, dressed, and will proceed to the Quinta Hall where the address will be presented by J. S. Stubbs Esq., the Chairman of the Committee. The procession will then return to the Britannia Inn, where an excellent dinner will be provided."

The Quinta celebrations were not organized by the Barnes family but by a committee of fourteen men plus a secretary with J. S. Stubbs of Brookside as its Chairman and T. Owen of Pentre as its Vice-President. They saw the occasion as a good opportunity to thank Thomas for the benefits he had brought to the area since moving to The Quinta in 1852. The report in the paper began by summarizing Thomas's achievements: "Mr Barnes, the father of the young gentleman whose attainment of his majority gave rise to these rejoicings, is the proprietor of the Quinta estate, which he purchased some years ago, and upon which he has spent a very large sum of money in improvements. The old hall was pulled down soon after Mr Barnes came into possession, and replaced by a mansion which forms one of the greatest ornaments of that portion of the county of Salop. The transformation wrought by Mr Barnes has by no means been confined to the re-erection and adornment of his country seat, but has extended to the whole estate. The land which is connected with the mansion is cultivated in such a manner as to entitle it to the designation of a 'Model Farm'—every modern improvement that experience, aided by science, has suggested, and wealth could procure, has been brought into operation, and in many spots on the rugged hills by which The Quinta is surrounded, has Mr Barnes been the means of 'causing two blades of grass to grow where only one grew before', which in itself renders him a benefactor to his species. But the worthy gentleman's first care, as he tells us himself, was, when he became proprietor of the Quinta estate, to look to the state of the dwellings of the labourers. These he found in a very dilapidated and disgraceful condition, and he at once caused them to be repaired, improved and made more worthy of being called—as all labourers' dwellings ought to be—'the cottage homes of England'. In addition to all this, Mr Barnes erected on his own estate, and at his own expense, a very beautiful chapel where public worship is conducted every Sunday, in accordance with the principles and forms of the Congregationalists, and several of the ablest preachers connected with the Congregational body have preached to large and attentive audiences since the chapel was erected.

With regard to Mr Barnes' antecedents, we would just state that he is a wealthy Lancashire manufacturer, and now carries on large works at Farnworth, where he is much respected, as well as in the neighbourhood of The Quinta. He at one time sat as member of Parliament for Bolton, but lost his seat in the same election which saw Cobden and Bright and other distinguished men ostracised for a time. Within the last few years Mr Barnes has been appointed Chairman of the Welsh Provincial Insurance Company, an appointment he has filled with great ability."

The committee for the birthday celebrations soon raised £200, more than they actually needed. Apparently some people must have felt affronted by not being approached for a contribution. Mr Stubbs mentioned this at a dinner in the Britannia Inn on the Tuesday afternoon following the celebration.

The celebrations around the village of Lodge began early on the Saturday morning with the firing of cannons from a nearby piece of high ground. The first part of the celebrations was the procession which actually left from the Britannia Inn in Bronygarth around noon. Opposite the Britannia Inn hung a large banner with the words "Much happiness to the Heir of Quinta", and printed slogans such as "Prosperity to the Quinta family", and "Long life and happiness to J. R. Barnes, Esq." were handed out and worn by the people in the procession. There were decorations marking the route to The Quinta and music was provided by the Llangollen Brass Band. The committee had now managed to buy three oxen, not just the two announced the previous week, and they and the sheep were displayed on three wagons provided by members of the committee—Mr John Owen of Pontfaen, Mr Jones from Trehowell and Mr Rogers from Vron. With the Llangollen Band leading the way, followed by the committee, the three wagons joined the procession with the tenants, friends and well-wishers bringing up the rear. The procession first called at the Chairman's house, Brookside, where Mr J. S. Stubbs and several guests joined it. They included Mr H. Stubbs from Manchester, Mr Lambe from Bowden, Mr Long from Manchester, Mr A. Reid from Llantysilio, Mr C. Stubbs, Mr Kinchant, junior, Rev. J. C. Philips from Tyn-y-rhos, and Mr R. S. Perkins. Only men walked in the procession. The women who wanted to take part had already made their own way to The Quinta.

When the procession arrived at the Hall, the second part of the celebrations began—the presentation of the congratulatory address. They were met and received by James Richardson and his parents. The procession was arranged in a semi-circle, the committee in front. Mr Stubbs stepped forward and said that, as Chairman of the committee, he had been deputed to present a congratulatory address that had been prepared on the coming of age of the Heir of Quinta, from the tenants and neighbours, and he never had greater pleasure in doing anything in his life. The address, beautifully engrossed with illuminations, and surmounted by the arms and crest of the Quinta family, was as follows:

"To Thomas Barnes, Esq., and Mrs Barnes, of The Quinta

We, the tenants upon the Quinta Estate, as well as your neighbours and friends, beg leave to congratulate you upon the coming of age this day of your only son and heir, James Richardson Barnes, Esq.

We are deeply sensible that your son has the best example set before him that parents can give and have no doubt that he will follow in the footsteps of his excellent father, and thereby retain the respect of all parties.

Mr Barnes,—

We feel deeply the great good you have done in this neighbourhood since you purchased the Quinta Estate, the vast improvements you have made, and the number of artizans and labourers you have employed, thus diffusing great social benefits, and amongst all your works, you have not omitted the most important—to build upon your estate, at your sole expense, a Church where your tenants and neighbours can meet together to hear the Gospel preached unto them.

Mr James Barnes,—

Your father's tenants upon the Quinta Estate are desirous of congratulating you upon your attaining your majority this day. From the high character we hear of you from a distance,—the honours you have already obtained, as well as your participation in all manly and healthful pursuits amongst your neighbours, and your urbanity and kindness to all,—we have the utmost confidence that you will further rise to eminence, be a blessing to your parents and an ornament to society.

Wishing the Quinta family long life and happiness in this world, and that which is to come.

Signed by the Committee

on behalf of the tenants and neighbours of the Quinta Estate

Mr Stubbs read a number of verses of poetry which he stated had been prepared in commemoration of the event. Then came another presentation of an address and a gift of a three-volume Bible bound in morocco leather from a separate group, the Friends of Temperance at The Lodge.

To Mr James R. Barnes, Esq.

"Sir,—We, the friends of temperance, resident in the Lodge, desire to approach and offer you our most hearty congratulations on this most auspicious occasion. We cordially felicitate you upon this day entering upon the full rights and duties of manhood, and we sincerely pray that your future career may be long, prosperous, and honourable, and that every act of your life may be worthy of a man and of a Christian, and as a slight permanent token of our esteem and regard we beg you to accept this accompanying Bible with our fervent prayers that as you have been instructed in its precepts during youth, so its principles may be your guide through life, and its precious promises your comfort and support in declining years.

Signed on behalf of the society and friends of temperance,

David Roberts, President, Donald Nicholson, Secretary."

Thomas then said: "Mr Stubbs, friends, gentlemen, tenants, and labourers—I feel most deeply the kindness which you have exhibited this day,—and on behalf of Mrs Barnes, and on my own behalf, I beg to express the deep feeling of gratitude we have on receiving this complimentary and kind address, which you have been good enough to present to us. I feel the kindness exceedingly, and if I am unable to give expression to my feelings, it is because of the depths of the emotions which at the present moment agitate my mind. That this day is an important one for me, there can be no question. I thank you that you have shown so much interest in this family event, and that you express such kind interest in my son, now that he has just come to the time of manhood. You have spoken so kindly of his past life, and expressed such kind anticipations for the future, that they cannot fail to affect my mind very much. I hope that those anticipations will be fully realised, and that if his life is to be continued, it may be a life of usefulness. You have also alluded to my own conduct. You have made some kind allusions to what I have done for the improvement of the estate, and you have been good enough to say that I have conferred great benefits upon the residents in this neighbourhood, and especially the labouring classes. It has been a source of great pleasure to me to do that, which I believed was for my interest for improving my estate; and if I have thereby contributed to the well-being of those who are around me, I may say I am doubly paid. I do, and I always trust I shall feel a great interest in the welfare of those around me, especially of the working classes. It would be a most serious drawback to my pleasure not to see those by whom I am surrounded in a state of prosperity, and as you have said what I have done has been a means of doing good—if it has, it is a source of great pleasure to me. You have alluded to the effort I have made for the spiritual welfare of my neighbours,— and that I have built a house for the worship of God,—a place where all around may receive instruction in spiritual things. I have built that Church in connection with the denomination to which I belong, and for which I feel a great respect. It is not antagonistic to any other. That place was not built to promote any denominational interests whatsoever, but it was done purely for the purpose of promoting the spiritual welfare and interest of those around. It would be improper for me to detain you any longer to-day, as I know that to-day I am only of secondary importance and the 'rising son' is the great object of interest. It would not be proper for me to occupy a more conspicuous position now, especially as the heavens above us are not of the most favourable character. I again express to you, on behalf of Mrs Barnes and on my own behalf, our great thankfulness for the kindness you have shown, and the anticipations you have expressed in the address you have presented to us." His speech was punctuated by cheers, cries of "Hear, hear" and occasional laughter and was applauded when he finished.

It was then James's turn. He said: "My friends—I do not commence like my father by saying, gentlemen, neighbours and tenants, as I have so many friends before me, and not one enemy. I begin again, and say—My friends, I am obliged to you for the address you have presented. I have been so busy with other matters that I have not been able to prepare a formal speech, and therefore I hope you will excuse the shortness of my address; but what I say I hope will be to the point. I had made one or two memoranda, but when I saw so many friendly faces, I almost forgot what I put down to say to you. I am deeply obliged to you for the exhibition of this feeling towards me. No acts of mine have deserved it, and what I have done for the public good has been very small. I hope that the good wishes you have expressed— most of them, if not all of them, will be realised, and that I shall be able to do something for the benefit of my fellow creatures. My father has done a good deal, and I am sure he intends doing more, and, if God spares my life, I will endeavour to second what he has commenced. This is an occasion in which my feelings overcome me, as it is the first occasion on which I have spoken in manhood, and I hope you will excuse the shortness of what I have to say on the present occasion. I must thank these temperance friends for their address—which came quite unexpected to me—and their good wishes. I am doubly obliged to them. I hope I shall remember their kindness whenever I open that Bible,—and I hope I shall study its precepts and abide by its laws. I again thank you all, and hope that God will bless you and all your families." James's speech was received with cheering. Then three hearty cheers were given for Mr Barnes, followed by three more for the young squire, and three still more hearty ones for Mrs Barnes. Ale was then handed out before all the men returned to the Britannia Inn for the next stage in the celebrations—the public dinner. It had been difficult to find a room big enough for the meal but by some alteration in the construction of the building, they had managed to make a room big enough to seat upwards of a hundred people. The dinner was laid on the table at half past three. Before that time, however, the seats were nearly all occupied, as the number of refusals the committee had been compelled to give to applications for tickets gave the general impression that it would not be safe to be behind time.

For the meal Mr Stubbs, the Chairman, and Mr Owen, the Vice-Chairman, were joined by Mr J. Girdwood, Thomas's estate agent at The Quinta. The ninety or so guests represented a wide range of interests—there was an MP, a minister of the Church, the estate agent from Chirk Castle, a solicitor, a doctor, Thomas's bailiff, representatives from trades such as an iron founder, a plumber, a hatter, an innkeeper, two saddlers, the blacksmith from The Quinta, people from as far away as Manchester and Liverpool, as well as many tenants and other friends. They included: Mr G. H. Whalley MP, Rev. J. C. Philips, Tyn-y-Rhos, Mr A. Reid, Llantysilio Hall, Mr Henry Kinchant, Park Hall, Mr R. S. Perkins, Mr B. Long, Manchester, Mr Henry Stubbs and Mr Charles Stubbs, Mr E. Bellyse, Chirk, Mr John Lambe, Bowdon, Mr Evans, Trevor Hall, Mr Thomas Minshall, Oswestry, Mr John Edmunds, Chirk, Mr Moorhouse, Ellesmere, Mr S. Winter, The Quinta, Mr Faulder, Preesgweene, Mr Kenrick, Wynn Hall, Mr Jones, The Hayes, Mr Evans, iron-founder, Ruabon, Mr J. G. Hughes, Weston Rhyn, Mr Williams, Tynycelin, Mr Whitfield, Halton, Mr Lloyd, Maesgwyn, Mr Thomas Rogers, Mr T. Hill, Mr E. W. Thomas, Mr T. Dale, Mr Askew Roberts, Mr G. J. Saunders, Mr Owen Jones, Mr Joseph Jones, Mr Williams, Cerney, Mr Turner, Mr T. Davies, plumber, Mr John Ellis, Mr B. Atkins, Mr Higham, Mr John Jones, hatter, Mr Edmonds, Mr Thomas Hughes, and Mr R. Roberts, Oswestry, Mr Moses Edwards, Lodge, Mr E. Williams, Pentrekendrick, Mr Sands, Cross Lanes, Mr E. Roberts, Pentredavid, Mr Philips, Lodge, Mr S. Williams, Vron, Mr Edwards, Weston Hall, Mr Sidos, Tyucha, Mr Foulkes, Queen's Head, Glyn, Mr E. Hughes, Liverpool, Mr Humphreys, Glandwr, Mr John Walworth, Liverpool, Mr Thomas Roberts, Lodge, Master Roberts, Lodge, Mr E. Griffiths, Chirk Castle, Mr Jos. Edwards, Chirk, Mr R. Moses, Chirk, Mr S. Morgan, Trehowell, Mr Job Edwards, Selattyn, Mr S. Williams, Stanwardine, Mr James Morris, Whittington, Mr Hughes, saddler, Lodge, Mr Jones, Rossett, Mr T. H. Richards, Chirk, Mr Jones, Chirk, Mr Lewis, Daywell, Mr Davies, Pontfaen, Mr Edwards, Glyn, Mr Drury, Mardu, Mr Buckley, Trehowell, Mr Parry, Tynddol, Mr R. Rogers, Vron, Mr Owen, Pontfaen, Mr D. Thomas, Vron, Mr Edward Arthur, Craignant, Mr W. Lloyd, blacksmith, The Quinta, Mr Jones, Birch House, Mr Jacks, Selattyn, Mr John Williams, The Quinta, Mr Jones, Trehowell, Mr Lever, Chirk, Mr E. Edwards, saddler, Chirk, Mr Owen, junior, Pontfaen, Mr Lloyd, Tynrhyd. Mr Parry, Mr Jones, Glyn, Mr Thomas Edwards, Glyn, Mr John Capper, Glyn, Mr Jackson, Park, Mr Vaughan, Vron and Mr Thomas Evans, Berllandeg.

Grace was said before and after dinner by Rev. J. C. Philips. When the tables were cleared, the Chairman, Mr Stubbs, began with the toast list. He gave in succession the Queen, the Prince of Wales, the Prince Consort, and the rest of the Royal Family, all of which were warmly received. The next toast was the health of the Army, Navy and Volunteers. Mr Kinchant, as an officer of the Shropshire militia, responded to the toast. Mr Reid responded to the next toast, the Yeomanry, and Rev. J. C. Philips acknowledged the toast to the Bishop and Clergy of the Diocese, and Ministers of all Denominations. The Chairman commented, "Without these I do not know how we should get on, they are all necessary but now we are coming to what may be termed the nerves and sinews of the country. Gentlemen, the toast which I am going to give you is the health of our friend Mr James Barnes, in honour of whose coming-of-age we have assembled this day. I trust he will live long to be a blessing to the neighbourhood, and to be an example to all who know him. We know he has been well brought up, he has distinguished himself at college, he has obtained all his degrees. His father has been kind to him, and has brought him up in the fear of the Lord. He has brought him up in that path which is right for every man to go who hopes to be respected by his friends and neighbours. We have every confidence in Mr James Barnes. He is Mr Barnes's eldest son; and he is likely to inherit a large estate; and he has planted in his bosom that excellent seed that will bud and bring forth such fruit as will prove a blessing to himself and those around him. He has sufficient to make the most ambitious satisfied. He knows the destination before him. I hope he will represent us, or some of our descendants in the House of Commons. He will be one of those who advocate the liberty of the subject, without which liberty a country is not worth a rap. He is one who will seek to the best of his ability to ameliorate the distress and burdens that press upon the inhabitants of the kingdom. I have no doubt he will represent some of our descendants in Parliament. He is a soldier too. He is a Volunteer, and an officer in the Yeomanry, and if the dignity of our country is assaulted, I know that he will come forward with that manly heart which is inherent in every true Englishman. He lives under a virtuous Queen, and I know he would support her as heartily and well as the highest Tory in the land. I propose the health of James Richardson Barnes,— may he live long and be a blessing to this neighbourhood, and I have no doubt we shall have him as one of our legislators before long." The toast was drunk with musical honours and followed by rapturous applause. No doubt the number of times glasses had been raised accounted for the cheering, applause and laughter which accompanied the Chairman's speech.

James's reply was longer than the speech he had made in the morning: "I am much obliged to you for the kind way in which you have drunk my health. I must plead the same excuse as I did this morning—that I have been so busy, having had personally to superintend the arrangements for the workmen and tenants at Farnworth, that I have not had time to make a set speech. I have had scarcely a moment to spare some weeks. In saying this I am telling you the truth,—I always like to tell the truth. I hope you will take the will for the deed, and whatever I may say, that you will multiply it a thousand fold. First, then, I repeat that I am much obliged to you for your kind feeling to me—not only to-day but always since you have known me. To-day you have shown great kindness in getting up this demonstration,—in going to such great expense,—and in presenting that beautiful address from the committee,—and the address from the temperance gentlemen at the Lodge; and also in getting up this dinner. During my short life, I have not experienced half so much kindness as I have experienced from my friends here, since I have known them. It is not many years ago since my father and mother came amongst you,—and still fewer since I came, as I was then in school, and afterwards in college, but since I have been here, you have always shown your good will and your good feeling, and I do not know that I have ever had one single word said against me—and have not had one word said against me to myself. I do not mean to say that I deserve this, because I have said things or done things that may not be pleasing to all of you,—but I thank you for overlooking my faults—and being so kind to me on this and every other occasion. Mr Stubbs was good enough to say that he proposed first the toast of the Queen, the Army and the Navy, the Bishops and Clergy, but they were of secondary importance to-night. The inference is that for the present I am of more importance than they are. That cannot be, as if I were away not more than one dozen individuals would miss me. (A Voice—'Two hundred here at least.') I must express the same wishes as I expressed this morning—that you all, tenants and friends, and everyone present,—may have much happiness and a due portion of this world's good, and happiness in the world to come. (Cheers.) I know that I have been placed under no ordinary circumstances. My father and mother have done the best they possibly could in bringing me up, and I should think myself an undutiful son if I did not endeavour in some way to carry out the good wishes they have entertained for me. I hope, with God's help, I shall be able to carry out some of those anticipations and hopes you have to-day expressed, if not all of them; and I hope you will never have occasion to regret this day's proceedings. I again beg to thank you for your kindness, and if at any time I am able to render you any public service—I do not mean by being member of Parliament for I am not fit for that—I should do it to the best of my ability and shall be much obliged to you for thinking me worthy of so serving you."

Mr Perkins then proposed the toast to Thomas: "I respond to the call of Mr Stubbs, but I am in no way prepared to propose this toast, and I am sorry it has not fallen into abler hands than mine. It is the health of Mr Barnes. There is an old adage which says—'A prophet has most honour out of his own country'. I do not think this is true in this case. I am one of his nearest neighbours, and I have witnessed his general movements in this district. His coming amongst us was a great blessing to this neighbourhood. This property which he purchased laboured under the disadvantages of an absentee landlord,—therefore, the tenantry on it were in anything but a prosperous condition, because they had no assistance in carrying out the necessary improvements in their various occupations. Mr Barnes has devoted himself to the improvement not only of his farms, but of his cottages. No man could have done more for the labouring classes on his estate than Mr Barnes has done. It was my lot only a week or two ago, to receive an invitation from him to be present at a rent dinner, when I saw him preside at a table, with all his tenants around it. I must say that I never saw a more contented scene, and one that gave me more pleasure. A good, kindly feeling seemed to exist between landlord and tenant. I only wish that Mr Barnes's example was more generally followed,—and that their tenants could on such occasions always sit down with their landlord and enjoy a hearty meal. As a neighbour and a friend, I cannot speak too highly of Mr Barnes, and as an agriculturist, I can speak of him as one who has done much good for this district. I have great pleasure in proposing his health." This was drunk with three times three and more cheers.

Thomas replied: "I thank you most sincerely for the enthusiastic manner in which you have received the toast. To make use of a common phrase we have in Lancashire, I may say—that I am obliged to play second fiddle to-day, but you will readily believe me when I say that I have no feelings of envy or jealousy for him who plays first fiddle. I wish I really deserved all the complimentary phrases which Mr Perkins has been good enough to use in reference to myself this evening. I cannot say I do deserve these praises. Ever since I came here I have endeavoured to do what it was my duty to do, and therefore I claim no merit for what I have done as the owner of the Quinta property. It is true that the first thing I directed my attention to was the state of the cottages, believing that the labourers were a most important portion of those on the estate, and their houses in the worst state. I have often thought of a phrase made use of by the Duke of Wellington, when an estate was presented to him, called Strathfieldsaye. He used to say— 'It would have ruined any other man'. When looking at the cottages I often thought of the phrase; but, as I say, I believed it was for my own interest to attend to the cottages of the labourers first, and make them comfortable. Then I took those of a higher class and so on; but it will take some time to do all that is wanted to be done. In doing this, I claim no merit because I believed it was my interest to do it. It is well that interest and welfare go together. If a man intelligently does that which is right for his own interest, it is almost sure to be for the interest of the community also. He is the best man who does this,— his memory will scent like a rose when he is dead.

I thank you, Mr Chairman, and you, Mr Perkins, for the manner in which you have proposed my health, and you all for the demonstration you have been pleased to exhibit on behalf of my son. I hope he will realise all your most sanguine expectations, and that he will grow in the expectation of those with whom he has anything to do. When he was a boy, I did not know what choice he might make as to future employment. If it was a professional life, I thought it would not be a bad thing for him to have such a place as this to come and spend his leisure time; if he chose an agricultural life, I thought this would be as good a place as any other for him to follow his agricultural pursuits. If he chose a commercial life, I hoped he would take my place, and so enable me to have more leisure time than I have had up to the present time, and enable me to devote more attention to the moral and physical interests of the country, and of the world at large. As far as I have been able to judge, he has been disposed to choose a commercial life. Whatever he might have chosen, I should have been content with it,—I only wish him to choose what he likes best, and that he will pursue it with all that activity his strength will enable him. Should he make commerce his permanent choice, I hope he will meet with a large amount of intelligent success. If it is his choice, then I shall be glad to have a little more time to attend to the physical and moral condition of those around me that I know, and that I may be able to benefit. I ought not, and shall not, say much in his praise before his face,—I feel rather disposed to 'pick holes in his coat', and tell him he might mend here, and mend there. But this is not the proper time to do that, and I will simply express the hope that your most sanguine anticipations for him will be realised, and that his future career will give satisfaction to everyone around this table. I thank you for the cordial and hearty welcome you have given him, and for the demonstration we have this day witnessed. He has, as he said to-day, made his first speech in manhood. Last night I left him, what the lawyers call 'an infant',—he was a simple infant, and this morning I saw him a full grown man. I hope his conduct and every act of his life will be, as was beautifully expressed in one of the addresses presented this morning,— 'worthy of a man and of a Christian'." As usual, Thomas managed to raise several laughs in his speech, especially at his son's expense. His speech was loudly cheered.

The meal ended with another series of toasts, including a toast to the health of Mrs Barnes by Mr Girdwood, responded to by Thomas, another to the House of Commons, responded to by Mr Whalley, to the tenantry by Mr Reid, responded to by Mr Owen, to Agriculture and Commerce by Mr Hill of Oswestry, responded to by Mr Rogers of Oswestry, to the Chairman by Mr Girdwood, responded to by Mr Stubbs, to the Committee by the Chairman, responded to by Mr Owen, to the strangers by the Chairman, responded to by Mr Long, to the subscribers to the festivities by James Richardson Barnes, to the Ladies by the Chairman, responded to by Mr Kinchant, to the Lord Lieutenant of Shropshire and Denbighshire by Mr Kinchant, responded to by Mr Minshall, to the Press by Mr Evans of Trevor Hall, responded to by Mr Askew Roberts, to the health of Mrs Biddulph by Mr R. Roberts, Oswestry, responded to by Mr Lever, and finally to the temperance friends at the Lodge by Mr Minshall, responded to by Mr Whalley. By now it must have been quite a rowdy affair, certainly not one that the friends of temperance would have approved of!

That was where the participation of the Barnes family ended. They now had to prepare themselves for the feast they had arranged in Farnworth on Monday. The committee in Shropshire had not finished their celebrations. They still had to distribute meat and bread to the poor in the neighbourhood. This was done at lunchtime on Monday. There was a huge amount—more than 1,000 lb of beef and 395 loaves. On Monday afternoon 163 women were treated to tea "and its usual concomitants", an event which turned into a dance and went on until nearly midnight. On Tuesday the committee, the workmen, the cottagers and others sat down to a substantial dinner at the Britannia Inn. Mr Owen was the Chairman and Mr Lloyd of Tynrhyd, and Mr Griffiths of Chirk the Vice-Chairmen. Just as dinner was over Mr Stubbs dropped into the room, and was asked by the Chairman to give several of the toasts. After giving a toast to the Queen and other loyal and patriotic toasts Mr Stubbs gave a toast to the health of Mr James Richardson Barnes. He said the subject of the toast would likely at some future day become proprietor of the Quinta estate, for he did not think the present proprietor was ever likely to dispose of it during his lifetime. Mr James Barnes, whom he had the privilege and pleasure of knowing for some time, was a young man of very great promise. He had good natural abilities—he had been brought up with the strictest regard to his morals, and had received an excellent education, and it was his opinion that he would one day become a very distinguished man. The occasion of a young man attaining his majority must be a time of peculiar interest to the parents, and no doubt the parents of Mr James Barnes would be very much pleased with the good feeling that has been shown by the inhabitants of that district. He did not know when they should be called together again as they were then, unless Mr Barnes should take to himself a wife, when, no doubt, all parties would be prepared to give him a bumper. This was greeted with loud cheers, followed by three times three. Mr Owen then gave a toast to the health of Mr Barnes, who, he said, was a good landlord, and a large employer of labour. This, too, was drunk with due honours. Mr Stubbs sang a song, followed by a song by Mr Lees.

Mr Stubbs next proposed a toast to the Committee, coupling with the toast the name of Mr Owen. They had worked together with the greatest unanimity, and with the greatest success, for they obtained £200 in a very short time. He thought it was a very handsome sum to obtain in so short a time, for they must remember they were not so rich in the district on the south of the Ceiriog, as they were on the other side of it.

A number of other toasts followed, including one to the Workmen on Mr Barnes's estate by Mr Lloyd, to Mr Winter, Mr Barnes's bailiff, by Mr Stubbs, and one to the Chairman by Mr Lloyd. The company separated early after a very pleasant evening. In spite of all the glasses raised, *The Wrexham and Denbighshire Weekly Advertiser* was able to report that "the utmost decorum prevailed throughout". The very last event was on Thursday evening when a ball took place at the Britannia Inn, attended by a very large number of people.

On Saturday evening the end of the birthday was announced in Farnworth by the booming of twenty-one cannon and the ringing of the bells at St John's Parish Church. By Monday the whole of the

Barnes family was in Farnworth ready to take part in the lavish celebrations there. B. T. Barton described the festivities in his history of the town. The cooks' headquarters were at Mrs Tonge's, the Golden Lion Inn. Here they prepared food for the 1,450 workmen and their wives and the invited guests who came not only from Farnworth but from Manchester, Bolton, and other places. A huge amount of food was bought for the dinner:

> 32 rounds of beef
> 200 lbs weight of ribs and sirloins of beef
> 30 legs of mutton
> 28 hams
> 30 cows' tongues
> 20 couples of fowls
> 6 turkeys
> 8 loads of mashed potatoes
> 2 butts of butter (120 lbs)
> Gallons of new milk
> 600 sticks of excellent celery
> 600 lbs weight of rich plum pudding, garnished with almonds
> 2 milk kits full of brandy sauce (prepared at the express wish of Mrs Barnes)
> 3 fine cheeses, weighing 224 lbs, made at The Quinta
> 400 4–pound loaves of plain bread

For tea later there were 715 lbs of currant bread.
Drinks were provided:

> 20 dozen bottles of ginger beer
> 20 dozen bottles of lemonade
> 20 dozen bottles of cider
> 7 load barrels of ale (containing 36 gallons each)

For dessert there were 3,000 apples and 2,500 oranges. In addition, there were other fruits and dainties in equal profusion, and wines for the principal tables, supplied from the host's own stores.

A spring-cart went four times between the Dixon Green Mill and the inn, laden to the full each time with plum pudding alone, and five times laden with celery. On Monday morning 70 gallons of new milk and between 300 and 400 plates of the sweetest, freshest dairy butter, moulded into beautiful devices were brought from The Quinta.

Mrs Tonge's son and son-in-law, Mr John Tonge and Mr Richard Holt, were in charge of the removal of the food from the inn assisted by James Crompton, Robert Roscow, John Hall, D. Parkinson, and others. It took from half past four in the morning, and was completed and the food laid out for the meal by eleven o'clock.

In the morning national flags (the St George's Cross) flew from the roof of the first mill at Moses Gate, from the Golden Lion Inn, and from Dixon Green Mill.

The feasting was in two large rooms in the Dixon Green Mill, the cotton room and the cloth room. They were decorated with garlands and festoons of real and artificial flowers, blue and white draperies, banners and evergreens. On the wall near the head table were the family's armorial bearings—lions rampant on an azure shield.

The event was under the superintendence of Mr William Holden of Farnworth Mills and Great Lever. 1,420 feet of tables were fitted up under the directions of Mr W. Coope, builder. The tables were covered in cloth. There were hundreds of yards of forms for seating the diners. On the platform were seats for a dinner party of about 80. Before the dinner there was a procession from the Golden Lion Inn to the Dixon Green Mill of 'The Royal Company of Carvers', fifteen men, including the butcher who had supplied the meat, whose duty it was to cut up the meat. The meal began in the afternoon at half past three. Thomas and Ann arrived in the cloth room at three o'clock, to rapturous cheers. The guests followed, then James Richardson Barnes. He then went on to preside at the dinner in the cotton room.

At the end of the meal came the speeches. The toast to James Richardson was proposed by Edmund Ashworth of Egerton. Robert Lawton, the oldest servant of the firm, presented an address on behalf of the workpeople. James Richardson acknowledged the gift. Robert Heywood proposed the toast to Mr and Mrs Thomas Barnes. Thomas responded to the toast. Other influential figures who spoke were Harrison Blair, a local magistrate and industrialist, William Ashworth and John Collier, two of the firm's employees, Thomas's nephew Alfred Barnes, the Mayor of Bolton John Harwood, Mr W. Hinmers, Captain Topp, Mr D. Crossley and Mr A. Ferguson.

In the evening there was a brilliant display of fireworks. At the end of the week all the work people received their wages for Monday as a free gift from Thomas.

When he responded to the toast to his health Thomas surprised everyone by offering part of the estate he had inherited from his father as a public park for the use of the people of Farnworth. He said: "I have looked with considerable interest on the building of mills and cottages. I have seen the price of land rising from three farthings to something like two pence and three pence per yard. The question has often occurred to me, shall not we have a single place in which the children can enjoy a breath of air? I have looked upon the children running about the roads and streets endangered by the carts and vehicles passing, and it has occurred to me, what a blessed thing it would be if these little creatures could skip and play without being in danger from these carts and horses; and seeing that there is a considerable prospect before long of cottages and factories being built on every square inch of land, I have made up my mind—and I wish to declare it in connection with my son coming of age, and also out of respect and reverence to his grandfather, to set aside a large portion of the Birch Hall estate, and lay it out and dedicate it to the public, and present it to the township of Farnworth. Of course it must be under certain conditions, so as to secure the property and privileges of this land in perpetuity to the people of Farnworth."[1]

The land which had been known for ages as the Birch Hall estate had been bought from Mr Lomas. At the opening of the park in 1864 one of the invited guests was Rev. Holland Lomas, formerly of Birch Hall and now a rector from somewhere near Liverpool. Soon after 10 December 1860 Thomas engaged William Henderson, a landscape gardener from Birkenhead, to design and lay out the grounds. Henderson had already laid out the Corporation Park in Blackburn which was opened in 1857, and went on to lay out Alexandra Park in Oldham (opened in 1865) and Queen's Park in Bolton (opened in 1866). Thomas had already used Henderson in 1857 to design the gardens at The Quinta. Work on the park in Farnworth began in the spring of 1861. However, Henderson did not complete his engagement in Farnworth and Robert Galloway from Liverpool who had trained with Henderson was taken on to finish the work. Even before the park was officially opened and presented to the people of Farnworth it was used as a public promenade and for instrumental concerts performed by the band of the Farnworth cotton mills. This was also the band of the 27th Regiment of the Lancashire Volunteer Rifles. James Richardson Barnes was the band's musical director as well as its conductor and was the driving force behind the concerts. The fact that the park attracted people from nearby Bolton was obviously a source of great pride to the Farnworth people.

Although Thomas's original gift of about twelve acres was not a huge piece of land, because it was in a prime position in the middle of Farnworth where building land was in great demand, its estimated value at the time was £11,284. It consisted of 11 acres, 2 roods and a few perches of rich arable land and 4,427 yards of leasehold, held for

999 years and for which a chief rent of one penny per yard had to be paid to the executors of the late Samuel Heywood. A later gift of an additional piece of land doubled the area of the park. Thomas had already spent another £2,000 on laying out the park before it was opened, and the work was not finished then. An entrance on Manchester Road had not yet been built because of complications with the raising of the road surface on Manchester Road. This is how a visitor described the park at this time: "The surface of the ground is very irregular, rising in one part into a kind of plateau, and at another dipping rather abruptly into a miniature valley, at the bottom of which there is a sheet of water, formed by adapting a small rivulet which flowed through the property. Here and there the area is diversified by small shrubberies, and flower beds. On one side the park is overlooked by the factory of Mr Barnes, as well as by that of Messrs Wallwork and Sussum—square red-brick blocks of the regular cotton factory type, specimens of which are to be seen plentifully scattered about the town."

Note

1. B.T. Barton *op. cit. History of Farnworth and Kersley* (pub. 1887, Bolton)

CHAPTER 7

1861–1862

The return to Parliament

After Joseph Crook's re-election in May 1859 he had succeeded in getting his bill, The Bleachers' Short-Time Bill, passed, and by December 1860 had let it be known that he was intending to retire mid-term. Liberals in Bolton held several meetings to decide on a replacement candidate. Thomas was still unpopular because of the ill-feeling created at the 1859 election and feelings ran high between the "Radical" Liberals represented by the Manhood Suffrage Association and the group from the Reform Association who supported Thomas, called the "Whigs" by their opponents. Comments such as the following were typical of the opposition: "A representative of such a place as Bolton ought to have a knowledge of the science of ethics and the laws of currency, banks, and the monetary system. Of these Mr Barnes knew nothing at all. Mr Barnes had been weak-minded; and on that account he [William Taylor] didn't like thrutching a man into a place he was not capable of fulfilling, and who might be bought over—not with money, he was too independent for that—but by invitations to dinners and balls, and such aristocratic influences." Thomas's supporters presented him with a requisition signed by 500 electors inviting him to stand again. Thomas was reluctant at first, believing that it was more important to keep the Liberals in Bolton united than to send him to Parliament again. However, he agreed and his letter of acceptance was printed in *The Bolton Chronicle* on 2 February, the day Joseph Crook officially announced his resignation:

TO THE ELECTORS OF THE BOROUGH OF BOLTON

GENTLEMEN—Your highly-esteemed Representative, Mr Crook, having expressed his intention to resign the office he now so honourably fills, it will become your duty to elect a successor when the vacancy occurs.

In anticipation of this event, a numerously-signed requisition has been presented to me, inviting me to become a CANDIDATE for your suffrages, with which I feel it to be both a duty and an honour to comply.

In appearing before you, I beg respectfully to say that my political opinions, which are well known to you, have undergone no change.

I regret that the improvements in the representation of the people, so long and so often promised, have not yet been obtained. We are still where we were nearly thirty years ago. The present is as favourable a time as we can have to consider this question, and I think there should be no further delay in effecting such changes as are necessary to secure a fair and full representation of the people in the Imperial Parliament. A greatly-enlarged constituency, with a more equitable distribution of representatives, and adequate protection to the voter against all undue and improper influence in the exercise of his right, I regard as essential to the satisfactory settlement of this question.

The public expenditure of the country has risen to an enormous sum, and now that we are happily at peace again, calls for a reduction.

With a wise and peaceful foreign policy, which this country should ever follow, I believe large reductions may be safely made.

In the commercial prosperity of the country, I am, along with yourselves, deeply interested; and such questions as may affect it will at all times have my most careful consideration.

Hoping to have an early opportunity of more fully stating my opinions at a public meeting,

I am, Gentlemen,

Your faithful servant

Thomas Barnes

Limefield, 1 February 1861

Joseph Crook was granted the stewardship of the Chiltern Hundreds on 5 February 1861 and Thomas met his supporters. He knew that his opponents resented the decision to put him forward without any consultation and insisted on facing the electors at a public meeting before the election. He added: "With regard to the representation of the borough in Parliament, he would emphatically repeat that if it would be the means of cementing a union of the Reformers in the borough, and the choice of a better and abler man, he was even now quite willing and ready to retire. True, he had been desirous of being in Parliament, but that feeling had become less ardent, especially during the last year or two—on seeing how public affairs were disposed of. Had he been inclined to take some trouble in the matter, he believed he could have been in Parliament then, having had offers from more than one borough. He was glad to hear that they had decided upon going with him before a public meeting. He had nothing to conceal— nothing to crave for—nothing to fear."

The public meeting was held in the evening of 7 February and was attended by a very angry group of opponents, the Radical Liberals from the Manhood Suffrage Party on the one hand and representatives from the Licensed Victuallers and Beersellers on the other who felt threatened by Thomas's support for a proposed bill—The Permissive Bill. In a two-hour speech Thomas set out his policies, the main one being his support for Parliamentary Reform. "Whether I remain a private citizen and have nothing more to do with the House of Commons, or whether it shall be my honour to go again into that House, wherever I may be, my object and purpose will be to get as wide and broad an extension of the suffrage as it is possible to extract from the present or any other Government". He was also in favour of a secret ballot: "For my part I cannot conceive of any man having any valid objections to the ballot who does not intend to influence or intimidate voters in some way. If I care nothing about how a man votes why trouble myself whether he does so openly or secretly?" He wanted a redistribution of seats in Parliament to give places like Lancashire a greater number of MPs and hoped to see more representatives of commerce in the House of Commons and fewer members of the upper classes: "In that house we find one-third of the members are either peers, sons of peers, cousins of peers, brothers of peers, or related to peers by marriage; so that full one-third of the people's house is under the direct power and influence of the peers of the country." As always, he wanted to see a reduction in the national expenditure and as usual, believed that savings could be made in the armed forces. Britain was not at war, and he saw no likelihood of an invasion by the French especially now that Cobden had successfully negotiated a trade treaty with them.

In the second half of his speech he defended his previous conduct as a politician. Votes he had given or not given on five occasions were still used as ammunition against him. In the years he had been in Parliament he had voted between six and seven hundred times. He had no regrets: "I am here to say that I repent of no one thing that I did, and that with the best of my judgement and ability all those things that have been criticised were, in my opinion right and good." He gave satisfactory explanations of his votes on the grant of public money to the Catholic Seminary at Maynooth, on the Bleachers' Bill, the

Hosiery Bill and the Combination Bill. He also took the opportunity of explaining about the Government grant, the regium donum, given to several religious denominations but no longer received by the Independent Congregationalists, the group to which Thomas belonged. He had fought hard when in Parliament to prevent this grant going to the Presbyterians in Ireland: "I do not think it right to give money to religious bodies. I think religious bodies should every one maintain and sustain their own religious denominations."

After two hours he concluded: "If it shall be my fortune to become again your representative, I can promise you, what I promised you before, the most conscientious devotedness to the duties of the office and to your interests. I am well aware that you may find a man that may serve you with more ability, but you cannot find a man that will serve you with a more honest intention." However, the meeting was not over. His chief opponent, Thomas Grimshaw, attacked Thomas's committee for trying to keep out the real Radicals by supporting what he called the one-and-one system—sending one Tory and one Liberal MP to Parliament for Bolton. Questions and accusations were still being fired at Thomas at half past eleven but he responded to each one. The hall was finally cleared at half past midnight. The longest political meeting that Thomas ever had to face in Bolton was over. He was not going to have to fight a contested election but he had not won over many of the electors.

The Editorial in the Conservative *Bolton Chronicle* gave its verdict: "The long-expected public meeting has been held, and Mr Barnes in a very lengthy speech, has vindicated his past Parliamentary curacy, and forged his claims to the renewed confidence of the constituency. Whilst Mr Barnes has undoubtedly conciliated some by his public explanation, the Radical opposition are more than ever embittered against him by the refusal of the committee to take the sense of Thursday night's meeting as to his eligibility for the candidature."

The election took place on 11 February at the hustings in the Market Place. Thomas was nominated by Robert Heywood in a rather restrained speech. "I have again the honour, and I may say, very great pleasure, of proposing Thomas Barnes, Esq., as a fit and proper person to represent this borough in Parliament. His conduct whilst in Parliament was, I believe, generally very satisfactory. In some few instances he differed in opinion with some of his constituents—a circumstance that I believe occurs with every Member of Parliament. [... ...] In his address on Thursday evening, my friend not only defended his Parliamentary conduct, answering the various questions put to him in a straightforward manner, but he also showed that he was no way the cause of or responsible for those misunderstandings that occurred at the last election. That meeting will, I trust, have smoothed the way to a better understanding among the Reformers, and I also trust, that in the course of time, union will be further promoted by the re-election of a gentleman of good abilities, with great application, and a most sincere desire to discharge faithfully all the important duties which may devolve upon him. In conclusion, everything considered, I trust, and indeed I have no doubt we shall find, we have put the right man in the right place."

Thomas then spoke for forty minutes, repeating much of what he had said at the public meeting and adding comments about education and the tax on paper. "Gentlemen, the paper duty is a tax upon knowledge. It prevents its spread—it prevents its extension." He also emphasised the need for a peaceful foreign policy: "Gentlemen, I am in favour of a peaceful foreign policy. I believe that our interest is to keep our own hands to ourselves. You know what a great boxer once said was the best attitude of self-defence. When he was asked by a young man as to the best attitude of self-defence, he replied, 'Keep a civil tongue in your head!' And, gentlemen, if we conduct ourselves civilly towards other nations, I am sure they will be peaceful to us, and orderly too. And I believe our foreign policy, if a policy of peace, will preserve peace abroad." He made an interesting comment about the English Channel separating England and France: "I hope the time is not far distant when that strip of water which separates France from England will be something like the Mersey between us and Cheshire. I hope it will no longer be a thing to divide, but a medium of increased communication and extended trade; when ships and steamers will ply constantly with men and merchandise, exchanging our goods more largely than hitherto, and that we shall no more think of going to war with the French, or quarrelling with them, than we now think of going to war with the people of Cheshire or Yorkshire. Why shouldn't we have as unrestricted and free intercourse with France, as we have with the counties adjoining this? I hope the time is not far distant when that will be the case, and no effort of mine shall be wanting to facilitate that end." In fact, within a few years Thomas was involved in a scheme to build a Channel Tunnel, proving that he was as good as his words.

At the end of his speech, in spite of some objections, the crowd confirmed the vote of confidence in Thomas and he was accepted as Bolton's Liberal MP. His opponents continued to fight the battle in the Correspondence columns of *The Bolton Chronicle* which added fuel to their anger by adding its support of Thomas: "We say that while in politics Mr Barnes differs from us greatly, yet that his personal qualities entitle him to the esteem of all parties. He is for a much larger extension of the suffrage than we advocate,—more the pity. He is for triennial Parliaments,—we are not. He is for the ballot,—we are sorry for it. But while these are the opinions which make him acceptable to a Liberal constituency, it is not to be concealed that for his private worth, uprightness of conduct, liberality to the poor, knowledge of business, and social standing, he is to be esteemed and honoured by men of all parties. Mr Barnes and his father before him have lived long in our neighbourhood, and have been among the greatest of the employers of labour in this locality. He has also for five years represented Bolton in Parliament. Now, as a speaker shrewdly said at the non-electors' meeting, if a man has a hole in his coat it is pretty sure to be found out under such circumstances. There are no keener detectors of sham philanthropy and sham liberality on the part of an employer than the men whom he employs. Yet at the electors' meeting it was boldly stated and never contradicted that Mr Barnes was an honourable, just, and kind-hearted employer, while Mr Grimshaw signally failed in his attempts to put forward a formidable list of his political shortcomings when in the House of Commons."

And so, as a result of this uncontested by-election, three months after his son's 21st birthday celebrations and the gift of land for a public park, Thomas went back to Westminster leaving the Liberals in Bolton still divided. On 12 February he fulfilled an engagement at the Mechanics' Institution in Bolton to preside at the second lecture on religious voluntaryism given by Rev. Alexander Thomson, "The Scriptural Argument for National Church Establishments examined". It was the day following his election. When the new session started on Monday 18 February his address was the Reform Club, Pall Mall, S.W. A long unbroken seven-year period as Liberal MP for Bolton was beginning. His return to Parliament coincided almost exactly with the outbreak of the American War of Secession which had such disastrous results for the Lancashire cotton industry. It was on 8 February 1861 that Jefferson Davis was elected as provisional President of the Confederate States of America.

At the time of the 1861 Census, on 7 April, Thomas and Ann were at home at The Quinta. Thomas was 42 years old, described as a gentleman and MP, and Ann was 50. Their son, James Richardson, who had come of age the previous December, was not with them. After he finished at university James Richardson had thrown himself into the business at Farnworth and into the life of the chapel at Halshaw Moor where in 1865 he was on the General Committee.

Thomas and Ann were living in style at The Quinta. They had five living-in servants: a cook and four housemaids. The estate was managed by 61–year-old Samuel Winter, Thomas's estate bailiff, who lived in a cottage in the Quinta farmyard. Samuel Winter had been brought over to The Quinta from Farnworth as estate bailiff when Thomas bought the estate in 1853 to "superintend the improvements and alterations". He was born in Cheddiston in Suffolk in 1800. He was probably the same Samuel Winter who worked for Thomas's brother George up to 1844 as it was stated in his Obituary in September 1871 that he had worked for the Barnes family for almost forty years. His son, also called Samuel, was one of the pall bearers at the funeral of Thomas's wife, Ann, in Farnworth in August 1880. His brother, Joseph, became a partner in the firm after Thomas Paterson's partnership ceased in 1865. Around 1830 Thomas's father, James Rothwell Barnes, had brought three wagonloads of families and their belongings from Suffolk to work in his expanding business. The Winter family was one of them and the men obviously remained faithful workers for the Barnes family for the rest of their lives. When Samuel Winter died he was said to "have been much esteemed by members of the Barnes family".

Staying with them in April 1861 was a visitor, John Dobson Riley, an unmarried man aged 29 born in Bradford. Although he was described in the Census as the Independent Minister of the Quinta Chapel, he actually did not accept the invitation to become the first minister of the Chapel until June 1861 and did not begin his duties until July. Thomas later built a beautiful manse for the minister but in April 1861 John Riley was living in The Quinta as a house guest.

After his re-election Thomas was soon back at work in Parliament. On 10 April 1861 about a dozen members of Parliament, including Thomas, presented petitions in favour of parliamentary reform. On 22 April it was announced in *The Times* that he had joined a provisional committee set up to provide a fund, the Kossuth Defence Fund, to enable Louis Kossuth to fight a legal battle in the Court of Chancery against the Emperor of Austria. Amongst the names listed on the committee were those of the MPs Thomas Bazley, George Hadfield and William Scholefield, the Treasurer. John Cheetham, no longer an MP, was also on the committee. Thomas continued to be involved in the question of church rates but was absent from the committee of supply at the end of July 1861 when Mr Dillwyn asked the Secretary of State for the Home Department a question on Thomas's behalf. It was whether his attention had been drawn to the state in which the town of Accrington had been placed by the Vicar of Whalley seizing the household goods and other property of poor parishioners and selling them by auction to enforce the payment of small sums of money claimed by him for Easter offerings. Mr Hadfield seconded a Motion on the question but as the action was not considered to be a breach of the peace, the Motion was withdrawn.

When the annual stocktaking at Farnworth Mills was held on 30 June 1861 Thomas and his partner Thomas Paterson were joined by James Richardson Barnes. On 1 January 1861 James had received £10,000 from his father's account which he must have invested as capital into the business. The amount was recorded in the firm's accounts in June. (Thomas had had £10,000 invested in the Huddersfield Banking Company from which he received annual interest. This was possibly the amount he transferred to his son.) During the year James Richardson drew £340 in cash from the Petty Cash account. Although James Richardson received a share of the profits from now on, he was not named separately in the share-out and must have received a portion of his father's share. His separate account at the back of the book shows that on 1 July 1861 after the previous day's share-out James Richardson received 5% interest on his £10,000 capital plus one-eighth of the year's profit, bringing his balance up to £11,458 1s. It was not until 30 June 1866 that James Richardson was recorded in the account book as having received a share of the profits and even then his share came out of his father's allocation. In 1861 James Newhouse and Joseph Winter were again recorded in the accounts and again Joseph Winter was given a gift of £636. The huge profits of £15,133 were divided between Thomas and Thomas Paterson and this year Thomas Paterson's share had doubled. He was now receiving one-third.

During the summer recess Thomas was able to attend the Denbighshire Assizes and on 31 July 1861 was again on the Grand Jury. It was two years before he attended again, on 28 July 1863, again during the recess. He was now described as Thomas Barnes MP, of Craignant, Oswestry. In the same year, before Parliament reassembled in November, he appeared as a magistrate at the Denbighshire Quarter Sessions on Thursday 22 October 1863 at Wrexham Town Hall. He was not on the jury on the Friday when cases were heard.

In 1861 Thomas and Ann found time for an annual holiday. They stayed in the week 17 to 24 August 1861 at the George Hotel, Bangor Ferry. Many of the other guests had very distinguished titles. Thomas had another engagement during the summer recess during the last week of August when he supported John Cheetham who was canvassing for a seat in Parliament as a representative for South Lancashire. Thomas was on the platform in the Concert Hall in Mawdsley Street, Bolton, when John Cheetham addressed the public on Monday 26 August.

A few days later on Thursday 29 August Thomas was back at The Quinta for the ordination service of the new minister, Mr J. D. Riley. He had trained at the Lancashire Independent College in Manchester. The ordination prayer was offered by Rev. J. Gwyther of Manchester, Mr Riley's former pastor. Rev. S. Martin of Westminster also took part in the service. After the service up to a hundred friends were invited by Thomas and Ann to a luncheon in a large room adjoining the mansion specially erected for such events. Although present at the luncheon, Ann was said to be suffering from an indisposition. Thomas was reluctant to give toasts after such a solemn ceremony but began with one to the Queen: "They ought to feel grateful and express their good wishes to their sovereign. On looking abroad and seeing there was great disturbance on the earth, some nations on the brink of revolution, and others in the agonies of civil war, they ought to be grateful that there was peace and order in their own kingdom, and he doubted not but that this was owing to their being ruled by such a sovereign." He went on to welcome Mr Riley: "The Quinta church was sacred to him, and he could assure Mr Riley he had their hearty welcome, their sympathy and prayers. There was a great sphere of usefulness before him—a large population scattered over a wide district, and his hopes were that his success would be so great that their place of worship would become too small for him." One of the speakers was Mr John Crossley of Halifax. Another was Rev. S. Martin who had taken part in the service. Apparently he had come into contact with James Richardson when he was a student in London. He said: "It was my honoured privilege to receive the only and dearly beloved son of our guest [sic] into church membership when in college in London. I watched him with a father's eye and I care for him with a father's care; and next to my own children I love him." The guests were invited to spend the rest of the day in the Quinta grounds, if they wished.

On 14 September 1861 John Girdwood, Thomas's agent at The Quinta, died at Sudbury near Derby, of diphtheria. He had been agent to Colonel Myddleton Biddulph at Chirk Castle before becoming agent at The Quinta. John Girdwood was present at the dinner in the Britannia Inn on the afternoon of 2 December 1859 on the occasion of the rent audit for the Quinta estate. He was described in the press report as "the respected agent".

On 1 October 1861 Thomas was in Oswestry to chair an evening meeting of the Baptist Missionary Society in the Baptist Schoolroom. He outlined the progress the Society was making in India and the West Indies. In 1861 he also laid the foundation stone for a new Baptist Church in Astley Bridge on a site in Eden Street.

Thomas was involved in the work of the Temperance League in the Quinta district. On Tuesday evening 5 November 1861 he was the Chairman at the annual meeting of the Wrexham Temperance League which met in the Music Hall.

On 18 and 19 November 1861 he attended a Reform conference in the Civil Court in Leeds Town Hall where John Bright and Richard Cobden had been expected to speak. They were unable to attend. However, Thomas was one of the three speakers, the others being George Wilson of the Anti-Corn Law League and Mr Baines MP. The aim of the conference was "to initiate such an agitation as will prove conclusively that the working classes are not indifferent on the subject of reform, and to adopt such measures as will cause the agitation to result in that extension of political privileges to the working classes which they desire".

On Friday evening 3 January 1862, as one of the chief subscribers to the building fund, he spoke at a tea party in the Temperance Hall in Bolton in aid of raising even more funds for building a new Congregational Church in St George's Road, Bolton. Thomas had contributed £500. Prince Albert had died not long before, the civil war in America was underway, they were surrounded by misery, but Thomas managed to find all sorts of reasons for optimism: the Queen's religious faith, the £4,200 already collected towards the building of the new church, the news received that day that the Federal Government in America had decided to send the Southern Commissioners to England, but most of all, the fact that they had survived the previous year. "I sometimes think that the commencement of the New Year is like setting out in a vessel for some distant land; when we get into it we know that we have to land on another shore, but that we have numerous difficulties and trials to undergo, and we know not whether we shall arrive safe. So it is with the New Year: we have set sail now,—we have got to buffet with the stormy billows of life, and although we all have set sail together, yet no one knows who will land safely at the end of the voyage. We set sail on the New Year's Day in 1861; and, thank God, we all landed safely on the 31st of December; and we are now setting forward on another voyage, which I hope may be a prosperous one to all, and that we shall all meet and congratulate each other again at the commencement of another year." He encouraged them to be even more generous, to double their subscriptions to the building fund. Although another speaker had said that he hoped they would be able to clear their debt before the church was finished, Thomas disagreed. "I am not over anxious for this, for I am of opinion that where there is a little bit of debt remaining on a chapel, it is like mortar between bricks—it makes the people stick together". He recommended congregations in England to adopt the American system of building churches: "In America we are told that some persons will raise up a splendid church, at a cost from £5,000 to £10,000, appoint a minister, and ask nobody for a shilling. They don't give the money, but let the building to the congregation at a rental,—the seat rents going towards the payment of the rent, and the surplus to keep the building in repair. They never think of paying the minister out of the seat rents, but levy a voluntary tax for his support." He was very critical of the English system of pew renting: "The chapels are never filled, and if you make inquiries as to the cause—inquire whether the ministers are good preachers, you will learn that they are excellent speakers, and that the thinness of the congregations is attributed to the bad system of renting the pews. Is that system right which allows our chapels to be sometimes only even a third full? Do we build chapels in order that some man may occupy one pew himself? That is the case in many places, and it is a system that should at once be corrected, for not until it is shall we see our chapels full." He also referred to an event which was to be celebrated on 24 August that year—the bicentenary of the dissolution of the Nonconformist ministers from the Church of England. He used the opportunity to express his views on what it meant to be a Nonconformist, a Dissenter. He said it was "the anniversary of that day when an immense number of our Nonconformist forefathers went out to maintain their independence in another land,—nay, not went out, for they were forced out—and we as Nonconformists and as Dissenters should bear this in mind, that we are Dissenters because we were forced out of the Church of England. There is a feeling that the Dissenters are a set of people who *don't* go to the Church because they *won't* go; but I object to the words Dissenters, as I don't go to the Church because I dislike it; and I don't think anybody living has a right to call me a Dissenter, for this reason—that I have as much right to keep up my standard of state, and say that every man who does not profess my faith is a Dissenter. [... ...] These men went out because they would not bow to the will of the Church; and from that circumstance we owe all our privileges—our liberty of conscience—our liberty of worship—and our very freedom. We have to thank and bless those patriotic and noble-hearted men for the privileges we are enjoying at this moment, of being allowed to utter what thoughts we like upon this subject and others of vital importance. I wonder what those barbarous men of the Church would have done to me, if I had said the things in the year 1662 which I have said this evening. I fancy that I should have been in a dungeon before another night." He hoped that they would use the coming year to make a greater effort to spread religion and to strengthen the Nonconformists. A few months later on 18 April 1862 Thomas laid the foundation stone of the new church in St George's Road and was presented with an engraved silver trowel. The new church was officially opened in April 1863.

On the morning of Wednesday 15 January 1862 he attended a meeting at the Borough Court in Bolton about proposed improvements to the Infirmary and Dispensary buildings. He made a speech and moved a resolution which was seconded by John Hick: "That a subscription be now opened and the inhabitants of Bolton and neighbourhood be earnestly invited to assist in raising the sum required, which is estimated at not less than £2,000". He donated £105 for improvements in the existing building, and a further £525 for a new Infirmary and its endowment. This very generous donation was matched by Lt-Col. Gray, Bolton's Conservative MP.

On the evening of Tuesday 21 January 1862 Thomas chaired a public meeting in the Temperance Hall in Bolton and gave a long speech on the subject of financial reform. The meeting was organised by the Financial Reform Association based at 46 Church Street in Liverpool. It had been advertised in the previous Saturday's *Bolton Chronicle*. Admission was free and reserved seats were available for "ladies and gentlemen" from the offices of *The Chronicle* and *The Guardian*. A special invitation was extended to "the working classes, both male and female, as the subject of taxation concerns everybody". The main speaker was Mr Hicks of the Financial Reform Association but before he spoke, Thomas set out his own views on the taxation system and on the relative merits of direct or indirect taxation. He was happy to act as Chairman at the meeting but he had to say "he was not what could be called a thick and thin follower of the Association in all it said and did". However, he did think that most of its principles were good. As usual, his speech was full of statistics. He showed how wasteful indirect taxation could be, and how it particularly affected the working classes. However, he could not agree with the Association if it recommended a taxation system based entirely on direct taxation—he did not think it could raise the amount needed. With the illustrations he chose he managed as usual to raise cheers and sometimes laughter. He suggested a revolutionary form of income tax—taxing outgoings rather than income. He did agree with the Association that public expenditure should be reduced and after Mr Hicks' speech promised to try to carry out the reforms the Association thought necessary.

A week later on Tuesday 28 January 1862 he gave another speech in the Temperance Hall, this time to his Bolton constituents. This was the first of what was to become a regular annual event until his defeat in 1868. In 1862 his nephew, Alfred Barnes, was one of the platform party. The purpose of these meetings was for Thomas to give an account of what had gone on in the previous year's Parliament, to explain how and why he had voted for the various bills, and to discuss some of the main issues of the day. This meeting lasted until nearly ten o'clock, probably having started at seven thirty.

Prince Albert had died a few months before, and Abraham Lincoln had been American President since the previous March. The effect that the year-long American War of Secession and the blockades were having on cotton exports was beginning to bite deeply into the Lancashire cotton industry. Bolton, however, had been spared the worst effects because most of its cotton came from other parts of the world and Richard Cobden's recent trade treaty with France had provided outlets for Bolton's cotton, especially in Bradford. Thomas was against breaking the blockade, even if it would have provided temporary relief. He was concerned with finding other sources of cotton and pointed to India, a sadly-neglected British possession, as the best source. Here cotton could be grown without the use of slave-labour, something which Thomas was passionately against. "My determination will be to take that course which appears best calculated to promote the happiness of all mankind—to do that which will open the prison doors and set the captives free, which will strike the manacles from the slave, deliver us from the odium and stain of slave grown cotton, and secure a lasting peace both in America and throughout the world."

During the last Parliamentary session 347 private bills had been discussed and debated and 268 of them passed into law, and 171 public acts passed, not to mention many matters which were debated but came to nothing. He described the session as average, not brilliant, but one in which a great deal of work was done. Amongst the questions he selected for discussion were how to assess income tax, Church rates,

Reform measures such as the £10 county and £6 borough franchise, the ballot, and redistribution of seats. All these measures were defeated. Successful measures included a Poor Law Improvement Bill and a bill to establish Post Office Savings Banks—something which Thomas approved of as being "most beneficial to working people all over the country". Thomas was delighted that the Chancellor, Mr Gladstone, had managed to repeal the duty on paper, one of the "taxes on knowledge" which Thomas had always fought against. Several bills were concerned with Indian government and administration and Thomas read an interesting extract from a letter from Mr Heywood (probably G. R. Heywood, the Secretary of the Cotton Supply Association) who was in India on matters concerning cotton supply. This extract allowed Thomas to discuss the state of India's communication links, especially its railway system which was still in its early stages. After his hour and a quarter long speech Thomas faced questions from the floor which he answered with confidence and without evasion. His old political enemy, Thomas Grimshaw, stood up to grudgingly acknowledge his approval of the way Thomas had voted in the last session: "Now, he had looked very closely after the conduct of Mr Barnes since he was last returned,—he had watched him, and especially his votes, every one of them, subject and date as well, like a cat watching a mouse; and they might depend upon it, had he found anything he didn't approve of, Mr Barnes would have been told of it." Councillor John Heaton who proposed the resolution "That the best thanks of the meeting are due and hereby given to Thomas Barnes, Esq., MP, for his address this evening; and that the meeting expresses its fullest confidence in him as one of their representatives", was far more positive in his praise. He said he had "long been a supporter of Mr Barnes, and he was sure that the manner in which he had acquitted himself to-night—the sterling abilities and sound judgement which he had manifested in the performance of his arduous and onerous duties— had given satisfaction to every candid person". He thought if they were open to conviction, Mr Barnes was the man to convince them. The meeting ended with Alderman Robert Heywood who had nominated Thomas at the 1861 election supporting the resolution: "He said he could not but express the feelings of deep satisfaction he felt that he was an honoured instrument in bringing before the Bolton electors so distinguished a representative. Not only had Mr Barnes extensive information, enabling him to answer any question on any subject; but he had a most happy and pleasing way of conveying what he had to say. He congratulated the meeting on having secured a gentleman who reflected such honour and credit on the town; and who had given such universal satisfaction, that not one person appeared to dissent from his opinion". All in all, Thomas's first annual address to his constituents was a great success.

He was back in London on 13 February as part of a deputation of five men from the Congregational Board of Education who had an interview at the Privy Council Office with the President and Vice-President of the Committee on Education.

At a special ceremony in the Quinta Church on the evening of 27 February 1862 nine people—Thomas and Ann, John Thomas, John Williams, David Ellerker, John Broughall and Robert Salmon, and the minister, Rev. John Dobson Riley and his wife Judith—met to join in solemn covenant and Christian fellowship to constitute themselves on Congregational principles into an independent church. Rev. John Riley read from Ephesians 2 and led the prayer. Then Rev. John Lockwood from Oswestry gave an address on "The principles and discipline of a Congregational church", followed by a second address by Rev. F. B. Brown of Wrexham: "The requirements for Church Membership". Rev. Riley then read the Covenant, and after that the twenty principles of religion and the thirteen principles of Church order and discipline as declared by the Congregational Union of England and Wales. When the nine people had held up their right hand to show their agreement they took communion as a pledge of the covenant they had entered into with one another and with God. They ended the ceremony with hymns and prayers. The covenant at the end of the list of Church members and the thirty-three principles were included at the front of the Church Book.

In the Lancashire Record Office is a letter from Thomas to his sister Jane Haslam, the only one of his five brothers and sisters still alive. Jane was married to James Haslam, of Manchester. The letter is dated 9 March 1862, one year into Thomas's term of office. Number 17 Pall Mall, was probably the address of the Reform Club which was Thomas's London address printed in *The Bolton Chronicle* after his re-election in 1861. It sounds as if he was feeling the strain of life in London as a member of Parliament.

17 Pall Mall, March 9 1862

"Dear Jane

My letter writing is so abundant, that if I were ever capable of being made into a "ready" writer I should have become one. But this is not possible, I am slow and consequently my time is mostly consumed in writing what is not very important but must be replied to. That is my reason for not writing sooner or longer than I did in my last. I have plenty to do here. Though alone I am by no means dull. I sometimes wish for a few spare moments when I could think I had nothing to do. My position here is a very important one, and opens a fine sphere for useful and important labour. But I have often thoughts of giving it up. I am halting between two opinions—having a desire to be more at home and more with the two nearest and dearest. My wife complains of being seperated [sic] from me and James does not like to be alone at Farnworth and she wants to be in two places at the same time which she cannot be. In our present circumstances we should do without the Quinta. If I could have foreseen that James would take to business and that I should be an MP I would not have bought the place. But now neither James nor his mother want to be without it. But it adds to my labours and furnishes me with more work than I should have if I had not it. I am rather perplexed what to do. James had medical advise [sic] last Saturday. Dr Perkins said it was the liver and would have been worse probably if he had not had assistance. I hope he will soon be well again.

In reference to the formation of the Church. Ann excited herself more than was necessary, but she is apt to do that, as all people are who have got livers out of order. Livers and nerves are sometimes very troublesome. The Church was formed by very few. Only 8. Mr Riley had of course to be the judge in the first instance. We have had a little difficulty through S. Winter *though this is private*. He has acted inconsistently in the matter of "drink". That great slayer of reputations, morals and life. He has had to be "left out", and in consequence his wife will not come in, and so neither of them are members. And through this, one or two others have not joined in the first instance. But at the formation we had a most impressive and instructive service, and many spectators and strangers. I had a long conversation with Lady Wynn the other day in the train about our denomination and its form of worship and creed—of which I must tell you particulars when I see you. I hope you feel better. Will you be likely to go to Bath. If you do I will try to go there during your visit. A little change would do both you and our dear friend at Hopefield good.

I am very sorry to hear a less favourable opinion of Mr Hinmers. I heard about a week ago and have heard nothing since. Today I have been to Mr Martin's Chapel and have dined with Mr and Miss Mary Hadfield— I have spent a very instructive and pleasant afternoon. The services both morning and evening were crowded to excess. Indeed it is uncomfortable now in the over 8' especially. But perhaps I am getting old and testy and particular and looking more to "comfort"—an Englishman's God.

I suppose you have received a Card of the Death of cousin John Grundy. Would that one could think it was a loss to any one!! He has been a lost man for many years. Another of our old acquaintances, Mr Richard Cross, you see is gone also. He was committed to his long Home yesterday. He was a man whom I much respected, for he was a sterling character. A sickly body—a weak frame, ever struggling for life, and yet he has outlived all his brothers and sisters. Our old chapel friends drop off, one by one.

Dear Mrs Lord, a mother in Israel, is now feeling the effects of age and is sinking I fear under the weight of age and infirmities. What a blessing that she has such a bright hope of the future.

> "Like a fine setting sun
>
> She wakes richer in grace."

These things tell us how *our* sands are running. When I think of the departed worthies, I sigh and feel sad."

The letter stops at this point with no conclusion or signature. Being based in three places, London, Limefield in Farnworth and The Quinta in Shropshire, was obviously causing difficulties for the family. Keeping the estate going as well as Limefield in Farnworth must have been quite a problem. Not only had Thomas built himself the new mansion but he had also greatly improved the estate, rebuilding many of the houses and outbuildings, and improving his tenants' properties. In 1864 it was reported that Thomas spent the Parliamentary vacations at The Quinta. Lady Wynn was the wife of Sir Watkin Williams Wynn MP who was one of the Trustees of the Provincial Insurance Company of Wrexham of which Thomas had been Chairman of the Board since 1860. Sir W. W. Wynn also used The Quinta on occasions for hunting. Mr Hadfield was Mr George Hadfield who had been Treasurer of Blackburn Independent Academy in November 1838 before it became the Lancashire Independent College, another establishment with which Thomas had close connections. He was now, like Thomas, a Liberal MP. The references to the opening of the Church in Thomas's letter are to the formation of the church at the Quinta Chapel on 27 February 1862.

It is not clear what Samuel Winter's inconsistencies in the matter of drink were. At this time Thomas had an easy-going attitude to alcohol even though he was not a drinker himself. However, he was not a teetotaller and The Quinta did have its own brewhouse so that the workmen could be paid part of their wages in beer. In these early days the Britannia Inn was the only public house in Bronygarth, the hamlet adjoining the Quinta estate. In 1851 it was kept by Richard Orford. Thomas used the Britannia Inn on the afternoon of Friday 2 December 1859 to treat his principal tenants to a meal on the occasion of the annual rent audit. *The Wrexham Weekly Advertiser* commented that it was "a splendid dinner, served up in a style which reflected great credit on the abilities of Mr and Mrs Orford". Thomas must have been satisfied with the catering as he ended the occasion with a toast "To our next merry meeting" and a year later used The Britannia Inn to celebrate

James Richardson's coming-of-age. Three days after writing to his sister Jane, on Wednesday 12 March 1862 Thomas presented a petition from Bolton in the House of Commons in favour of closing public houses on Sundays. This was probably part of the useful and important work he referred to in the letter. However, he was not present on Christmas Day 1862 when a Temperance Tea meeting was held in the Quinta Schoolroom at The Lodge. His daughter-in-law, Ellen, became very involved with the Temperance Movement and on 29 March 1869 organised a Temperance coffee supper in the schoolroom belonging to her. She gave a party the following day to the children who also were given a talk on temperance and invited to join the Band of Hope. This was all followed up by a Band of Hope meeting three days later in the Quinta Schoolroom at The Lodge. Thomas's attitude to alcohol must have hardened because later, as a result of his influence, the Britannia Inn lost its licence and was taken over by The British Workman Public House Company, a non-sectarian and non-political temperance organisation. They operated it as a coffee house. In 1885 Thomas Frith was the manager and in 1891 Thomas Higginson. On 2 May 1892 Ellen Barnes presided over a meeting held at the British Workman to hear a speech by Mr A. T. Jebb.

Just two weeks after presenting the petition about Sunday closing in March 1862 Thomas and his fellow Bolton MP, Captain Gray, were part of a deputation on the subject of the 1860 Bleaching and Dycing Works Act who met Sir George Grey at the Home Office on 21 March. Four days later he and Captain Gray were in another deputation with chairmen of Quarter Sessions who met Sir George Grey again, this time to discuss the cost of prosecutions.

When *The Nonconformist* completed its twenty-one years of publication on 14 April 1862 its editor was Edward Miall. It was decided to use the occasion as an opportunity to set up a testimonial fund for Edward Miall to thank him not only for his contributions to journalism, but also for the part he played in setting up the Liberation Society, for his support for Liberal politics, for serving as Liberal MP for Rochdale, and for supporting voluntaryism in education. John Crossley from Halifax was the Chairman of the Testimonial Fund Committee which had collected well over £4,000 by 15 April. Although Thomas was not one of the Executive Committee he was one of the major donors, giving a £50 subscription.

When the annual profits for the mills in Farnworth were announced at the end of June 1862 Thomas Paterson again received a one-third share. According to the accounts at the back of the book James

Richardson Barnes again received interest on his capital and drew £721 from the Petty Cash account. In 1862 his father also paid £1,208 into his son's account. He was not listed in the share-out of profits but obviously was receiving funds. James Newhouse and Joseph Winter continued to be listed in the accounts and again Joseph Winter received a payment out of the final balance. More improvements had been made at the mills. Higher Mill had had new steam engines at a cost of £61 5s and more had been spent on flagging and a new shed. During 1862 the firm extended even more by adding a new cloth room and a new cotton room.

Thomas must have got over his weariness and sense of becoming an old man which he described in his letter to his sister. After all, he was only 50. He continued adding to his public commitments. In 1862 he contributed £1,000 towards the Chapel Building Fund in connection with the Bicentenary movement. A few days before Thomas laid the foundation stone at St George's Congregational Chapel in Bolton, a meeting had been held on 15 April 1862 at the Independent Chapel in Denbigh to mark the Bicentenary of the Great Ejection on St Bartholomew's Day 1662. Thomas was one of the principal supporters. The conference began on Tuesday with sermons on the evening before. After the morning's conference there was a dinner in the Assembly Room followed by an address in the chapel. Thomas was one of the guests at the tea before he chaired the public meeting in the Independent Chapel in the evening. The purpose of this meeting was to deliver addresses on the ejectment of the 2,000 Dissenting ministers. Thomas spoke in English and apologized for not being able to speak Welsh. Much of the meeting was conducted in Welsh. He was thanked for presiding over a meeting where so much had been said in a language which he did not understand.

On 21 April 1862 he was in Shropshire to lay another foundation stone, this one at the Congregational Chapel in Prees when he donated £50, a sum he often donated to the Congregational chapels around The Quinta.

What Thomas had not mentioned in his address to his constituents was that in the whole year after returning to Parliament in February 1861 he had made no speeches in the House. It was not until May 5 1862 that he spoke at a Committee of Education to discuss the revised code of regulations. He supported a resolution by Mr Baines which aimed to ensure the Government grant went to support the poorest children in schools, and not the children of the middle classes. After his long break from the subject his argument had not changed. He said he would support the resolution on the ground that the grant went now in a considerable degree to the education of a class of children for whom it was never designed. The House would not have consented to the first grant of £20,000 had it not been distinctly stated that it was for the education of the poor. On that account it appeared to him that the House had shut its eyes to the facts, for it was under the delusion that by granting large sums of money it was promoting the education of the children of the labouring classes. He held in his hand a statement which showed that at a school of considerable reputation near the metropolis, which received large grants from the public purse, the children of a superior class of tradesmen, who could as easily afford to pay 1s as 3d a week, were being educated. In Lancashire and Yorkshire, and all the large towns, it was well known that the pupils attending the schools were in a great measure the children of parents well able to pay. In a school with which he as well acquainted, which was attended by 250 scholars, and received no grant from the State, the balance-sheet of last year showed a loss of only £8, and at a little distance was another school which received a large public grant, but which had no more necessity for it than the other". When he mentioned the school with which he was well acquainted he must have been referring to Queen Street Seminary in Farnworth.

On 4 July 1862 he was in Westminster at a debate to agree to the Second Reading of the Mersey and Irwell Protection Bill. He tried to delay the reading by supporting an amendment to replace the word "now" by the phrase "to this day in three months". He said it would be most unfair to deprive the proprietors of their rights without compensation and thought a Committee should be appointed to investigate the whole question. However, the amendment was not accepted and the bill received its Second Reading.

On Monday 14 July 1862 Thomas laid the foundation stone at Queen Street Welsh Congregational Chapel in Wrexham and was presented with a silver trowel on which was engraved: "I Thomas Barnes, Ysw., AS., ar sylfaeniad capel Ebenezer Gwrecsam, Gorphenaf 14, 1862" ["to Thomas Barnes, esq., MP on the foundation of Ebenezer Chapel, Wrexham, July 14, 1862"]. This was followed by a soirée and a public meeting in the evening.

In 1862 Thomas and Ann managed to have another holiday. They were in Llandudno staying at Mr H. Duke's Moseley House on North Parade in the week 23 to 30 August. Soon after that he became involved in matters much further away from home when he subscribed £5 to the Garibaldi Surgical Fund which by the end of September had collected nearly £942 to send to General Garibaldi "for the benefit of his wounded comrades".

On 24 September 1862 Thomas was part of the platform party at the inauguration of the Crompton Statue in Nelson Square, Bolton. The statue cost over £1,900, raised by public subscriptions. Following the ceremony he was a guest at the déjeuner given by the Mayor, J. R. Wolfenden, to 300 guests in a marquee at his home, Westwood. It was now thirty-two years after Crompton had died in poverty, having given his invention, the mule, to the world. Samuel Crompton's son John, aged 72, and unable to stand during the unveiling of the statue, was so obviously in need of assistance that another meeting was held on 13 October, called by Mr Gilbert French to set up a fund to help John Crompton and his wife. The proposal was made by the Mayor and seconded by Thomas.

When Mr Gladstone visited the new offices of the Provincial Insurance Company in Wrexham on 29 October 1862 Thomas, the Chairman of the company, was not able to meet him as he had another pressing engagement in Manchester.

CHAPTER 8

1856–1890

Thomas the farmer

After moving to his estate at The Quinta Thomas tried to keep up with the latest developments in agriculture. On 23 November 1856 he was one of a large number of noblemen and gentlemen who were appointed at a public meeting held at Chester to arrange the 1858 meeting of the Royal Agricultural Society of England which was to be held in Chester that year. The Chairman of this Committee was the Marquis of Westminster and the Vice-Chairman the MP Sir Philip de M. Grey Egerton. In 1858 Thomas subscribed £10 to this Royal Agricultural Society of England. On 12 March 1861 he was with some local leading agriculturists and landed proprietors and others interested in agriculture from the neighbouring English counties who met on the home farm of Mr Whitehall Dod at Bryndinarth to witness the introduction of steam into Wales by means of Beard's Steam Ploughing Apparatus. When Thomas gave the toast "Prosperity to Agriculture" at the dinner in the Britannia Inn on 2 December 1859 after the rent audit of the Quinta estate he said: "He himself was no agriculturalist— he knew very little about it; but he was doing his best to improve himself and was gathering knowledge from every possible source. He knew, however, what farming was, and was very fond of taking his gun, not so much for the sport derived from it, as for the opportunity it offered for inspecting the different farms. He often missed a covey of birds, being too intent on examining the thistles, weeds and hedges; so that if his tenants wished him to become a good sportsman, they must keep their hedges properly trimmed and their thistles down." The local paper included occasional references to Thomas's farming activities. When the list of meat available for Christmas 1859 in the Oswestry butchers' shops was published, Mrs H. Jones of Willow Street had two sources of meat—a Hereford heifer, fed by Mr Hughes of Escob Mill and four excellent black-faced sheep fed by Mr Barnes of

The Quinta. In January 1861 Mr J. Lloyd was the farm bailiff at The
Quinta and Thomas still had his flock of black-faced sheep. It was
possibly this same flock which received a special mention in *The
Wrexham Weekly Advertiser* on 10 March 1860: "Mr Barnes of the
Quinta has in his possession 6 ewes, which in the course of 2 days
produced 19 lambs, 16 of which are living, viz: 1 ewe yeaned 5 lambs
and 4 living; 1 ewe yeaned 4 lambs and 3 living; 2 ewes yeaned 3 lambs
each and 5 living; and 2 other ewes yeaned 2 each, the whole living."
In July 1863 one of his shepherds was a William Roberts who was a
witness in a case involving sheep stealing at Denbighshire Summer
Assizes. Oswestry Second Annual Agricultural Show was held on the
Smithfield, Oswestry, on 1 October 1863. Thomas was highly commended
for a pair of chestnut mares in the show. Whether by design or by
accident, I do not know, but this entry was missed out of the list of
prizewinners and added as a postscript.

The farming side of the Quinta estate must have been quite considerable.
When one of the farms, Tynyrhyd near Selattyn, came to be let, some
of the stock was sold by auction on 24 September 1866. The auctioneer
advertised "100 Splendid Shropshire Stock Ewes, 41 Capital Fresh
Bullocks, 4 Waggon Horses and 3 Cart Colts". Six months later the
farm had been re-let and the whole of the livestock came up for sale.
This time there were 106 Prime Shropshire Down Ewes, in lamb, 250
Welsh Ewes, in lamb, 115 Yearling Sheep, 67 Fat Welsh Wethers and
40 Cattle, principally calving cows and heifers. Before the sale at the
end of March 1867 some of the cattle must have been sold as the cattle
which actually came up for sale were: 5 Calving Cows, 5 Calving
Heifers, 5 Good Barrens, 2 Yearling Bullocks and 4 Yearling Heifers.
The three horses in the sale were a Prime Cob Horse, 7 years old,
good in harness and saddle, a Splendid Chestnut Cart Colt, rising 3−
year-old, and a Cart yearling. In addition, the sale included all the
"Implements of Husbandry and Brewing and Dairy Vessels". A farm
sale on 8 November 1870 at Penlan Farm, Llangollen, included a 3−
year-old bull which had been bred out of the pedigree bull owned by
Thomas at The Quinta. When the meat on offer in Chirk for Christmas
1871 was listed in the local paper the magnificent display in Mr Griffiths'
butcher's shop included "two very neat pork pigs and a small Ayrshire
calf, all three fed by Mr T. Barnes, The Quinta".

In October 1870 an advertisement in *The Wrexham Weekly Advertiser*
gave an indication of another source of income on the estate: "To be
sold by tender, a quantity of Larch Poles, standing; also a quantity of
Elm, Ash, Sycamore, Oak and other timber, standing. The Oak may

remain till May next. Sealed tenders to be sent to the Quinta Office, near Chirk, on or before 14th day of the next." According to a list of principal landowners in Denbighshire in 1873, Thomas Barnes of The Quinta owned 1,761 acres with an estimated annual rental of £737. Although large, his estate was dwarfed by the nearby estate at Chirk Castle which was many times greater.

By 1883 he had obviously established a name for himself as a stock breeder. On 4 November 1883 Mr Richard Humphreys, formerly of Beddgelert, and now landlord of the Penrhyn Arms Hotel, Bangor, disposed of his herd of pedigree Welsh cattle. Standing round the auction ring were representatives of the leading breeders of stock in North and South Wales, notably Earl Cawdor, Lord Penrhyn, the Marquis of Anglesey, Lord Harlech, Lord Bagot, Major Platt, Mr Assheton Smith, Mr Oakley from Plas Tanybwlch, Mr Barnes, formerly member for Bolton, Capt. Mitchell, and Mr Pope Q.C. (This was Samuel Pope who had stood with Thomas as Liberal candidate for Bolton in 1865 and 1868.) Eight heifer calves by "Prince Llewelyn IV" were bought for Thomas at 15 guineas each, and were regarded as one of the best bargains secured during the day. At the 17th annual spring sale of pedigree cattle and bulls at the Oswestry and Western Counties Sale in March 1890, a bull, "Caroline Duke the Second", owned and bred by Thomas, was sold for 31½ guineas. At the 28th Annual Oswestry District Agricultural Show on 18 September 1890 Thomas won a First Prize (£2) for a pig in the class "Berkshire or other blacks of intermediate size".

CHAPTER 9

1863–October 1864

The years of the Cotton Famine. Cotton in Jamaica

Life at Westminster, Farnworth and The Quinta

On 8 January 1863 Thomas gave his second annual address to his constituents in the Temperance Hall in Bolton. Amongst the large party on the platform were his son, James Richardson, and a group from Farnworth. Alderman Robert Heywood was the Chairman on this occasion. Even though a royal wedding was imminent, the effect that the American war was having on the cotton towns, now including Bolton, cast a gloomy atmosphere over the meeting. One of the bills passed during the session was one for the relief of Lancashire which had assumed that the worst would be over by the end of October. Now, two months later, things were even worse, and Thomas predicted that he could see no end to it until they had a new source of cotton supplies. He did not tell them that in December 1862 he had bought a 100–acre former sugar plantation in Clarendon parish in Jamaica with the intention of trying to grow cotton there. It was not until January 1864 that he told his constituents about this venture.

It was not surprising that Thomas became involved in an attempt to grow cotton in Jamaica. He was already involved with the Cotton Supply Association as one of its Council Members. This Association had been inaugurated on 21 April 1857 to encourage the production of cotton in countries other than America. Its aims were printed in an article in *The Mechanics' Magazine* on Saturday 11 July 1857. Its first annual meeting was held on 9 April 1858 in the large room at the Town Hall in Manchester. There was a very large attendance and several important speakers, including the Rajah of Sarawak and several MPs. John Cheetham MP was asked to preside. There was no mention of Thomas on this occasion. In the report of the Third Annual Meeting of the Cotton Supply Association held in Manchester Town Hall on 11 May 1860 Thomas was listed as one of the Council members. The situation had not changed at the Fourth Annual meeting a year later on 11 June 1861. John Cheetham was President of the Association when it met on 13 August 1862 to discuss new sources of cotton and was still its President at the Seventh Annual Meeting in Manchester Town Hall in June 1864. The Cotton Supply Association had been sending cotton seed to Jamaica in 1861, if not earlier, to an organisation in Hanover parish in the north-west of the island, the Hanover Society of Industry. This seed was distributed to people willing to experiment with growing cotton. The Cotton Supply Association sent a second batch of seed in 1862, together with gins for separating the cotton from the seeds. In 1862 they also supported the Jamaica Cotton Company and reported that another company was about to be set up in Glasgow. This was presumably the Glasgow Cotton Company which, like Thomas, bought Jamaican estates in Clarendon parish.

Long before this Thomas had been involved with another company hoping to promote the growing of cotton. In June 1850 he was on a committee which planned to form a joint stock company, the British Colonial Cotton Company, by raising £50,000 in capital and using half of it to promote the cultivation of cotton in Jamaica.

Thomas became involved with a third company, the Manchester Cotton Company, when it was first launched on 14 September 1860 at a meeting in the Mayor's Parlour in the Town Hall, King Street, Manchester. It was to be a cotton-purchasing company whose aim was to encourage the growth of cotton in various parts of the world, particularly India and Australia. This first meeting was presided over by Thomas Bazley MP. The company was to be considered formed as soon as one half of the capital of £100,000 was subscribed. Thomas was named as one of the provisional Directors. Once the company was formed, Hugh Mason was elected its Chairman. In his first speech to his constituents in January 1862 Thomas was most optimistic about the prospects of cotton from India. However, this venture was not a success and the Manchester Cotton Company never managed to obtain any cotton from India. Anthony Burton wrote in his book *The Rise and Fall of King Cotton*: "The Manchester Cotton Company was formed with plans to raise a million pounds: by July 1862, they had just a little over £40,000. But they were able to collect enough cash to buy cleaning and pressing machinery which was duly despatched [to India]. Unfortunately, a promised new pier and new roads in India were scarcely begun, and the expensive machines were left to rust on the beach. The scheme came to nothing—not one pound of cotton was ever brought to Lancashire by the Manchester company." They had originally offered shares at £100, but had to reduce them first to £20 and then to £10.

Soon after his election as MP for Bolton in 1861 Thomas was appointed chairman of yet another company, the British Cotton Company, a long-established company which was already in existence in 1830. Its purpose was to buy cotton in Jamaica, Natal, Queensland and India. In 1862 its shares were on offer at £1 each to encourage poorer people to get involved.

Thomas does not appear to have had anything to do with the London-based Jamaica Cotton Company which was also well established by the time he bought his estate in Clarendon. The Jamaica Cotton Company's estates were further east in the parishes of St Thomas in the East and Portland. However, Thomas must have been well aware of the activities of this company, launched in 1859 with the aim of growing cotton once again in the British Colony of Jamaica. The driving force behind this company was Stephen Bourne, a man who had been a magistrate in St Andrew parish in Jamaica at the time of emancipation and had lived there with his family for over six years. Once back in England, he combined his knowledge of Jamaica with his skills as a journalist and kept up a regular correspondence with the daily papers giving detailed accounts of the progress of the Jamaica Cotton Company. He made regular appeals to the cotton manufacturers in Lancashire. For example, on 22 May 1862 Thomas could have read in *The Manchester Times* in one of Stephen Bourne's letters: "The Lancashire manufacturers have then a remedy within their reach. Let them heartily co-operate with us and before this time next year they may have from Jamaica alone a large supply of very superior cotton, at a much less cost for labour than that produced by means of slave labour." In October 1862 when Thomas must have been considering buying his estate, Stephen Bourne made another appeal, this time in *The Daily News*: "How little do our Lancashire manufacturers know what they have lost by slighting our West Indian colonies." This company was also supported by Thomas's fellow Liberal MP, Thomas Bazley, who had links with The Manchester Cotton Company. Thomas would have come into contact with Stephen Bourne who had met Lancashire cotton manufacturers in Manchester on several occasions before 1862.

Thomas bought his Jamaican estate in Clarendon parish in December 1862. Clarendon parish is in the south of the island, about halfway between the west and east points. At the time it was still separate from the parish of Vere to the south, and practically without any coastline.

The two parishes became one in 1866. Near May Pen, the present capital of the parish, is a place called Denbigh, named after Denbigh in North Wales. Could this perhaps be a link with Thomas and his estate at The Quinta on the Welsh border between Denbighshire and Shropshire?

In March 1861 Rev. Mr Fletcher, a missionary with the London Missionary Society, wrote from Chapelton, then the capital of the parish of Clarendon, to Mr Hayward, the Secretary of the Cotton Supply Association in Manchester. He had met Mr Hayward in Manchester in the summer of 1860 before leaving with his family for Jamaica in December that year and had been inspired to grow cotton on the island. Thomas had been an active supporter of the London Missionary Society since his early days. In 1864 he was a director of the Society and regularly chaired meetings linked to it. It is most likely that Thomas Barnes and Rev. Fletcher in Clarendon knew one another.

Thomas also supported the Baptist Missionary Society, the body which in 1865 was accused of having played a part in inciting the negroes to revolt through the writings of one of their missionaries, Dr Underhill.

By September 1862 the war in America had brought the cotton market in England to a standstill. Even working men had become involved in trying to find new sources of cotton and had set up a Working Men's Cotton Supply Association in Manchester. Mr Bazley was involved in this, too. By now there were organisations trying to obtain cotton from India, Western Australia, Queensland, Algeria, Jamaica and Natal. In Jamaica the Jamaica Cotton Company was expanding and had just bought a 2,000–acre estate. Various private individuals were also attempting to grow cotton there. One of these was a shareholder of the Jamaica Cotton Company who had 300 acres. Another was The Honourable Mr Westmoreland, a leading member of the Jamaica House of Assembly who had 40 acres on his estate at Temple Hall. Near to the Jamaica Cotton Company's estate at Manchioneal Governor Charles Darling had planted 83 acres of cotton at Weybridge, one of his estates. The Jamaican newspapers, which at first had been doubtful as to the Company's success, were now writing about their experiment as though they had always believed it would bring success, not only to the company, but also to the whole island.

By November 1862 the Jamaica Cotton Company was able to demonstrate their success by producing some items of clothing from their first cotton crop. Several eminent men including Lord Brougham, Earl Fortescue, the Marquis of Normanby, Mr J. B. Smith MP and Mr

Gurney MP had had waistcoats made up out of this cloth which they were wearing as an advertisement for Jamaican cotton. There were also plans to encourage experienced agricultural workers to emigrate to Jamaica from the United States and Canada. Soon after that, another scheme was launched by a relative of Stephen Bourne to move 50,000 to 100,000 negroes from North America by paying their passage and providing them with a house and small plot of land in Jamaica. It must have seemed an ideal opportunity for Thomas to find himself a source of cotton in the bleak days of the Lancashire Cotton Famine and to make a reasonably safe business investment whilst at the same time avoiding using slave labour to do so. *The Christian World* wrote a eulogy of Thomas which was quoted in *The North Wales Chronicle* on 2 December 1865: "Mr Barnes was an active member of the Cotton Supply Association. Long before the recent glorious emancipation of the blacks in the Southern states of America, Mr Barnes was obtaining— and the only man in England obtaining—cotton, cultivated by free blacks on his own estate." I am not sure that this was strictly accurate as there were other private individuals trying to grow cotton in Jamaica. However, it could be that he was the only cotton spinner in England who was trying to produce his own cotton in this way.

The Morning Post reported on 6 July 1863 that there were now two other cotton companies and many private individuals planting cotton in Jamaica with every prospect of success. Governor Darling had about 70 acres cultivated, Thomas Barnes 130 acres, Mr Dunsford 100, and expecting to put in 800, and another gentleman from Lancashire had 100. Unfortunately, there had been extremely wet weather during the picking season and less cotton was picked than had been expected. However, what cotton there was, fetched a higher price than the American cotton. On 1 August 1863 *The New York Times* was able to report that the cotton-growing experiments on the Clarendon estate in Jamaica had been highly satisfactory. Presumably this included Thomas's estate.

In January 1862 when he gave his speech to his constituents Thomas was still looking to India as the main source of cotton grown without the use of slave-labour. He was a fierce opponent of slavery. The war in America had begun in February 1861 and the effects of the blockade were beginning to be felt in the cotton manufacturing areas. As a user of cotton he must have felt an obligation to find an alternative source of cotton. During the 1862 Parliamentary session there were several debates on the situation in America, including one questioning the efficiency of the blockade and another demanding British recognition of the Southern States. Thomas was not prepared to recognise the South, chiefly because he believed Britain should continue to be neutral, but also because he saw Washington as the constitutional government. Nor could he accept the South's attitude to slavery. He said, "The South presents itself before me as a nation declaring itself to be a slave empire, the cornerstone of which is founded upon slavery. They say that their government is based upon the acknowledged principle of difference between the black and the white man; and they say that the black man is doomed by nature to serve the white man, and that they are the only kingdom in the world based upon this principle. Nothing will induce me to acknowledge slavery or [the] right to maintain slaves. Nothing will induce me to acknowledge a power which is claiming the right, as some of their leading men are, to reopen the slave trade and to have as free a traffic in slaves for the South as the North has in importing mules from Malta—to use the expression of the Southerners themselves." He also believed that the North was moving towards emancipation of slaves, having abolished slavery in Columbia and in the so-called "territories"—districts not yet formed into states.

In his annual speech to his constituents in January 1863 Thomas described the session as a not very brilliant one—but unlike the previous year, it had not been an active one either. They still had not managed to pass a bill to allow affirmations to be allowed in courts instead of oaths, nor a bill to settle the church rate question, nor the introduction of the ballot at elections, and moves to reduce the duty on fire insurance had only reached a half-way stage. (When an Association was formed in the December of that year, the Association for the Abolition or Reduction of the Duty on Fire Insurances, Thomas was listed as one of its many Patrons.) Thomas had taken an interest in the education debates on the funding of the British Schools. He was not satisfied that the system was working properly. "The system as now existing has been justly described by Mr Tremenheere, another of the school inspectors, as a system expensive, unsuitable, squandering public money, accumulating vested interests, and destroying rather than extending education to the children of the poor. This system, I say, demands careful watching and guarding against, and the country ought to keep their eye upon it, and if we are to have any check upon the expenditure we must take care that it does not go to those parties who do not want it, for whom it was never intended, and who would not ask for it if it was not given, so that it might not be wastefully applied."

As usual, he went into detail about the national expenditure, especially the amount spent on the army and navy. "If we want to be strong as a nation—able to defend ourselves from any foe, instead of squandering money upon navies and upon soldiers who are not required, we must reduce the number of them, harbour our resources, keep our money in our pockets, keep our finances square and straight, and then we shall keep the people of the country in a condition to meet any demand that may be made upon them to an unlimited extent." A more than adequate supply of Enfield rifles and Armstrong guns had been built up and was still being stockpiled. Nor should money be spent providing soldiers for the colonies: "We must have a change in our colonial policy. We must tell our colonies they must undertake their own defence. If they want soldiers they must either make them or pay for them." Lord Palmerston, the Prime Minister, was not interested in being thrifty. Thomas said of him, "I believe he conscientiously does his best for the good of the country, but still he is always for spending money, and is strongly in favour of keeping up our armaments. I believe it is his conscientious policy. I don't agree with it to a great extent."

After speaking for an hour and a half, he faced questions from the floor before a vote of confidence in him was moved by Alderman Ferguson: "That this meeting, having heard the very able address of Thomas Barnes, Esq., MP, in which he has described his Parliamentary conduct during the last session, desires heartily to express its satisfaction with the same; and while warmly thanking him for public services which are past, it extends to him cordial confidence for the future." It was seconded by Mr W. Thirlwind on behalf of the working men "because he believed Mr Barnes would do all he could for working men, to get them the suffrage. He believed distinctly and honestly, that a better representative England did not possess." A second resolution was carried: "That in view of the present state of the country, this meeting is of opinion that the national expenditure upon military and naval operations is extravagant in the extreme, and attended with the most pernicious results to the people, and it earnestly hopes that the Liberal members of the House of Commons will exert their influence to secure a large and permanent reduction of such expenditure." Presumably this was to be reported back to Parliament.[1]

Once back at Westminster, Thomas was kept busy with various deputations. On Saturday 28 February he was one of a group interested in the proposed Bristol Channel Docks who had an interview with the Right Honourable T. Milner Gibson at the Board of Trade. On the following Thursday he was part of a deputation from the Natal Central Railway Company who, accompanied by representatives of the Natal Land Company and the Nepal Cotton Company, met the

Duke of Newcastle at the Colonial Office. Shortly before this, on 22 January 1863, an announcement had appeared in *The Times* offering shares in a newly-formed company, the Cotton Plantation Company of Natal (Limited), naming Thomas as one of the eleven Directors. He was described as an MP, a member of the Council of the Cotton Supply Association and a Director of the Lancashire & Yorkshire Railway Company. Another of the Directors was the Bolton cotton spinner J. K. Cross. The company had been set up to buy land to grow cotton in the Colony of Natal. It had already made arrangements to buy some 130,000 acres of land, including 24,000 acres on the coast and intended employing Henry Milner, a former Member of the Legislative Council of Natal as their local manager.

On 12 April 1863 Thomas laid a foundation stone in Shrewsbury at the Abbey Foregate Church, having already donated £500 towards the purchase of the site. Two weeks later on 24 April he was back at Westminster as part of a deputation of civic leaders from Bolton, Bradford, Leicester and Halifax who met Sir George Grey at the Home Office.

That year, on 3 May, at a special church meeting, Thomas and David Ellerker were elected as the first deacons of Thomas's own church at The Quinta. On the day before this an announcement had appeared in *The Times* giving details of a new company, the Royal Sardinian Railway Company, naming Thomas as one of the five Directors in England and describing him as an MP and as a Director of the Lancashire & Yorkshire Railway Company. His fellow Directors were three men from London—Charles Bell, H. R. Grenfell and I. Leonino—and the MP John Pender. The Company's Council of Administration in Italy was composed of very grand names with its Honorary President General Count Alberto Della Marmora, two Marquises and a Deputy of the Italian Parliament, Signor Guiseppe Sanna-Sanna. This new company, guaranteed by the Italian Government, had bought the exclusive right to build a railway in Sardinia which was accompanied by guaranteed payment per kilometre of completed section of line. With the concession went the grant of a large area of freehold estate in Sardinia. It would appear that all did not go as well as anticipated with this company because three and a half years later on 1 December 1866 Thomas was part of a deputation together with H. R. Grenfell, Charles Bell, John Pender and Edward Langley representing the directors and shareholders of the Company who met Lord Stanley at the Foreign Office. They wanted Government help to redress wrongs suffered by the Company resulting from the Italian Government's non-fulfilment of the terms of their agreement.

In spite of the problems caused by the Cotton Famine Thomas was continuing to expand his business in Farnworth. The profits for the year 1862/63 of £9,591 were shared between Thomas and Thomas Paterson on the same basis as in the previous two years with Thomas Paterson receiving one-third. During the previous year two new offices had been built at a cost of £751, a new reservoir (later referred to as "Top Reservoir") had been constructed for £420, a new fly wheel installed at Lower Mill (£500) and a new iron safe bought for Higher Mill. There is a note in Bolton archives in Thomas's handwriting dated 30 June 1863 which describes the new offices as counting houses, each building measuring 46' 6" x 43' 6", a total of 223 square yards and incurring an annual ground rent of £1 17s 2d. Two items—"int. on offices £45" and "£25 for the reservoir"—suggest that the money had been borrowed at interest. Another note was: "increase rent for balances". The reservoir was an unevenly sided rectangle 245' (258') x 141' (185'), covering a total area of 4,554 square yards. Its ground rent came to £18 19s (rounded up to £19) in Thomas's calculations.

On 9 July 1863 Thomas spoke in the House of Commons to oppose the Augmentation of Benefits Bill which had come down from the House of Lords to receive its Second Reading. The aim of the bill was to authorize the sale of about 320 of the smallest livings in the Lord Chancellor's gift. Thomas objected very strongly to this and became involved here with religious controversy. He objected to the Bill because the principle of it was one which he thought was most dangerous and bad. "He believed it would be injurious to the Church of England as well as to the parishioners, because it would be injurious to religion, and because it sanctioned a practice which unfortunately prevailed to a great extent, but which was condemned by the almost universal voice of the Protestant Church. This Bill raised the question of buying and selling livings—and the House was now asked directly to sanction that practice of the Church of England, which was utterly opposed to the spirit of Christianity".[2] In spite of his efforts, the Bill received its Second Reading. For the next four years Thomas made no more speeches in Parliament.

He returned to The Quinta in the summer recess and on 28 July 1863 was on the Grand Jury at the Denbighshire Summer Assizes.

On Tuesday 4 August 1863 Halifax had a Royal visitor to open the new Town Hall. The royal party travelled by train on the Lancashire and Yorkshire Railway and Thomas, as one of the Directors, might have been with the Company Chairman and other Directors who travelled the last stretch of the journey in a gondola carriage attached to the front of the Royal Train. Because they had not informed the station superintendent in Halifax about the additional carriage, this gondola carriage was responsible for the train stopping twelve yards short of the specially erected platform. The Royal party had to clamber down and make their way along the platform and the dignitaries on the raised platform missed the show!

Another of Thomas's public commitments was the part he played in Farnworth's decision to set up its own Local Government. His nephew Alfred was a leading figure in this. At the meeting held on 25 August 1863 called by the ratepayers to consider and determine a resolution for the adoption of the Local Government Act 1858 within Farnworth, Thomas spoke in favour of Local Government as it would give them the cheapest form of government they could have.

In September 1863 Rev. John Dobson Riley, Quinta Chapel's first minister, resigned. He preached his farewell sermon on 27 September and at a separate meeting on 30 September an expression of satisfaction of his two years' service was proposed by William Porter and seconded by Thomas. One of Rev. Riley's last duties had been to attend the funeral at Low Hill Cemetery in Liverpool of Dr Raffles on 24 August 1863.

On 22 October 1863 Thomas sat as a magistrate when the Denbighshire Quarter Sessions were held in Wrexham Town Hall. An article in *The Bolton Chronicle* on 24 October 1863 reported that Thomas had presided at the annual tea meeting of Railway employees held in the Baths Assembly Rooms.

Rev. Riley was replaced by Rev. Thomas Davison from Crewe. He began his ministry on Sunday 6 November preaching in the morning from Psalm 71:16 ("With the mighty deeds of the Lord God I will come, I will praise thy righteousness, thine alone") and in the evening from the Second Letter of St Paul to the Thessalonians Chapter 3:1 ("Finally, brethren, pray for us, that the word of the Lord may speed on and triumph, as it did among you"). He continued in the post until he retired over twenty years later.

Another company which Thomas was involved with in the 1860s was the Diphwys Casson Slate Company (Limited) whose First General Meeting was held at the Company's offices, 10 Bridge Street, Westminster, on 15 January 1864. Thomas was Chairman of this company but was unavoidably absent at this important meeting which was chaired by the Deputy Chairman, Thomas Savin. (Mr Savin was later involved in the construction of a railway line for the Wrexham, Mold, and Connah's Quay Railway.) Thomas was probably in Farnworth at the time as he gave his annual speech to his constituents on 18 January. The Diphwys Casson Slate Company had been registered six months previously on 16 July 1863 and was required by law to hold a meeting within six months of this date. They obviously had only just managed to do this. The company had taken on a quarry which would need at least three years to develop. The article in *The North Wales Chronicle* contains detailed information about the state and problems of the quarry. In his absence, Thomas was re-elected as Chairman. I have not found any reports about the company for the next eight years until January 1875 when it won a case it had brought against the Ffestiniog Railway Company who had contravened the Traffic Act by trying to impose unfair conditions.

On 18 January 1864 Thomas again gave his annual address to his constituents. Again, Alderman Robert Heywood acted as Chairman. Thomas began by referring to the sufferings of the previous year caused by the Lancashire Cotton Famine. "The year that has passed is one which will be remembered by many for years to come,—such a year as has seldom been experienced in this country—a year of suffering, a year of want, yet a year of patient endurance and a year of noble fortitude; a year in which many have been called upon to experience very much the same suffering and distress as a besieged and beleaguered city where there has been a want of bread; and yet those sufferings have been borne with a magnanimity and fortitude, a patient endurance and a quiet order that have extracted the admiration not only of this country, but of the whole world." He acknowledged that Bolton had not suffered quite as much as other towns and hoped that the worst was now over. The state of Lancashire had been debated in Parliament and one of the measures passed, the Public Works Act, promised to bring great benefits to areas which needed new sewers, pavements, streets, to improve the health of the inhabitants. Bolton had already arranged to borrow a large amount of money to make a start on the work. Thomas showed a concern for the state of the poor, a concern which his nephew Alfred and later generations of the Barnes family shared. "We hardly know—and working men do not consider—the evil effects of living in damp houses and in undrained streets—they do not consider how much it affects their health and comfort, and how much loss of labour and time as well as personal suffering it occasions them, or they would take away the cause of all this." Thomas had also been against one solution suggested to ease the poverty in

Lancashire—emigration at the public expense. "To send thousands of people and throw them upon a strange land with not more money than will keep them for a month, with no work for many of them, and for some not even a covering for their heads, would be considered a desperate remedy for Lancashire, and little less than consigning two-thirds of them to death within twelve months."

He mentioned the recent royal wedding when Edward the Prince of Wales had married Alexandra of Denmark. In spite of all the poverty, Bolton managed to provide a memorial of the Royal Wedding for all the young people in the town. Thomas dared to report "That good lady has made very quick work of it, for she has already brought herself and her husband to Babbicombe Bay", a comment which was greeted with peals of laughter.

It had been a very quiet session when the Opposition did not even attempt to attack the Treasury benches. It was said "the Tories are in power, but the Whigs are in place". Thomas did not disagree. "Well, this to some extent is true, and describes the position of things. [... ...] How long this will last, I cannot say, but it is not generally the case that men are content to have the power without the pay and without patronage. [... ...] However, we know this—the house itself will not occupy very long; for if it go to the full extent of its legal life it will end next year, and then I suppose we shall have some sort of struggle and some sort of change, even if not before; and it will be most wonderful if all the elements of discord around us do not cause some split." Thomas's admiration for Gladstone, the Chancellor of the Exchequer, was unabated: "We have an excellent Chancellor of the Exchequer, who is, I believe, as anxious as any person here to bring down the expenditure of the country, and I believe he does all in his power for that purpose."

They had made little or no progress on the question of reducing the national expenditure or sorting out the Church rates question, and now another subject had been raised after lying dormant for many years—the question of the Irish Church. This was to dominate politics during the rest of Thomas's term in office. Thomas devoted a large part of his speech to the question and had done a great deal of work on it, providing statistics and examples to show the need "to remedy the evils which obviously are in existence at the present time". After being in existence for two hundred years, the Act of Uniformity had been brought up again—"a stumbling block and rock of offence for years past, and destined to be one in years to come, unless something be done, which many excellent Churchmen are anxious to effect, and I wish them success with all my heart".

Nothing had been done about Reform. Thomas gave a very descriptive metaphor: "This question of Reform seems to have gone to sleep; both in the House of Commons and out of it; in fact, the ministers say that it is a vessel that is becalmed: the man at the helm—the master of the vessel—sailed out in this fine vessel of Reform in 1859. He got into deep water, and there he cast anchor and folded his sails and says 'There is no breeze on the sail; we must wait until there is a breeze; the vessel cannot go without wind, as you know; we cannot turn a windmill without a pair of bellows'. They are waiting for a storm, and there must be something like a hurricane outside before the vessel will move again." He did believe that Palmerston intended doing something about it—but not yet, and only if the country pressurized him to do it.

In the budget the Chancellor had taken 2d off income tax and 5d off tea, and a little off tobacco. Thomas took this opportunity to set out his views on tobacco: "I am no friend to smokers, and especially to young men indulging in this practice. I could excuse our Chairman smoking, though he is not old; he is yet young—young in feeling, young in thought, young in judgement, and I hope he will be young and green for ever. But he is past fifty, and when a man gets to that age, especially if he is a working man, I can excuse him smoking; but I should like him to have a bit of good tobacco; and I don't see how he can have it when there is such a heavy duty on as at present. I believe there is an immense amount of smuggling in some way or other, and that there is a great deal of stuff put into pipes and smoked which was never grown as tobacco leaf. I only speak that as report, as I happen to be one of very few who never had a lighted cigar in my mouth, and never mean to have; for I learnt when young a good maxim, and that is, 'Never beget a want'. Take care of that—if you never learn to want it, you will never need it; and it will apply to many other things as well as tobacco; and you will never want it in after life."

Thomas had also become involved with a bill to stop the sale of alcohol on Sundays. He voted for the bill to pass but it was defeated by a huge majority. He believed he was acting in accordance with the wishes of his constituents as they had sent petitions to Parliament supporting the bill. When he faced questions at the end of his speech he was asked about a proposed bill which was to play an important part in the squabbles of the Liberals in Bolton for the next few years.

This was a bill due to be introduced by Mr Lawson MP for Carlisle, called the Permissive Bill and put forward by the United Kingdom Alliance for the Suppression of the Liquor Traffic. It would give the ratepayers the power to prevent or increase the number of public houses in their area. Thomas denied any knowledge of the bill but it was a question which had many repercussions for him over the next few years.

New sources of cotton were needed. Already it was coming from all over the world—Thomas mentioned Egypt, Turkey, Greece, Italy, Algiers, Queensland in Australia, Natal in South Africa and other colonies. Great efforts were being made in the West Indies, and more cotton was also coming from India. However, he was disappointed with India. In his speech in 1862 he had had great hopes of Indian cotton but he now had to report: "With such capacity to grow cotton, the system of rascality and dishonesty that is practised there has resulted in the cotton produced being of a description which nobody wants".

At last he told his constituents that he had decided to experiment with growing cotton in the West Indies and in December 1862 had bought a 200–acre sugar plantation which had been lying waste for ten or twelve years. He had employed an agent, Reverend Jones, to take charge of it and within six months 130 acres had been planted. He was hopeful that the venture would be successful and had brought some samples of his cotton to the meeting. "I entered upon the speculation, if I may so term it, in the first instance from a pressure on my own mind that we as cotton users had not done our duty to obtain cotton, the production of free labour, as in opposition to slavery. I knew nobody that had ever made the attempt, and in conversation with others I found the universal objection, 'It won't pay, and if you go into it you will lose your money', and that seemed to be the one great obstacle in the way of any free labour cotton. We want cotton, Sir, but we want it also as the result of free labour. I do not want to see us return again to slave labour, nor to countries where slavery exists. [... ...] I felt anxious to keep my own conscience clear in the matter, and I have bought property in Jamaica, and employ a person who has been resident there for twenty years as my agent. He enters into all my views on the subject of slavery; and he is anxious to raise free labour in opposition to slavery; he believes with me that free labour is cheaper than slavery, and that it is better economy to use free labour than slave labour. I bought the estate, and he has been working it. There has been great labour attending it. First we had to fence it round; it was covered over with brushwood and trees, and these had to be cut down or destroyed; and then we had to prepare the earth for the seed. He did all this with the spade, for it is impossible to use a plough. All this incurred an amount of labour that startled me when I heard so much about the negroes—that they would not work for the world. They tell you that these black negroes in the West Indies won't work, that they grow in their little plots of land their potatoes, etc., that they just dig a little bit, and then lie down and bask in the sun all the day, and that they want nothing and won't work, not even for money. This was a serious objection, but we had to prove it. There are 200 acres of land, and this cannot be fenced, cleared of trees and rubbish, and planted with shrubs eight feet apart, without an immense amount of labour. In December 1862 my agent told the people what he was going to do; and 32 men offered themselves next week; in the next fortnight, 50 offered themselves; and gradually the number rose up until he had in men, women, and children, 230 persons employed of those who it was said would not work. There is a secret about these men not working; we have given them a bad character, and they are a maligned and slandered people. They have always been willing to work for those that pay them, and the reason why they have not worked before is either that they have received no pay, or have been paid in meal and malt instead of money. My agent paid them week by week and always in money, which is not generally done, for the general rule is to pay when you can—and some can't pay often—and sometimes they have no payment for many months, until it becomes a question as to how much is owing; then they go before the magistrates. And so the slave has a system of self-defence, and he won't work for those who won't pay him regularly, and in money. I have observed that we paid regularly; and the result is we have been blessed with labour, and have had to turn as many as 100 away in one week because we could not find employment for them. That is a gratifying circumstance to state about these black people. They are willing to work if you pay them regularly, and on a system; and there is no lack of labour for lack of willingness to work. The young women there are just as fond of fine dresses as young women here; and they are quite as willing to work for those who will find them the means of obtaining them. The result of twelve months' labour has been the enclosing, cultivating, and planting of 210 acres of cotton; and my agent has sent me some of that cotton over, part of which I have brought to the hall with me, and shall be happy to show it to anyone at the close of the meeting. The cotton speaks for itself. But now comes the question—Will it pay? Ah! There is the rub—will it pay? We know it will not do to grow cotton upon benevolent principles, or upon generosity principles. It must be grown on commercial principles. I can hardly tell you now whether it will pay or not; but I can tell you next year. As far as I can judge now, I believe I shall be satisfied with the result of the speculation. If what the agent tells me is true, it will pay. It astonishes me from the facts given to me that our West India islands can all this time have been growing sugar when they have the best land in the world for growing cotton, and have never tried to grow cotton since they gave it up before. I ought to tell you that some 30 or 40 years ago, cotton was grown in the West Indies; but heavy duties were imposed to protect sugar, which made it so profitable, that everybody pulled up their cotton and substituted sugar. Then came Messrs Bright and Cobden, who repealed the tariff, and sugar at once came down to its former level; it would not pay then, and many people gave up their estates; the estate that I have bought is one of them; and it had been for 10 or 12 years lying in a state of wildness, doing nothing whatever;—it once grew sugar,—it now grows cotton. Even if cotton comes down to its ordinary price, I believe the result will be that it will pay better to grow cotton than sugar. Although it may not pay me, if I can only be the means of leading people to grow cotton in any one place, and if it is found to pay—though I get nothing—yet if I should be instrumental in growing cotton by free labour, I shall be satisfied. I hope that this allusion to my own affairs will be taken as intended—as an instance to show that cotton may be grown in places where it has been thought impossible to grow it, that it may be grown with benefit, and that those people who have been slandered and maligned are not deserving of the epithets which have been heaped upon them."[3] Later in his speech he mentioned that he could hire an able-bodied black man in Jamaica for 1s 3d a day—much less than the one guinea a week it cost to keep a slave. It was this part of his speech which found its way into other papers, even as far away as Jamaica. On 20 February 1864 *Harper's Weekly*, the most popular illustrated newspaper of the Civil War years, reported under the heading 'Common Sense: "Mr Thomas Barnes, a member of the British Parliament, lately made a speech to his constituents, in which he said a great many sensible things. One of them is particularly applicable to us at this time. In December 1862 he bought 200 acres of land in Jamaica and confided it to an agent who believed in freedom for the cultivation of cotton. He paid cash wages, and the first week 50 negroes applied for work, next week 50 more, then 230. They worked most willingly, so much so that frequently a hundred applicants were turned away, and in one year they had cleared, fenced and planted

210 acres of cotton, of which Mr Barnes laid samples upon the table before him." The article ended by quoting from a London paper: "This", said *The London Spectator* "is practical common sense, but it is odd that such an illustration should be necessary to convince an English audience that a negro, like every body else, works hard whenever it is made worth his while. Nobody ever saw an Englishman working until that point had been made."

Thomas's optimism was justified in the next few months after his speech to his constituents. An article appeared in *The Liverpool Mercury* on 20 May 1864 giving an assessment of the success or lack of success of the cotton-growing experiments in Jamaica. Apparently a letter in a morning paper in March 1862 had described the financial losses resulting from some failures in the cotton crops in Jamaica and had slowed down the whole experiment. However, in May 1864 things were much brighter and good quality cotton was now being produced. The article used Thomas as an example: "On an estate in Clarendon owned by Mr Thomas Barnes, MP for Bolton, 18,000 lb of cotton in the seed have already been picked, or about 5,000 lb of clean cotton. Some of this cotton has been sold at Liverpool at 3s 8d a pound." This price was higher than the price for cotton from other estates. Cotton from Mr Weguelin's Greenwall estate was selling at an average of 2s 9d a pound. The Jamaica Cotton Company which was also growing cotton in the east of the island had already picked 60,000 lb of seed cotton in May 1864. They had only sold nine bags as yet which fetched 2s 11d and 3s a pound. This company was experimenting with all kinds of cotton seeds and had just had some Peruvian cotton sent to England from their estate in Jamaica which had been valued at 4s per pound.

Various types of cotton were now being grown in Jamaica ranging from the choicest Sea Island cotton, the type grown in America, to the local Jamaican green seed cotton collected on the island. The Lancashire cotton spinners, in particular, were keen to obtain the Sea Island cotton and both Thomas and the Jamaica Cotton Company had concentrated on this type. However, by May 1864 the Jamaica Cotton Company was having difficulty with the Sea Island cotton. They discovered that it was not a perennial and only produced tender plants which did not thrive either in the extreme heat or the heavy rains of the Jamaica seasons. They had lost many acres of Sea Island cotton and had had to replant with the perennial green seed cotton native to Jamaica, a fine and long-stapled variety. They were now learning the best way to grow it and were now getting high prices for it in the English markets. By December 1864 the problems with Sea Island cotton were only too apparent. At the annual meeting of the Jamaica Cotton Company Stephen Bourne was asked whether their attempt to grow Sea Island cotton had been a complete failure. He had to admit that a great many Sea Island cotton shrubs had failed but said it had not been a total disaster as had been the case on Thomas Barnes's and the Glasgow Cotton Company's estates in Clarendon. A letter to the Editor of *The Standard* said that Thomas's agent, Reverend Jones, was not to blame. From the first he "went economically to work, and, if success had been possible, was the person most likely to have achieved it; but that the soil and climate were not favourable to the growth and production of cotton." In a follow-up letter Stephen Bourne said that his son, Alfred, had visited both Mr Barnes's and the Glasgow Company's estates, and had found that both were well-managed estates, and promised success.

In 1864 Thomas's views on the American War had not changed—Britain had to keep out of it even if the sympathies in the House of Commons were divided. "It is our best policy to have nothing to do with the war, but leave it in the hands of Him who controlleth the passions of mankind. I should rejoice to see it closed, and I would not quarrel with on whatever terms it was settled if I could only see the extinction of slavery—that secured, I should rejoice to see it closed upon any terms which the parties might wish to adopt."

He also mentioned the unrest in Europe—in Poland, Hungary, Italy, Schleswig and Holstein. "Denmark, with 2,000,000, was going against Germany with 40,000,000, and, as usual, he supposed England was going to sympathise with the little man, especially if he showed plenty of pluck." He hoped Britain would remain neutral in this conflict, too. He summed up his views: "Upon all such questions as these, I say our policy should be that of neutrality. We are surrounded with dangerous elements on every side, and I am anxious to see old England riding through the storm self-defended, protected by neutrality, with all our rigging right, looking upon the storm itself, but taking no part in it, preparing herself for the future and reserving all her strength for better times. I believe those times are before us, and that if we only keep at peace with all the earth, we shall have before us a brighter and more prosperous time than England has ever yet seen. Let us obtain a supply of that article necessary for the industry of our people, and having that, and harbouring our resources and maintaining peace, we may say old England is the most prosperous country on the face of the earth."

This meeting ended, like the two previous ones, with general approval of Thomas's conduct in Parliament in the previous year. "This meeting having heard the very able address of Thomas Barnes, Esq., MP, in which he has described his Parliamentary conduct during the last session, desires heartily to express its satisfaction with the same, and while warmly thanking him for public services which are past, it extends to him cordial confidence for the future."

At the meeting William Cross from Farnworth asked Thomas if he would be willing to take part in a Cotton Supply Conference in London, if one was called during the next Parliamentary session to consider how, when, and where they could get the best and the largest supply of cotton. He believed the subject was now being considered by several influential men in London. Thomas replied that he would be perfectly willing to join in a conference of that kind.

On the day after the annual address, Thomas's name appeared in *The Times* in a long list of influential people who had written on 16 January to Sir George Grey, the Governor of New Zealand, to express their concern about the problems caused by the war with the Maoris. The letter urged the Governor to try to end the war by negotiation and to respond to any offers of peace the natives might make. The suggestion to punish the Maoris by confiscating their lands horrified the writers of the letter, fearing that this might see the extinction of the Maori race.

On 25 March 1864 Thomas was unfit to attend an inaugural tea party and public meeting at the Temperance Hall to mark the opening of a Working Men's Club in Bolton. He had sent a letter and a telegram apologising for his absence. He was "confined to his house by indisposition".

On Good Friday 1864 Thomas presided at a tea meeting held in the Quinta Congregational Church for the parents of the children at the Sunday School to meet the teachers and other members of the Church. His son James Richardson was there together with W. Porter, D. Ellerker, J. Williams, J. Thomas, J. Broughall, and a Sunday School teacher, Mr J. Winter. James Richardson played a prominent part at this event, giving a speech about the importance of "Praise", offering to employ a singing teacher to improve the choir, and playing the harmonium.

Thomas wrote from The Quinta on 17 May 1864 to apologize for not being able to attend a Grand Review of the Prince of Wales Fire Brigade in Wrexham on 24 May because of a previous engagement. With his usual humour and as Chairman of a Fire Insurance Company he wrote: "I wish that you may be in every way successful, provided always that there is no real fire to extinguish."

The year 1863/64 was a bad year for the business in Farnworth and profits fell to just £1,011. Thomas received £674 1s 3d of this and Thomas Paterson his one-third share of £337 6s 7d. James Richardson Barnes again received an allowance from his father's account and interest on his capital. He also drew £1,068 9s 1d from the Petty Cash account plus £80 which was paid for the rent of his house. Presumably he had a house in Farnworth before his marriage in October 1864. In spite of the problems caused by the economic conditions more work had been done to the mills including £120 spent on a new steam engine hall. A note "Taken out" might mean that the steam engine had been moved out of the main building to its own building. Another expensive new fly wheel had been installed, this one at Higher Mill at a cost of £860, a shed at Higher Mill had been flagged (£120), additional buildings had cost £64 15s and £30 had been spent on the flue to the chimney at Dixon Green. This was the last time that Thomas Paterson's name appeared in the stocktaking accounts as a partner even though he continued to be listed as one of the four men providing the firm's capital. During the following year Joseph Winter replaced Thomas Paterson as a partner in the business.

In August 1864 Thomas became involved in another business scheme which was announced in *The Wrexham Weekly Advertiser* on 13 August 1864. Thomas headed the list of five Directors of a Lead Mining Company, the Pont Du and Waenlas Mining Company Ltd, incorporated under the Companies Act 1862, whereby the liability of each shareholder was limited to the amount of his shares. Two lead mines, Pont Du Mine and Waenlas Mine, held under lease from the Marquis of Westminster, which had been held under separate leases and worked by separate proprietors until then, were to be united in one newly granted 21–year lease and carried on under one management. £30,000 capital was to be raised in 6,000 shares of £5 each. The Company had agreed on a purchase price of £7,962 plus 1,480 fully paid-up shares. This covered the mines and the plant, the buildings and the machinery. In a very long description of the size of the ore deposits "in the heart of the richest lead districts in the kingdom", the potential of the mines was set out. At least £25,000 had already been spent in driving the adit levels and doing other necessary works at Waenlas. Several shafts had been sunk. There were also two pumping engines, together with a smith's shop, commodious offices and other buildings, and the shafts at both mines had been well-timbered and would require no more than a moderate outlay to put them in thorough repair. The notice concluded: "The prospects of these mines must be considered encouraging. Large deposits of ore are known to be left in the old workings of Pont Du." I do not know how successful this enterprise was, but when a list of the joint stock companies regulated by the Limited Liability Act which had been set up in the two years ending October 1866 in Shropshire and North Wales appeared in *The Wrexham Weekly Advertiser* on 3 November 1866 the Pont Du and Waenlas Mining Company appeared in the list together with Thomas's other enterprise, the Quinta colliery.

In the week ending Saturday 8 October 1864 Thomas attended the Autumnal meeting of the Shropshire Association of Independent Churches held at Whitchurch and as Chairman of the Association chaired the evening meeting. During the year he had laid a foundation stone at City Road Presbyterian Church in Chester.

Notes

1. *The Bolton Chronicle* [Bolton Archives and Social Studies]
2. Speeches in Hansard (hansard.millbanksystems.com)
3. *Bolton Chronicle* [Bolton Archives and Social Studies]

Opening of Farnworth Park

CHAPTER 10

October 1864–June 1865

The opening of Farnworth Park. James Richardson's marriage.
The aftermath of the Cotton Famine.

When a Local Board for Farnworth was elected in 1863 the town had a public body which was able to accept the gift of the park. The President of the Local Board was Thomas's nephew Alfred Barnes. On behalf of his uncle he negotiated the transfer of the Park to the care and keeping of the Board. This was one of the first matters which the newly-formed Board had to deal with and they were not sure about their powers. They had to ask Sir George Grey whether, under the Public Health Act, they could accept and maintain the Park. Apparently, under the 74th Section of the Act they did have the power to defray the cost of the Park out of the general District Rate. So, on 4 July 1864 Farnworth Local Board accepted the Park on Birch Hall Estate presented by Thomas Barnes "for the free use of the inhabitants of Farnworth for ever". This is repeated on the inscription on the monument in the Park: "In commemoration of my son's coming of age and in memory of his grandfather I present and dedicate this Park to the people of Farnworth for their benefit for ever". The conditions in the transfer deed are interesting: "Dancing in the Park is strictly prohibited; the sale of any kind of intoxicating liquors in or connected with the Park is forbidden, and there is not to be preaching, lecturing, or public meetings therein." Thomas objected to some kinds of games, such as bowling as he thought they "were likely to be less productive of good than injury". Apparently some sort of compromise was eventually reached on this point. Thomas said all he required was that "such conditions and stipulations should be made as would secure to the public the use of the park, in quiet enjoyment, free from nuisances and from misappropriation and abuse, and the maintenance of the park in an efficient manner".

The day originally chosen for the official opening of the Park was Wednesday 21 September 1864 but when W. E. Gladstone, the

Chancellor of the Exchequer and the Leader of the Liberal Party, agreed to attend the inauguration ceremony, the opening was postponed until 12 October. Gladstone had a prior engagement—with Queen Victoria at Balmoral. On 11 October Gladstone visited Bolton before opening Farnworth Park the following day. Thomas and Colonel Gray, Bolton's other MP, were amongst the people who met Gladstone at Bolton station just before five-thirty in the afternoon. They accompanied him to the Free Library which had been opened in 1843 and now had 21,000 books, and to the Market Hall, before he made his speech in the Temperance Hall. Thomas seconded the vote of thanks. Mrs Gladstone went straight to Green Bank for the dinner party in the evening. In Bolton Archives is a note sent on 17 September 1864 by Thomas's nephew, Alfred Barnes of Green Bank, to Robert Heywood inviting him to a dinner at his house on the evening of Tuesday 11 October to meet Mr Gladstone. There was a menu attached to the invitation.

October 11 1864

Menu

Vins

MILK
PUNCH

MADEIRA

SHERRY

STEINBERGER
CABINET
(*Die Braut*)
1857

CHAMPAGNE

POTAGES

Clear Turtle.   À la Reine.

POISSONS

Turbot and Lobster Sauce.   Red Mullet à l'Italien.

ENTRÉES

Ris de Veau piqué à la Turque.

Petits Croustades de Beurre aux Huîtres.   Filets de Lièvre à L'Ancienne.

Côtelettes de Pigeons à la Lucullus

RELEVÉS

Haunch of Venison.   Filet de Beef au Madère.

Turkey à la Financière.   Ham aux Haricots Verts.

GIBIER

Pheasants.   Grouse.

	ENTREMETS SUCRÉS
GRAND VIN (*Chateau Lafitte*) 1846	Gelée en Macedoine. Croqu'en Bouche à la Historie.
	Crême d'Abricot en Mosaïque. Suprême de Poires. Genois aux Fruits.
	Gelée de Madère. Gâteaux à la Cerito.
PORT 1820	Meringues à la Chantilly. Boudin à la Parisienne.
	Boudin Glacé à la Victoria, &c.
	DESSERT
𝕷iqueurs ____	Grapes. Pine Apples. Peaches. Pears. Apples.
COFFEE, &c.	Nuts, &c.[1]
	★ ★ ★ ★ ★

The opening of the Park was a very grand occasion indeed. From early in the morning cannons boomed and bells rang at St John's Church. It was estimated that there were a hundred thousand people there. Newspaper reports captured the atmosphere. This one from *The Border Counties Advertiser* describes the scene in very flowery prose: "The people of Farnworth did their part worthily and zealously. The display of bunting was most abundant, the quantity of evergreens used in the decoration and devices must have covered acres of shrubbery ground, gardens had been stripped of their remaining autumn flowers, and where the supply of these fell short, thousands of artificial ones supplemented them. Market Street and other main thoroughfares were crossed at frequent intervals by lines of streamers raised on ornamental poles, and the front of almost every house in the same quarters was decorated with more or less display according to means or taste. The weather was fine, but not sunny; at times the sun promised to break through his leaden shroud and illuminate the scene with his rays, but the expectation was transient. Nothing, however, daunted the vast multitudes bent on the day's enjoyment. From every quarter they poured into the place by rail, bus, private vehicle, and walking, and by half-past nine o'clock Market Street had become so thronged as to be almost impassable."

A report in *The Oswestry Advertiser and Montgomeryshire Mercury* ran: "The town, the township, and 'the country side' kept holiday. There were decorations, procession, ceremony, oration, banquet, attempted balloon ascent, evening entertainments, illuminations, fireworks, and fine weather. Nearly all the people of Farnworth, who could either walk or afford to ride, must have joined the procession, and eight or nine times the population of the township came from Bolton, which suspended business, and from the places surrounding Farnworth, to line the streets of the four-mile route which the procession traversed. Such a demonstration, for numbers, for organisation, for effective display, astonished even those who knew what Lancashire can do on such occasions. The chief ground of surprise was that the demonstration seemed so disproportionate to the size, fame, and population of the straggling, overgrown village, which has enjoyed local self-government only about twelve months. Perhaps its straggling character to some extent accounted for this by giving it so many neighbours to participate in the event."

This reporter did see a funny side to it all: "The decorations of the town were as characteristic of the locality as the procession and the gathering of spectators. The taste and liberality of a street did not exhaust itself upon a single device, nor was any continuity of decoration effected by neighbourly co-operation, except so far as streets were spanned by slender arches of evergreens, strings of streamers suspended from windows, chains of coloured paper, festoons of foliage and pendant crowns of flimsy flowers, and mottoes of welcome and praise, and good wishes for the guest of the day. But from countless windows and chimney stacks there fluttered flags and banners of every description; doors, windows, and balconies were ornamented with pictorial and floral devices; and the successive indications of individual enthusiasm, surmounting windows which were the frames of living pictures, and streets lined with spectators, were sufficiently connected to form one effective aggregate demonstration."

The report in *The Farnworth Observer* on Saturday 15 October was the most detailed of all. It described each street decoration along the circular route of the procession from the Local Board Office in Darley Street to the park entrance at Dixon Green. Mr Leach of Farnworth had created a particularly fine decoration over the entrance to Alfred Barnes's house, Green Bank, where Mr and Mrs Gladstone were to be entertained. It was a shield representing the Farnworth coat of arms with batons of flags and streamers to represent England, Ireland, Scotland and Wales. Barnes's new mill had a square ornamental porch at its door with the words "They that look after others' good, their own will follow". Its verdict on the decorations was that they were "light and beautiful, rather than substantial and gorgeous".

The day was to start with a procession at ten o'clock. There were ten separate venues for the various groups and half an hour had been allowed for them to assemble. That was an impossibility—the procession was not in marching order until eleven o'clock, an hour late. And what a procession it was! It was headed by an advance guard of yeomanry on horseback and The 27 Rifles with their band. Then came an unbroken line of nearly fifty carriages. In thirty-five were magistrates, the Bolton Corporation and Guardians, the Directors of the Farnworth and Kersley Gas Company, the Overseers of Farnworth, Kersley, and Little Lever, and the Farnworth Local Board. The carriage with the Chairman Alfred Barnes and Samuel Seddon of Lytham was followed by the carriage carrying Thomas and his wife and Mr and Mrs Gladstone. Then followed the carriages of the High Sheriff (Sir J. P. Kay-Shuttleworth), the Earl of Ellesmere, the Honourable Algernon Egerton, Lt-Col. Gray MP, Mr T. Bazley MP, Mr John Cheetham, and Mr James Richardson Barnes and Mr J. F. Cheetham, and in another carriage was Mr Wilfred Lawson MP. Mr and Mrs Blacklock of Hopefield, Pendleton, travelled with John Cheetham. Two representatives had come from the Quinta area— John Minshall from Oswestry and Anthony Dillon of Wrexham, the Secretary of the Welsh Provincial Insurance Company of which Thomas was the Chairman. Other carriages held William Hinmers and Thomas's two brothers-in-law Thomas Paterson and William Haslam. The carriages were followed by clergymen, ministers, and gentlemen on foot. After them came the Sunday School classes, with name-flags, banners, mottoes, and bands; and these formed by far the longest part of the procession. There were at least 4,856 children and their teachers taking part.

The reporter from *The Oswestry Advertiser and Montgomeryshire Mercury* was obviously not used to Lancashire customs: "The marching of the schools was not characterised by that compactness and regularity which distinguish school processions in towns in Whit-week. It could not fail to strike anyone who watched this part of the procession that the Sunday schools of the neighbourhood retain either as scholars or friends a very large number of adults of both sexes. The number of young men who walked as scholars was large; still larger was the proportion of young women; and, what seemed most extraordinary, numbers of middle-aged and probably married women walked, apparently as classes, with some of the schools, and evidently did so with the feeling that that they enjoyed a privilege and discharged a duty."

The procession continued. There were several wagon loads of children who were too young to walk, "all in the charge of men and women; and the vaulted ribs of the wagons were encircled with evergreens and paper flowers, whilst youthful postilions, in gaily coloured caps, smocks, and trousers, bestrode the leading horses, to the envy of all the other little boys who saw them." Towards the end of this section the procession was cut into two with the Roman Catholic schools being a considerable distance behind the rest.

The Farnworth Observer named each Sunday School and gave exact numbers in each procession. There were three Congregational Sunday Schools—Albert Road, Little Lever and Farnworth and Kersley Congregational Sunday School which was by far the largest with 808 people involved. James Newhouse, one of the managers at Barnes's mill and a relative of mine on my mother's side of the family, walked at the head of the 274 males, behind Rev. Handford of Bolton and together with Samuel Winter and J. B. Kay. The infants followed— 173 of them—in four wagons lent by Messrs T. Barnes & Co. and Mr Thomas Raynor who was driving one of the wagons himself. Alfred Barnes, one of the superintendents, had provided new banners with the arms of the new Farnworth Local Board "Be just, and fear not". Luke Boardman led a procession of 3,500 children from his Ragged School, an organisational feat for which he thanked his helpers in the Saturday paper.

The schools were followed by the Friendly Societies and five bands. There were Oddfellows, Gardeners, and Shepherds, and their banners, dresses, and insignia were to the spectators the most amusing part of the procession. "There was Eve tempting Adam, not merely on canvas, but actually as a *tableau vivant*; and six ancient shepherds, male and female, in patriarchal habit and holding pastoral crooks, created a little more sensation than a juvenile shepherd in a round crowned, very broad, circular-brimmed white hat." The huge procession ended with some trade societies carrying their emblems, and with one or two wagons carrying working models of machinery.

Right at the end were two neatly-decorated wagons containing 50 boys and 50 girls from the workhouse. The wagons belonged to William Haslam of Burnden Chemical Works who was Thomas's brother-in-law and one of the invited guests. Amongst others in a carriage with Mr Greenhalgh, the Governor of the workhouse, was Mr John Haslam of Bolton, probably William Haslam's younger brother.

The report in *The Oswestry Advertiser and Montgomeryshire Mercury* gave a detailed description of the park itself: "It was one o'clock before the procession reached the park—an irregular and indented oval-shaped plot of land, twelve acres in extent. Its east end is separated by a wall from the Manchester and Bolton Road. The Albert Road and Park Road, containing one of Messrs Barnes's mills, also that of Messrs Wallwork and Co. and the Grammar School constitute its northern and western boundary. On the south it is bounded by cottages, the gas works, and the Wellington Road. Entering it from the Manchester Road, asphalted footpaths lead right and left round a grass plot, and on the left there is an inviting valley. The paths meet again, and there is a broad central path through the park to a slope at the western extremity. The terrace gives a view of the whole park, and, on a clear day, of the country for miles beyond. On the south side is a lake, crossed by two bridges, with fowls, including swans (which have been presented) floating on its surface. There is an island upon which an artificial crocodile is endeavouring to land in order to devour an affrighted animal at the water's edge. From a rocky base in another part of the lake there springs a fountain, which was in full play on Wednesday. There are several seats round the lake, and in one or two places the park is ornamented by voluntary contributions of vases, from local residents; and in time, the example of the donors will be followed, and the park embellished by gifts of sculpture and other suitable objects."

The writer of one of the articles does sound as if he found the whole thing amusing, rather than awe-inspiring: "Had [the procession] been well marshalled, it might perhaps have passed a given spot in little more than half an hour, but, divided as it was, it took more than three-quarters of an hour to turn a corner that was not crowded, and where there was no impediment to progress save the startling of horses by amateur discharges of artillery, at the Kersley Moor toll-bar."

After the procession the children returned to the assembly points for refreshments which had been provided by the Local Board at the cost of 3d per head. This might sound generous but the lavish meal provided for the guests in the marquee after the ceremony cost 7s 6d. per head! The Independent School from Little Lever assembled for refreshments in Queen Street Seminary.

Even though Gladstone should have been the chief attraction, he failed to make the impression he might have expected: "It cannot be said that Mr Gladstone received an ovation in the sense in which the word would be understood of a reception in Manchester or the metropolis. The reason of this is simply that he was undistinguished and unrecognisable except by those who knew his features, and the carriage in which he rode passed many points without the spectators knowing at the time that they had seen Mr Gladstone. Sometimes there was a kind of half-cheer, prompted by enthusiasm mingled with doubt; but when a confident cheer was led by anyone who knew the Chancellor of the Exchequer, then it was taken up heartily and was duly acknowledged by Mr and Mrs Gladstone."

Nevertheless, the occasion was a real showpiece for Liberal politics. It attracted many distinguished people who came to hear Gladstone's speech. Thomas had even invited Richard Cobden who did not attend but did send a congratulatory letter which Thomas read out:

Midhurst, 14 September 1864

My dear Mr Barnes,

I am under an interdict which precludes me from attending any public meetings except those of the House of Commons and my own constituents, and I have pleaded this rule in so many quarters, that I could not without falsifying myself make an exception in your case; otherwise I need not say how gladly I should accept the invitation to be present at the ceremony of the presentation of a public park to the people of Farnworth. I have a very strong opinion in favour of the mode in which you have determined to indulge your public-spirited munificence towards your less affluent neighbours. I do not know how you could render a greater service to the health, happiness, and civilisation of future generations of a manufacturing town than in now rescuing from the hands of the builder and preserving for all time a plot of ground for the purpose of affording free exercise and fresh air to all classes of its inhabitants. To miss the acquisition of a park for our rapidly increasing town populations now might render it almost impossible at a future time, and hence the invaluable opportuneness of your liberality. I am glad that Mr Gladstone has promised to be present at the ceremonial. Personally, I know you shrink from any public glorification, but it is well that attention should be drawn to this interesting proceeding, if for no other reason because it may suggest to other wealthy and benevolent men to do likewise.

Believe me,

Yours very truly,

Rd. Cobden

Thos. Barnes Esq. MP

Gladstone's speech at the opening of Farnworth Park included a tribute to Thomas's philanthropy, which he described as an example of the new relations which had developed between employers and workers. By giving the land in what he called 'this busy hive of industry' for the 'rest and repose for the wearied limbs and exhausted minds of men', Thomas had performed a duty 'worthy to rank with all the efforts of the wisest philanthropists'. At the banquet held after the opening ceremony Thomas explained why he had decided to present the park to the town and provide an open green space for the people. "I have been for a long time impressed with the importance of reserving some portion of what were once green fields from, as Mr Cobden says, 'the hands of the builder', and keeping it as an open space or plot of land, where not only might be met green fields, but that reminiscences of these once beautiful flower-gardens, which I have seen in some parts of this township, might be preserved. I have done this; and I feel most, because I believed that it would have an improving bearing not only upon the physical but also upon the mental, and I believe indirectly upon the spiritual welfare of the masses of people who should enjoy it. [... ...] It appeared to me it was desirable now, if ever, some portion of land should be retained, and devoted to the object for which this park is devoted. The question was, who is to do it, and how is it to be done? I felt quite sure there was not ability to do it by public subscription, at least not in a short time. We had, no doubt, public spirit which would have done it in time, but it would have required time, and probably a whole generation might have passed away before this could have been accomplished by public subscription. In the meantime probably every inch of land which will now be reserved would be covered with buildings, and then the park would be placed at the outskirts of the population. I had myself become possessed of this piece of land to devote to that purpose. I fully knew that, in the midst of streets as it is, I could soon have covered it with buildings, and so have enriched myself, or I could devote it to the public, and confer a benefit on the poor, far greater than riches of any kind; and being deeply impressed with the importance, directly and indirectly, with the comfort as well as the physical condition of the people living in this neighbourhood, I resolved that it should not be any further built upon; that it should be reserved, at least that portion which has been marked out, for this purpose. And I have done this with the view that it will be found to contribute materially to the well-being of the people of this district. It will have, I trust, a tendency to elevate their moral conduct; it will improve their physical life; it will, I hope, benefit them morally. I trust that here working men may have an opportunity of walking with their wives and families on the evenings of summer days, and perhaps also on Sundays and days of rest, breathing as much fresh air as this smoky atmosphere can afford. I trust here to have the pleasure also of seeing young children amusing themselves with those games which children delight in, and which they may enjoy in perfect security. I hope here the sick and the feeble may be enabled to come in quietness and rest, and either rest themselves or find that gentle refreshment in exercise which a quiet place of this kind is calculated to give; and I trust that old and young—all classes of the community— will find that they do derive some advantage from the possession of a park which I consecrate to their service. I do it thankfully—thankful, that if I have had an opportunity of doing it, and if it does contribute to the happiness of the working-man, if it increases his health, if it promotes his convenience and his long life, then I shall myself be perfectly satisfied, feeling that the object which I have had in view has been fully accomplished."

The banquet for some 700 guests was described in detail in *The Farnworth Observer*. Messrs Jennison had erected a large marquee on the terrace at the west end of the park and had installed an oven, state-of-the-art boiling equipment, and even a bakehouse to prepare all the food on site. The arrangements and the preparation of the food "reflected the greatest praise upon the skill and enterprise of Messrs Jennison", but the same could not be said of the service which was very patchy. "So far as we could see, the provisions, as well as the waiters, were somewhat irregularly distributed. Whilst one table would seem loaded with all the good things of this life, with an abundance of prim-looking waiters ready to administer to the dictates of a keen and longing appetite, others could seem to be almost wholly destitute of these important *desiderata* to the requirements and comfort of dining." The meal began at three o'clock and took an hour. Alfred Barnes as Chairman of the Local Board sat at the head of the top table with the 46 invited guests sitting at each side of him. If they were facing one another, Thomas Barnes would have been sitting opposite Henry Ashworth. His son, James Richardson, was not at the top table. Presumably he was with his mother and other family members at another table. By the time a toast to him (and his bride-to-be) was drunk, he had left the marquee to accompany Mr and Mrs Gladstone and the High Sheriff to the station.

The Bill of Fare was included in the article in *The Farnworth Observer* and was, "we are sorry to say, somewhat inconsistent with its realisation".

BILL OF FARE

SOUPS

Mock Turtle, Cockie Leekie, and Ox-tail.

HOT JOINTS

Roast Ribs, Sirloins and Rounds of Beef

Fillets of Veal, with Boiled Ham, Roast Pork

Roast Haunches of Mutton

Boiled Legs of Mutton, Fore Quarters of Lamb

Stewed Rumps of Beef.

Venison Pastie. Jugged Hare.

Ducks. Geese. Boiled Fowles. Capons.

VEGETABLES

Potatoes. Cauliflowers.

TARTS, &c.

Green Gooseberry Tarts. Apple Tarts. Damson Tarts.

Preserve Tartlets. Cheese Cakes. Mince Pies.

Celery. Cheese. Butter.

DESSERT

Grapes. Filberts. Apples. Pears.

Wine Biscuits

The accompanying etching of the event gives an impression of the grandeur of the occasion. A Bolton photographer, W. Currey of 12 Higher Knowsley Street, was advertising photographs of the event at 1s each (supplied only on order). He had two views of the park before the ceremony began, one view whilst the 100th Psalm was being sung, and another view whilst Mr Gladstone was speaking.

It was not until 1867 that Farnworth Local Board applied for an Act to carry out the provisions made between them and Thomas Barnes in an indenture dated 12 October 1864. In the 1867 Parliamentary Session this Act of Parliament was passed "confirming the gift of a park by Thomas Barnes Esq. to the Local Board of Health of the District of Farnworth, for the Benefit of the Inhabitants thereof, and authorizing the said Local Board to maintain and regulate the said Park". That the gift of the Park was fully appreciated was shown by the fact that in 1889 on the 25th Anniversary of the Park's opening the Local Board presented Thomas with a congratulatory address assuring him of the high appreciation of the inhabitants.

Thomas had not intended to have such a fuss made at the opening of the Park. He said: "It was by no means my own wish there should be anything like such a demonstration as that witnessed today. [... ...] My own desire was rather that there should be a quick affair of signing the deeds, and then throwing open the gates to the public, and the public partaking of the use of it—participating in its advantage and pleasures, without any sort of demonstration whatsoever." However, he was overruled by Farnworth Local Board who wanted something special to mark the occasion.

Ellen Barnes

On the day after the opening Thomas had another important engagement. His son James Richardson was marrying John Cheetham's daughter Ellen in Stalybridge. In Farnworth the marriage day was marked by a continuous firing of cannon at the Farnworth cotton mills throughout the day. The band also paraded through the township, and in the afternoon sat down to dinner at the Golden Lion. In the evening the men who had been firing the cannon had a supper at the same place. At both of these entertainments the health of the newly-married couple was drunk "with great enthusiasm".

At The Quinta on the day of James Richardson's wedding Thomas's neighbours and tenants celebrated in style, ending with a dinner in the evening for one hundred male guests. They certainly gave him the "bumper" they had promised him when he married. Compliments were paid to the Barnes family in the after-dinner speeches. Mr Edmunds said, "In a neighbourhood where the bulk of the population are poor, it was a favourable circumstance that they had such neighbours as Mr Barnes, and as to Mr James Richardson Barnes, knowing him intimately, I can speak with confidence as to his moral qualities and disposition, and whenever he is called upon to succeed his father, which I trust will be in the far distant future, he will prove a worthy son of a worthy sire, and I am sure he will make it his study to benefit the district." Thomas's bailiff, Samuel Winter, responded to the toasts to their health on behalf of Thomas and his wife and said he had been in Mr Barnes's employ nearly 32 years and he had always found him a good master and a good man, and he could speak in equally high terms of Mrs Barnes." On the following day a huge tea party was given to 400 children from six neighbouring Sunday Schools and to 150 women.

October 1864 was three years after the American War of Secession had broken out and just before the winter of 1864–5 when the real pinch of the Cotton Famine was felt. On 1 November 1864 Thomas's partnership with his brother-in-law, Thomas Paterson, was dissolved by mutual consent. A notice in *The Bolton Chronicle* on 5 November 1864 read:

Legal Notice:

Notice is hereby given, that the partnership heretofore existing between us, the undersigned Thomas Barnes and Thomas Paterson, both of Farnworth in the County of Lancaster, carrying on business at Farnworth aforesaid as Cotton Spinners and Manufacturers under the name, style or firm of "Thomas Barnes & Company" was this day dissolved by mutual consent. All debts owing to or by the said Partnership will be received and paid by the said Thomas Barnes by whom the said business will in future be carried on.

1 November 1864

Although Thomas Paterson continued to work in the business at least until it became a limited company in July 1874, he no longer received an annual share of the profits but nor did he have to take responsibility for his share of the huge loss of £19,260 which the Company was about to declare at the end of the financial year on 30 June 1865.

The winter of 1864–5 was a very cold one and many people suffered extreme hardship. Thomas was forced to close down his mills in Farnworth for six weeks. The year ending June 1865 was the worst year in the firm's history. The average price of cotton was 1s 9d per lb but the mills were kept going as long as they could buy any cotton and only closed when supplies ran out. Years later *The Christian World* reported: "The family of Barnes is much respected and beloved by their numerous workpeople, for they take every means to promote their social happiness and prosperity. The story is yet to be told of the mental sufferings and anxiety which many of our kind-hearted manufacturers underwent on behalf of their 'hands' during the cotton famine, and the immense sacrifices which they made to keep them employed. Take the case of Mr Barnes as an illustration. In the height of the distress he observed to a friend, 'If I were to sell my cotton now, and shut up my mills till better times, I would realize a profit of £10,000; and if I go on working till Christmas, all will be gone'. That was the temptation presented to many—'Shall I sell for my own benefit, or go on working for my heavy loss, but for the benefit of my hands?' and in his and many other cases, disinterestedness prevailed. The mills were kept open; and in addition Mr Barnes was a very large contributor to the relief funds." At the time of his death it was reported that during the cotton famine Thomas contributed nearly £1,000 pounds to the funds of The Poor Protection Society. He also contributed £500 to the Bolton Relief Fund and £500 to the money raised in Farnworth. The Provincial Insurance Company of Wrexham also sent £50 to the Lancashire Relief Fund through Thomas their Chairman.

Amongst the Cobden Papers in the West Sussex Record Office there is a letter which Thomas wrote to Richard Cobden on 18 January 1865. It suggests that the relationship between Thomas and Richard Cobden was not purely a business one. In fact, in a list of subscriptions to the Cobden Fund in 1860 Thomas's name was one of half a dozen men at the top of the list who had contributed the huge sum of £1,000 each. The only person who gave more was Thomas Thomasson, one of the leading Bolton Liberals and a personal friend of Cobden's, who had contributed £5,000. Cobden had written in 1865 to ask if Thomas could find employment for a young friend of his, a Mr Ellis, and Thomas repeated an invitation to Mr and Mrs Cobden to spend some time at The Quinta "as you have kindly promised, sometime this year". He was concerned about Mr Cobden's poor health "the effects, I fear, of your exertions in Rochdale". "This is a bracing and comparatively dry place. [... ...] I feel confident the change of air will do you good, and the country around is very pleasant and varied in its scenery." It was in this letter that he mentioned the gun accident which had just occurred on 15 December. Captain Robert Phipps Dod from nearby Nant Isa Hall had been at the Quinta with a shooting party organized by Thomas's son. He was walking with the muzzle of his gun pointing downwards when the trigger caught on his watch chain and the gun went off accidentally, shooting him in the leg. He had to have his leg amputated the following morning but died on 9 January, shortly before Thomas wrote to Cobden. Thomas was clearly very upset by the incident, but did not refer to his own accident when he, like Captain

Dod, had to have an amputation. In his letter he also mentioned that he had just returned to The Quinta from Lancashire. He was about to return to Bolton to give his annual address to his constituents and was not looking forward to it: "I wish it was over. I feel far from easy at the prospect".[2]

However, this annual address on Thursday 27 January was a triumph for him. In a two-hour meeting in the Temperance Hall he gave a detailed account which included the previous year's Parliamentary business, the progress of Reform, and the war in America. There was none of the opposition from the Radical Liberals which had existed before his re-election in 1861. Even his political "enemy" Thomas Grimshaw managed to say they had all heard tonight a most splendid and eloquent speech, and seconded the resolution: "That this meeting having heard the address of Thomas Barnes Esq. MP explanatory of some of the principal measures which came under the consideration of Parliament during the last session, and also a statement of his views on Parliamentary Reform and other questions of deep public interest, begs to record its approval of his Parliamentary conduct generally, and pledges itself to render him all the support in its power in his future efforts, along with others, to promote wise and just legislation, and to secure such a reduction of taxation and economy in the public expenditure as may be found possible in the circumstances of the country."

Alderman Robert Heywood was again the Chairman but arrived half an hour late and Alderman Richard Harwood stood in for him until he arrived. Two months later Robert Heywood stood down as President of the Bolton Liberal Registration Association when it was decided to put forward two Liberal candidates at the next election. Richard Harwood then took his place again.

Thomas began his speech by explaining why he thought public meetings like this one were important, even if they were not easy for the speaker. "I saw in one of the newspapers—one of the weekly journals of London—of last Saturday, some remarks made by some one, somewhat depreciating meetings of this character, and rather representing them as a sort of trial or yoke or test, or something not very agreeable that members are called upon to go through once a year,—what we should say in that old-fashioned term that we used when we were boys, "passing through St Peter's needle". Now I don't look upon a meeting of this character in that light, though I am free enough to confess that it is not any very great pleasure to me to stand and address such an intelligent audience as that which I now see before me and have seen on former occasions. I am too deeply impressed with a sense of my own inefficiency and unworthiness to feel any great degree of pleasure in the duty which I have to perform. But I do look upon it as a very excellent thing for electors themselves, as well as their representatives, to be called upon once a year to meet and see each other face to face and to review in some manner the measures that have passed through or come before Parliament in the year that is gone, and to look forward also to some of the things which are to come in the year that is approaching. I do not myself desire to see a time come when either the electors or non-electors of this country will become apathetic in reference to acts of a political character and affecting the government of their country. I don't want to see people so careless and indifferent about the government and their members of Parliament and the affairs of this country as to care nothing about elections or annual meetings of electors or the subjects that are to be discussed. I think if we take a right view of the importance of these matters we shall see and feel that to a great extent our welfare in this world—our comfort, our happiness, nobody knows to what extent they hang upon the government of the country, and that is affected by the Legislature: and the best mode of securing a good and efficient government is for the people of the country to take an intelligent interest in the things that are brought before Parliament. I therefore rejoice at such meetings as these, because I believe they tend to excite the mind and to draw attention to subjects and keep alive an interest in political matters in the town or borough in which they are held. On this ground if no other I am sincere when I say I feel a pleasure in meeting you this evening."

After two years when his speeches reflected the depressed state of the cotton industry, this speech was more hopeful that cotton supplies were improving. "We see that efforts are being made everywhere, and that numerous sources of supply are rising up, and though little or nothing may be got from these sources this year, we feel quite certain we shall get more next year, and still more the year after; and though the increase so far may be small, we may say that the clouds are breaking, that the darkest hour is past, that there is a blue sky overhead, and a fair and prosperous time to be anticipated." He had already had disappointment on his Jamaican plantation but did not tell his audience until asked during the question time following his speech. All he said during the speech was a comment about the cotton plant: "It is a plant of such great delicacy, one that has so many natural enemies both in the earth and in the air, and requires so much care, that the first efforts of all new countries will be almost certain to disappoint us. It will take time for any person to succeed and grow it to any great extent in a new country."

He had finished his speech the previous year with fears that Britain would become entangled with the dispute over Schleswig and Holstein. It had very nearly ended in war in spite of a Peace Conference held in London. Eventually, however, the opinion of the country swayed the Government and the Opposition to vote for peace.

Two measures had been debated but not settled, both concerned with the admission of people into the universities—the Uniformity Act amendment and the Tests and Abolition Bill. Thomas voted to support the opening of universities, as far as possible, to the whole nation. He also referred to a measure which had been brought into the House of Lords by the Lord Chancellor who proposed to pass a bill to limit the liability to the payment of debts to twelve months. Thomas was decidedly against any such thing as being against the ordinary rules of honesty. He said, "If a man incurs a debt he should be ever liable until he discharges it, and an honest man will say so, and will never be easy until he has got rid of it; and if it is an old debt, that should only be an additional reason why he should discharge it." He told one of his anecdotes to support the point. "There was a man about Whalley who went by the name of 'Billy Whittaker', and who was notorious for getting in debt. This Billy got into debt everywhere, so much so that a neighbour said to him one day, 'Billy, I wonder how thou can sleep i' thi' bed, owing so much money as thou does everywhere'. To which Billy replied, 'I can sleep well enough if they'll let me alone, but I tell thee wot, I wonder how those foaks can sleep as I owe it to'. I am afraid there are a good many of that kind, and that is one reason why the laws ought to be made to encourage fair dealing and support the rules of honesty, and teach those who are disposed to be dishonest that they cannot be so without incurring the just penalty of the law." The anecdote went down very well with the audience.

As predicted, Mr Lawson's Permissive Bill had been introduced and had caused a great deal of excitement. It aimed to give a majority of ratepayers the power to prevent the sale of alcohol in their area. Thomas had voted for the bill, not because he approved of the bill as it stood, but because he approved of the principle of the bill, giving to ratepayers and residents in any place a voice in saying whether or not there should be public houses or beer houses in that particular place. At the moment, he thought it unfair that a magistrate or magistrates, or the Excise, should have the power of opening a public house or a beer house in any locality they might think proper, without saying one word to the people who lived in that locality. He supported the bill because it was based upon the principle of consulting the residents or ratepayers of the locality. He always asked himself how it affected the public good. "That is the principle upon which I have always gone, and I see no other that is capable of guiding me."

Questions of Reform had also been debated—the franchise, the ballot, the redistribution of seats in Parliament, the reduction of the national expenditure—and nothing had really changed there. Thomas spoke about the way in which the working classes had shown themselves capable of taking responsibility for having a vote. The fact that there had not been any recent agitation for Reform did not mean that people did not want it.

During the previous year *The Border Counties Advertiser* had reported on Thomas's experiment to test whether it was a practical proposition to grow cotton in the West Indies, something which "might make all Lancashire his debtor equally with Farnworth". However, when asked about his experiment during the series of questions which followed his speech, Thomas had to report a disaster. "I have had the same experience as a good many persons who have tried. I have found it has not been all sunshine. Up to the beginning of this year, the thing was going on as prosperously and as fairly as it could be, down to the month of May, and even after that. At that time, or soon after, they had very heavy rains in the island of Jamaica, followed by most intense heat, and this produced, it is supposed, what is called the bollworm, and a great portion of my cotton, which ought to have been coming into Liverpool, I believe is buried in the soil of Jamaica. The bolls, instead of ripening and coming to maturity, dropped off one after the other and left nearly every one of the plants without a single pod of cotton. Now, this is one of the incidents to which the cotton plant is liable, and we must all experience these contingencies, but we must go on and try again and see if we cannot overcome them."

Through his connections with the Cotton Supply Association he was also involved with cotton growing in Natal in South Africa. There, too, they were having problems. He continued: "I am connected with another cotton company, and our agent in Natal was in treaty to buy a field of cotton from a person there who had grown it, about 100 acres, and it was a very fine crop, within about three weeks of being ready to pluck. They could not agree as to the price, and in about a fortnight's time there came a shoal of insects—nobody knows where from—settled upon that field, and there was not one ounce of cotton left—all gone. That is another case; and there are others; and this shows us the difficulties that have to be contended with, and no doubt the loss too, because to that poor man who owned that field, it must have been a loss of several thousand pounds. But I hope he will go on again, as I am doing, and hope for better times."

He finished this meeting with his constituents by answering the rest of the varied questions from the floor confidently and with his usual good humour. He was in a very cheerful mood when he ended on this note: "I return you my sincere thanks for the expression of confidence which you have been pleased to vote to-night, and it will be an encouragement and stimulus to me to go on in the same course as that which I have hitherto pursued, and I hope that before long we shall see the desires of our hearts upon the question of suffrage and redistribution of members gratified. I have now the pleasure to move that a vote of thanks be given to your highly-esteemed townsman—the Chairman. He is ready on all occasions to render any service in his power for the good of the people, and I know no greater patriot or one more deserving of the thanks and approbation of his townsman than our esteemed friend. I have very great pleasure in moving that the thanks of this meeting be given to Mr Alderman Heywood for his services in the chair to-night; and we won't say one word about his coming too late; but we say that we are very glad to see him when he does come, whether late or not."

The Editorial in *The Bolton Chronicle* on the Saturday after his annual address also reported on the cotton-growing experiment and concluded: "It is gratifying to know that Mr Barnes is not disheartened, but is going on again, 'hoping for better times'. We heartily wish him success. On the general question of cotton supply, though reminding us that the attempt to grow cotton in a new country will be almost certain to disappoint the planter, Mr Barnes, we are glad to see, speaks in a tone of confident encouragement. Next year, or at the latest the year after, he is quite certain that we shall have an ample supply."

Coupled with the crisis in the cotton market, Thomas had another financial set-back when on Thursday 2 February 1865 there was a fire at one of his mills, Higher Mill at Dixon Green, which caused £5,000 worth of damage. Thomas was not in Farnworth on the day of the fire but arrived in the afternoon of the following day. *The Bolton Chronicle* on Saturday 4 February contained the following article:

"An alarming fire broke out shortly after three o'clock on Thursday afternoon, in the Higher Mill, top of Dixon Green, belonging to T. Barnes Esq. MP. The mill contains spinning mules, throstles, and power-looms; and that portion which has suffered from the fire is two storeys in height, situated at the east end. Upon the ground floor of this were placed three scutching machines, five carding engines, a roving frame, a slubbing frame, and a drawing frame,—the whole of this machinery being used in the preparation of the raw cotton for manufacturing. Over this was the mixing room, which contained a "double opener" (also employed in the preparatory process), and a large quantity of cotton, American, Surat, and Japan,—either in bales or mixed bulk. At one side of this room, but separated by a partition, were a pair of self-acting mules. Each department of the mill was in working operation at the time the fire commenced, which is supposed to have arisen by some hard substance coming in contact with the beaters in one of the scutchers. The flames darted out at one end of the machine and communicated with great rapidity from one machine to another, and thence to the cotton room, which was soon in a complete blaze. The fire commenced so suddenly and spread so quickly, that the workpeople were obliged to make great haste to get away from the scene of peril; and it is supposed that no more than five or ten minutes elapsed ere it reached the mixing room. Here the flames from the ignited cotton flashed up in an entire sheet, catching the ceiling of the upper storey, and thus the whole block was on fire.

As soon as the alarm was given, a quantity of hose was run out from several jets of water in the room where the fire occurred, as well as in those adjoining. These, about ten in number, were attached to the Bolton Corporation mains, and were of essential service in keeping the flames in check within the building where the fire commenced; but the pressure was not sufficient to feed the whole, hence they were not as effective as they might have been if a fewer number had been used. In addition to these measures, by direction of James Barnes, the overlooker, a number of pipes were broken, and steam turned into the room, but all seemed of no use in subduing the flames, which by this time had got hold of the entire building. The *Firefly* engine, from the Lower Mill, was immediately brought to the scene of action. It was stationed at the front of the mill, and the hose dropped into a well made for this purpose; but from some cause or other, the engine did not get into play for a long time after its arrival. Shortly before four o'clock a telegraphic message was forwarded from Moses Gate Station for the Bolton engines. The telegram was received by Inspector Beech at ten minutes past four, and in a very few minutes from that time the *Jesse* and *Bumble* fire-engines, with the fire brigade, were on their way to Farnworth, horses having been promptly procured. These engines were got into play by twenty minutes or a quarter to five o'clock. The *Jesse* was stationed upon the bank of a lodge, and in a portion of the garden attached to the residence of Alfred Barnes Esq., Greenbank. The *Bumble* took up the position in front of the mill occupied by the *Firefly*, and was fed from the same well; the latter engine, at the suggestion of Mr Alfred Barnes, being removed to the back of the mill, near to where the *Jesse* was stationed. The *Deluge* from the Farnworth Paper Mills together with about sixteen men, under the superintendence of Mr James Wolstenholme, was the first to arrive, and was stationed near the boiler-house behind the mill, obtaining a supply of water from the engine well in the yard. This engine is a powerful one, and did its work well, as may also be said of the others.

In about half an hour from the period when the fire commenced, and notwithstanding the greatest exertions, the roof of that particular block fell in with a fearful crash, and the flames darted into the thick murky atmosphere with a startling and appalling effect. All hope of saving this section of the building was obliged, therefore, to be abandoned; and the efforts of the firemen and those aiding them were accordingly directed towards saving the main portion of the mill, as well as the weighing room, communicating with the mixing room by a large slide door, and containing about 100 bales of China and 20 bales of Smyrna cotton, together with 18 bags of waste, which were saved. On the west side was another large block of two-storey buildings, the ground floor being the card room, and the second filled with self-acting mules. To prevent the fire extending into these rooms caused a good deal of anxiety to those concerned. Fortunately, the wall separating these rooms from the burning building was fire-proof. There were two communications—one above and the other below—both of which were covered by iron slide doors. In making an investigation and rendering some assistance James Barnes, the overlooker, rushed through a dense volume of smoke, which, just as he was about to retire, overcame him, and he would have sunk down and been suffocated had not another person rushed to his assistance. To prevent the fire from spreading in that direction, four jets—two from the engines, and two from the hydrants—were carried on to the roof of the spinning room. Notwithstanding these vigorous efforts, however, the fire quickly caught the roof—four bays of it being damaged; two of them indeed being destroyed. The falling *debris* also seriously injured a pair of mules at the end of this room. Had it not been for the precautionary measures, the whole of that part of the mill would soon have gone also.

The scutching-room and the cotton-mixing room—forming a block of building about 80 feet by 84 feet—with the whole of their necessary machinery, were completely destroyed, together with a quantity of cotton. A considerable stock of cotton was pitched out into the street, some of it damaged by the fire; and other portions would suffer much depreciation through lying in the road, which was exceedingly muddy and sloppy, and from the rain which fell heavily at intervals. The night was foggy—exceedingly so at one time, and rendered the operations of the firemen and their auxiliaries anything but easy. Huge fires were improvised on the ground in the mill yard to afford light to enable the men pumping at the engines to perform their arduous work,—relays being ready at frequent intervals in order that there might be no intermission during the most critical period. The fire was got under between half-past five and six o'clock, and was extinguished about seven. The manager of the mill, Mr James Newhouse, was in Bolton transacting business when the fire originated, but information soon reached him, and he lost no time in hurrying to the scene of the accident in a cab. Mr Alfred Barnes was promptly at hand, and rendered efficient assistance in directing the operations of the firemen. His residence is immediately contiguous to the works, between which there is a direct means of communication, and a low railing separates the mill lodges from his garden and grounds, within which two of the engines were stationed. Large crowds of old and young hastened to the spot, and contemplated with awe the brief but terrific ravages of the fire, speculating both as to its cause and effect—many and diversified being the utterances and opinions it called forth. Two of the fire-engines—the *Jesse* and the *Firefly*—remained in attendance all night. The damage is estimated at about £5,000, and is stated to be only partially insured. In the salvage, some of the cotton is expected to be saved in good condition. Mr T. Barnes arrived at Farnworth at two o'clock yesterday afternoon. As the news of the fire spread, a number of gentlemen from the neighbourhood proceeded to the mill to render any assistance in their power, including William Hargreaves Esq. of Darley Hall, and Charles Ainsworth Esq. of the Wellington Cotton Mills, Great Lever. Mr Ferrier Clarke, surgeon, of Farnworth, likewise hastened thither so as to be able to render medical assistance, if it should be needed; but except here and there a few scars and bruises—unavoidable under the circumstances—those engaged in the laudable work escaped without personal injury. Mr Superintendent Scott, with Inspector Read, Sergeant Holland, and seven men of the County Constabulary, rendered great aid in keeping back the crowd, and in facilitating the operations of the firemen and others in various ways. The number of hands employed in the various departments of the mill is 550; and of this number about 200 are thrown out of employment by the fire, but these may find employment for some time in clearing the *debris* and similar incidental work. The weavers can go on with material from the other mills of Mr Barnes, situated at a short distance.

The mill was supplied with gas by the Farnworth and Kersley Gas Company, and the meter was unfortunately in the immediate vicinity of the fire; but Mr John Smith, the manager of the gas works, took prompt measures for preventing any damage, by stopping the supply from the main pipes, and drawing off the remainder. Some of the mill hands lost their coats in the fire, and with them their wages which they had been paid that afternoon, and which they had placed in their coat pockets."

It is likely that this was the fire referred to in another article which said that Farnworth formed its own fire brigade after a fire at Dixon Green Mill which destroyed a two-storey building and put ninety people out of work. Before that the town had had to rely on the amateur fire brigades at Barnes's Mills and Crompton's paper works. After the formation of the Town Fire Brigade the mill brigades continued to turn out to assist. This article gave the date for the formation of the Farnworth Fire Brigade as 1864 which would appear to be an error. There was no Farnworth Fire Brigade called to the fire in February 1865. The fire engine from Barnes's Mills was regularly used to fight other fires in the district. On Tuesday 21 June 1870 it was sent to a fire at Mossfield Mill, Farnworth, and on the afternoon of Sunday 10 December 1871 it went to a fire at Trencherbone Mine, Little Hulton.

The reference to the mill manager, James Newhouse, is of special interest to me as he was related to my mother's family. He was not mentioned in the annual stocktaking accounts on 30 June that year and probably left the firm soon after the fire to set up business on his own.

Thomas was back in Farnworth on Wednesday 22 February 1865 to make a speech at the annual soirée of the Bolton Mechanics' Institution held this year in the Baths Assembly Room. A long report in *The Bolton Chronicle* described the event—a "tea party" for 400 people in a room decorated with flags and streamers, with music to accompany the meal, and a group of glee singers who punctuated the speeches with four songs. After the President had given his annual report the main business of the evening began—the start of a campaign to raise funds for a badly needed new building for the Institution. Thomas was there to move the resolution to agree to the campaign. He was concerned that the committee was intending to erect the cheapest possible functional building. He wanted something that was both functional and attractive: "He hoped it was not going to be as plain as a barn, or like those dead walls which we saw about our railways, and some other buildings in the town which he could name. But he hoped there was going to be a bit of ornament about it, something that would make it attractive, and do credit to the good taste of the people of Bolton, or else he thought it would be a sorry reflection on the committee if they did not intend to put up a building of some respectability and pretensions. [... ...] He did not think money was thrown away when spent in such a way as to be attractive, ornamental, pleasant, and handsome to look upon." Although the committee was planning to spend no more than £4,000, Thomas recommended aiming at raising £10,000. "In fact, he thought he might venture to say that anything it cost above that, if they went about it in an economical manner, he would be answerable for it. [... ...] If they would engage to raise £10,000, say in five years, he would be very glad to give £500." At the soirée he also gave an insight into his attitude to money: "He would tell them what he found in the course of his life. He had always found that by applying for a high sum, they always got more than by aiming at a low sum. There was a good old saying, 'He that shoots at a star will shoot higher than he that shoots at a man', and if they aimed at a high figure, they might depend upon it they would get more money." The speech Thomas made on this occasion was more light-hearted than many of his political speeches, but his style of rhetoric was the same—he managed to get audience reaction which included a great deal of laughter and cheering. His description of Gladstone's visit to Bolton when he came to open the Park in Farnworth is a typical example of his style: "When the Right Honourable Member visited Bolton, the Ex-Mayor did take him to the Market Hall, and he saw there something worth looking at, and that pleased him; he also went to the Temperance Hall, and that was also worth looking at, especially when it was filled as it was on that occasion; and he likewise went past the Working Men's Club, and though he did not go into it, still it was pointed out to him, and that also was a place which they could take a stranger to and point out with pleasure. But when he went past the Mechanics' Institution, he (Mr Barnes) wondered whether the Ex-Mayor showed him that (laughter and cheers), and if he did, he wondered whether he felt any particular pride in saying, "That is the Bolton Mechanics' Institution", (renewed laughter). He rather thought the Ex-Mayor drove quickly past there and said nothing about it; and he was sure if it was not pointed out to him, Mr Gladstone would never see it himself (laughter)."

On the evening before this soirée the Liberal Registration Association had held their annual meeting at which the question was raised as to whether two Liberals should stand at the next general election. On the Friday of that week there came the news that P. R. Arrowsmith, one of the leading Bolton Liberals and a cotton spinner like Thomas, had incurred losses of £200,000 through over-importing cotton. (James Newhouse had business connections with P. R. Arrowsmith, and like him, lost a great deal of money on speculations.)

Richard Cobden never recovered from the illness referred to in Thomas's letter in January. He died on 2 April of bronchitis at his apartments in Suffolk Street in London. Thomas attended his funeral on 7 April 1865 at West Lavington Church and at a meeting of the Reform Association held in Bolton on 11 April 1865 gave a eulogy of Cobden. On the same day he was in the Temperance Hall at a public meeting held to promote the National Reform Movement where he moved a resolution and made another speech.

On 15 April 1865 *The Manchester Times* reported that as President of the Bolton Sunday School Union, Thomas had presided during the previous week at the 18th Annual Conference of the Sunday School Union of Lancashire, Cheshire and Derbyshire which took place in Bolton. The whole of Good Friday was spent in conference on the question "Have Sunday Schools failed in the object for which they were initiated?" Special sermons were given on Sunday in most of Bolton's chapels and in the afternoon there was an aggregate meeting in the Temperance Hall.

In April Thomas's nephew Alfred opened an Industrial Exhibition linked to the Congregational Young Men's Improvement Society in the new church hall in Farnworth. Several members of the Barnes family, including Thomas, had lent items for the exhibition. Thomas had sent some pictures and two bronze statuettes, *Justice* and *Peace*. Another item of Barnes family memorabilia was also on display—"a somewhat primitive-looking set of blue and white tea-service with no pretensions to be beautiful". A label explained that it was valued and revered because it had once belonged to Thomas's grandmother. Presumably this grandmother was Mrs Jane Topp, the landlady of the Golden Lion, who had struggled to bring up her son James Rothwell Barnes after being widowed three times. It is interesting that the family did not in any way try to hide their humble origins and were just as proud to display this homely pottery as bronze statuettes. Also on display at this exhibition in 1865 were photographs of the family—pictures of Thomas and Ann, of James Richardson and Ellen, of Ellen's sister Agnes Cheetham, and of Alfred.

In 1865 Thomas's wife, Ann, spent seven weeks from around 24 April to 2 June in Llandudno, this time on her own. She stayed at Brinkburn House, 7 Glan y Mor Terrace, run by a Miss Donkin. Mr William Barber, Miss Barber and Miss M. A. Barber from Dirk Lodge, Ayrshire, and Mrs J. T. Jones from Brynhafod, Shropshire, were also at Brinkburn House during the whole period. I do not know if they were friends of Ann's. In the first week of May Thomas laid the foundation stone of the new Welsh Independent Chapel in Queen Street, Wrexham.

On 30 June 1865 when the annual stocktaking was held the firm had to face a huge loss of nearly £20,000, the largest loss in its history. As Joseph Winter was now a partner he had to accept his £6,419 share of the loss. Thomas's share was double that—£12,895. James Richardson Barnes again received an allowance of £759 5s from his father and interest on his capital. By resigning his partnership in the previous November Thomas Paterson was not involved in all this. It is tempting to think that Thomas Barnes had deliberately encouraged his resignation to protect his brother-in-law from the financial losses.

However, the year was not all gloom and doom. In October 1864 there had been the opening of the Park and James Richardson's wedding and a considerable amount of work had been done at the Farnworth Mills. After the fire in February £1,960 had been spent on a new Scutching Room and a new Mixing Room at Higher Mill. Messrs Coope, the builders, had had the £1,519 building contract. The rooms had been fireproofed by using ironwork costing an extra £243. Musgraves had supplied the pulleys for £89 and the firm had done the shafting themselves at a cost of £113. As well as all this £658 4s was spent on a new boiler house and pipes and £82 16s on building a wall round the boiler yard at Lower Mill. Boiler cleaning apparatus had cost £42, a Green's Economizer £345 12s, and alterations to the McNaughting of the engine had cost £580. (Thomas's firm was keeping up with the major advances in steam engine technology which had taken place since the introduction in 1845 of William McNaught's design for the first compound engine which effectively used the energy from the hot steam twice. By using a high-pressure cylinder and a secondary smaller low-pressure cylinder he had produced a highly efficient recycling system which was referred to as "McNaughting" an engine. Green's

Economizer, also patented in 1845, was another device used to increase the steam-raising efficiency of the boilers of stationary steam engines.)

By the end of June Thomas had agreed to stand again at the election in July and was preparing to fight his next election campaign.

Notes

1. ZHE/60/2 [Bolton Archives and Social Studies]
2. Cobden Papers Ms 8 f21 *op. cit.* West Sussex Record Office

CHAPTER 11

June 1865–February 1869

The third term at Westminster. The Jamaica Committee.
The end of a political career.

In July 1865 Palmerston's Government with Gladstone as its Chancellor of the Exchequer was due to reach the end of its term of office and a General Election would have to be called. In Bolton archives are two documents written just before this election. The first, dated 30 March 1865, is a copy of a letter to Thomas from Robert Heywood who was resigning as President of the Reform Registration Association because attempts were being made to put forward two Liberal candidates in Bolton at the next election.

Bolton, 30 March 1865

My dear Sir,

At a meeting last night of the Reform Registration Association we had a Deputation from the Reform Union urging us to unite with them in obtaining two liberal members for this Borough. After their retirement I expressed a strong opinion against the attempt being made with a show of only a majority of 130 liberal voters based upon a favorable estimate of many hundreds entirely new electors—this with the furious opposition we might expect from our opponents left us no chance of success with almost a certainty of losing you. I was one of those who preferred being non represented rather than doubly misrepresented. Some cried out for two Tories as the only means of rousing us and leading to future success, this I said had not attended the present state of South Lancaster and I could not believe so favorably in the result of defeat. Mr Thomasson being mentioned I said I had had the most positive assurance from that gentleman that he would never attend evening debates. After a long discussion a resolution was moved and seconded that the meeting pledged itself to bring forward two reform candidates. This appeared going too far in the opinion of W. Mellor and J. K. Cross (brought to the meeting after very long absence by the prospect of sending two liberals) and they suggest an alteration viz. recommending such course to be adopted which was carried without dissentions.

I then rose and expressed my deep regret that such a resolution should have passed, my entire disapproval of their proceedings and the consequent necessity of resigning my office of President after which I immediately left the room. I learned today that my successor is Mr Richard Harwood who has I am sorry to say [has] taken a leading part in these unfortunate proceedings as he says with your concurrence. I am well aware of the serious responsibility I have incurred. The attempt will I feel sure prove an entire failure and the blame will ultimately rest upon me for refusing my early co-operation. I have seen W. Martin today and find he quite agrees with me in the preposterous pursual and has has [sic] it on knowledge that it will bring out Mr Hick causing us all an immense deal of trouble and expense ending in worse than nothing.[1]

The second letter is Thomas's reply, written on the following day, 31 March 1865, in which he discussed his prospects in a contested election.

March 31 1865

My dear Mr Heywood,

I have received your very kind letter and beg to say that I am very sorry to hear that anything has occured [sic] to cause you to retire from the office you have held. The subject on which their [sic] is a difference of opinion in the Registration Association is one on which I can express no opinion.

If the Association think they are strong enough to carry two, they will no doubt wish to do so and will make the attempt. All I can say is, that I shall be very glad to have a colleague on my side of the house. Whether it is prudent to bring out a second candidate or not I cannot say. The responsibility must rest on the Committee to decide.

It certainly would not be unreasonable to ask those who are anxious to have a contest to provide the "ways and means" that will be demanded for such a contest. No doubt it will be a fierce one and our friends will not win without a hard fight. I dare say there are some who would like a fight if they have nothing to find, but perhaps something to receive. Bolton *ought* to return two Liberals but we know it has not hitherto been able to do so twice together.

I must be quite still in this matter and leave it entirely to my friends in Bolton. This is what I have told Mr Harwood. I have never said more than that I should be glad to have a Colleague if our party can carry one. But I have never recommended that a second should be brought out because I never felt myself able to give an opinion whether or not it would be wise to do so.

I hope the counsels of the Committee will be ultimately guided by wisdom and prudence. I shall leave it entirely to them and be quiescent in the matter. It will be a pity if they play the fable of the Dog and his shadow.

I am very sorry you have to retire.

If the man Peter Rothwell is under 25, he had better call on me. If he is above 25, he will not be eligible for any situation on the Railway.

With my best thanks and kindest regards

I am yours truly,

Thomas Barnes[2]

Unlike the previous few elections, this one was not to be fought on any particular matter of policy but simply as a straight fight between the two political parties. The Bolton Liberals saw this as an opportunity to put forward two Liberal candidates and to return to the 1857–59 position when Thomas and Joseph Crook, both Liberals, had represented the borough. They invited Samuel Pope, a lawyer, to stand together with Thomas. However, Samuel Pope was a firm teetotaller and an active member of the United Kingdom Alliance against alcohol. The decision to invite him had an immediate effect on the election. The Licensed Victuallers and Beersellers put forward a candidate of their own, William Gibb of Swinton Park, a wine and spirit merchant, to stand as a supporter of their trade. He and the Conservative Lt-Col. Gray fought a joint campaign. The result was that an election where the two existing MPs could have been returned unopposed now had to be fought out between the four candidates. Not only that, but some Liberals changed their allegiance to vote for Mr Gibb and presumably some teetotal Conservatives voted for Samuel Pope. In spite of pleas from all four candidates for electors to vote for the candidates' political views, the question of alcohol played a large part in the election campaign.

Thomas and Samuel Pope addressed a meeting in the Temperance Hall before receiving the electors' formal approval of their candidature. Thomas gave a very competent speech summing up the achievements of the last Government and concluded: "If there should be prosperity at home and peace preserved with nations abroad, if they [the electors] desire that there should be a reduction of our national expenditure, if they desire that there should be progress in our legislation, if they desire that there should be equity in the administration of justice, and in the measures of legislation that we presented before the House of Commons, if they require that those civil and religious disabilities that still hang over a portion of our community be removed—if they desire these things to be done, how is it to be effected? There is only one way, and is that you should send members to Parliament who are in favour of them and will vote for these measures when they are brought before them."

Samuel Pope's views coincided with Thomas's on all questions. He was new to political campaigning but had been a Liberal supporter for many years. He and Thomas knew one another already. Samuel Pope explained how: "I have received my political education at the hands of the men who founded the Lancashire school of politicians, and who have left upon the history of this country the impress of their giant intellect and their great energy; the men with whom your present member has been associated, and of whom I aspire to be a humble follower." After the two men had faced questions about the proposed Permissive Bill and Samuel Pope had explained his views on teetotalism, the decision to put them both forward was almost unanimous. Immediately after this meeting the two candidates issued their addresses to the constituency. Thomas wrote:

TO THE ELECTORS AND NON-ELECTORS OF THE BOROUGH OF BOLTON

GENTLEMEN,—The present Parliament will be soon dissolved, and you will be called upon to exercise your constitutional functions in electing two members for another.

Having served you as your representative for several years and having been again honoured with an invitation to present myself as a CANDIDATE for the same responsible position, I venture to do so, and to ask for your support at the impending election.

I have so frequently had the opportunity of addressing you, and have so fully expressed my political opinions on those occasions, that it is not necessary I should repeat them at present.

I will only say my views are unchanged, my votes have been in accordance with them, and what they have been in the past, they will be in the future, if I am again honoured with your confidence.

I still think that an alteration is called for in our representative system, which will widen its basis, and give to the populous and commercial parts of our country a fairer share of political power.

I am also still of opinion that protection should be given to the voter by the use of the Ballot.

The interests of the borough, both in Parliament and out, have received my best attention and services, and will continue to do so if I am again placed by your votes in the honourable position I now occupy.

I am, gentlemen,

Your faithful servant,

THOS. BARNES

Limefield, 30 June 1865[3]

Nomination Day was 11 July. All four candidates appeared on the hustings in the Market Place where their nominations were proposed and seconded. Robert Heywood again proposed Thomas saying: "After such long and valuable services, I need not enlarge upon his merits. With high moral standards and active business habits, he possesses great commercial knowledge and considerable ability in expressing his opinions on all important subjects." He was seconded by Richard Harwood. Samuel Pope was nominated by Thomas Thomasson and seconded by Joseph Crook, Bolton's former Liberal MP. Thomas made a long statesman-like speech which began: "I stand before you not as an adherent of Lord Palmerston, but I stand before you as an adherent of those great principles in foreign policy, in commercial policy, in home policy, which have made this nation one of the most prosperous nations in the world and have given it the greatest wealth. I have never desired to be a man attached to any party except that party which has made the good of the people its first object; and I now appear before you to say that I am in favour of that commercial policy which has been pursued in this country now for many years. I can point, gentlemen, to what has been done by the party that is now in power, and when I say that party I don't mean simply Lord Palmerston and those that are with him, but I mean those who have been urging on, forcing on, driving on Lord Palmerston and his Ministry to measures which they would not have undertaken but for that pressure. I will simply give you a list of some of those measures which have been advocated and passed by the Government of the day, urged on by the Liberal and extreme Liberal and Radical party of the country, obstructed and prevented and hindered by the gentlemen who sit on the opposite side." He went on to refer to about twenty successful measures brought about by Liberal pressure. The excitement of the crowd was mainly good-humoured as they accompanied the speeches with cheers, hisses or hoots of derision.

After the speeches, a show of hands was taken. To prevent confusion, the Town Clerk held up a placard with the name of each candidate as the crowd was asked to vote. The reporter for *The Bolton Chronicle* estimated that nearly half voted for Colonel Gray, almost the same number for Thomas, fewer for Samuel Pope and about the same number for William Gibb as for Thomas. A considerable number of people did not hold up their hands at all. The Conservatives immediately greeted the result with cheers even before the Mayor announced his decision in favour of Colonel Gray and Thomas. A poll was then demanded for the following day by Mr Crook on behalf of Samuel Pope and by

Mr Richardson for William Gibb. The Liberals were not happy with the Mayor's decision even though he had been supported by James Knowles of Eagley Bank, a Liberal who had previously been Mayor himself and had had to make a similar decision at an election.

Polling was on the next day. For some time the two Liberals were at the head of the poll with Thomas in the lead but around ten o'clock Colonel Gray moved into second position. By quarter past eleven Thomas and Colonel Gray were neck and neck, followed by Samuel Pope and then William Gibb. For half an hour Thomas again took over the lead but at noon Colonel Gray was ahead of Thomas by one vote—and this position was then held by the four candidates to the end of the poll. When the poll closed Colonel Gray and Thomas had won. The result was very close. Colonel Gray was returned at the head of the poll with 1022 votes and Thomas came second with 979. The two defeated candidates, Mr Pope and Mr Gibb, received 864 and 727 respectively.

The official results were declared the following morning and Thomas made his last speech of this election. In it he set out what he intended to do when he returned to Parliament: "I go there to give a consideration to every question that comes before us, and I shall do so, whatever side of the House it may come from. I am fully aware there are some gentlemen who sit on the opposite side of the House than I sit on that are also much interested in the good government of the country, and are anxious to bring forward good measures, and they shall have from me a fair and impartial consideration of any measures they may bring forward, and I do trust that measures will be brought forward that will carry on that progressive improvement in legislation which has signalised the legislation of this country for some years past."

And so on 12 July 1865, nine months after the opening of the Park, Thomas returned to Parliament for the third time, having won his second contested election. He had last been elected in 1861 just as the war in America broke out and was now being re-elected just as the Cotton Famine in Lancashire had finally ended. Palmerston, now over 80 years old, was to head the new Government until his death in October that year. Thomas said at his next meeting with his constituents: "We entered the House of Commons at the start of last session with what we considered a strong Liberal party, with a strong Liberal Government in it, expecting great things."

In August, one month after his re-election, Thomas was back in Shropshire laying yet another foundation stone, this time at Church Stretton Congregational Chapel. He had made a generous donation of £295 towards the High Street site and still had links with this chapel twenty years later when he attended a bazaar and again made a donation, this time of his usual £50.

In the second week of October 1865 he and John Cheetham (both of them now MPs) attended the funeral of a Church of England clergyman, Rev. Canon Stowell of Salford, and were the first names in the long list of distinguished people who formed the mile-long funeral cortege. In this same month Palmerston died and Lord Russell took over as Prime Minister.

On 6 November 1865 the launch of a new company, the Grand Hotel Company Scarborough Ltd, was announced in *The Times*. Thomas was named as one of the fourteen men forming the Provisional Committee set up to run the business. Apart from Thomas and one man from Liverpool, all the rest of the Committee were Yorkshire men. Three of them were, like Thomas, Directors of the Lancashire & Yorkshire Railway, one of them its Chairman, H. W. Wickham. The Company was offering a capital of £100,000 in 1,000 shares of £100 each. It had bought the unfinished hotel in its imposing position of the cliffs at Scarborough from the Scarborough Cliff Hotel Company for £43,600, with the vendor taking 100 paid-up shares and £10,000 in ordinary shares. The estimate for completing the hotel designed by Mr Brodick with its 30 sitting rooms and 312 bedrooms, its "spacious and noble" public rooms and accommodation for a club, was nearly as much as the company had paid for the unfinished building. However, the hotel's potential as a holiday destination was emphasised in the prospectus. I do not know whether Thomas ever became one of the proposed eight Directors of the Company or if the launch was successful. Applications for shares had to be submitted four days after the announcement appeared in the paper.

Thomas was in Manchester on Wednesday 22 November 1865 to attend the Liberation Society Conference. He proposed a vote of thanks to Mr Miall for giving a paper, and also moved a resolution at the end of the meeting.

On 29 November 1865 he and John Cheetham were at a public banquet of members of the Liberal party at Blackburn Town Hall to present a testimonial to James Pilkington, the former Liberal MP for Blackburn. John Bright made a speech and Thomas proposed a toast at the end of the meal.

Now that the Cotton Famine was over, the need to obtain cotton from Jamaica was no longer as urgent. However, Thomas's cotton-growing experiment in Jamaica had just had a set-back. As news in those days took between three and four weeks to reach England Thomas would only have heard about the event in mid to late November. About three weeks into October 1865 disaster struck in Jamaica in St Thomas in the East where the Jamaica Cotton Company had their Elmwood and Muirton estates. Many of the blacks in the town of Morant Bay went on the rampage, killing and looting. At first rumours of insurrection in Jamaica were played down in the British press. The Jamaica Cotton Company had received a letter from their agent written on 9 October with no hint of any disturbances. In fact, he wrote that the weather was fine and they were just about to start cleaning the cotton fields. The agent was also excited about the finding of a vine in the woods which promised to be a new source of fibre for paper-making. Even on 4 November no news had reached Britain to affect the price of Jamaican goods in the market.

However, on the same day that all this appeared in *The Liverpool Mercury*, another paper, *The Belfast Newsletter*, had much more serious news. They had received their information by magnetic telegraph from a telegram sent by *The Times'* Own Correspondent in China. Shortly before 26 October the Governor of Jamaica had sent a despatch reporting a rebellion of the black population in the Eastern district of the island, and requesting immediate naval and military reinforcements.

On 23 October the Correspondent for *The Dundee Courier and Argus*, someone with the initials J.S. who lived in Port Marie in the parish of St Mary, wrote a long account of the insurrection which was published in the paper on 20 November. He gave a graphic and bloodcurdling account of the events which started "Barbarous rebellion has, in our beautiful island, imitated the Sepoy atrocities of the east." He went on, "Almost every white and coloured man in the parish of St Thomas in the East, where the insurrection broke out, has been butchered, and the churches and court houses burned to the ground".

Dr Underhill, a Baptist missionary, was blamed for starting the unrest with a letter he had written to the Colonial Secretary contrasting the present state of the blacks with their position some years before. He described them as people "willing to labour, but unable to obtain employment, as being ground down by class legislation, and unjust and oppressive taxation, and as being destitute, naked, and starving". Many years before he had written a book "showing how well the black population were getting on, how liberally endowed with houses and lands and horses, how they went to church and market well fed, well clad, and well mounted, how many of them had their small sugar estates and coffee plantations, and were quite independent of work on the sugar estates." He now saw "the same people persecuted, afflicted, tormented, ragged, and hungry, in want and woe". The sense of grievance aroused by this letter resulted in a series of meetings often held at Baptist chapels. On the night before the insurrection hundreds had met in a Baptist chapel before pouring into the town of Morant Bay. All the magistrates and town officials were assembled in the town. The mob went via the Police Office to steal weapons, then on to the Court House where they began to murder the dignitaries one by one. Twenty-two were massacred on the spot, first the parish curate, then Charles Price, an elderly black man, the only black member of the House of Assembly, then the Police Inspector, the Custos of the parish, and the Leader of the Volunteers. The Volunteers had turned out immediately but only managed to fire one volley before the Court House was set on fire. The mob only spared the doctors, thinking they might need them. One man, Mr Georges, the Custos of a neighbouring parish, managed to hide and eventually to send a message to the Governor in Kingston. The mob then went on to free the prisoners in the local jail and they all then went on the rampage, plundering and murdering. When news reached the Governor, Edward John Eyre, he immediately ordered military intervention. The Governor then sailed on a French commercial steamer from Kingston to Morant Bay. The soldiers shot large numbers of the rioters and took many more prisoner. After trials by court-martial scores of them were hanged on the gallows in the towns involved. The writer of this report had nothing but praise for the Governor "who acted throughout with praiseworthy energy". "We are thankful there was no weak indecisive hand at the helm, but one equal to the emergency. The Governor had previously been unpopular among a certain class; and whatever he said or did was wrong in their eye. At the present crisis no one says an ill word of him. He is the right man in the right place."

Rewards were offered for the capture of the ringleaders and 500 dollars were offered as a reward for the arrest of a mixed-race man, George William Gordon, a Member of the House of Assembly, who was believed to have encouraged the uprising. In fact, Mr Gordon gave himself up and was taken to Morant Bay. "He studied his Bible and hummed hymns all the way, munching biscuit and sipping water— that being his restricted fare." When this report was written the writer could only say that he had heard a rumour that Mr Gordon had been hanged on a gibbet in front of the ruins of the Court House at Morant Bay. The rumour was true and this summary execution of Mr Gordon was to play an important part in the case brought by the Jamaica

Committee (of which Thomas Barnes was a member) against Governor Eyre.

The sugar and cotton estates suffered. "In some places they saved the estates, because they said they would want them to make sugar and rum for themselves; in others they not only burned the buildings, but slew the very cattle and sheep. In the adjoining parish of Portland they have burned a good many places. [... ...] Elmwood, the Jamaica Cotton Company's estate, was burned to the ground. Their other estate in Portland, called Whitehall, we passed through some time since. It lay like a sluggard's vineyard, and displayed all sorts of wild brush flourishing luxuriantly, but with newly-built walls around the fields. Nature was busily engaged stifling the cotton plants with overwhelming masses of wild creepers and worthless vines. The hand of man was idle, and the race of ruin and desolation unchecked and unrestrained."

"J.S." knew that many people in England, especially the Anti-Slavery Society, would take the side of the black man. He, however, spoke for the frightened white people in Jamaica: "I would not be surprised though the Anti-Slavery Society were to sympathise deeply with those amiable creatures whose amusements in killing and mangling the white inhabitants were interfered with, and themselves rudely strung up to a tree, or shot down by a ruthless soldiery. We are used to their misrepresentations."

Thomas was one of these people criticised by "J.S.". Soon after the Morant Bay rebellion the Government in Britain appointed a Commission to look into the events. At the same time a Committee was formed in London, the Jamaica Committee, with which Thomas Barnes became involved. It had three aims: to watch the progress of the official inquiry; to bring about a searching parliamentary inquiry into the past and present condition in Jamaica; to provide Mrs Gordon (the widow of the man hanged after the court-martial at Morant Bay), and the many others who might have unjustly suffered from the proceedings of the civil and military authorities in Jamaica with competent legal assistance to conduct their several cases before the Commission. When the Committee was first formed its Chairman was Charles Buxton MP, and among the members named in the first notice were John Stuart Mill MP, Lord Alfred Churchill, John Bright, Sir Thomas Fowell Buxton, Professor Cairnes and Professor Goldwin Smith. The Secretary of the Committee from the start to the end was F. W. Chesson. When a longer list was published on 31 January Thomas Barnes was one of the thirteen MPs named. Also amongst the members were Titus Salt, Reverend Newman Hall, and Thomas Thomasson of Bolton. The

Jamaica Committee eventually included some more well-known British Liberal intellectuals such as Charles Darwin, Frederic Harrison, Thomas Hughes, Thomas Huxley, John Tyndall and Herbert Spencer. A rival committee was set up by Thomas Carlyle for the defence, arguing that Governor Eyre had acted decisively to restore order. Its supporters included John Ruskin, Charles Kingsley, Charles Dickens and Alfred Lord Tennyson.

This rivalry was played out in the newspapers, both in Britain and Jamaica. A letter written around January 1866 by a clergyman in Jamaica was published in *The Standard* on 5 February 1866. He began: "The outcry against the Governor and military authorities is as ungenerous as it is unreasonable. Both the Governor and Colonel Hobbs are men who have much more than the form of religion, and so are exceptions to an almost general rule. It is impossible that they could have had any of the blood-thirsty feeling or animosity to the blacks which have been attributed to them." He criticised those people who took the side of the rebels: "Had matters been allowed to gather to a head, and a couple of regiments sent out to pieces [= *plots of land*], with numerous other painful incidents, those good people who sit at home so quietly in their arm-chairs by their firesides—who have lost no relatives, nor been hunted into the bush, and exposed for days to weather and starvation—would sing quite a different tune."

This writer had no sympathy for the executed man, George William Gordon. "It seems now very generally admitted that his capture and execution were illegal, but never was sentence more just. The Governor will be able to prove that within his dying hour he perjured himself, [... ...] and that he was cognisant of all that was about to take place."

The same clergyman disapproved of the stance being taken by the Radicals in Britain. "Had the Governor not openly written and asserted his belief that the rebellion, if not brought about, was fermented by the Baptists, and Underhill especially, I do not believe that the English Radical papers would have taken up the matter as they have."4

Once the Government Commission had made its report, the Jamaica Committee no longer needed to monitor its progress. However it continued its campaign, now concentrating on trying to have Governor Eyre brought to justice. This was quickly criticised by the press. *The Glasgow Herald* reported on 27 June 1866 that the Jamaica Committee had resolved to urge upon the Government the prosecution of Mr Eyre for the "murder" of George William Gordon. The Editor commented: "One is led to ask whether these gentlemen who are full of, no doubt, genuine philanthropy as regards the black man, quite understand what is meant by vindictiveness towards the white." This article regarded what the Jamaica Committee was doing as "vindictive persecution" of Mr Eyre.

Charles Buxton who had been the Chairman of the Jamaica Committee since its foundation in December 1865 obviously agreed with this sentiment. In a letter published in *The Daily News* on 29 June 1866 he confirmed his resignation saying, "I think we ought to be satisfied, so far as Mr Eyre is concerned with his dismissal and disgrace." On 9 July 1866 at Hadley's Hotel John Stuart Mill was elected as the new Chairman of the Jamaica Committee. (Most reports about the Jamaica Committee describe John Stuart Mill as the organiser and Chairman of it. In fact, he only became Chairman when the Committee launched into this second phase of its activities.) Soon after this on 27 July the Jamaica Committee issued a statement signed by John Stuart Mill as Chairman. Another document, an Address to the Friends of the Jamaica Committee was issued on 12 October 1866 naming Thomas as a member of the Committee. When the Jamaica Committee launched its Ten Thousand Pounds Fund in January 1867 to provide money to pay for an indictment for murder against Mr Eyre and the other people involved in Mr Gordon's trial and execution, Thomas was listed as one of the 100 chief members of the Committee. Another 600 men, not named individually in the announcement in *The Times*, were also on the committee.

On 19 July 1867 in the House of Commons John Stuart Mill asked the Chancellor of the Exchequer whether any steps had been or would be taken to bring to trial Lieutenant Adcock, Captain Holt, Lieutenant Oxley, Ensign Cullen, Dr Morris the stipendiary magistrate, Attorney-General Hislop, Lieutenant Brand, Captain Toke, Captain Field, General O'Connor, and Colonel Nelson, for certain illegal acts committed by them in the suppression of the insurrection in Jamaica; and whether any legal proceedings had been or would be ordered to be taken against Mr Edward John Eyre, late Governor of Jamaica, for complicity in all or any of the illegal acts, and particularly the illegal trial and execution of Mr George Gordon; and if not, whether Her Majesty's Government were advised that these acts were no offence under the criminal law.

Governor Eyre was charged with murder twice but neither case came to anything. It was reported in the press on 15 May 1868 that he had again attended Bow Street. Presumably this was the second occasion. Soon after that the attempt to prosecute Eyre was abandoned. On 15 July 1868 the Jamaica Committee published their final document addressed to Members of the Jamaica Committee. As the attempt to call Mr Eyre to account was at an end now that the Grand Jury of Middlesex had thrown out the Bill, the duty of the Jamaica Committee had now been performed. They had all along been "trying to guard public liberty and vindicate the law."

I do not know what happened to Thomas's cotton estate after the Morant Bay Rebellion. The Jamaica Cotton Company was never the same again even though it tried to diversify by growing coconuts, plantains and fibre for making paper. In 1866 the only references I have found in the papers are to the sale of their shares at a fraction of their original price. I wonder whether Thomas also gave up his attempt towards the end of 1866. On 9 April 1866 his son presided at a soirée in the Music Hall in Wrexham to celebrate the 25th anniversary of the opening of the new Chapel in Chester Street. Thomas had intended presiding but had been called back to London. One of the speakers, Mr R. C. Rawlins, gave a talk on the history of Jamaica and referred to the appalling incidents which had recently taken place. James Richardson then remarked that "as his family possessed three estates in the island, he ought to know something about it. He contradicted the assertion that black people were extremely lazy: when they knew they would be paid in money for their labour, and not in kind, they were always ready to work. A proof of this might be gathered from the fact that lately the Messrs Barnes wanted labourers, and such was the rush for the work that they were immediately supplied with sufficient hands and had to turn many away without employing them." This is the only reference I have found to the three estates in Jamaica. I wonder if James Richardson was including John Cheetham, his wife's father, as "family". It is possible that he, like Thomas, had bought land in Jamaica as a new source of cotton. Anyhow, in April 1866 Thomas would appear to have still owned property in Jamaica. However, on 28 May 1866 the Reverend F. Jones of Clarendon was reported as being the agent for the Jamaica Mutual Life Assurance Company in Clarendon Parish. On 20 July 1866 polling began at the Chapelton Court House in Clarendon for the election of two Churchwardens and ten Vestrymen. Reverend F. Jones was elected as one of the Vestrymen. If this was Thomas's agent, perhaps this was the time when Thomas abandoned his experiment and his agent on the cotton estate had to find an alternative source of income.

In the week ending Saturday 17 January 1866 Thomas was expected to chair a meeting in Oswestry when Mr Samuel Bowly from London, a Director of the Temperance Provident Institution, gave a lecture for the Oswestry Temperance Society. Thomas did not give his annual address to his constituents in January this year, presumably because he had addressed them on several occasions before his re-election in July and would only have been able to report on a few months' business.

On 21 January 1866 he was one of the many guests at the Hand Inn near The Quinta when a public dinner was given to mark the coming of age of C. R. W. Tottenham, the son of Colonel Tottenham of Plas Berwyn.

On Thursday 15 February 1866 Thomas and John Cheetham were amongst the minority of fifty Liberal MPs who followed John Bright into the lobby to vote for his amendment on the Cattle Plague Bill to obtain the owner's consent before slaughtering cattle which had been in contact with other diseased animals.

On 5 April 1866 the Bolton Liberals held a public meeting in the Temperance Hall to debate the Reform Bill introduced by Gladstone on 12 March which proposed extending the franchise by another 400,000 electors, most of them working men. Thomas attended to second the first resolution of the evening in support of the bill. There was a large turn-out, proving, as both the Chairman, Robert Heywood, and Thomas pointed out, that there certainly was no apathy in the country about this new bill, as many people claimed. This meeting of Liberals welcomed the bill, not as a complete measure, but as a step on the way to true reform. They felt it was a safe amendment to the 1832 Reform Bill. This was also Thomas's view. "I will take all I can get, and I will not say I am content until I get all I want." He called on the meeting to petition Parliament. He was also asked to take a petition setting out the support of this meeting. He stressed the importance of the bill. Lord Grosvenor had declared his intention to introduce an amendment. "The Government mean to fall or stand by the bill. They have declared that this amendment shall be considered as a vote of confidence, and upon the carrying of it or not the Government will stay in or go out." He was not over-confident of success. "My own opinion is that the majority of the House do not want a reform bill." There was already a split in the Liberals with a breakaway group, the "Cave of Adullam" led by Robert Lowe, siding with the opposition against Russell, Gladstone, Bright and others. The meeting in the Temperance Hall ended with a resolution to hold another meeting, this one in the open air, in support of the bill before its second reading.

Thomas was unable to chair a meeting in the Music Hall in Wrexham on 9 April 1866 because he had gone to London to be present at a meeting of Liberal MPs called by Earl Russell. His son chaired the meeting in his absence. On 12 April the second reading of Gladstone's bill was moved but was not carried until several weeks later after a series of amendments were introduced. After seven debates, all on Lord Grosvenor's amendment, the Government won by a small majority.

For the two next two months before the Government's defeat on another amendment to this bill Thomas was busy at Westminster. On Friday 11 May 1866 he and six other MPs accompanied a deputation from the Lancashire District Sunday School Unions Association and other associations who met the President of the Poor Law Board to discuss the proposal to charge rates to Sunday Schools. John Cheetham MP introduced the deputation and spoke as a fellow-labourer and Sunday School teacher, saying that if the Government did not see its way to secure the object sought by a new act, if necessary, he, along with others, would feel it their duty to do all they could by preparing a bill or otherwise to accomplish it. Thomas and the other MPs present were in full agreement with this.

On Saturday 12 May 1866 the Congregational Union rounded off their annual assembly with a breakfast which Thomas attended together with distinguished representatives of various denominations and over two hundred pastors and delegates of the Congregational churches of England and Wales. Rev. Newman Hall presided, and amongst those present were Lord Ebury, the Dean of Westminster, Sir Francis Crossley MP, Thomas Chambers MP, Harvey Lewis MP, C. M. Norwood MP, G. Leeman MP, the Rector of Christchurch, Blackfriars, the President of the Wesleyan Conference, Rev. Thomas Alexander of the Presbyterian Church, Rev. Dr Thompson from New York and Rev. Sella Martin, delegates of the Congregational churches of America, Rev. W. Ellis, from Madagascar, Rev. Dr Mullens from India, Rev. R. Sewell from Londonderry, L. Kossuth, son of the Hungarian patriot, Hon. A. McArthur, Samuel Morley, W. R. Spicer, H. Wills, C. Jupe, Professor Hoppus, Rev. J. Stoughton, Rev. H. Allon, Rev. T. James, Rev. E. White, Rev. R. Ashton, and Rev. Dr Massie. The meeting was simply a gesture of good fellowship with representatives of other religious bodies. As one of the speakers, Thomas caused controversy when he said that the Chairman, Rev. Newman Hall, was neither Churchman nor Dissenter, because of the use by his congregation of the Liturgy. The Chairman responded to this, amidst applause, by saying, "Certainly, we belong to the Holy Catholic and Apostolic Church". The Chairman then said that while Congregationalists made no secret of their views on ecclesiastical questions, and altogether disapproved of the connection between church and state, they disclaimed the unfair inference that they were opposed to any church as such which might happen to be so connected. It was the principle they condemned, and they would equally condemn it if proposed to be applied to their own body. He wished it to be understood that the representatives of other churches present that morning in no degree compromised their own distinctive views. They knew how to hold and how to utter conscientious and strong convictions, and yet most heartily respect those who differed. I am sure Thomas had no criticism of these words.

On the following Monday morning 14 May 1866 Thomas was at a very large gathering of important people connected with the Congregational Union which met at Hadley's Hotel in Blackfriars to present a testimonial to the Rev. Dr Robert Vaughan who was retiring from *The British Quarterly Review*. Thomas was one of the four MPs who made speeches on the occasion.

On Thursday 24 May he was back in Bolton where he made a brief speech at the opening by the Earl of Bradford of Bolton's new public park, the Heywood Recreation Ground on Bolton Moor. He was also at the banquet in the afternoon at the Baths Assembly Room and briefly acknowledged the toast at the end of the speeches. On 26 May he had been expected back in Wales to lay the foundation stone of a new chapel at Cefn Mawr but special engagements prevented his attendance.

He was back in Westminster on Wednesday 30 May 1866 when he and John Cheetham were amongst nine MPs who introduced a deputation from the Lancashire Butchers' Association who had travelled to London to meet the Right Hon. H. A. Bruce at the Privy Council Office. They wanted some relaxation of the restrictions imposed during the Cattle Plague to make it easier for cattle to be moved from Salford cattle market to adjoining towns. Their mission was successful—on the following day a new order was issued allowing cattle to be sent alive from Salford market to places within a twelve-mile radius. If the distance was more than five miles, they had to be sent by railway.

Where the Reform Bill was concerned, the Government managed to remain victorious until Monday 18 June when Lord Dunkellin's amendment that rating, not rental value, should be the basis of the right to vote defeated the Government by just eleven votes. Thomas was one of the 304 Members of Parliament who voted for Lord Dunkellin's amendment to the £7 borough franchise clause of the Reform Bill which was to leave out the words "clear yearly value" and insert instead "rateable value". As a result of its defeat Earl Russell's Government resigned to avoid dissolution on the question of Reform, fearing that this would split the Liberal party. That was the end of this Reform Bill. Lord Derby then formed his third ministry.

On Saturday 23 June 1866 Thomas was back in Lancashire to lay the corner stone of the new Independent Schools and Chapel House at Stand. He was presented with an inscribed silver trowel and mention was made of his former connection with their Sunday School. In his speech he said he was prevented by present circumstances from taking any active part in Sunday School management but he hoped to take up the work again some time. Thomas and his sister Mrs Jane Haslam were guests at the Jubilee Meeting at Halshaw Moor Chapel on 26 June. During that year he made a second attempt to give Queen Street Seminary in Farnworth to the Church at Halshaw Moor to be used as a Denominational School. Again, nothing came of this offer.

In the year 1865/66 business at the mills in Farnworth was better than in the previous year but the firm made another loss, this time of £3,861. On 30 June 1866 Thomas and Joseph Winter shared the loss on the same basis as in the previous year except that this time part of Thomas's share (£428 19s 8d) was allocated to his son. Thomas made a note that he paid off the previous year's loss, which presumably included the £6,400 owed by Joseph Winter. For the first time, James Richardson added his signature. He did not receive an allowance this year but continued to draw out of the Petty Cash.

Thomas was in Richmond on Saturday 21 July at a formal dinner at the Star and Garter Hotel chaired by W. E. Gladstone to inaugurate the Cobden Club. (He attended the same dinner the following year.) Amongst the many guests were John Cheetham and his son J. F. Cheetham.

Around this time in 1866 there were moves in Denbighshire to invite Thomas to stand as a Liberal candidate in that area at the next election. A Reform Meeting was held in a field near Brymbo Church, chaired by Rev. W. Jones MA of Tredegar. He said that he saw no reason why ministers should not become involved with politics. Another minister, Rev. J. Jones of Brynrhug, called for the removal from Parliament of their three present Members: the Conservatives Mr Mainwaring and Sir Watkin Wynn and the Liberal member for Denbighshire, Colonel Biddulph. He believed the Liberals in Denbighshire could return any Liberal member they might want. He believed that the Dissenters in the parishes of Wrexham and Ruabon if true to their principles could turn the scale in favour of "a gentleman in whom the Liberals confide, and who at all times would vote in favour of reform—that gentleman was Mr Barnes of The Quinta". This remark was greeted with loud cheers.

On 8 August 1866 Robert Heywood again wrote to Thomas Barnes at the House of Commons about the possibility of a contested election.

My dear Sir,

I have had Mr Thomasson with me this morning as one of the committee to make arrangements for the next election. They seem resolved upon a contest and mention our *townsman* Richard Harwood and Mr Pope. The former has had his fancy tickled by having been named on some emergency but is quite out of the question having hardly the ability or likely to have any great support from the liberals, and the other is seriously damaged by his honest and noble principles. I told Mr T. that I could not see any chance of altering our position unless he would come out himself and exercise all his enger [sic] and influence in stirring up the new constituency. This he positively declines till you keep to the hours of delight. My opinion is that the attempt will utterly fail and leave us unrepresented.

When I think of the Tories so wealthy, so unscrupulous and so united and our party so *crochetty*, I feel convinced that the attempt will utterly fail and leave us misrepresented which I consider worse than non represented. However I am desired to write to you upon this matter so as to lay your views before the committee. They express themselves quite satisfied with your services and only wish to strengthen you and the liberal interest by the course now proposed.

Yours very truly, RH[5]

Thomas's reply on the following day was no more positive for the Liberals:

9 August 1866

Dear Mr Heywood

I am much obliged to you for your letter which I have just received. In reference to the matter of it, I beg to say I think it is rather premature to discuss at present either the question whether there shall be two candidates for our party, or the other question, who they shall be. We are not to have a general election until 1869. I think it would be wiser to wait until we see what will be the character of the new register. If there are to be two candidates for our party Mr Thomasson should be one if possible. But seeing how the Tories have acted—how completely they have become Radicals—had we not better say, we are satisfied with their new policy. They have "turned over a new leaf" and we hope they will go on in their New ways. What can we say against Col. Gray after his votes in support of the New Reform Bill!!! Should we not embrace him and his party with open arms, as allies!! And so long as they go on in this way, can we oppose them!

For myself, I beg to say that I begin to think I ought now to retire. I have occupied this honourable position a long time, and now I should make way for some gentleman in Bolton, who may aspire to the office and emoluments. The great object which I have been seeking for fifteen years is now attained. A Reform Bill on the basis of Household suffrage has been gained. The franchise is greatly extended. A large number of new Voters will come upon the scene, and the stage should be made clear and free for the New constituency to choose their own candidates without bias or influence.

I should not like to stand in the way of the new constituency making a free choice of their future representatives and I think that to make it quite open and free it is necessary I should say "Othello's work is done" and slide behind the scenes.

But there is time enough yet to talk about arrangements for the future and I have only one wish which is that Bolton should be well represented.

I am, my dear Mr Heywood, yours very truly

Thomas Barnes[6]

A report in *The Cheshire Observer* on 8 September 1866 reported that Thomas's wife, Ann, described as "the lady of Thomas Barnes Esq., MP for Bolton", was one of the three patrons of a grand fancy fair bazaar which was to be held on that Saturday and the following Monday and Tuesday in the School Rooms of the Presbyterian Church, City Road, Chester. The other two patrons were the Mayor and Mayoress of Chester. The report does not state whether or not she attended the bazaar.

In 1866 a report in *The North Wales Chronicle* on Saturday 29 September linked Thomas with the Liberation Society which had arranged a conference in Denbigh on Friday 21 September 1866. In the evening a Public Meeting attended by 2,000 people took place in the Calvinistic Methodist Chapel. Thomas was expected to be Chairman of the meeting but was unable to attend, owing to a serious attack of illness. He sent a letter which included the following paragraph: "I venture to hope that the visit of the deputation will lead to some effort of a decided character being made to rectify the anomaly which now exists in Wales, the most decidedly liberal and Nonconformist constituencies being represented almost entirely by the most illiberal and High Church members. The Welsh representatives do not represent the Welsh people, the Welsh constituencies. They represent only a small class and that the upper one, and one that ignores the feelings, the principles and rights of the real constituents. It is time this was put an end to, and Wales become really and correctly represented."

This illness probably also accounts for his absence on Monday 24 September from a demonstration in Manchester organised by agents

of the London Reform League. Several public meetings had already
been held and the mass demonstration was at Knott Mill fair ground,
Camp Field. This was described as "the largest political demonstration
in Manchester since the days of the Anti-Corn Law agitation". In the
evening John Bright made a speech in the Free Trade Hall while other
demonstrators were holding a torchlight meeting outside. I was surprised
that Thomas was not mentioned in reports of this event but his letter
to the conference at Denbigh on the previous Friday would explain
his absence. He was still unfit on Monday 22 October when he was
unable to preside at a tea party for a thousand guests at the new
Congregational Church at Plaskynaston in Cefn Mawr.

However, he was fit and well again by the evening of Tuesday 20
November when he attended a Reform Banquet in the Free Trade
Hall in Manchester, chaired by its President, George Wilson. On the
Thursday of the same week he was present at another grand occasion
near The Quinta, this time a Ball given by Sir Watkin and Lady W.
Wynn in the Grand Hall at Wynnstay. Another Society Ball had just
been given by Mr and Mrs Peel at Bryn-y-Pys. The one at Wynnstay
with an even larger number of the elite of the County outshone it.
Thomas's wife does not appear to have been present at the Ball.

When Thomas gave his annual address to his constituents in the
Temperance Hall in Bolton on Thursday 31 January 1867 he reported
on the previous year's struggles in Parliament with the second Reform
Bill, which still had not been passed. "I stand again before you, not,
I must say, so much to give an account of what has been done in
Parliament as on this occasion to review our position, to look back to
the past, and to look forward to the future." He confined his speech
to just three main topics—the suspension of the Habeas Corpus Act,
the Cattle Plague Bill and the question of reform. He also reported
that he had been ill for two months during the recess. This had given
him the opportunity of reading Macaulay's *History of Britain* and he
used quotations from this in a brilliant piece of oratory to prove that
no-one need have any fear of the masses. Quotations from Macaulay
were being used by the opposition to the Reform Bill to prove just
the opposite view. Thomas kept the information that his quotations
were also from Macaulay's speeches right to the end of his address and
received a round of applause when the name was finally revealed. "And
with such a high authority as that, I think we may be very well content
to go on, as going on we are, and going on we shall do, with agitating
for this Reform Bill."

A month later on 27 February he was speaking as Chairman of the Board of the Provincial Insurance Company at Wrexham when he said of the year that had just ended that it "had been about the most disastrous to commerce and to everything connected with commerce that he at all events, or men who were much older than himself had known in the course of their lives—a year marked by disasters and losses in almost every branch of business".

After four years of silence in the House of Commons Thomas put a question to the Under Secretary of State for India on 11 March 1867 to ask about the progress of a delayed report on the famine in Orissa. He received a very uninformative reply. That was the last time he ever spoke in the House. For the next eighteen months until his defeat at the 1868 November election, he remained silent.

On the afternoon of Thursday 21 March he was one of the 278 Liberal MPs who had an hour-long meeting at Gladstone's private house in Carlton House Terrace. On the following day he and Colonel Gray introduced a deputation of seven men from Great Bolton who met the Right Honourable Gathorne Hardy at the Office of the Poor Law Board in Whitehall.

On Tuesday 26 March he was in Lancashire to attend the opening by Lord Caithness of a Working People's Exhibition in the new hall of Pendleton Working People's Association. He moved the vote of thanks to Lord Caithness. Amongst the many exhibits were works lent by the South Kensington Museum and some porcelain from Mr Gladstone's collection. The proud President of the Association was Thomas's friend W. T. Blacklock who also spoke to praise the work done by its members.

Then came a busy few months. On Friday 10 May 1867 he and four other MPs were at a conference in the Reform Club in Pall Mall to discuss the question of Sunday School rating which had still not been settled. It was attended by superintendents and secretaries of Sunday Schools from various parts of the country and resulted in an agreement that John Cheetham and two of the other MPs present, Hibbert and Graves, would bring in a bill to exempt Sunday Schools from the liability to pay rates. On the same day Thomas appeared before a Select Committee in the House of Commons to give evidence at the first reading of the Bill for the Wrexham, Mold and Connah's Quay Railway.

On the following afternoon, Saturday 11 May 1867, he was one of the deputation who met Gladstone at his house in Carlton House Terrace on Saturday afternoon to discuss the Reform Bill. There were 300 people present, including several MPs. Some of Thomas's Liberal colleagues were also there—J. Cheetham, J. Bright, George Hadfield, E. Baines, and Mr Bazley. It was described in the report in *The Manchester Times* as "one of the largest and most influential reform deputations that have appeared in London during the present session". Thomas was asked during the 1868 election campaign: "When the Conservative Reform Bill of 1867 was going through the House of Commons, what course of action were you, with Mr Gladstone's party, intending to take with regard to the second reading of that bill before the meeting of the tea-room party?" Thomas replied that before the meeting of the tea-room party there was a conference at Gladstone's house, at which it was decided not to vote against the second reading. The resolution they came to was to express an opinion that certain parts of that bill must be reformed in order to make it a good measure; and to secure the bill being made a good one, it was decided that Mr Coleridge should bring forward a resolution for that purpose, and that they should vote for the second reading with that understanding. Mr Gladstone did not intend to throw out the bill on the second reading.

Thomas and other Liberal MPs also attended a public meeting called by the National Reform Union on the following Wednesday evening, 15 May, in St James's Hall, where the speakers included John Bright and John Stuart Mill. This meeting was described by the paper as "the most enthusiastic and impressive of all yet held in London".

Yet another Great Reform Meeting was called for the afternoon of 28 June in St James's Hall to protest against the Government's scheme of redistribution and to demand adequate representation for the large Borough constituencies. George Wilson was to be the Chairman and Thomas was one of the eight MPs expected to address the meeting. The others were John Stuart Mill, Isaac Holden, Sir John Gray, George Hadfield, Dr Brady, Charles Gilpin and Thomas O'Donoghue.

30 June was as usual the day of the annual stocktaking at the Farnworth Mills. This year the business had made a huge profit of £32,220, at 62½% the highest ever return on the capital. Out of it Thomas paid his share of the loss made in 1865/66 and Joseph Winter his £1,286 18s.

In the first week of July he attended two dinners, the first, a breakfast with between 300 and 400 guests in St James's Hall given to Mr Lloyd Garrison to congratulate him and his friends in America upon the abolition of slavery there. As at the Reform dinners, ladies were also present, and *The Manchester Times* noted that there were probably more "persons of colour" there than had ever before been the case at a single meeting in London. A few days later another dinner in honour of Mr

Lloyd Garrison was given in Bolton. Thomas did not attend this one, possibly because on Wednesday 3 July he and John Cheetham were amongst the 160 guests at the Anniversary Dinner of the Cobden Club at the Star and Garter Hotel in Richmond with Earl Russell presiding.

An Editorial in *The North Wales Chronicle* on Saturday 20 July 1867 indicated that Thomas was being seriously considered as a Welsh Liberal MP: "Radicalism, after a century's somnolency, is beginning to show signs of returning to life in North Wales, and the dead body is being galvanized by sundry quack practitioners. The political dissenters of Denbighshire, headed by Mr Gee of Denbigh, have just covertly commenced the electioneering campaign to oust the present Conservative members—Sir Watkin [Wynn] and Mr Mainwaring—and to return in their stead Mr Miall (or any other sufficiently advanced political Dissenter who can be made the subservient tool of the Liberation Society)." The writer named as possible Liberal candidates Mr Miall and Mr Biddulph, or Mr Biddulph and Mr Barnes.

Thomas was continuing to perform official duties at various chapels near his home at The Quinta. On Thursday 25 July 1867 he was Chairman at the opening of Broad Oak Chapel and on the following day laid a memorial stone at Wollerton, a small Independent Chapel between Hodnet and Market Drayton, where he was presented with a silver trowel.

On 16 September 1867 Recognition Services were held at the English Congregational Church in Ruabon for the new minister Rev. J. Lewis. Thomas chaired a public meeting in the chapel in the evening. He explained that the reason for Recognition Services was that there was no law to prevent any man calling himself an Independent minister. Therefore public recognition was important. The Church in Ruabon was very pleased to have Thomas as their Chairman as it was the first opportunity they had had of welcoming him since he had made a generous contribution to the building fund ten years earlier.

Three days later on 19 September he was at a very grand event when the town of Barrow-in-Furness celebrated the opening of the new docks built by the Furness Railway Company. The town which had grown rapidly from just a small village with a few farms and small cottages now had docks only rivalled in size by the docks at Birkenhead. Dignitaries had been invited to the banquet from all the corporate towns of Lancashire, Yorkshire, Cumberland and Westmoreland and Thomas was there together with his fellow MP for Bolton, Colonel Gray. However, all the directors, managers and secretaries of all the railway companies in the country were there, not to mention all the merchants and commercial men of importance, all the JPs in Lancashire, Cumberland and Westmoreland, and all individuals prominent in social, political and trading circles. Thomas would have qualified for an invitation on several counts. Gladstone was one of the chief guests and made a speech. The Chairman was the Duke of Devonshire and the Vice-Chairman the Duke of Buccleuch. Messrs Jennison of Manchester who had done the catering for Thomas at the opening of Farnworth Park also supplied the food on this occasion.

On Friday 25 October 1867 Thomas chaired a lecture in Oswestry Public Hall by the Rev. G. W. Condor MA from Manchester with the title "Past and Present, or, Steam, the Civiliser". The proceeds were to go to the British School in Oswestry.

He gave his annual speech to his constituents on 23 January 1868— a celebratory occasion because a new Reform Bill had now been passed. The borough vote was now given to all rate-paying occupiers and to those occupying lodgings of £10 value. In the counties the vote was given to those occupying houses rated at £12. The effect was to almost double the electorate. 45 seats were redistributed by removing one member from each borough with a population below 10,000. Shortly after Thomas gave his address to his constituents the Reform Association in Bolton began to prepare for the next election by recommending on 3 February that moves should be made to select a second candidate to stand alongside Thomas when that election came. This idea had first been mooted in August 1866 when Robert Heywood wrote to Thomas to express his disapproval of the idea. Nevertheless, after Lord Derby's third ministry ended in February and Disraeli took over, it was Robert Heywood who chaired a second meeting of Bolton Reform Association on 28 April to appoint a Selection Committee.

With the passing of the Reform Bill Thomas had time for other issues. On 5 March 1868 he was one of many MPs who accompanied a deputation to the Duke of Marlborough to apply to the Government for a grant to build an extension to Owens College in Manchester. He was also in the group who met the First Lord of the Treasury on 24 March to apply further pressure for the grant to Owens College. They did not receive a very positive answer—Disraeli assured them of government attention and said that in any case, he was sure the people of Lancashire would help out if necessary.

At the beginning of January 1870 when Thomas was no longer an MP, a reference was made at a meeting of Wrexham Town Council to another enterprise with which he had been involved whilst still MP for Bolton—the building of a Channel Tunnel. On 25 January 1870 the main item of business at the monthly meeting of Wrexham Town Council was the approval of a letter to be sent to Gladstone in support of a plan put forward by Mr Low, one of the Members of the Board. The letter was in support of a committee of Frenchmen and Englishmen who were hoping to build a tunnel under the sea to connect England's railways with those of France and the Continent. Mr Low and two other engineers, Mr James Brunlees and Mr John Hawkshaw, were the three English engineers for the tunnel. When they had been in France Senator Michael Chevalier suggested that before the committee presented the Emperor with the finished plan it would be a good idea to accompany it with an address signed by several important Englishmen asking for the Emperor's support for the undertaking. They would not make themselves responsible for the work but would point out that it could form a bond of union and strength between the two nations when finished. The first signature on the address was that of Sir Watkin W. Wynn, the second that of Colonel Biddulph, and the third that of Thomas Barnes, at that time MP for Bolton.

On Tuesday 5 May 1868 the Eighth Triennial Conference of the Liberation Society began in Cannon Street Hotel in London. Thomas, who had been too ill to attend the conference in Denbigh on 21 September 1866, was present at this one and chaired the conference in the evening. The full name of the Liberation Society was The Society for the Liberation of Religion from State Control. Samuel Pope, another of its members, explained: "It is not a society for the disestablishment of religion. It is not a society intending to interfere with the internal management of the Church, but it is a society liberating or wishing to liberate religion from State control. Why? Because we believe that religion is not benefited, but is hindered, by being associated with the civil power."

On the night of Friday 29 May 1868 Thomas was one of the MPs who voted with Gladstone in the majority when the House divided for the second reading of Gladstone's Established Church (Ireland) Bill. Colonel Myddelton Biddulph, the Liberal member for Denbighshire, paired in favour. The other MPs in the Denbighshire area, Mr Mainwaring, Lord Hill Trevor and Sir W. W. Wynn voted in the minority against the Bill.

At the end of May the Bolton Reform Association was busy preparing for the next election. After two Selection Committee meetings they were unable to come to a firm decision about the choice of the second candidate and were still debating the merits of the two men Robert Heywood had mentioned in August 1866, Richard Harwood and

Samuel Pope. Eventually, on 17 June, the Committee's two recommendations were put before a full meeting of the Association's members, chaired by Thomas Thomasson, not by Robert Heywood. There was a very definite and acrimonious division in the ranks of the Liberals. Joseph Crook reappeared on the political scene after a long absence to propose Samuel Pope who had failed to be elected in 1865. When the vote on the resolution was taken, the teetotallers swung the vote clearly in favour of Samuel Pope.

Thomas was still busy officiating at church occasions. On 1 June 1868 he laid the foundation stone at the new Independent Chapel at Maesbury and was presented with a very handsome inscribed trowel. A hermetically sealed bottle was placed in a cavity in the stone together with a parchment and three newspapers—*The English Independent, The Oswestry Advertiser* and *The Nonconformist*. This was followed by a public meeting in the evening. When the Maesbury Congregational Chapel finally opened, Thomas was Chairman and Rev. Davison, the Minister from Quinta Chapel, gave the address.

At the annual stocktaking on 30 June the profit of £10,763 was shared as usual with Joseph Winter receiving his one-third share. For the first time the amount allocated to James Richardson out of his father's share was set out in the accounts. (He received one sixth of it.) In that year, 1867/68, a new name appeared in the accounts, that of Samuel Horrocks who appears to have had about £1,100 invested in the company. (His separate account at the back of the book does not begin until 1871.) The only new types of cloth mentioned in the inventory were cords and calicos. It was not mentioned in the annual accounts that the firm probably made a loss when two bills, each for £1,000, belonging to the company and dated 14 April, got lost in the post between Manchester and London. Bankers were warned in a notice in *The Times* on 24 April not to negotiate the bills. I do not know whether they were ever traced.

On 8 July 1868 Thomas was again involved in a stone-laying ceremony, this time in his Lancashire constituency, at Claremont Baptist Chapel, St George's Road, Bolton.

On 11 July, a public meeting of Bolton Liberals was held in the Temperance Hall, again with Thomas Thomasson in the chair. Thomas Barnes and Samuel Pope were formally adopted to fight a joint campaign just as they had done at the previous election.

On 15 July 1868 the Jamaica Committee was wound up after the attempt to have Governor Eyre prosecuted had failed. On 16 July Thomas was back in London as one of a deputation of noblemen and gentlemen from the cotton districts at a ceremony in the Guild Hall to present a new window to the Corporation of London. It had cost over £1,000 and was the gift of the workpeople in Lancashire and the cotton districts to commemorate the assistance given during the Cotton Famine by the Mansion House Relief Fund. By the end of the month Thomas was back in Shropshire to act as Chairman on 23 July at the re-opening service at Ruyton Congregational Chapel and on Friday 31 July he was again on the Grand Jury at the Denbighshire Summer Assizes.

Later that year, on 22 September, the build-up to the election began in earnest in Bolton at a crowded meeting in the Temperance Hall, chaired by Joseph Crook, when Thomas and Samuel Pope were invited by the Reform Association in Derby Ward to set out their views. As municipal elections were also due to be held on 2 November, election fever was already evident with many National Reform Union banners festooning the room. Party colours—blue for the Tories and red for the Liberals—were also in evidence. The Liberals were keen at this election to show their patriotism and that they were not trying to undermine the British constitution in any way. This meeting began and ended with verses of the National Anthem, something which I have not come across before in reports of their meetings. Thomas tackled the question of the British Constitution in his speeches during the election campaign. He discussed what was meant by it and showed how important it was that it should be altered and improved when necessary. "Macaulay said the English Constitution might be compared to a good old ship, always sailing over the waters, but now and then requiring a fresh plank to keep it right. New ones were put in, the old ship was repaired, still kept afloat, weathering every storm, and at the present day so many new planks had been put in that no one could tell where the original planks were." At this meeting in the Temperance Hall Thomas and Joseph Crook discussed in great detail the main question to be considered at this election—the position of the Established Church in Ireland and the question of religious equality before the law. All sorts of issues were involved including the grant to the Catholic seminary at Maynooth and the grant of State money, the Regium Donum, to Dissenters. Gladstone's Suspensory Bill prevented new appointments being made in the Irish Church until Parliament had decided the question of the disestablishment and disendowment of the Irish Church. Gladstone had also made it clear that if the Irish Church was disendowed, then all grants of every kind both to Catholics and to Presbyterians would have to be discontinued. However, the two candidates had many other issues to tackle at this election arising from attempts to cloud the main questions by personal squabbles and slanders. They stressed that the Liberals were going to try to fight this campaign on principles, not on personalities, and the two men did put a great amount of effort in the many speeches they made during the campaign into setting out the differences between the political parties. For example, on one occasion Thomas said he agreed with the definition of Toryism given by the Chairman, that the many were born to serve and the few to govern, or, as it was quaintly described by a public speaker, "Some men were born with saddles on their backs and bridles in their mouths, and other men were born to ride them". He tried to define Toryism: "Mr Disraeli once said a sound Conservative Government was 'Whig measures and Tory men'. Tories in power, carrying out Whig measures." His colleague, Samuel Pope, also showed himself to be a talented speaker who skilfully defended the many personal attacks made on him. Both men agreed that the working men who had now been given the right to vote would determine the outcome of the election. Thomas said he wished to see the working men of this country the most ardent and earnest politicians, and if they were true to their interests they would be so. They would determine the sort of Parliament the country got. The meeting was a great success. Derby Ward had given the two candidates a rousing send-off.

In the following week they had campaign meetings every night from Monday to Thursday in different wards of the borough and Thomas even managed to fit in a separate engagement on Wednesday morning, 30 September, when he made a speech in the Temperance Hall at the opening of a bazaar to raise funds for the building of a new Baptist Church in St George's Road, Bolton. On one of the stalls a Miss Vickers had a scent jar for sale which she had painted "very elegantly". I wonder if this was perhaps the first reference to Elizabeth Vickers who had become Thomas's housekeeper at Limefield around 1861. The minister of this church, Rev. T. W. Handforth, was one of several local ministers who had become involved in the politics of the election and had spoken out to support Liberal policies, especially in relation to the Irish question. This caused responses by Anglican clergymen and led to remarks made by Thomas about provision for the poor in Anglican churches being taken up in the press by his opponents. It ended with Rev. W. M. Hurst, the Vicar of the local Anglican church at St Martin's near The Quinta, being drawn into the dispute with long letters in *The Bolton Chronicle* justifying the number of pews available for the poor in his church. His parting line was: "I do feel deeply pained at our being thus rudely singled out and put on our defence on the occasion of a Parliamentary contested election". Quite unintentionally, Thomas's election campaign in Bolton was having repercussions near The Quinta.

At the meeting in East Ward on the Tuesday evening Thomas gave a very carefully researched speech on the topic "Who gave Reform?" arguing that the Tory Government could not take full credit for the passing of the Bill. It was the Liberals who had given the bill its final shape: "By the motions made on the Liberal side of the House, that bill was moulded into something like its present form." At the meeting on Thursday at Astley Bridge the Chairman, A. Pilling, listed Thomas himself as one of the great names in the Reform movement: "Had it not been for Thomas Barnes, John Bright, William Ewart Gladstone, and others of the same school, that Reform Bill would never have been obtained."

Whilst Thomas and Samuel Pope were holding their campaign meetings, another group of Bolton electors, both Liberals and Conservatives, were holding their own meeting. They were members of the Licensed Victuallers' Association who were alarmed by Samuel Pope's teetotalism and membership of the United Kingdom Alliance. They appealed to everyone interested in the future of Bolton's licensed trade, regardless of their politics, to vote against him. This underlying problem of Samuel Pope's teetotalism caused several Liberals to change their allegiance on voting day.

On Wednesday 7 October 1868 Thomas was one of the guest speakers at a Grand Banquet held in the evening at the Board Room in Hotel Street, Bolton, to commemorate the opening of the Bolton Gas Company's new offices. For an evening the political squabbling was put on one side as the two MPs were complimented on the work they had done for the town. The Mayor said: "When the party spirit and the strife of the present time (which, he was sorry to say, was pretty strong) had passed away, and the history of these times came to be written, it would be considered by the calm and thoughtful inhabitants of Bolton that they had never had two better members than Messrs Gray and Barnes." In his speech Thomas made an interesting comment on the Gas Company: "I think the Bolton Gas Company is an instance of the way in which prosperous concerns in this country can be carried on. They have been begun by cautious, and careful, and excellent men of business, who have been a great deal more anxious about success than about show, and have worked on patiently and slowly, but always surely, not making haste to be rich, but seeking to make a progress safe and steady as they went on, and now they have the proud satisfaction of seeing one of the most successful and prosperous gas companies in the United Kingdom." Very much the same could be said about Thomas's own business in Farnworth.

Meetings of various sorts continued over the next three weeks and the Municipal Election was held on 2 November. The two Liberal candidates continued to argue their policies with Thomas sticking firmly to principles but Samuel Pope having to defend himself even more forcefully from personal attacks made by supporters of John Hick, the second Conservative candidate who had been brought in as Colonel Gray's colleague (and who, in the end, was responsible for both Thomas and Samuel Pope being defeated). Thomas continued to impress upon the voters how important this election would be: "If the Tories gained the coming Parliamentary election, it would stamp a character upon the borough for many years to come—it would be, they might expect, a Tory borough for a great many years hence; and the borough would not be advanced in the van of the boroughs of the nation, but would be hanging back and left behind as one of the unimportant boroughs of the community."

At the end of October Robert Heywood, the President of the Bolton Reform Registration Association, who had supported Thomas Barnes throughout his political career, died at the age of 82. At his funeral on 31 October there were 36 carriages. Thomas Barnes was in the fourth one, immediately behind the relatives.

After the Municipal Elections and before the election of the Mayor a second Great Reform Meeting was held on Thursday 5 November in the Temperance Hall, five weeks after the one in September which had marked the start of the campaign. The Chairman was Thomas Thomasson who had not appeared at meetings during this election campaign since he chaired the meeting in July when Thomas and Samuel Pope were formally adopted as candidates. This huge enthusiastic meeting was the last such mass meeting Thomas was ever to address, although he did not yet know it. He said: "I have had the opportunity of addressing a great number of meetings since the agitation in connection with this election commenced, and I must say I have never seen yet on any occasion an audience like the present. I can only compare it to a story told in reference to the battle of Waterloo. It is said that during that battle, some of the best British soldiers were laid down, either upon their bellies, or upon their knees, behind a little rising eminence, and that at one particular period, when the Duke of Wellington saw that the battle required a particular impulse, he went to those soldiers, and said, 'Up lads, and at 'em'. Well, it appears to me that that is the feeling prevailing in this audience. This is not a time for speech making, but really a time for action." There was just time for one last political meeting on Saturday 7 November at Astley Bridge at which Thomas worked his way through the main questions of the election and made another speech on the history of Reform saying "he appeared before them as a real Radical Reformer, and one who was not born yesterday, but who made his first political speech when he was in his teens, and when they were agitating for the first Reform Bill; therefore he stood before them as an old Reformer." In the following week the Queen announced dissolution of Parliament and 17 November as the date of the election. Canvassing now began in earnest.

On Nomination Day, 16 November, between thirty and forty thousand people, many more than at previous elections, gathered in the Market Place in front of the hustings. Even Richard Cobden's widow and her daughters, friends of Thomas Thomasson, were there to support Samuel Pope. People were wearing the party colours of blue and red; there were many political "squibs" in evidence and various mock demonstrations such as one by the Conservatives of a young man "washing his hands" which appeared to be directed at Thomas Barnes for not voting for the Bleachers' Bill when a division was called. The Liberal supporters got their own back. An effigy of a soldier, stripped to the waist and being whipped by another man, was held up above the heads of the crowd and pointed towards Colonel Gray. Then a man dressed in military uniform was lifted up on to the shoulders of his friends who pretended to flog him. Another Liberal demonstration involved a young man holding up and twisting a bright new screw-key. A piece of bacon on the end of a pole was held up labelled "The original Tory bacon". The Liberals had their own cry of "Barnes and Pope" in opposition to the Conservatives' "Gray and Hick", and they sang the political song "Shout boys, shout, and tell the Tories".

Thomas Thomasson had stepped in after Robert Heywood's death to nominate Thomas: "I have known Mr Barnes from his youth upwards, and I have seen him gradually advance from the ardent enthusiasm of youth to the rank of a benevolent philanthropist, and of a cautious and enlightened statesman. The poet says—'That Satan is grown wiser than of yore, and tempts by making rich, not making poor'. Well, he has passed undamaged through the temptations of wealth, and not his wealth alone, but his time and his talents have been constantly placed at the service of his countrymen. His public character is pure and spotless, and the shafts of calumny itself fall harmless at his feet. As a politician he has served this borough long and faithfully, and he can point to a long list of public measures which he has supported. During the political paralysis in which Lord Palmerston was the mere tool for carrying out the policy of Lord Derby, and when many so-called Liberals offered every obstruction to every Reform, Mr Barnes steadily adhered to his principles—'Amongst the faithless faithful always he'. And in the late mighty contest which I rejoice has ended in the enfranchisement of the ten thousand householders in whose presence I have the honour to stand, when others crept under tea-tables, or sought shelter in caves, Mr Barnes consistently supported the great Liberal leaders, Gladstone and Bright, and steadfastly adhered to those great principles of human progress, to the promotion of which his entire political life has been devoted. His past public conduct is before you. His future policy he has explained with the most transparent candour and sincerity, and he has done so without hesitation, or evasion, or equivocation, or double dealing, or deception, or concealment, and has challenged the fullest and most free, public or private, inquiry, on every point. I esteem it a peculiar honour to be allowed to nominate him as a fit and proper person to represent this borough in Parliament."

In his speech Thomas concentrated on examining past Conservative policy. He ended: "Now gentlemen, that party in the past has done nothing to deserve your support, and in the future it promises to do nothing whatever. It is, then, for you now to say from which party you will choose your future representatives. Of my own past career, you are witnesses, and I say nothing. What I have done I may say I shall do in the future. I shall ever seek to promote those laws which I believe will be beneficial to the mass of the people. I shall be totally opposed to all class legislation, and all privileges to any party. I shall seek to deal out even-handed justice to all classes of the people, and to secure for the whole of this United Kingdom peace, contentment, and happiness; and I shall seek in the policy of the Government, to secure retrenchment, and peace, and happiness for all."

After all the speeches the Mayor called for a show of hands for each candidate in turn. *The Bolton Chronicle* summed up the situation accurately (of course with the benefit of knowing the actual result by the time of publication): "There was not as great diversity in the numbers as we have seen on former occasions. Still there was a very decided majority for Colonel Gray, and a still larger number for Mr Hick. The numbers for Messrs Barnes and Pope were less than for either of the other two candidates, the Liberals voting about equal numbers for

Messrs Barnes and Pope." The Mayor did not have the advantage of hindsight and the closeness of the numbers for each candidate coupled with the large numbers involved was a problem for him. However, he finally declared the show of hands in favour of Colonel Gray and John Hick and the nominators of the two Liberal candidates demanded a poll for the next day.

This time there were fifteen polling booths throughout the borough and polling went on without major problems. There was no unruly behaviour around the booths although in other parts of the town rival gangs went on the rampage, fighting, breaking windows and damaging property so that the Riot Act had to be read. There was one very interesting incident at this Bolton election which might even be the first historical record of a woman voting. "Much enthusiasm was created in Derby Ward by the fact of a woman named Frances Wharton, of 131 Cannon Street, voting for Messrs Gray and Hick at the Commission Street booth. She arrived in the neighbourhood of the booth in a conveyance, and was escorted to the booth by Colonel Gray, amid the plaudits of the spectators. The woman's name appears on the register as 'Francis' Wharton, but the deputy returning officer had no power to reject the vote."

When the poll closed at four o'clock it was clear that the Conservatives had won but, in fact, the support for all four candidates was fairly equally balanced. The votes cast were 6,061 for John Hick, 5,848 for Colonel Gray, 5,451 for Thomas Barnes and 5,436 for Samuel Pope, making a total of 22,796 votes—a very high turn-out in a constituency of just over 12,000 with two votes each. However, only in Exchange Ward and West Ward did Thomas have a very slight majority over John Hick. Otherwise the election was a clean-sweep for the Conservatives. To the very end the Conservatives maintained that the Liberals had brought the defeat upon themselves by putting two candidates in the field. Colonel Gray said when the official result was declared: "The contest that has taken place was not one of our seeking. Our opponents had, in the last session of Parliament, one gentleman to represent their opinions. They were not satisfied with that, but must needs try to monopolise the representation of the borough, and the challenge they threw down, we could not refuse to take up." For the first time in its history, Bolton now was to send two Conservatives to Westminster.

The Liberals were disappointed and surprised by the result. Thomas did not blame the working men: "Working men of Bolton,—We have fought a great fight. It has been fought well. We have not been successful; we do not know why, but the fault is not with you. I feel perfectly satisfied with the manner in which you, the working men of Bolton, have worked and fought in this election. You have been striving for your rights. You have been working for what you believe to be the advantage of the State. You have done it in the most legitimate manner. Perfectly spotless and pure, I believe, has everything been that you have done." He did not sound too disappointed at finally being able to leave national politics. Perhaps as he had written to Robert Heywood he was relieved the time had come for him to say "Othello's work is done" and slide behind the scenes. He said: "I stand before you as one of the candidates that has not been successful. It does not depress my spirits one bit. I was fighting along with you for what I believed to be great and good principles of good government,—a good policy for a great nation. I have been fighting with you for what I believed would have elevated this country,—for a policy, which, if carried out, would elevate this country to the highest pitch of glory and honour in the world." He was convinced that over-all, the Liberals would be successful in this election and in this he was quite right. "Sound principles will progress; they will advance; they will go on. Every place is not like Bolton, over-ridden by stupid, ignorant Toryism. Intelligence exists in Birmingham, and it exists in many other places if it does not exist in Bolton, and I hope the day will not be very far off when the rising generation will read, and inquire, and think for themselves, and then a higher tone of political morality, and political knowledge and sentiment, will arise, and we shall see a different result in the borough of Bolton." The last public words spoken by Thomas at this, or any other election, were: "I have nothing more to say but again to thank you for your noble and devoted exertions, and to wish that the next time those exertions may be crowned with greater success. You have worked for success, and you have richly deserved it, but the righteous cause does not always succeed, and a devoted Liberal is not always successful. Don't lie down; rise again and make yourselves ready to fight on another day."

And so the 1868 election was over. It had been hard-fought, and never before had the candidates had to make so many speeches and for so many weeks. After the county elections had taken place it was clear that the picture in Bolton was not typical of the country as a whole. A Liberal Government, led by Gladstone, came into power. Thomas Barnes's political career came to an end just when what he had been fighting for since his early days as a member of the Manchester School became a reality—the extension of the franchise to a wider section of the population, the working men. After this, he never returned to national politics. Perhaps his political life can best be summed up by Rev. Hewgill who said at his memorial service in 1897, "He was an ardent, earnest politician of advanced views at a time when the country was sorely in need of such men to educate and mould the opinions of the people and their representatives to right and good action. He threw himself heartily into the great political and economical movements between 1840 and 1860 (for example, Liberalism, Free Trade and social progress), not without occasional doubts as to how far a Christian man may engage in public work."

The end of Thomas's political career was formally marked on 23 February 1869 when he and Mr Pope were presented with silver epergnes and illuminated addresses at a huge meeting of Liberals, mainly working men and women, which was held in Mr Pablo Fanque's Alhambra Circus in Ashburner Street in Bolton. Before the ceremony two thousand people had been entertained to tea in two sittings at the Temperance Hall and at the Congregational Hall on St George's Road. Another two thousand people bought sixpenny admission tickets for the ceremony itself, so that four thousand people were in the circus to hear the speeches. Alderman Wolfenden, the Chairman, and other prominent Bolton Liberals sat on a temporary platform on one side of the circus ring. Thomas's son, James Richardson, was also present. The Darwen Brass Band provided music and the supporting timbers were decorated with evergreens and artificial flowers. There were banners with appropriate mottoes around the building. The centre-pieces were the two epergnes, valued at £110 each, made of frosted and burnished silver with figures at the base and branches springing from the stem. They, too, had been decorated with flowers. Each had an inscription. The one for Thomas read:

> Presented to Thomas Barnes, Esq., by the Liberal working men and women of Bolton, in remembrance of his faithful services as their representative in Parliament during a long series of years, and of his consistent advocacy of the cause of civil and religious freedom.
>
> Bolton, 23 February 1869

Although the meeting was not officially a political demonstration, the huge turn-out and the tone of the speeches made it a very significant occasion for the defeated Liberals of Bolton to show that they were not depressed by the result of the last election and intended to fight on. Although Bolton and much of Lancashire had lost their Liberal members of Parliament, the Government was in the hands of Liberals, and Liberal Reformers at that, led by Gladstone. There was a warning that the Tory opposition in Bolton planned to interrupt the ceremony by a false fire alarm. The audience were told to ignore it, but actually, nothing of the sort took place. John Bright had written from his home in Wakefield to James Vickers, the Secretary of the Bolton Reform Association, apologising for not being able to attend:

Heath, Wakefield, January 18, 1869

Dear Sir,

There is no chance of my being able to accept your invitation to meet Mr Barnes and Mr Pope about the middle of February. I shall be compelled to be in London at that time, and my many and pressing duties make it impossible for me to accept invitations to public meetings unless under very special circumstances. I need not tell you how much I regret that Mr Barnes and Mr Pope were not returned to Parliament at your recent election. I hope and believe the time will come when the present verdict of your constituency will be reversed.

I am, very respectfully yours,

John Bright

The tribute paid to Thomas by Mr Joe Cooper speaking on behalf of the working people of Bolton summed up many of his political achievements: "Few boroughs have been honoured by having a representative for so lengthened a period who has commanded such universal respect, such universal confidence and even the respect of those who were politically opposed to him. In Mr Barnes we recognise one of a body of men who have embalmed their names in the country's history—a band of men who leagued themselves together that they might obtain for the toiling multitudes of their countrymen the great, the untold blessings of cheap and untaxed bread—a band of men who, by dint of large sacrifices of time and money, and of unwearied effort, succeeded in breaking down the bulwarks of monopoly, and of inaugurating a new era in the history of the commercial policy of the country. To Mr Barnes also belongs the high honour of forming one of a comparatively small but distinguished body of men who, many years ago, when friends were few and opponents were many, laboured earnestly and banded themselves together for a high and holy object, to secure the liberation of religion from State patronage and State control. I should be trespassing upon your patience were I to enumerate all the labours and all the good causes which have had the benefit of Mr Barnes's advocacy. Compulsory Church-rates have ceased to exist. Mr Barnes has the honour of having for years advocated the abolition of compulsory Church-rates. To Mr Barnes also belongs the high honour of advocating the cause of Reform. Mr Barnes has never been one that has talked of the great body of the working men of this country as the great unwashed or the swinish multitude. On the contrary, he has ever regarded the great mass of working men, being sober, intelligent, educated, and God-fearing, as the basis upon which the column of his country's greatness must be reared, to be reared safely and effectively. Mr Barnes has laboured to promote the great causes of retrenchment, vote by ballot, and the education of the people; and every other great and good measure that has been before the people during the last five-and-twenty years has found in our late distinguished member an eloquent and distinguished advocate."

The beautiful address illuminated and engrossed by John Watson of Bolton had apparently been the idea of the women of Bolton. Mr Cooper read it out on behalf of the working men and women who had collected all the money and arranged the whole ceremony.

An Address to Thos. Barnes, Esq., J.P.,

from the Liberal Working Men and Working Women of Bolton

Dear Sir,

We desire you to accept this humble expression of the gratitude we feel for the great services you have rendered to us, and of the high admiration with which we view the ability, straightforwardness, and consistency which have distinguished your political career.

As the Liberal representative of this borough in Parliament, during a period of nearly sixteen years, your conduct was an honour to the constituency. Your annual review of your labours in the House of Commons, and the intelligent exposition which you favoured us with on those occasions, of the true policy of legislative action and administrative Government, increased our confidence in you, and enhanced our esteem for you from year to year.

Within the time during which you held a seat in the Legislature many and great questions arose; and we remember with deep thankfulness your earnest and cordial support to all measures for extending the liberties and promoting the happiness of the people.

Most gratefully would we acknowledge the indefatigable and energetic manner in which you have supported—through many years when others evinced coldness and indifference—the enfranchisement of the working men; and we take the opportunity of publicly recording the fact that it is to you, and to the great Liberal party with which you have cordially co-operated, that we owe the concession of the right to vote for Parliamentary representatives.

Your exertions to establish government by the many and not by the few; to abolish all class distinctions; and to realise perfect civil liberty and religious equality, demand our warmest praise; while your persistent efforts to reduce the extravagant expenditure of our country, to banish war, and hasten the reign of peace amongst the nations of the earth, will, we trust, at no distant day, yield to us rich harvests of blessing.

In all times and on all occasions we have found you our faithful friend and representative; and, whether in relation to questions of local or national bearing, we believe you have honestly advocated and supported those measures best calculated to ensure to us and to our children, the fullest freedom, prosperity, and happiness.

We therefore ask you to accept this address and the accompanying epergne, as a humble acknowledgement of your services during many years in the cause of popular progress. We trust that God may long spare your life, and that soon your presence may again grace the Parliament of this nation, that you may assist in the consummation of more of those measures you have helped forward, which are so calculated to elevate, and bear fruits of beneficent blessings to the people of this country.

On behalf of the Liberal working men and women of Bolton,

We remain, dear sir, yours truly,

J. R. WOLFENDEN, Chairman.

JAS. VICKERS, Secretary.

Bolton, Feb. 23, 1869.

Thomas was obviously very moved by all this. "To see such an audience as this, and to receive the spontaneous address of so many hundreds, and I may say, thousands of working men and women, is a most gratifying thing to me, and I wish I could utter all that I feel and tell you how deeply I appreciate your kindness and generosity." In his reply he said his politics had always been dictated by a desire to promote the interests of the working classes. "When I started life as a public man, I was impressed with the sense that the labouring classes of England had been for many years most unfairly governed and most unfairly dealt with, and that they were suffering greatly in consequence, and my ambition was to do something to strike off those things which oppressed them and which caused much dissatisfaction."

He added a few other campaigns that he had been involved with. One was the long struggle to take the tax off bread which had begun in 1836 and eventually achieved in 1846. Another was to see the children of the poor get a better education, something which had not yet been fully accomplished. He had also been interested in the free press believing it gave "food to the mind, abundance of cheap literature, and plenty of instruction and knowledge". He was amongst those Liberal MPs who fought for the penny newspaper. "It was done for the benefit of the people, and because we believed the people would derive great advantage from it." He also referred to his constant struggle to force the Government to reduce the national expenditure, something which was of vital importance to the working classes, and to working women in particular. "Who suffers more, indirectly though they may see it, than the sisters of our country by that lavish and extravagant expenditure? Who have to buy provisions for the house? Who know when the money is short and can hardly reach as far as it ought to do, and who have to scheme and contrive to spin it out and make both ends meet? It is the women that have to do that, and I say that a great deal of the suffering, and a good deal of those things which we now lament in the state of society in this country, arise indirectly and partly from the lavish expenditure of the country."

Then he made an interesting point. He was not in favour of cutting the salaries of the highest paid—he believed they should be properly rewarded for the work they did. Underpayment resulted in a poor job being done. "I am of Joseph Hume's opinion. When he was alive, he always advocated paying men well who did work well; but he disapproved of having two men to do one man's work, and neither of them well paid. Dismiss one and pay the other well, and then you may have the work right well done."

He was pleased that Gladstone's Government had made a start on reducing the expenditure. He urged the people of Bolton to let the Government know that they supported them. "To you they look, and on you it will in a great measure depend whether those measures are carried or not."

He finished his speech by thanking Bolton for their support during his political career. "I believe no member of Parliament ever represented a borough that was more generous, more kind, or that gave him less trouble. I have never desired, to change my constituency, and never should if it had been the pleasure of the people of Bolton to return me."

On the Friday following this event, 27 February 1869, Thomas was unable to perform his annual duty as Chairman of the Provincial Insurance Company at their Sixteenth Annual General meeting because of a "sudden indisposition".

Notes

1   ZHE/61/12 [Bolton Archives and Social Studies]
2   ZHE/61/14 [Bolton Archives and Social Studies]
3   *The Bolton Chronicle* 1.7.1865 [Bolton Archives and Social Studies]
4   References to the Morant Bay Rebellion from *The Liverpool Mercury, The Belfast*

Newsletter, The Dundee Courier and Argus, The Standard, The Glasgow Herald are all from 19th Century Newspapers online.

  5   ZHE/63/1 [Bolton Archives and Social Studies]
  6   ZHE/63/2 [Bolton Archives and Social Studies]

CHAPTER 12

1869–1874

Life after Westminster.

Thomas lost his seat as MP for Bolton on 17 November 1868 but soon came close to being adopted as a Liberal candidate for Denbighshire. Only a few days later on 20 November a group of the most influential Denbighshire Liberal electors met to consider putting forward two Liberal candidates for Denbighshire at the next election. Their member of Parliament, Colonel Biddulph, did not want to fight a joint campaign but had promised not to use his influence against the second candidate. The two men proposed as this second candidate were Thomas and George Osborne Morgan. There appeared to be some uncertainty as to whether Thomas would consent to stand or not, and as time was short, and George Osborne Morgan had already issued his address, his name was adopted by a large majority and Thomas was not put forward on this occasion. However, he continued to take an active interest in Welsh politics. In the week ending Saturday 13 February 1869 a committee met in London at the Freemasons' Tavern to discuss arrangements for a Welsh Liberal Banquet. Thomas was one of the many men of high status and influence who had agreed to act as stewards.

On 16 April 1869 the Liberals in Oswestry held a preliminary meeting to set up the Oswestry Branch of the North Shropshire Liberal Association. James Richardson Barnes was now also becoming involved in Liberal politics and was the Chairman at this meeting. The decision to set up this association was the result of a conference of Liberal delegates from the whole of North Shropshire which had already been held at Shrewsbury with Thomas as the President. At this conference it had been decided to try to establish a Liberal Association for North Shropshire. There were four main aims: to promote the adoption of Liberal principles in the Government of the country, to return Liberal members for the Northern Division of the County, to improve the register, and to circulate information by public meetings, lectures, and so on. After the meeting in Oswestry on 16 April James Richardson issued an invitation through the local paper to all the Liberals in the district, electors and non-electors, to enrol as members. So as not to exclude anyone the minimum subscription was fixed at 2s 6d per annum, but as the working expenses were expected to be heavy, and as they intended to establish a permanent fund, they hoped that the Association would be generously supported. A second meeting was arranged for these newly-enrolled members in the Double Class Room at the Public Hall in Oswestry on Friday evening, 30 April, to elect a General Committee for the Oswestry district.

The next annual stocktaking at the mills in Farnworth on 30 June 1869 was the first after Thomas had left Westminster. The profits of over £14,000 were again split on a one-third, two-thirds basis between Thomas and Joseph Winter and again Thomas paid part of his share to his son. (James Richardson's capital still only stood at £10,577.) Samuel Horrocks' name now joined the usual list of Thomas Barnes, James Richardson Barnes, Thomas Paterson and Joseph Winter in the list of those who had invested in the firm. Samuel Horrocks was paid a 2½% commission on his capital out of the balance. One new type of cloth, "Jeans" was mentioned in the inventory.

On 27 October 1869 Thomas presided at the 46th annual meeting of the Chester branch of the London Missionary Society when a missionary from the South Seas spoke. Thomas had been a director of the Society at least since 1864 and regularly chaired meetings linked to it.

When members and supporters of the National Reform Union met on the evening of Tuesday 1 February 1870 in the Free Trade Hall in Manchester in support of Gladstone, Thomas and John Cheetham were amongst the platform party. George Wilson chaired the meeting and speeches were given by Thomas Bazley and Jacob Bright. *The Manchester Times* described the meeting as "a gathering altogether unprecedented in the history of the National Reform Union".

On 17 February 1870 Thomas took the chair at a public meeting when Oswestry Old Chapel Sunday School held a tea and public meeting in the Public Hall in Oswestry.

On the evening of 20 April 1870 North Shropshire Liberals held a meeting in the Public Hall in Oswestry which Thomas chaired. His son sent a letter of apology for absence. At this meeting Thomas gave one of his long political speeches containing, as usual, detailed statistics to support his facts. "The meeting had two objects: to do something towards forming the Liberal party in that part of Shropshire into a compact union, and to express their opinion of Mr Gladstone's administration." He believed they had never had a minister of equal capacity to the present premier. He also referred to the passing of the Irish Church Bill the previous year. He believed it was for the interests of the church itself that it should be emancipated from the position in which it was formerly placed for the sake of Protestantism and religion. Gladstone had reduced income tax by 1d in the £, had knocked off 1s duty on corn, the last remnant of the protective duty, and had abolished tea licenses and taxes on locomotion. In addition "the Admiralty had set to work to see where there was extravagance and they found it abounding on every side."

Profits at the mills in Farnworth were low in the year 1869/70, only £1,788 18s, but were shared out as before. Again, at the stocktaking on 30 June James Richardson received some of his father's two-thirds share but this was only £198. He had continued to draw an annual amount out of the Petty Cash but this year a much larger amount— £1,610 3s 9d. It was also the last year (up to 1873 when the stocktaking account book ended) in which this amount drawn on Petty Cash was recorded. In 1870 his father gave him a £1,000 allowance. Thomas had a separate account at the back of the book from 1870 to the end of 1872. In 1870 he would appear to have had a total of £58,866 invested in the business made up of a balance of £46,902 19s 5d plus the previous year's share of the profit of £9,160 13s plus £2,803 interest.

On 4 November 1870 Thomas had been expected at a meeting of Liberal electors in Wrexham Town Hall to hear George Osborne Morgan QC, now the MP for Denbighshire, give an account of the past parliamentary session. Thomas was to have proposed a motion expressing appreciation and support of the MP's parliamentary services. However, he had written to say that there was no prospect of his being able to attend the meeting.

He devoted a great deal of time and money to supporting the Nonconformist churches and chapels in Lancashire and in the area around The Quinta. Between 1861 and 1885 he was Treasurer of the Salop Association of Ministers and Churches linked to the Congregational Church movement. He was one of the largest contributors to its funds and on several occasions went on tours round the churches in the county to try to whip up enthusiasm. For example, when meetings of this Association were held on Monday and Tuesday 28 and 29 April 1873 at Castle Gate Chapel in Shrewsbury Thomas presided at a meeting of the Committee of Finance and Management on the first day.

He also supported the local Welsh chapels. *The Christian World* reported: "Mr Barnes has proved quite a father to the Welsh Independent churches in that locality, and from far and near they come to him for aid in their struggles. In fact, his presence amongst them has given the struggling Nonconformist churches a status which they never had before." On Christmas Day 1869 he lent the Quinta Congregational schoolroom for a tea party and literary meeting in support of the Welsh Calvinistic Methodist Sunday School. This literary meeting at which prizes were awarded for pieces in Welsh was the first Welsh literary meeting ever held at the village of Lodge within living memory. There was a full turn-out and more than three hundred people were crammed into the room. When Rev. D. Roberts, the minister at Lodge Welsh Calvinistic Methodist Chapel died in May 1870, both Thomas and James Richardson sent their private carriages to his funeral on 17 May at the Zion Chapel burial ground in Oswestry. In June that year there was a joint Sunday School excursion from Cefn and Rhosymedre to The Quinta. Children from the English Independent and the Welsh Wesleyan Sunday Schools arrived in six large canal boats. They lined up and sang in front of Quinta Hall in English and Welsh, then had fun in the Park before having tea in the Quinta schoolroom. When the foundation stone of the Welsh Presbyterian Chapel at Lodge was laid by Mrs Jones of Oswestry on 20 July 1871 Thomas threw open Quinta Park for visitors to enjoy after the ceremony and public tea meeting. James Richardson and his wife attended the ceremony. On Christmas Day 1873 the Welsh Presbyterians held their Annual Festival at the Lodge in the large schoolroom built by Thomas and lent for the occasion. The newspaper article reporting the event added that Thomas and his son James Richardson had taken great interest in and shown great kindness to the Welsh church.

Around this time Thomas became involved with cricket clubs, both in Farnworth and at The Quinta. Farnworth Cricket Club began negotiations with him at the end of 1870 to rent some land and by May 1871 they had laid out a pitch and erected fences and a pavilion. Two years later they added a bowling green. The Earl of Ellesmere was the Club's first President. Thomas then held the position of President until his death in 1897. The report of the origins of the club in *The Grand Bazaar Newsletter of Farnworth Cricket Club* on 20 March 1901 added that Thomas's interest in everything that affected the pleasure and well-being of his fellow-townsmen was manifested in many ways. In Shropshire, Lodge Cricket Club had been playing matches in Quinta Park at least from May 1868. For example, on 9 July 1870 a match,

Dee v. Lodge, was played in the Quinta Park. On 20 January 1873 an amateur concert was held in the Quinta schoolroom in aid of the club. On 29 April 1874 a team from Lodge played one from Trevor Hall at Quinta Park. On 12 February 1875 the annual meeting of Lodge Cricket Club was held at the Lodge Inn. Elections of officers took place. All the previous officials were re-elected. Thomas was the President and his son one of the Vice-Presidents. Cricket matches were played regularly in summer 1875. On 29 May 1875 they played against Wynnstay, on 7 June against Anstice Memorial, and on 5 July against Trevor Hall. By then the cricket ground in Quinta Park was referred to as Lodge Cricket Ground. By 1882 a football team was also using Quinta Park. On 25 March 1882 the Quinta Swifts played Selattyn Blues on the Quinta ground.

On Wednesday 4 January 1871 Thomas was in Manchester to attend the funeral of George Wilson, the President of the Reform Union. He had also been a Director of the Lancashire & Yorkshire Railway Company and Thomas, another Director of the Company, was in the long funeral procession in one of the three carriages carrying the Company Directors.

Since December 1868 Farnworth had had its own Liberal Association, led by David Crossley. On 9 January 1871 Thomas chaired a meeting in Moor Hall, Church Street, Farnworth, at a soirée given by the Farnworth Liberals. After tea Thomas made one of his political speeches which was reported in *The Wrexham Advertiser*. "He expressed his pleasure at seeing such a large audience, and said that the last session of Parliament had been a most distinguished and valuable one. He had not expected so much to have been accomplished. Parliament had passed a measure for Ireland which might be expected to have a pacifying influence over that country, and would probably do more, united with the measure which preceded it, to unite Ireland as an integral and substantial part of the United Kingdom than any other measure that had yet passed the House of Commons.

Another important measure passed during the last session was the Education Act. There were, no doubt, different opinions with respect to that measure. His opinion was that the Education Act should not have been passed during last session. If it had been postponed they would have had a better measure. But the bill was passed, and they had now what the country had been demanding for more than one generation. The measure had to be taken as it stood, and all the good possible extracted from it, and he had no doubt, notwithstanding many imperfections, that its effect would be highly beneficial.

But they looked forward to the coming session, and expected that more would be done. The ballot had not yet passed, but he believed it would be law before the close of next session. They were undoubtedly indebted to Mr Leatham, the member for Huddersfield, for what he had done. That gentleman had brought the question very prominently before Parliament and the country, and had extracted something like a promise from the Government that it would form a part of their schedule in the coming session. For one he would be greatly disappointed if the Government did not take it up. But whether they did it or not, Mr Leatham would be at his post and would take care that it was passed with or without the concurrence of Government.

He was very much afraid that as soon as Parliament opened they should find persons who were deeply interested in the expenditure of the country, and who would be pressing Government by questions and motions to an increased expenditure on the army and navy. These persons would be heard croaking about war on the Continent, and telling them that England was in danger and that they must be prepared for all contingencies. He did not give these people credit for attaching so very much importance to the security of England as he did to their making it a mere plea for an enlarged expenditure. Their remedy for every evil was 'Spend more money'. (Hear, hear, and applause.) They would hear that the army was not prepared for war and far from perfect. That had been the cry ever since he had anything to do with politics. That cry came especially from the Tory section of the community, who were always interested in a very large expenditure, who never looked to the interests of the taxpayers, but always to the interests of the taxeaters. (Applause.) But he thought before the country consented to any enlarged expenditure on the army a rigid examination of the way in which the money was expended ought to be insisted upon. They were told by persons who knew, that the army was the most expensive of any army in Europe. (Hear, hear.) They were told that the army cost a great deal more than the army of Prussia, which had proved itself so efficient, and yet they were told by those who seemed to know that the army was inefficient and unfit for active service." He continued on this topic to the end of his speech.

David Crossley moved a resolution and J. T. Cross seconded it: "That this meeting hails with satisfaction the fact that during the present complications on the Continent of Europe, a Liberal Government has been in power in this country; and desires to express its approbation with the manner in which, whilst striving to maintain and make peace, the honour of the country had been maintained." The resolution was supported by R. C. Rawlins from Wrexham. Mr Topp moved a motion supporting Gladstone and was supported by R. N. Philips MP.

A month later Thomas was back in Manchester on Wednesday 1 February 1871 when he appeared on the platform at a great meeting of the National Reform Union in the Free Trade Hall in support of the government policy of non-intervention.

On 2 April 1871, the date of the Census, Limefield House, Thomas's house in Farnworth, was left in the care of his housekeeper, 43–year-old Elizabeth Vickers, and a servant, Sarah Ann Holland. They were looking after a 4–year-old visitor, Ernest J. Arrowsmith, from Tunstall in Staffordshire. Ernest Arrowsmith was still at Limefield, and still a visitor, in 1881. He was then working as a warehouse boy. In the 1901 Census he reappeared as a steam engine brake fitter in Hanley in Staffordshire after having spent some time in Australia. I wonder if his return around the time of Thomas's death and his job with a railway company were in any way connected with Thomas?

Thomas and Ann were at home at The Quinta in April 1871. It was a huge estate. Records held by English Heritage relating to the sale of the estate in April 1929 list the properties in just the Bronygarth part of the estate: Brookside, Brookside Gardens, Bryntirion, Oakfields, Bronygarth Post Office, Penybryn, Bronygarth, the Lime Works, Quarry Cottage, Gibraltar Cottage and Little Gibraltar Cottage, Brynwel, Rose Cottage, Park Cottage, The Hollow, Ceiriog View, Castle View, Field Cottage, Old Gate House. The 1871 Census refers to more properties in Weston Rhyn near Quinta Hall such as the Gardeners' Cottages and Tynypistite where William Lloyd, the blacksmith, William Ellis, the coachman, and Edward Williams, the groom, lived. C. Neville Hurdsman's book *A History of the Parishes of St Martin's and Weston Rhyn* contains photographs of many more properties which were part of the Quinta estate when it was finally sold. Fron Farm, a 17th century house, was part of the estate when Thomas bought it in 1852. It was described in the sale as a dairy and cheese-making farm and might have been the farm which provided the butter, cheese and milk for the Farnworth feast to celebrate James Richardson's coming of age. Another old farm was Redcastle Farm, another dairy farm. There was Wern Farm which had the last tithe barn in St Martin's parish, Pentre Farm in Bronygarth, Pontfaen Farm which had once been part of the Chirk Castle estate, three farms let to the Richardson family—Trehowell Farm, Ty'n-y-Celyn Farm and Little Trehowell Farm, another dairy farm—, and Fron Ganol Farm. At a rough calculation, these farms alone had a total acreage of over 580 acres, all paying annual rents to the Quinta estate. Then there were the houses and cottages—Summerfields, Bryn Ceiriog, a large double-fronted house on the outskirts of Weston Rhyn, Dalescot and Hillside, two semi-detached cottages at Bronygarth, Park Cottage, a brick-faced stone building with 2 acres of land, and Retford Villas, a row of six cottages near Preesgweene Farm. Numbers 1 and 2 Woodfield Cottages were two semi-detached houses, one of which was let to the superintendent of the adjacent Free Churches' Burial Ground. I was told when I visited the Church in 2006 that one semi, originally occupied by the caretaker at the School and Church, had been sold fairly recently for £135,000. The list goes on: there were the two Ty'n-y-Fron Cottages on the Wern road, two three-bedroomed semis called Celyn Cottages, the Nursery House with its 2 acres of land, Ashfields, a stone cottage in Weston Rhyn village, Quarry Cottage at Bronygarth, the Dongre, a 3–acre smallholding on the Bronygarth road, Bryntirion, a brick-built house with 9 acres of land, Northgate which was used as a lodgekeeper's house for the estate, and Trehowell Cottage. Mr Richardson of Trehowell Farm was also renting South View, a large house at Upper Chirk Bank which had been built in 1872 as the manager's house for Trehowell Colliery. There was also another large house, Oaklands Hall on Chirk Bank built in the Victorian Gothic style. Many of the properties appear from the photographs to have been built in a similar style with dormer windows and protruding bays and were probably the products of Thomas's building scheme for the estate.

Staying as a visitor at The Quinta at the time of the 1871 Census was a 27–year old woman, Oswald C. Caddell, born in Antigua in the West Indies. I wonder if this visitor had anything to do with Thomas's interests in the growing of cotton. Oswald's father, Patrick Caddell, born in Glasgow around 1814, was described in the 1851 Scottish Census as a West Indies merchant. Their son William had been born in Antigua in 1840 and their daughter, Oswald, (christened after her mother), two years later. In 1845 they were back in Glasgow, but a year later another daughter was born in St Kitts in the West Indies. They had returned to Glasgow by 1850. I have not been able to trace the rest of the family after this.

In Quinta Hall itself Thomas was employing seven servants in 1871— a cook, a lady's maid, three housemaids, a kitchen maid and an errand boy. Although in each of the four censuses between 1861 and 1891 the house staff changed, there is one name in the 1871 census which recurs in 1881 and 1891—Sarah Hume, born in Glencairn in Scotland. She was a housemaid in 1871, a waitress in 1881, and housekeeper at

Limefield in Farnworth in 1891. Samuel Winter who had been inconsistent on the question of alcohol "that great slayer of reputations, morals and life" when the Quinta Church was formed, was still going strong in April 1871 at the age of 72 and working as Thomas's land bailiff.

James Richardson Barnes was living at Brookside on his father's estate at Bronygarth at the time of the 1871 Census. He was now 31 years old, a JP and a landowner in his own right, and a Captain in the Denbighshire Yeomanry Cavalry. He and Ellen had not had any children since their marriage in 1864. They had four living-in servants: a cook, a housemaid, a kitchen maid and a footman. For the next thirty years he, too, played his part in the life of the estate and the Quinta Church.

I wonder if it was around this time that Thomas handed over the Quinta estate to his son? When his brother-in-law James Haslam wrote his Will on 17 June 1872 and named Thomas as one of his Executors and Trustees, he gave Thomas's address as Limefield in Farnworth. There was no mention of The Quinta. When James Haslam died ten years later on 7 November 1881 Thomas was still referred to as "cotton spinner of Limefield, Farnworth". On 18 April 1882 James Haslam's widow, Thomas's sister Jane, wrote her Will, leaving her brother a £100 legacy in acknowledgement of his services as a Trustee under her late husband's Will. She, too, referred to Thomas as a cotton spinner of Farnworth. James Richardson wrote his last Will on 9 October 1895, eighteen months before his father died. It is clear that by then James Richardson owned the vast estate. His instructions in his Will for the administration of his estate in the event of Trustees having to take charge made all the provisions which were missing in Thomas's Will written in May 1887. Thomas only left just under £13,000 when he died, his son nearly £211,000. A suggestion made around July 1887 that Thomas might have gone bankrupt at some stage could perhaps be explained by his having transferred the estate to his son.

On 30 June 1871 the firm's annual profit of £9,776 was shared out as usual between Thomas and Joseph Winter (and presumably James Richardson who had signed his name which had then been crossed out). Samuel Horrocks received his 2½% commission. The new cloth "Jeans" introduced in the previous year now appeared in a version called "Jeanettes". Between 1870 and 1871 the firm built a warehouse in King Street in Farnworth and in 1871 made further additions to the Gladstone Road works.

On Thursday 10 August 1871 the Fourth Annual Oswestry Institute Fête was held in the grounds of The Quinta, "by the generous permission of Thomas Barnes". About 4,000 people enjoyed themselves on a day of glorious weather. Four large refreshment tents had been erected and all sorts of entertainment were provided, including a one-mile bicycle race and dancing to a "quadrille band" on the croquet lawn in the corner of the park. James Richardson acted as guide to those people who chose to have a tour of the Hall. Others sat on the terrace in the shade and watched what was going on in the park. The exquisite gardens with their varied coloured blossoms were laid out with a taste which "did great credit to the gardener Mr Louden".

Samuel Winter, Thomas's land bailiff, did not live long after the 1871 Census. He died on 16 September 1871 and his funeral was attended by nearly all the tenants and workmen on the estate and by many of the neighbouring farmers and friends. As a last tribute of respect for an old servant, Thomas joined the procession in his carriage. It is possible that Samuel Winter's successor was Alexander Grant who was already Thomas's farm bailiff in October 1874 when he organised a new event, the Bronygarth and Weston Rhyn Ploughing Match, at Bronygarth. On 29 May 1875 details of an arrest were printed in *The North Wales Chronicle*. Alexander Grant had been dismissed by Thomas at the beginning of 1875 and had managed to obtain horses and bullocks from a cattle breeder in Scotland by pretending they were for the Quinta estate. The whole report makes interesting reading: "Alexander Grant, who a few months ago was dismissed from the service of Mr Thomas Barnes, The Quinta, was arrested at Wrexham on Thursday May 20 under peculiar circumstances. He had been employed by Mr Barnes for three or four years and the utmost confidence had been placed in him. However, on Mr Barnes's return from America a few months ago, he thought it advisable to examine Grant's accounts. The consequence was that he was discharged. It appears that in his capacity of bailiff, he had many transactions on behalf of Mr Barnes with Mr Robert MacWilliams, a large cattle dealer residing at Strichmore, Stranraer, Wigtonshire, Scotland. A few days ago Grant went to Scotland and informed Mr MacWilliams that he had been sent by Mr Barnes to make purchases. He succeeded in obtaining three horses and ten bullocks which he had conveyed to Chester by railway. He took one of the horses to Mold fair and sold it for £50, and thus he was provided with money sufficient to enable him to take the remainder of the animals to Wrexham, where they were offered for sale at Mr Lloyd's auction mart at the fair on Thursday 13 May, and sold for £180. The auctioneer did not give Grant a cheque, and he was told to meet Mr Lloyd at the Feathers Hotel on Thursday. In the course of the morning Mr MacWilliams arrived in Wrexham and communicated with the

Deputy Chief Constable, Mr Bradshaw. Subsequently, they went to the Feathers Hotel and Grant was apprehended by Mr Bradshaw and locked up. Sergeant MacMillan of the Scottish police arrived in Wrexham on Friday, with a warrant from the Prosecutor Fiscal for the arrest of Grant, who, during the day, was conveyed to Stranraer. Upon the prisoner was found a £5 Bank of England note, £2 18s in cash, a watch and two pawn tickets for four suits of clothes, the latter indicating that he had been much pressed for money. He had also in his possession a ticket per mail to Dublin, dated Saturday May 15, it apparently being his intention to escape to America by way of Ireland. He appears to have become afraid during the interval between the selling of the cattle and the receipt of the cheque, and had got as far as Holyhead, but on second thoughts had returned. He is married, and has a wife and seven children." Another local paper, *The Wrexham Weekly Advertiser*, reported in its edition on 4 September 1875 on Grant's conviction: "Alexander Grant formerly in the employ of Mr Barnes as a farm bailiff at The Quinta and who was arrested in Wrexham in May last on the charge of purchasing cattle in Scotland in Mr Barnes's name and disposing of them with intent to defraud, pleaded guilty yesterday at Dumfries and was sentenced to nine months' imprisonment."

In the autumn of 1871, on Tuesday 17 October, there was a soirée in Manchester to inaugurate the new building for the Manchester Reform Club. This was followed by a dinner in the Club House in King Street on Thursday, and finally by a banquet in the Free Trade Hall. Amongst the guests at the banquet with Thomas were John Cheetham and Samuel Pope who had fought the joint campaign with Thomas in Bolton at the 1868 election. The Club had been established at the end of 1866 when one of its members was John Stuart Mill. Until now it had occupied temporary premises on three floors of an old warehouse lying between Spring Gardens and Brown Street.

On Friday 20 October 1871 Thomas was at Hunt's Bank in Manchester at a Special General Meeting of shareholders of the Lancashire & Yorkshire Railway Company to consider and possibly approve the amalgamation of the London & North-Western Railway with the Lancashire & Yorkshire Railway Company. The Chairman who moved the resolution for amalgamation was R. Dugdale. Thomas seconded the motion and the resolution was carried.

On 27 and 28 November 1871 a conference of Welsh Liberals was held at Aberystwyth. It opened with a public meeting on Tuesday when a letter of apology for absence from Thomas written at The Quinta on 24 November was read out: "I am much obliged to you for your note, and the papers relating to the proposed Welsh Liberal Conference at Aberystwyth. I am sorry it is not convenient for me to attend, in consequence of previous engagements which compel me to be in Manchester on 28th and following days. I heartily approve of the proposed Conference and hope it may result in securing the objects especially named, and the ballot above all. That I consider most essential for the good and fair representation of Wales. I cannot but think it was a great blunder of the Government in not placing it first on the list of Government measures for last session, and trust that the Conference may be an effective means of inducing them to give it the most prominent position in their measures for the next session."

On Wednesday 6 March 1872 he attended one of the most imposing events that had ever been witnessed in Bury when Thomas Wrigley of Timberhurst began his term of office as High Sheriff of Lancashire. He was the first ever High Sheriff to have come from Bury and there were great celebrations in the town. Thomas Wrigley had invited several hundred men to breakfast at his home at 11 o'clock in the morning.

The firm made a huge profit in the year 1871/72, declaring a 44½% return on the capital of £36,799 out of which Samuel Horrocks' £384 commission was paid. According to his separate account he was also receiving a salary of £300 and more commission of £22 7s on £1,788. He also received commission of £224 10s on a sum of £9,776 and £65 5s interest on this balance. James Richardson again received a £1,000 allowance from his father and continued to earn interest on his £10,000 capital. A new type of cloth, "Patent Velvet" appeared in the inventory.

In September 1872 there was a fire at one of Thomas's mills which cost the firm about £5,000. A document in Bolton archives records that £1,355 12s 2d was spent restoring the mill after the fire. £1,305 12s 2d had been paid to the firm of W & S. Coope, presumably the same firm who had repaired the damage after the fire in February 1865. Another £40 was spent on shafting, pulleys and fixings and £10 on steam pipes from No. 3 Mill.

On 17 May 1873 Thomas was back in the Farnworth area for yet another stone-laying ceremony, this time at Little Lever Congregational Sunday School.

On 19 June 1873 another church, the English Congregational Church in Mold, had a trip to the Chirk area. Teachers and friends of the Church visited the Parish Church, the aqueduct and viaduct, the beautiful Congregational Church, and The Lodge, and then walked round the grounds of The Quinta. They had tea in the new schoolroom at Bronygarth. Sir W. W. Wynn had just made a donation towards paying off the debt on the church in Mold which now only owed £400. Thomas had promised £40 if the remainder could be raised during the next twelve months. The church clearly made a great effort to raise the money. On 29 December 1873 Lord Richard Grosvenor MP for Flintshire opened a Bazaar and Christmas Tree in the Assembly Room in Wrexham Market Hall to reduce or wipe out the debt on Mold English Congregational Church. £516 had been raised since Christmas 1871, leaving £200 still to collect. Lady Patronesses included the Marchioness of Westminster, Lady Williams Wynn, Lady Cunliffe, Mrs Ann Barnes of The Quinta and Mrs Ellen Barnes of Brookside. Ann and Ellen sent money or articles and were probably at the bazaar but were not specifically named. £70 was raised at the event. Meetings were held from Sunday 12 July to Wednesday 15 July 1874 at the Church to commemorate the final clearing of the £800 debt the church had incurred for its new building. Thomas chaired the public meeting on the Monday evening.

On 30 June 1873 the profits of £20,542 made by the business were divided as usual between Thomas and Joseph Winter. Samuel Horrocks received his usual commission. He continued to be paid a £300 salary and receive more interest on a separate account recorded at the back of the book. Three additional names appeared this year of men who seems to have invested money in the firm: William Crowther (£323 16s), Mr Rate (£1,709 15s 11d) and Samuel Winter, Joseph's brother and a weaving manager at one of the mills (£92 2s 1d).

Thomas continued to support the temperance movement. On Monday 21 July 1873 a demonstration of Good Templars was held at Lodge. They marched in procession through the village, had tea in the schoolroom, then went on to Quinta Park. Here they held a public meeting presided over by Rev. T. Davison. In October 1874 while Thomas was away in America it was decided to hold a Grand Bazaar to raise funds to buy and furnish a Temperance Hall in Wrexham. Both Thomas and his son James Richardson were amongst the seventeen Patrons, the chief one being the Duke of Westminster. Another Patron was William Low of Roseneath, presumably the engineer who was involved with Thomas on the Channel Tunnel project. Fourteen women, mainly the Patrons' wives, were Patronesses. Thomas's wife and James Richardson's wife were amongst them. The Grand Bazaar took place in Wrexham Town Hall from 17 to 19 November 1874. It was a great success. There had been twelve months of preparation.

The ladies had held sewing meetings, paid many visits to collect items, and had written many begging letters. The men had had conversations, conferences and committee meetings. Great trouble had been taken over the decorations in the Hall. There were four stalls, each with articles worth up to £200. Contributors had been found all over the country. On Stall Number 2 a walnut chair was bought by the Duke of Westminster who also bought from Stall 4 an Afghan rug made by Miss Thomas of the Vicarage. On Stall 2 were books provided by the Duke of Westminster including some copies of Dickens. Thomas Barnes was one of the main contributors to this stall. Mrs Barnes and Mrs J. R. Barnes were amongst the contributors to Stall 3. On the first day they raised £227 16s 6d. Mr and Mrs J. R. Barnes were present on the first day. The total raised for the three days was £569 18s 10½d plus money from the sale of tickets. Thomas and Ann did not attend. Thomas was on his American tour and Ann was in poor health at the time.

During 1873 Thomas spent around two months in Germany but was home by October. On 23 October 1873 he was one of the platform party in the Town Hall in Wrexham at an evening meeting of Liberals when their member of Parliament George Osborne Morgan QC delivered his annual address to his constituents. Thomas seconded a motion and made some comments about his views on the temperance movement. "I have been called upon to second the resolution which has been so ably moved by Mr Balfour. Mr Balfour is, I think, an advocate of the temperance cause. I have met him a few times, but I cannot claim any personal acquaintance with him. Mr Balfour reminds me, as temperance speakers generally do, of a story told of a certain painter who was engaged to paint the portrait of anyone who would pay him for it. But his paintings had this peculiarity, whatever subject he was engaged to paint, it always came out with a red lion (laughter). And so it is with our earnest and able temperance speakers. They will speak upon any subject, but they always drag the red lion into the picture. (Loud applause.) Now I do not say this by way of reproach, because the subject on which they speak is a vitally important one, and it shows the intense earnestness which actuates them upon that subject. (Applause.) Let them go on; there is a great evil to be cured, but it will not be cured by men who are not in down right earnest.

I'm very glad to have the opportunity for the first time of being present on one of these occasions when our esteemed and valuable representative makes his appearance before his constituents. I am glad to have the honour of being one of Mr Osborne Morgan's constituents, and I most heartily second the vote of thanks to Mr Morgan as one of the most valuable and excellent members of Parliament in the House of Commons—(applause)—and I think it was a lucky thing for Denbighshire when he was elected as the representative of it. (Applause.) I hope the day is not very far distant when he will be separated from us as our representative. He is a lawyer, and they say our lawyers are like Scotchmen—they are always a-looking up. (Laughter.) If Mr Osborne Morgan has any ambition in his soul, and if he follows the old advice to a person about to shoot, 'Shoot high—(laughter)—aim at the stars and not at a man, if you mean to hit anything'; and if Mr Morgan is really looking towards the woolsack, and if the day will ever come when he will be Lord Chancellor—(loud laughter)—I hope that it will be at the time when he ceases to be our representative. And I would only ask him one favour, and that is, when he does become Lord Chancellor 'Don't forget Joseph'. (Loud laughter.)

Great questions lie before us. The Liberal party has not done its work. It has done great things. No Ministry of five years' duration has done as much for this country as the Gladstone Ministry has done in the past five years. (Applause.) No measures of equal importance have ever passed the legislature in the same space of time. Thanks to Mr Morgan and those who have been with him to support those measures. But there are great questions still to be settled. [... ...] I believe that he will do that which he believes to be just and right and we need ask no more. I would never call in question the particular vote of any member of Parliament upon a particular occasion. Knowing a little of it myself, I know twenty reasons, good reasons, may exist for a member of Parliament to vote against a measure which may be before the House, and which he himself may desire to carry. [... ...] I believe that had Mr Bright been in the House of Commons he himself would have opposed the Education Bill which passed the Legislature two years ago, although he has always been an advocate for measures for the education of the people."

He went on to examine two questions—the lavish expenditure of the country, especially on naval, military and warlike matters—and the substitution of arbitration in the settlement of difference for the other "bloody and wicked" way. He continued: "I have from necessity been spending about two months in Germany this year, and when there I was somewhat surprised and much delighted to find the deep interest which the people in Germany took in the motion of Mr Henry Richard for the substitution of arbitration, and their delight in finding that the motion had passed the House of Commons. They, ignorant of course of all the peculiarities connected with the causes which led to the passing of that motion, attribute great importance to it. [... ...] I name the motion to show that on the continent amongst masses of the people and those who serve as soldiers, there is a deep and earnest desire for the success of the motion. Why is there not in this country a public voice strong enough to prevent England ever going to war? (Applause.) Why is there not a voice which says that peaceful modes of settling differences should always be resorted to and that the sword should be sheathed? [... ...] And what is it we ask now, but that before war is commenced, every reasonable means should be exhausted for the settlement of differences, and that if we cannot settle them ourselves, an independent party should be called in to settle the differences by arbitration, and make an end of it. [... ...]" He ended his speech with the words "On earth peace and good will amongst men."

On Wednesday 12 November 1873, at a meeting of the Lords of her Majesty's Privy Council in the Court of Exchequer in Westminster, the Sheriffs for various counties in England and Wales were nominated. There were three nominations for Denbighshire—William Chambres of Dolben, John Cu(a)rstairs Jones of Gelligynan, and Thomas Barnes of Craignant. Why Thomas gave his address as Craignant, I do not know. It is the village closest to The Quinta on the west side. I do not know who was chosen on this occasion.

On Thursday 8 January 1874 Thomas was probably present at a grand event held at Gisburn Park when the first turf was cut to mark the start of the building of the Chatburn & Hellifield Railway by the Lancashire & Yorkshire Railway Company, to open up a rich agricultural district which up to this time had had no railway connections. When Lord Ribblesdale performed the opening ceremony he particularly thanked Mr Barnes for "his liberality and public spirit in giving us this festivity". Lord Ribblesdale, the Directors and officials of the railway company and the gentry of the neighbourhood had met at the Ribblesdale Arms and led by a band and children from the National School marched in procession to the park where they were greeted by a salute of guns. Thomas was at this time Chairman of the Railway Company but he was not specifically mentioned in the report of the event except by Lord Ribblesdale.

At the end of January 1874 the dissolution of Parliament was announced and again Thomas was considered as a prospective Liberal candidate in Denbighshire, especially as the present MP, Mr Watkin Williams Wynn, had upset supporters of the Permissive Bill by a recent statement. Mr J. M. Jones proposed that Mr Barnes of The Quinta be requested to become their candidate, he being a man who would unite the whole party. Mr Lewis seconded the amendment. Another man, Mr Thomas, believed Mr Barnes was the only man who could heal the breach. However, Mr Minshall said he was sure Mr Barnes was too good a Liberal to do anything to injure the Liberal cause by coming forward in opposition to Mr Watkin Williams.

Four months later on 26 May 1874 Thomas was proposed as a possible permanent President of a newly-formed Association, the Ruabon Parish Nonconformist and Liberal Association. Whether or not he accepted this position, I do not know.

In May 1874 he became involved with another local church which was building new premises. For many years the United Methodists had held services at Chirk in a small room at Chirk Green. Then, through the generosity of Mr R. Myddelton Biddulph of Chirk Castle, who provided a piece of land, and of Thomas Barnes and others, they were able to start building a church of their own at Chirk Green. Thomas "with his usual kindness" consented to lay the foundation stone. He was presented with a handsome silver trowel on which was inscribed "Please accept this as a small token of the respect in which you are held by us as a resident gentleman in this district, and as a faithful advocate and warm supporter of all measures tending to commend our Protestant religion to the attention of the inhabitants of this and of every other land." The new church was opened a year later on 7 June 1875 and at the end of the ceremony a tribute was paid to the men who had helped so much in the undertaking—Mr Biddulph, Mr Barnes and Mr E. Griffith.

There is a note in *Shropshire Congregationalism* that on 24 June 1874 Thomas was unable to attend the foundation laying ceremony at Madeley Congregational Church. On 30 June 1874 he was in Farnworth to sign the accounts at the annual stocktaking in Farnworth which had taken place on that day of the year ever since 1836 and probably ever since the firm started keeping records in 1812. This year, 1873/4, was the last year before the business was converted to a limited company. The profit of £14,176 was again shared between Thomas and Joseph Winter and Samuel Horrocks received his £354 commission but was not listed as one of the investors.

Several handwritten documents in Bolton archives appear to relate to this period when Thomas was working out the finances of converting to a limited company. He was working on a basis of 14,000 shares divided between the workpeople (2,366), himself (6,334), James Richardson (1,000) and Joseph Winter (4,300). He had a nominal capital of 20,000 shares at £10 each and in his calculations was banking on calling up shares either to the amount of £140,000 (which would have been their full value) or £115,000. He was also building into his calculations £20,000 credit at the Bank of Bolton, borrowing £50,000 capital as debentures and £10,000 from Thomas Paterson who had continued to be listed as an investor up to the last entry in the stock book in 1874.

In documents where he was working out the value of the business Thomas listed No. 1 and No. 2 Mills with their four cottages and land as worth £50,354. A mill on King Street was valued at another £7,000. A plot of land in Brackley Street between King Street and Brackley Street was possibly worth £300. (This amount had been added in pencil.) The firm had just bought a mill in Queen Street from Messrs Martin & Johnson. Queen Street Mill's engines, shafting and machinery were valued at £10,500.

Accounts, cloth, machinery, cotton etc. at No. 1 and No. 2 Mills were valued at £122,000. For No. 3 Mill the figure was £1,400. The freehold of No. 1 and No. 2 was worth £52,000 and No. 3's freehold £6,000. (I think No. 3 Mill might have been the mill at Dixon Green originally built for George.) This brought the assets to a total of £194,600. In his calculations Thomas had added in pencil three figures of £500 plus £98,000 capital for No. 1 and No. 2 Mills and £10,000 for No. 3 Mill. He had miscalculated the grand total of £176,654 as £175,654. Once he had deducted the £60,000 he intended borrowing he was left with a figure of £115,654 which seems to tally with the £115,000 or £140,000 he would have raised by calling up shares. I cannot be sure that I have interpreted these figures correctly but they give an indication of what was going on.[1]

On 13 July 1874 Thomas chaired a public meeting at the English Congregational Church in Mold. Shortly after that he set off on his trip of a lifetime, spending several months touring America and not returning until December.

Note

1   Uncatalogued material *op. cit.* [Bolton Archives and Social Studies]

CHAPTER 13

1856–1889

The Quinta Coal Company

When Thomas bought the Quinta estate it included two small collieries—Quinta Colliery in Bronygarth and Trehowell Colliery, both of which had been established when Frederick West sank shafts into the coal deposits on his land. The first reference in *The Wrexham Weekly Advertiser* to the Quinta Coal Company was on Wednesday 5 November 1856 when Thomas laid on a celebration at The Lodge after a first-rate bed of coal had been found on the estate. Several of the proprietors of the new colliery were at the celebration—Mr Morgan, Mr Udell, Mr Jones and Mr Halbert, all of Wrexham, Mr J. Rogers of Coedpoeth, and Mr Farish of Chester. A couple of weeks later on 25 November Mr Morgan was again mentioned when he appeared as the defendant in a court case at Wrexham County Court charged with not having paid for eight 9" pipes and pumps he had received on behalf of the Company from a Mr Jukes, the proprietor of another local colliery. Because Mr Morgan had not received an invoice, as he expected, he had not paid, and now Mr Jukes wanted the pipes back as the price had gone up. However, the pipes were already installed down the shaft. The judge decided there had never been a contract and the case was settled with Mr Morgan paying just £20, the price for second-hand pipes. The new colliery flourished and in the following February and March put a large advertisement on the front page of *The Wrexham Advertiser*:

COAL! COAL! COAL!

The Quinta Coal Company are now prepared to supply the public at
the usual market price, with their very superior
COAL and SLACK.

This coal will be found well adapted for Blacksmiths' use.

All orders punctually attended to.

N.B. The Teams will turn by the Wesleyan Chapel, Lodge, direct
for the
QUINTA WORKS.

One of the figures connected with the colliery was a William Seabrooke Chalkley who was convicted around June 1860 in a scandalous court case of forgery and embezzlement. He had been the Secretary of the Liverpool Tradesmen's Loan Society as well as being a well-known figure and Wesleyan preacher in Lancashire and Shropshire, regarded before the scandal as "a man of the utmost respectability and as a local preacher whose piety and eloquence made him a great attraction even on special occasions". He was also a partner in the Quinta and Preesgweene collieries and was understood to have provided a large portion of the capital for the working of these collieries. However, *The Liverpool Mercury* reported that it was said that the undertaking had also been assisted, "from the most praiseworthy motives", by Thomas Barnes.

In April 1870 Thomas subscribed £5 to an appeal made by the Denbighshire and Flintshire Geological Survey Association who wanted to make a public presentation to the Secretary of the Association in recognition of the work he had done for them. They had been asked to provide data for a Government survey of Denbighshire and Flint. Because the Association felt that the landowners and mineral owners and lessees would benefit so much by the survey they were asked to subscribe. Thomas's £5 subscription was not the largest, nor the smallest. The late Earl of Westminster, the main landowner in the area, had subscribed £25.

Several fatal accidents happened at the colliery. An elderly man, David Rowland, who was employed at the Quinta Colliery had a serious accident on 22 March 1871. He was doing some repairs to the pit head and had started to lift a piece of timber when he caught his foot and fell backwards. The timber fell on to his chest and crushed it badly. He died at home, leaving a widow and a large family. David Lomax, the manager of the Quinta Colliery, gave evidence at the inquest held at the Britannia Inn when a verdict of accidental death was given. On 2 September 1875 another inquest was held, this one on John Ellis, aged 54, who was killed whilst shunting wagons at the Quinta Colliery on 26 August 1875. The first witness was David Lomax, the colliery manager, and the second witness Edward Morris, a banksman. Again, a verdict of accidental death was reached. Yet another inquest was held at the Bridge Inn, Chirk Bank, on Wednesday 22 March 1876 on the body of Thomas Prodger, aged 30, a collier employed at the Quinta Colliery. David Lomax, still the manager of the colliery, was present. James Morris, another collier, was working with Prodger in the three-foot-six mine on 9 March. Prodger went to "hole" under a lump of rock (which he had already "holed" from above) when the lump fell on him. He had not put in a prop. He died on Monday, having said on Friday that the accident occurred entirely through his own fault. Again, the verdict was of one of accidental death.

In the 1870s there were several reports in the local paper that miners' wages in the area were to be reduced. However, on each occasion it appears that this did not happen at the Quinta Colliery. For example, on Saturday 2 May 1874 miners in the Chirk district went on strike. The notice for a reduction of 15% given at the different collieries in this district expired on that day. "The men, around 1,200, not feeling disposed to accept the reduction, brought home their tools on Saturday, and have not yet resumed work. The notice for the reduction was withdrawn at the Quinta Colliery on Saturday, and the men there are at full work. But Brynkinalt and Preesgweene Collieries are closed, and Black Park partially."

In August 1877 Quinta Colliery Company appeared as plaintiff in a case before the County Court. Mr Joseph Williams, Secretary of the Company, said that the defendant, Elisha Duckett, owed the Company 17s 5d for a load of coal. The defendant said that he did not owe the Company a farthing. If the coal was supplied, it was to his mother at the Mill, who was now dead. The executors to the Will had given notice to all creditors to send in their accounts and the plaintiffs sent in theirs, which was paid, and now they came upon him for a bill that purported to be owing some time before the last receipted bill, which he produced. If the account had been sent in at the proper time, it would have been paid by the Executors. The witness was not an Executor himself. What little surplus remained was divided amongst the children. Judgement was given for the defendant without costs.

It appears that around April 1880 the Quinta Colliery Company agreed to go into voluntary liquidation. It was involved in a law case in the High Court of Justice, Chancery Division, at Lincoln's Inn on April 29 1880. This was a motion under the 138th Section of the Companies' Act, for the Court to determine the amount owing by the Quinta Colliery Company to the Great Western Railway Company. Mr W. Pearson QC, speaking for the Quinta Company, said the Company had agreed to a voluntary liquidation, and the Great Western Railway Company had made a claim upon the winding up. The purpose of the application was to determine how far the claim of the railway was a good one, and how much, if any, was owing. The reason that the case was not decided on that day was that the Vice Chancellor who was hearing the case could not take it upon a motion there and then because it was "a short denial of an action". The case was arranged to stand over until Saturday 8 May to give the Great Western Railway Company time to contact their area manager. I have not traced any article reporting the outcome of the case but I think that from now on the Quinta Colliery was merged into the Trehowell Colliery.

There was another fatal accident at the colliery on 1 October 1888. The colliery was now referred to as the Quinta or Trehowell Colliery. "On Monday morning about 11 o'clock, a collier named William Randles, aged 39, met with his death while at work in the Quinta or Trehowell Colliery near the Lodge. The unfortunate man was felled to the ground by a piece of rock, which dislodged itself from the roof, and death took place in a few moments. The body was conveyed home, to the Palace near Gobowen. On Tuesday an inquiry into the death was opened at Mr Roberts' at Daywell Farm. The inquest was adjourned for the attendance of the Government Inspector. His widow and children have been left in needy circumstances." In Flintshire Record Office archives there is a copy of a report on Trehowell Colliery and Brickworks dated 1888 by Nathaniel R. Griffith, a mining engineer of Westminster Chambers, Wrexham and Plasnewydd, Ruabon, sent to Colonel James Richardson Barnes at The Quinta. Originally the brickworks had been associated with the Quinta Colliery, not with Trehowell Colliery.

There were two very interesting articles in *The Wrexham Weekly Advertiser* on 19 and 26 January 1878 taken from the publication *The British Architect*. It is possible that the articles were the work of T. Raffles Davison, the son of the minister at Quinta Church, who was a regular contributor to *The British Architect* before becoming its editor in 1878. They were entitled "The Fire Clays and Fire Clay Productions of North Wales" and gave an account of the clays associated with the various coal seams worked in the district. The introduction explained why brick making and coal mining went together. "Every considerable seam of coal rests upon a bed of fine mud or clay, the upper portion of which, usually of a darker colour than the rest of the deposit, formed the soil out of which grew the vegetation of which the coal bed is made. [... ...] The clays of the "Coal Measures" are usually denominated "fire clays". Their power of resisting the action of fire is, however, very variable. Even the best of them have their fire resisting quality increased by the addition of sand from the beds of the millstone grit;

indeed, the bricks made from the "gannister" beds of that series are most largely used in the manufacture of iron and steel." The article then added that Thomas Barnes of The Quinta and J. C. Edwards of Trefynant had both made some interesting experiments in the admixture of these sandstones with the clays worked by them. When T. Raffles Davison designed the Quinta Schools for the Barnes family in 1882 J. C. Edwards' products were used in the building. The same firm also sent exhibits of encaustic tiles to the Ceiriog Vale Industrial Exhibition in 1892. The second article in *The Wrexham Weekly Advertiser* gave an account of the different brickworks in the North Wales coal mining area. The Quinta Colliery and Brick Company was described as follows: "Six miles to the north of Sweeney are the brick works of the Quinta Colliery and Brick Company. The clay of the "yard coal" was worked here for some years, but latterly the underclay of a lower coal, probably that of the "lower yard" has been substituted. The former clay contained an appreciable quantity of oxide of iron which occasionally gave a reddish tinge to the bricks. An improvement has ensued with the working of the lower clay and a nice sound brick with rather more colour than those of Sweeney is the result. The manufacture here is not confined to bricks, but includes pipes, tiles, etc."

These two articles explain why Thomas was able to use the clay layers between the coal seams to produce bricks. This clay produced chimney pots, pipes and distinctive cream-coloured bricks which can still be seen today in many of the houses in the neighbourhood. C. Neville Hurdsman in his *History of the Parishes of St Martin's and Weston Rhyn* gives a detailed account of Thomas's collieries and brickworks. The Quinta/Trehowell brickworks were already producing bricks by 1860. It was quite a large-scale enterprise with four firing kilns. Thomas could have got his goods on to the Great Western Railway line at their siding at Preesgweene but he appears to have preferred to transport the bricks, and possibly also the coal, by canal, rather than by rail, as it was cheaper. There was a short tramway from the works to a canal wharf at Chirk Bank, built in 1870, with a stone bridge (now demolished) over the old Chirk Road as it ran through Chirk Bank. This means of getting the coal and bricks to the canal was probably not really used as the steep chute which was needed to drop the goods into the canal boats damaged them. In 2010 I found a photograph on a website showing the site of this wharf. The bank slopes steeply down to the edge of the canal and the site of the wharf is marked by the gap in the stone facings to the side of the canal. After 1873 Thomas had an alternative route to the canal using a tramway to the canal wharf at

Gledrid which had been brought back into use by the Glyn Valley Tramway Company. Thomas paid the company a small fee of 3d per ton to use this line and in return they paid him a similar fee to run a branch line across the Quinta land to the Barnes private railway siding at the Trehowell Mine. The Glyn Valley Tramway line also stretched back up the Ceiriog Valley and Thomas was able to use it to take his goods to local markets. This arrangement continued, even after the Glyn Valley Tramway Company altered its route in 1888 away from the wharf at Gledrid and no longer needed the tramway Thomas was using. He persuaded them to leave the old line in situ from Pontfaen to Gledrid for his own use. Apparently his involvement with the Glyn Valley Tramway was very minor considering how close to it his collieries and brickyards were. His interest probably did not extend beyond the arrangement he had with them for using their disused line to reach the canal wharf at Gledrid. He built the imposing house "South View" at Upper Chirk Bank for the colliery manager. A row of terraced cottages, now known as Quinta Terrace, housed the mine and brickyard workers. In 1885 The Trehowell Colliery Brick and Fireclay Works was registered under the name of David Lomax, formerly the manager at the Quinta Colliery, who was possibly then leasing the works from Thomas Barnes on a partnership basis. The coal-mining side of the Trehowell works closed down in 1889 but brick production continued up to the turn of the century.

C. Neville Hurdsman describes Thomas as "an early environmentalist" as he was careful to remove the unsightly spoil from the works and take it to the river Ceiriog near Pontfaen where it was tipped into the river at high water, and so dispersed without trace. Coming from the blackened industrial towns of Lancashire, he was obviously keen not to spoil the beauty of the Shropshire landscape. Legend has it that he built the tunnel under the Pontfaen-Weston Rhyn road as a route for the spoil, but this is highly unlikely as he already had the old Glyn Valley Tramway track. The tunnel, quite elaborately built in dressed stone is more likely to have been one of the several ornamental features he built on the estate.

Mr Hurdsman also relates another local story, probably apocryphal, about Thomas. A former employee told a tale of how in 1895 (when Thomas was, in fact, housebound) he was an office boy in charge of the powder magazine keys and was sent with workmen to get explosives for use in the mine. They used a pony and tub running on rails and the noisy clatter disturbed the game birds in Trehowell Woods just as Mr Barnes and his shooting party arrived—to find their targets had already flown! The story goes that Mr Barnes was so angry that he swore to close the colliery and the brickyards, and level them, so that nobody would ever know they had existed. Allegedly he did just this, and dismissed between 350 and 400 men in the process! The story had obviously lost nothing in the telling over many years and was most unlikely—unless, of course, the Mr Barnes in question was James Richardson Barnes. It is also true that by 1889 the collieries had ceased production, and the brickworks around the turn of the century. Whether so many men were ever employed, I do not know. The behaviour of the angry man in the anecdote does not fit the picture of Thomas who was always known as a real philanthropist who earned the respect of his employees.

When the estate was put up for auction in 1928 another business was offered as a going concern—the lime quarry with its kilns and weighbridge. This business appears to have been added to the estate after Thomas's death, and possibly also after James Richardson's, but it functioned until the mid 1920s when it closed down.

CHAPTER 14

1874–June 1880

The trip of a lifetime. Thomas Barnes & Company Limited.

Recognition in business and society.

In 1874 Thomas went on a long tour of America, returning at the beginning of December. He said in his speech he had been considering this trip for eighteen years but he could very well have been further encouraged by a lecture he chaired in Wrexham Concert Hall on 29 September 1870. A popular lecturer, Henry Vincent, gave a lecture entitled "Impressions of a Fourth Visit through the United States of America". Thomas also had the example of Robert Heywood in Bolton who had spent three months in America in 1834. On 12 December 1874 *The Wrexham Advertiser* gave Thomas's return from America special coverage, even including it in the Editorial Comment: "Mr Barnes's tenants have given him a hearty welcome home to The Quinta on his return home from an extended tour in the United States. The event is not only interesting to those of the immediate locality, but to the whole country for two reasons, first the example shown of the cordiality and sympathy existing between landlord and tenant, and secondly, inasmuch as it afforded Mr Barnes the opportunity of saying something about America. Numbers of Englishmen have 'done' America, but they by no means agree in their verdict of it. The testimony of a thoughtful discerning man like Mr Barnes, will, however, carry weight, and we feel sure his remarks on that great country, which we publish today, will be read with attention."

Thomas's tenants wanted to use the occasion of his safe return home as an opportunity to show the esteem in which they held him. A committee decided to confine the operations strictly to the estate's tenants. The first event was a tea party for around 300 schoolchildren from the Quinta Congregational and Bronygarth Schools, followed on Friday evening by a dinner at the Britannia Inn, when Thomas was presented with a congratulatory address. Mr J. Gittins Hugh presided;

and Messrs Dempster Jones (Pentre) and Rogers (Vron) were the Vice-Chairmen. More than fifty people sat down to the meal. Amongst those present were James Richardson Barnes, Dr Box, A. Kelly (Tyn-Rhyd), E. Griffith (Hand Hotel, Chirk), F. Edwards (Lodge), J. Edmunds (Pentre Kendrick), Evans (Graig), Lomax (Quinta Colliery), Jones (Rossett), Roberts (Pentrecruggin), Pierce (Wern), Pugh (Wern), Parry (Tynymaryn), William Griffiths (Cross Keys), Clark, J. Broughall (Preesgweene), Baines, John Williams (Quinta Colliery), Grant and Hardy (The Quinta), Evans (Lodge), Evans (Craignant), Pugh (Vron), Evans (Caedae-cws), Hughes (Lodge), Edward Thomas (Oswestry), Jones (Trehowell), Edward Edwards (Pentre), David Jones (Wigginton), Jackson (Caegwynion), Williams (Bronygarth), Robert Roberts (Bronygarth), Humphrey Jones (Halton), W. Hughes (Lodge), T. Murdoch (Pentre Newydd), W. Lloyd (Bronygarth), James Edwards (Lodge), Richardson (Tynycelyn), Edward Whitfield (Oswestry), R. Rogers (Fron), T. H. Richards, J. Louden (The Gardens), R. Porter (Oswestry), T. Lewis, T. Davies (Oswestry), John Thomas (Lodge), Richard Parry (Bronygarth), D. Roberts (Craignant), Robert Jones (Rhos) and W. Ellis (Trehowell).

After the usual toasts T. H. Richards read the following address:

To Thomas Barnes, Esq., The Quinta

We, the undersigned, being tenants on the Quinta estate, beg most sincerely and respectfully to congratulate you on your safe return from your tour through the United States of America, which, we trust, has proved both beneficial to your health and conducive to your enjoyment.

It affords us much pleasure and gratification to find that the health of Mrs Barnes has so much improved as to admit of your taking the tour, and it has been equally pleasing to us to learn that she has not suffered from your absence from her, the loving attention of your son and his amiable wife no doubt tending in a great degree to make her feel your temporary loss the less, and to alleviate her anxiety about you.

It is now upwards of twenty-one years since you became our landlord and we can truly say that our respect for you as a gentleman, and as our landlord, has not suffered through length of years under you, for we know, by past experience, that you are ever ready to meet our wants and redress our grievances.

Such being our feelings towards you, we have embraced the present opportunity of expressing them in this congratulatory address, trusting it will be acceptable, not so much for its intrinsic value as a joint expression of our esteem and respect for you.

We most sincerely hope that the Divine Providence may ever watch over yourself and Mrs Barnes, and that you may long be spared to live among us.

4 December 1874

Thomas was received with loud applause and said he could only return to them his sincere and heartfelt thanks for that unexpected expression of their opinion. He had not expected anything of the sort would have been thought of. He returned home last Saturday evening expecting to go about his work as usual on the following Monday, and when he was informed that there was something to be contemplated on Thursday and Friday he was quite taken aback. He could assure them that he valued it all the more highly for its being so unexpected.

They reminded him in the address of the long time he had spent among them—more than twenty-one years, and that added to any man's life, at any period of his life, made a great difference. That allusion was useful in telling them of the way in which time was flying, and of the use it behoved them to make of it. (Hear, hear.)

When he came to speak of America, it was such a great subject that the difficulty was where to begin and where to leave off. It was no new wish of his to go to America that had led him to attempt the journey. It had been his intention to go for the last eighteen years, but it was only recently that he had been able to see his way to leave this country and to traverse the Atlantic Ocean, spending somewhere between nine and twelve days at sea. It was true that there was still some danger in making the journey, but since steam was invented that had been very considerably lessened, and he felt that the same Providence that had watched over him on land would continue to watch over him at sea. (Hear, hear.) He did not know if anyone there had been sea sick. (Laughter.) For some time after leaving Liverpool he enjoyed himself very much, but then he began to feel the effects of the tossing, and some unmistakeable tokens gave him to understand that all was not right, so that he was glad when evening came, and he had some excuse for going to his berth. After the second day, however, he got over his sickness. He found that the majority of the people on board got over the sickness in one or two days. There were some old sailors on board who were not in the least affected, and there were also some sensitive persons who went below and were never seen until they arrived at their destination, but the majority appeared, like himself, to suffer for a short time. There were several Englishmen upon the vessel and he found them very amusing and communicative. On arriving in the Bay of New York he was very much surprised to see the word "sozodont" painted in large white letters. He could not understand what "sozodont" meant, and did not like to show his ignorance, but he asked his next neighbour if he knew what it meant and he said he did not. In New York he saw the same word staring at him in the face in every direction, and all along the road to Boston it was written up in every available spot, the grass on the side of the road even being cut in the form of the letters spelling the word. It was not until he was returning from the tour through the greater part of the United States that he discovered that the word meant nothing more nor less than tooth powder. (Laughter.) That was their way of advertising. That was characteristic of the Americans. As soon as anyone discovered any new article, he at once set his head to work to discover some novel mode of bringing it before the public, and this rather suggested to his mind that the article was not very good, as a good article would recommend itself to the public.

The Americans were most energetic, and they seemed scarcely to stop at anything in effecting their purpose. They worked very hard, and even men of great property in New York worked from eight in the morning till eight or nine at night, with the exception of two months in the year when the heat was too great to permit them, and during that time every one able to do so leaves New York. It was remarkable that being so far north, New York should be so excessively hot. It was hotter than many cities further south. He could not explain how it was, but he was down at Charlestown, and there it was not as hot as in New York, and it was the same with many other cities of America.

In England it was a common thing to say that Americans boasted. Well, they had something to boast of. If an American spoke of lakes, there was Lake Michigan, not the largest lake in America, which was as large as our country. Then their rivers, where had they such large rivers as in America? Or such prairies? As to their cities, there was not a country in the world having cities like American cities. The wonder was that they had had time to build their cities. Two hundred years was not a long time in the history of nations, and very few would think that all those cities had been built during that time. The time when the Red Indians pitched their tents on the spot which was now nearly the centre of New York was in the memory of the grandfathers of some of the people now living in that city, and at the present time New York had more than a million of inhabitants.

Mr Barnes than passed to an even more remarkable city, Chicago. In 1829 there were not twelve houses there with white faces in them;

at the present time it contained as large a population as Liverpool, having 450,000 inhabitants. Since 1829 Chicago had been half burnt down once, and a quarter of it burnt down on a second occasion. He then referred to a large hotel at Chicago, the Tremont Hotel, an engraving of which he sent down the table. It was first built of wood, and was soon burnt down. It was next built of brick, as its proprietor was determined it should at any rate not be burnt so readily next time. The present hotel was six storeys high and was capable of holding something more than 400 beds. Some time ago it was discovered that the streets of the city were built too low, and that the health of the people was suffering [in] consequence. The city was built upon the borders of Lake Michigan and on the level of the swamp, and it was undoubtedly too low. They at once asked themselves what they were to do, and they quickly decided to raise the streets and houses ten feet. The first house raised was that immense hotel, and during the whole time that operation was going on, all the business went forward as usual. The man who did this was Pullman, who was still alive, and an active man. After this a great many other houses were raised and in the greater part of the town the streets were raised. By this time the proprietor was 72 years of age, and he had begun to think of disposing of his hotel, and retiring from business, but the last disastrous fire again burnt the hotel down to the ground. Nothing damaged, however, he himself plunged into the midst of the ruins, and recommenced building the present hotel which he was now carrying on with great spirit, and he (Mr Barnes) hoped with great success. That fire burnt three miles of houses in length and one mile in width, and it was started by a woman, who kept a cow, going to milk with a lamp. The cow kicked the lamp over, the shed was set fire to, and the flames ran along from house to house and soon became uncontrollable. A person was at the time erecting a building without any wood whatever, but of iron, stone and marble, and although there was no other building within three hundred feet of this, to show the intense heat, the great iron beams were twisted into shapes resembling the letter S, and the marble scorched and cracked, and the stones melted. The bricks were the only thing that appeared to stand the heat, which was so great that the people fled to the shores of Lake Michigan, and even here were driven back into the water. They went in up to their chins, and kept their heads cool by dashing water over them. To show that they were inclined to make the best of their misfortunes, he mentioned the case of one man who was burnt out, and who put up a little hut by the side of the lake, and erected a pole on the ruins of his former abode, bearing a placard on which was drawn a kicking cow, and over the words, "Removed to such a street in consequence of"—a kicking cow! (Laughter.)

In Chicago some of the streets were eight miles in length, and some had six miles built upon. It was a practice with them to name the streets by the number beginning at one side, and the cross streets were at right angles, so that all the blocks were square. This rendered it easy for a stranger to find his way.

Mr Barnes then proceeded to refer to the number and magnificence of the churches in New York and other American cities. In the former city was being built a church which would cost 300,000 dollars or £60,000. The whole of the churches were most magnificently furnished, and were rendered as comfortable as private homes. He also remarked that he heard an Episcopalian Bishop preach in a Presbyterian Church.

Passing on to the subject of schools, Mr Barnes explained the way in which education was carried out in America. In every town there was a School Board which had the entire management of all schools, and in that Board was rested the power of providing all accommodation, and they were obliged to provide for all the children in the town, so that as a town rose, new schools were built, and every child in the country could be educated at these schools, freed of any charges except for books, and if the parents were too poor to provide books, these were given by the State. This state of things existed not only in the large towns but in every village.

Thomas said before he sat down he must make a few remarks on the farming in America. He supposed they considered a farm of five hundred acres a very tidy farm in this country, and one of a thousand acres was certainly an exceptionally large one. But what would they say to a farm of forty thousand acres? Farms of that size were not uncommon in America, and farms of twenty thousand acres were ordinary sized farms. There the farmer put his seed into his drill and drilled for fourteen miles straight ahead. (Laughter.) He only took two drills a day on a farm of that sort. He had met a man who had raised last year 500,000 bushels of corn on his farm which was situated in Illinois. The clearing of farms was attended with some danger, for persons engaged in that occupation were subject to ague and other sufferings. Nearly all the farms were owned by the occupier. He had spoken to some experienced men on the subject of farmers going out and taking farms in the State, and they appeared to be of opinion that the first thing necessary would be to unlearn a good deal of what they had learnt in England, and they recommended that anyone going out should, before taking a farm, reside some time there and learn how things were done.

The Americans had struck him as being a very abstemious people; and from his own observation he found that they almost invariably drank water with their meals. What drinking was done was at other times, and no doubt there was a good deal of it, and he believed they greatly injured themselves by drinking whiskey of not very good quality, but he had seen very little drunkenness. He had seen agricultural shows just like those in England, with one exception: there was [sic] not so many facilities for drinking. The great beverage with the Americans was iced water. This was provided in every place, and it was no uncommon thing to see a man get up in church in the middle of the service, walk to the door, take a drink of iced water and then walk back to his seat.

In conclusion, he referred to the very civil and obliging disposition of the Americans, ever most willing to render every assistance to strangers, and expecting nothing in return, and stated that he had come away with the firm impression on his mind that America would become a great country in the future. It now contained between thirty and forty millions of inhabitants, and could contain double as many without any fear of being inconveniently crowded. He firmly believed that it would have God's blessing resting upon it. He was much obliged to them for listening so attentively to his remarks. (Loud applause.)

On 1 January 1875 he was one of twelve men who formed a new company, the Fleetwood Estate Company, which paid £120,000 to Sir Peter Hesketh-Fleetwood's Trustees for what remained of his estate in and around Fleetwood. The company consisted of Sir John Hawkshaw of Westminster; Thomas Hargreaves Carr, John May Jameson and Philip Turner, all from Fleetwood; Captain Henry Turner and Sturges Meek from Manchester; Thomas Barnes of Farnworth, James Whitehead of Preston, Joshua Radcliffe of Rochdale, Samuel Burgess of Altrincham, William Barber Buddicom of Penbedw, Mold, and Samuel Fielden of Todmorden. The twelve men had each subscribed £10,000. Negotiations with the Trustees of the Hesketh-Fleetwood Estate had begun the previous year when a Memorandum of Agreement to transfer the estate was signed on 16 May 1874 by Harry Smith Styan, the last Trustee of the Hesketh-Fleetwood Estate, and Thomas Hargeaves Carr and John May Jameson for the new company. The Articles of Association of the Fleetwood Estate Company were actually dated 9 June 1874, six months before the sale was officially concluded. Several of the men in the new Fleetwood Estate Company were civil or railway engineers and others

were connected with the Lancashire & Yorkshire Railway. John May
Jameson had been agent to Sir Peter Hesketh-Fleetwood and his
successor and was now to be agent to the new Fleetwood Estate
Company. A few years earlier in 1871 Thomas would have been
involved as a Director of the Lancashire & Yorkshire Railway Company
in similar negotiations when the railway company bought 600 acres
of land in Fleetwood near the railway line from the Fleetwood Estate.
Thomas's involvement with this company appears to have been purely
financial. As a shareholder he received annual dividend on his twenty
shares which came as an interim dividend in the summer and a second
instalment in February. On his £10,000 investment he made between
1.44% and 1.49% per annum in the three years for which I have figures,
1878/79, 1879/80 and 1880/81. I have not found any references to
Thomas in the Company's archives after February 1881. He was not
one of the eight shareholders who agreed to the Directors' request on
11 June 1880 that they should pay up to the full amount of their shares
to clear the mortgage debt of £56,000 on the estate. By 5 July 1881
those who agreed had had the third call made on their shares and had
paid the final instalment of their £10,000. In December 1879 another
of the shareholders, James May Jameson, had put his twenty shares up
for sale. I do not know whether Thomas also disposed of his shares
around 1881.

On 14 January 1875 he sent a letter of apology for absence to a
meeting in Wrexham Town Hall in support of a proposal to put a
training ship in the river Dee. The speaker at the meeting was Mr
Plimsoll MP. Thomas's son was also unable to attend this meeting.
However, on 25 January he was able to attend another engagement,
this one to lay a foundation stone at the Congregational Church at
Nantmawr.

There was a very sad accident on 29 January 1875 in the kitchen at
The Quinta. It was reported in *The Wrexham Weekly Advertiser*: "We
regret to record a sad accident at The Quinta. On Friday week, one
of the servants, a young girl of nineteen, named Elizabeth Evans,
kitchen maid, was standing with her back to the cooking range when
she said to a fellow servant that she thought she was scorching. Her
companion found that such was the case, and pressed her hand against
the girl's dress, and, as was imagined, placed her out of danger. In a
short time, however, Evans felt that her underclothing had taken fire
and rushed from the room, and as she lost command of herself, some
time elapsed before the flames could be extinguished. Medical assistance
was at once secured and everything was done to alleviate her pain but

the unfortunate girl was badly burnt about the lower part of the body and she died early on Monday morning. It was not considered necessary to hold an inquest."

Thomas offered to give a lecture "Impressions of America" in Wrexham on the evening of 8 February for the funds of the Working Men's Institute. His son had been at a meeting in Wrexham Town Hall in April 1869 when it was proposed to establish a working men's club in the town. James Richardson had proposed names for a provisional committee.

In 1875 the business in Farnworth was converted into a limited liability company under the name of Thomas Barnes & Company. It was also to be run on a profit-sharing basis for the benefit of the employees. Members of the family continued to retain a considerable interest in it. Thomas's son, James Richardson, was Governing Director at the time of his death in 1899, after which his great-nephew Harold Alfred took over. Thomas laid on a celebration for his employees to mark his return from America and gave another talk about his trip. The scheme to share the profits of the firm with the employees was celebrated by his workpeople and he was again presented with an illuminated address. One of the employees who took 3,000 shares was Joseph Winter's son-in-law, Henri Edouard Platé, who was working at the time the firm became a limited company at the warehouse at 21 Marsden Square in Manchester. He later went into business on his own as a general shipping merchant, exporter and shipping agent but soon got into debt and was declared bankrupt in 1890. His father-in-law had become one of the managing directors of the limited company and had been helping him financially for three years, unaware of his insolvency. He, too, had incurred large debts before Henri Platé appeared at the bankruptcy hearing.

On 22 March 1875 Thomas chaired a public meeting in the Congregational Chapel at Ellesmere organised by the Oswestry District Congregational Association.

In 1875, just as Thomas took over as Chairman of the Lancashire & Yorkshire Railway Company on the death of Thomas Dugdale, an advertisement appeared in *The Wrexham Advertiser* on 17 April, naming him as one of the five Directors of a newly incorporated company which was trying to raise £10,000 capital in 1,000 shares, each of 10s. This company was called The Wrexham District Tramways Company and had its offices at 10 Temple Row, Wrexham with J. Oswell Bury as its Secretary. The Chairman of the Company was the Honourable George T. Kenyon of Gredington, Whitchurch, and the other three

Directors were William Low of Roseneath, Wrexham, (who was involved with Thomas in the Channel Tunnel Project and the Grand Bazaar for Wrexham Temperance Hall), James Sparrow of Gwersyllt Hill, Wrexham, and Peter Walker of Coedyglyn, Wrexham. Almost all the institutions involved were local to Wrexham:

Bankers:	North and South Wales Bank, Wrexham
Solicitor:	Mr Evan Morris, Arcade Chambers, Wrexham
Engineer:	Mr Henry Dennis, Hafodybwch, Wrexham
Brokers:	Messrs Parr and Rae, B11 Queen Insurance Buildings, Liverpool
	Mr John Bury, Temple Row, Wrexham
Auditors:	Mr T. H. Jones, North and South Wales Bank, Wrexham
	Mr Snape, Lion House, Wrexham

The Company had been formed to construct and run three tramways, which, as the Prospectus maintained, were "now becoming generally adopted in populous districts". The three tramways would run from Wrexham to Rhosllanerchrugog (3 miles 15 chains), from Wrexham to Broughton (2 miles 9 chains), and the third, a branch tramway to replace the stage carts currently in use, would run to the bottom of Summerhill (1 mile 3 chains). The Company had postponed raising the capital and constructing the tramways until this time because of the high price of iron and other materials. It believed this delay would have saved 40% in the price of the iron required. I have not found any more references to this company and do not know if it was successful, nor whether the tramways were ever constructed. However, a short item in *The Wrexham Weekly Advertiser* on 3 March 1883 stated that the Wrexham Tramways Company had just declared a dividend of 1s 9d per share.

On 14 December 1875 Elizabeth Davison, the wife of Rev. Thomas Davison, the minister at Quinta Congregational Church, died at her home, The Manse at The Quinta. Like her husband she had worked untiringly for the church and had been involved in all sorts of good works in the neighbourhood.

By 1875 Thomas had connections with the University College of North Wales. On 21 January 1875 a meeting was held in the Library of the University College of Wales to elect the Governors of the University College. They had already met in October 1874 to form and adopt the Constitution of the College. The Governors were chosen from men who had subscribed to and had shown an interest in the College. Thomas was one of these men chosen as Governors. He was also a Trustee. At a meeting at the University College of Wales on 24 October 1875 when the first year's report was read, Thomas Barnes, Lord Aberdare, David Davies MP, and T. Jones of Manchester were appointed Trustees for the purposes of eisteddfod scholarships. The sum of £250, the surplus of the Mold Eisteddfod, was directed to be invested in the Trustees' names. At a meeting of the Governors of the University College on 25 January 1876 a letter from Thomas was read out. The building at Aberystwyth had been opened in 1872 and cost £15,000. It had 25 students when it opened but by July 1877 it had 100 and was hoping to get an annual Government grant of not less than £2,500 towards the maintenance of the University College at Aberystwyth, and a grant of not less than £5,000 towards the completion of the college building. On 18 July 1877 Thomas was one of a large deputation representing North and South Wales who had an interview with the Lord President of the Education Department to present a memorandum asking for this grant. He had been interested in universities for over twenty years. He had subscribed £100 to the 1851 Auxiliary Fund of £10,000 in aid of Owens College, Manchester, and one of the first causes he supported when he first went to Parliament was a movement by the Friends of the University of London who wanted the university to be represented in Parliament. On that occasion he sent a letter to a meeting on 1 December 1852 approving of the movement.

On Tuesday evening 3 January 1876 George Osborne Morgan, the local member of Parliament, gave his annual address to his constituents at Wrexham. Letters of apology for absence were received both from Thomas and from James Richardson. However Thomas was able to preside at a meeting in Oswestry Public Hall on 14 February 1876 when Rev. J. B. Heard MA, late rector of Pinner, spoke about a clergyman's reasons for Disestablishment.

The North Wales Chronicle reported on 19 February 1876 in a list of the new Welsh Sheriffs that Thomas Barnes of The Quinta, Oswestry, was to be High Sheriff of Denbighshire for 1876. The three names nominated for the position had been announced in *The London Gazette* on 12 November 1875. The other two nominees were Henry Potts of Glenravon and James Goodrich of Eyarth House, Ruthin. At the 22nd Annual General Meeting of the Provincial Insurance Company at the end of February 1876, reference was made to Thomas's new appointment. On 4 March 1876 it was reported in *The Wrexham Weekly Advertiser* that the new High Sheriff of Denbighshire, Mr Thomas Barnes of The Quinta, Chirk, had appointed Mr Llewelyn Adams, a solicitor from Ruthin, his Under-Sheriff, and another solicitor, Mr F. W. Adams, of 32 Essex Street, The Strand, as his deputy in London. His chaplain was Rev. D. J. Jones, incumbent of Lodge, near Chirk. In the afternoon of 15 March 1876 when the Judge for the Denbighshire Spring Assizes, Mr Justice Lush, arrived at Ruthin Station, he was met by Thomas as the High Sheriff of Denbighshire and taken in his carriage to the Judge's Lodgings. Thomas had probably also arranged for the javelinmen and trumpeters who greeted the carriage. When his son, James Richardson, made his first appearance on the Grand Jury at the Assizes on the following day Thomas, as High Sheriff, was also present, reappearing at the Denbighshire Assizes after a gap of nearly ten years. Three months later on Monday 17 July this ceremony was repeated when another Judge attended the Assizes. This report gave more details: "They rode in the Sheriff's carriage, preceded by trumpeters and escorted by the usual posse of javelinmen, and drove to the Judge's Lodgings in Castle Street."

At the end of March 1876 anniversary services were held at the Quinta Congregational Sunday School. On Sunday two sermons were given in the Chapel by Rev. R. G. Leigh of Farnworth. On Monday there was a tea-meeting in the Quinta Schoolroom which was judged to be "the best and most successful anniversary tea meeting". Thomas's son and daughter-in-law were in charge of the arrangements for the tea meeting. After this, Thomas presided at a public meeting.

On 20 April 1876 Thomas sent a letter to a conference of the nobility, gentry, clergy, magistrates and guardians of North Wales which was held in Rhyl Town Hall to discuss topics such as the closing of public houses on Sunday, Sir Harcourt Johnstone's Bill to reduce the number of public houses and to suspend further issues of licences to sell alcohol to be drunk off the premises, and the reduction in the hours of sale of intoxicating drinks. Whether Thomas had written in his capacity as High Sheriff or because of his interest in the subject, I do not know because his letter was not read out. He presided at the closing of an Art Treasures Exhibition in November 1876 and as High Sheriff, presented the main promoter of the exhibition with an illuminated address. The last mention I have found of Thomas as High Sheriff was when he attended the Denbighshire Hilary Quarter Sessions at Ruthin Town Hall on Thursday 4 January 1877.

There was an interesting letter in *The North Wales Chronicle* on 25 October 1879. The post of High Sheriff must have led to some correspondence in *The Times* and this unsigned letter was from an ex-High Sheriff of North Wales. He set out the situation very clearly. The office entailed great expenses. He had had to employ an Under-Sheriff and pay him. He had to pay for lodgings in the assize town for the Judge and had even to buy a suitable carriage to carry the Judge in. He had to find liveries for the javelinmen and trumpeters. There were constant charitable appeals. All in all, holding the office cost him £1,300. He went on, "Once a gentleman is appointed High Sheriff he has no option in the matter, he must submit to the extortion, as it is impossible for him to attend to the legal details of the office. He is also responsible for the laches and errors committed by the Under-Sheriff and his bailiffs. [... ...] The only compensation which the High Sheriff receives in return for a large expenditure of time and money, and the great and inevitable risks to which he is exposed from the laches of his Under-Sheriff and bailiffs, is the questionable honour of the office and the social privilege of precedence in the county—not excepting the Lord Lieutenant—during his year of office." This letter was not written by Thomas but possibly reveals what his one year in office cost him.

Both Thomas and James Richardson were involved with the Welsh National Eisteddfod. In April 1876 it was reported that Thomas and many other local well-known people had agreed to support the holding of the National Eisteddfod at Wrexham in August. Thomas had just subscribed five guineas to the fund which already stood at £700. In February 1876 at about the same time as Thomas was appointed High Sheriff of Denbighshire he had become a Vice-Patron of an Art Treasures Exhibition which was planned to coincide with the Eisteddfod in Wrexham. He subscribed £25 and was also a Guarantor of the event. Queen Victoria agreed to be Patron. The Exhibition was on a very grand scale. Its stated aim was "to allow the working and middle classes to inspect the treasures preserved in the mansions of the noble and wealthy families of our country" and works of art were rounded up from all parts of the country. The exhibition included a display of paintings by the Old Masters, water colour drawings, engravings and etchings, works of Modern Artists, a gallery of portraits of "Welsh Worthies", and a Museum of Ornamental Art and Antiquities. It was to open on 15 July and was to remain open three months. By August 1876 when the Eisteddfod was held in Wrexham, Thomas and James Richardson were both Vice-Presidents. Thomas was one of the platform party when the Eisteddfod Pavilion opened for the start of the Eisteddfod. He presided at a musical conversazione on the evening of 27 November when the Art Treasures Exhibition finally closed and presented an illuminated address to Major W. Cornwallis West, the Lord Lieutenant of Denbighshire, who was the chief promoter of the exhibition. The exhibition had been a success in every way except financially as people had not supported the high class music concerts. Also, it had been a mistake to offer 6d half-price admission tickets to people brought by the railways on cheap excursion tickets. Most of the 75,000 visitors had only paid this half-price admission. Thomas said the deficit was only £1,500 and he thought that could soon be met. By the end of the evening subscriptions had begun to come in for the fund. He also suggested a movement to provide a permanent art gallery for Wrexham. On the evening of the 5 December both Thomas and James Richardson were stewards at a Grand Fancy Dress Ball held in the Exhibition Hall, still surrounded by the valuable pictures and art treasures which had not yet been removed. When the National Eisteddfod was again held in Wrexham in August 1888, Thomas had agreed to act as one of the Patrons and Honorary Presidents. By that time he was in poor health and making few public appearances.

On 17 February 1876 there was a happy event at The Quinta when one of the servants married. The local paper reported: "A pleasant event happened here on Thursday week when Mrs Barnes of The Quinta showed her regard for a valuable and faithful servant, Miss Harriet A. Smith, who was married at Quinta Congregational Church to Mr Joseph Horley of Chester. The wedding took place from The Quinta and Mrs Barnes lent her private carriage to convey the bride to the church. After the ceremony the wedding party sat down to a sumptuous breakfast in the dining room at The Quinta. Mr and Mrs T. Barnes and Mr and Mrs J. R. Barnes were present, and presented the bride with valuable gifts."

On Monday 13 March 1876 Thomas, now Chairman of the Lancashire & Yorkshire Railway Company, attended the funeral at St Annes Church in Turton near Bolton of his old friend and Liberal colleague, Thomas Thomasson. Thomas Thomasson was a Quaker and a special dispensation had been granted by the Bishop of Manchester to allow the service to take place in an Anglican church. Amongst the mourners were the Right Honourable John Bright, Mr J. K. Cross MP for Bolton, and Jacob Bright MP for Manchester. When the coffin was lowered into the vault, John Bright took the cord at the head, and "was much moved".

On Friday 14 July 1876 Thomas and Thomas Thomasson's son, J. P. Thomasson, were part of a large and influential deputation who met the Earl of Derby to present a memorandum signed by MPs, magistrates, ministers of religion, manufacturers, merchants in various parts of the country, and representatives of numerous associations in London, Manchester, Birmingham, Liverpool, Bristol, Leeds, Sheffield, Rochdale, and other places, in favour of strict neutrality by Great Britain in the Eastern complications. Leading the deputation were John Bright MP, Jacob Bright MP, T. B. Potter MP, and J. Crossley MP. Thomas was described as Thomas Barnes of Bolton. This is odd because during that year he held the office of High Sheriff of Denbighshire and it might have been expected that some reference would be made to this.

On 2 October 1876 Thomas was one of a few special guests who had reserved seats at a soirée given by the President of the Manchester Reform Club, Mr Benjamin Armitage, to the members of the Club. John Bright MP was a guest speaker and so many people had responded to the invitation to attend that the club which could only hold between 600 and 700 standing had to find room for 800. George Hadfield had sent a letter of apology. He was unable to attend because of "weakness of age". The main item for the speeches was still the Eastern Question which had been the subject of the memorandum handed to the Earl of Derby in July.

On 9 December Thomas had been expected to chair the annual parents' meeting at Bronygarth School, the school that his daughter-in-law Ellen had had built. However, he was ill and his place was taken by his son, James Richardson. This illness was probably the reason why he did not attend the annual meetings of the National Reform Union in Manchester on 13 December 1876. A crowded and enthusiastic meeting was held in the evening in the Free Trade Hall with Jacob Bright MP in the Chair. Thomas's nephew, Alfred Barnes, was amongst the large group of supporters on the platform.

However, just before Christmas on Saturday 16 December Thomas, now referred to as Mr Thomas Barnes JP, did make an appearance at a meeting of Liberals in the Co-operative Hall at Little Lever near Bolton. The meeting was reported in *The Manchester Times*. The MP for Bolton, J. K. Cross, had sent a letter of apology which explained the reason for this meeting: "If anything could tend to cheer the Liberal party in these times of political lassitude, it ought to receive some encouragement to hold fast to the articles of its faith when we see so many of the other side going out of their way to apologise for the damnable atrocities of the Turkish soldiery simply because they think it is necessary to support the traditional policy of England in the East of Europe. Politically, Little Lever and such like places have no voice in the National Assembly, but the time must come, and that ere long, when the accident of locality shall not prevent a householder from exercising his due share of influence on the Government of the day."

Shortly before his year in office as High Sheriff of Denbighshire ended Thomas was at the Hilary Quarter Sessions on Thursday 4 January 1877 at Ruthin Town Hall to hear the Surveyor's Report. This contained an item about Pontfaen involving James Richardson: "Mr Barnes, Brookside, has requested me to bring before you the unsafe state of the approaches, and to ask for a grant to help subscriptions now being made to put the road in good order. It is now in a deplorable condition, but the 200 yards on the Glyn Ceiriog road have never been made over to the county."

On 30 January 1877 Thomas made another public appearance. Still described as Mr Thomas Barnes JP, he accompanied J. K. Cross, Bolton's Liberal MP, on to the platform at a meeting in the Temperance Hall, Bolton, promoted by the Liberation Society in favour of the disestablishment of the Church of England. Because so many people attended, an overflow meeting was held in the Co-operative Hall, chaired by R. S. Ashton JP. Thomas was one of the three speakers at this meeting.

In 1878 the business in Farnworth expanded even more when the weaving shed in Glynne Street was built. It was here that my grandmother, Minnie Green, began work as a half-timer around 1890 and it was this connection which began my research into the Barnes family of Farnworth.

As Chairman of the Lancashire & Yorkshire Railway Company Thomas received an invitation to the opening ceremony of the new Manchester Town Hall on 13 September 1877. He wrote his acceptance of the invitation from the Board Room in Manchester on paper with the Lancashire and Yorkshire Railway Company heading on 14 August. His handwriting at the time was that of a man in a rush. The letter was concise and had clearly not been checked before being sent.

> Lancashire & Yorkshire Railway
>
> Board Room, Manchester
>
> Aug[t] 14 1877

Dear Sir Joseph

I am much obliged for the invitation to the proposed Ceremony of the Public Opening of the Town Hall which I have much pleasure in acception

> and am Yours very truly
>
> Tho[s] Barnes

Sir Joseph Heron, Town Clerk[1]

He was amongst the many guests at the banquet on Friday 14 September 1877.

When the members of the Reform Club in King Street, Manchester, gave a Club-house dinner to their fellow-member, the Mayor of Manchester, Alderman Heywood, on 4 October 1877, Thomas sent a letter of apology for absence (as did John Cheetham).

In early May 1878 Thomas's name appeared on a list of people who intended attending the public luncheon on 20 May at the Lion Hotel for the Duke of Westminster who was going to lay the foundation stone of the new schoolroom and manse for the English Congregational Church in Mold. However, I could not find Thomas's name on the list of people who were at the luncheon and suspect he was again having health problems. I have not found any references to him for the next two months or so until August when he appeared with his son at the Tenth Annual Meeting of the Denbighshire County Rifle Association at the Abbey Range, Llangollen. They were both Vice-Presidents of the Association and James, Captain Barnes, was one of the Officers in charge of the firing competition. It is rare to find references to Thomas being involved with his son's activities as an officer in the Denbighshire Yeomanry Cavalry.

At the Half-yearly General Meeting of the Lancashire & Yorkshire Railway Company on 21 August 1878 it was reported that their Chairman, Mr Barnes, was "very much improved in health, but he still deemed it prudent not to take his place among them on that occasion". By Friday 25 October that year he was well again and appeared in Lancashire on the Grand Jury at the Winter Assizes of the Northern and Salford Divisions at the Assize Courts, Strangeways. He was referred to as Thomas Barnes, of Farnworth.

On 4 December 1878, a Wednesday, he was in Farnworth when a fire broke out at the No. 1 Mill in Gladstone Road. There was a graphic report of the incident in *The Bolton Journal* on the following Saturday: "On Wednesday afternoon, at 5 o'clock, a fire broke out in the mixing room at Messrs T. Barnes & Co's No. 1 Mill, in Gladstone Road, Farnworth. The portion in which the fire occurred is in the yard at the back of the boilers, a building which was originally used as a foundry. It is three storeys high, and the fire commenced in the top storey, in which position it was practically confined. The mixing rooms are separated from the scutching and carding rooms by iron doors, and about the time named a person was engaged unfastening some bales of cotton in the top room. The bales are bound round with iron, and the hoops are cut with an axe. The man had just cut the last hoop and a bale flew open when fire ran along the cotton. He and his son endeavoured to stamp the fire out but finding that to be impossible, they raised an alarm and at once closed the iron fireproof door. Recently a very powerful donkey engine has been placed in this mill for emergencies such as fires or break downs, and on Saturday the brigade belonging to the firm tested its capabilities as a fire engine, and found that it would throw water from four jets several feet higher than the mill. As soon as the alarm was given, three jets were placed to this engine, and the brigade got their fire engine, four jets being immediately played on the burning room. Information was also sent to the Farnworth Brigade, who were speedily on the spot, and before half an hour had passed, two more jets were pouring water upon the burning portion of the building, work being of course suspended as soon as the alarm was given. Mr T. Barnes was early at the scene and interested himself in the work of extinguishing the fire. This, however, was no easy matter, for there were over one hundred bales of cotton in the room in which the fire occurred and the one immediately under. In the floor of the top room is a trap door and through the crevices burning cotton kept dropping, so that great care had to be taken to prevent it getting hold in that room also. In less than an hour after its outbreak, it was well under control, but some of the firemen had to remain upon the scene till near midnight, as the fire kept breaking out now and again. The vast volume of water thrown into this portion of the building of course found its way through all the rooms, but fortunately there was not so much cotton on the ground floor. There was a large supply of willing hands, and great praise is due to all who helped for the active and zealous manner in which they worked. Neither the roof nor the flooring was damaged to any extent by the fire. It is estimated that the damage to stock is about £1,000 which is fully covered by insurance in the Alliance and other offices. The effect of the fire will be to close the mill for a few days, this portion being that from which the hands are primarily supplied with material for work."

At the beginning of that year, on Saturday 16 March 1878, the mill's fire brigade had attended a fire at Messrs Crook Brothers' cotton mill in Cawdor Street, Farnworth.

In 1879 Thomas was spending more time in Lancashire. In the autumn he was invited again by the selection committee of Bolton Liberal Registration Association to contest the borough at the next Parliamentary election together with J. K. Cross, the current Liberal MP. In the report of this in *The Manchester Times* he was described as Mr Thomas Barnes, cotton manufacturer of Farnworth, Chairman of the Lancashire & Yorkshire Railway Company. On 23 October Thomas declined the invitation "on account of the necessity of his being free from additional work and anxiety". The Bolton Liberals selected J. P. Thomasson, Thomas Thomasson's son, to stand instead of Thomas.

For many years Thomas was a Director of the Bank of Bolton. In a Copy of Returns Pursuant to 7th and 8th Victoria Cap 32 for the Bank of Bolton printed in *The Manchester Times* on 16 February 1850, and in *The Manchester Examiner and Times* on 15 February 1851 and on 16 February 1853, the names of about one hundred Bolton men and women "Persons of whom the Company or Partnership consists" included Thomas Barnes of Farnworth, spinner. Thomas's brothers-in-law, the three Haslam brothers, James and John, manufacturers of Bolton, and William, chemist of Burndon, were also in the list. In his book *The Cotton Masters* Anthony Howe mentions that Thomas was a Director of the Bank of Bolton by the 1870s. He played an important part in the bank's development in January 1879. On Wednesday 22 January a special general meeting of the shareholders of the Bank was held in the Co-operative Hall in Bolton to consider the scheme of reconstruction which had been prepared by the promoters of the new Bank. There were 200 shareholders present, "and the proceedings were marked with the utmost unanimity". Thomas presided in the absence of Mr P. Martin of Rivington, the Chairman of the Board of Directors of the Bolton Bank. He explained the scheme, and expressed the belief that if it was heartily taken up the proposed new bank would become one of the most successful banks in the country. It was Thomas, as Chairman of the meeting, who moved that the existing company be wound up voluntarily, and that Mr P. Kevan, public accountant of Acresfield, Bolton, be appointed liquidator for the purposes of such winding up. This was agreed to by the meeting. Thomas then proposed a detailed description of the new bank: "That the following scheme of reconstruction be and the same is hereby approved—namely, that a new company be incorporated under the Companies Acts 1862 and 1867, as a company limited by its shares, by the name of the Bank of Bolton Limited, with a capital of £1,000,000, divided into 50,000 shares of £20 each, of which 15,000 shares shall be ordinary shares, and 35,000 shares shall be preference shares, entitling the holders to a preferential dividend at the rate of 5 per cent per annum on the amount for the time being paid up thereon, and to share rateably with the ordinary shares any further dividend which the profits may be sufficient to pay after making such contribution to a reserve fund as the directors may think fit; and the reconstructed company is to have power to acquire and take over the business, property, and liabilities of this company."

Anthony Howe also mentions in his book that by the 1870s Thomas was a Director of the Royal Sardinian Bank. Thomas was one of the principal promoters of the Sardinian railway network which was built by the British engineer Benjamin Piercy. Mr Piercy bought Marchwiel Hall in the Wrexham area in 1881 and invited Thomas to his daughter's wedding in January 1883. Mr Piercy had begun the railway scheme in Sardinia in 1862 and also bought large estates there. It is likely that Thomas's connection with the Royal Sardinian Bank had something to do with this. Around June 1880 Thomas spent some weeks along the course of the line just before it was ready for opening at the beginning of July. Mr Piercy also worked as an engineer on the Wrexham, Mold and Connah's Quay Railway of which Thomas was the Chairman. On 16 September 1884 he presided at the lunch after the celebrations at Connah's Quay to mark the start of work on the new wharf at the port.

Note

1. M68/4/16 [Manchester Archives and Local Studies]

Ann Barnes

CHAPTER 15

July 1880–1883

The end of a long marriage. Building the Quinta Schools.

On Tuesday 25 May 1880 Thomas was in Oswestry Public Hall to open a three-day Bazaar in aid of the Christ Church Building Fund. The church had been built seven years earlier at a cost of £6,500 and still had a debt of £1,800. The Bazaar reduced the debt to below £1,000.

Around June that year he was in Sardinia inspecting the new railway network. His wife, Ann, died shortly after this on 30 July 1880. There was an announcement of her death in *The North Wales Chronicle* and a short report appeared in *The Wrexham Weekly Advertiser* on the following Saturday. "Many of our readers will regret to hear of the death of Mrs Thomas Barnes of The Quinta. The deceased lady, who was 76 years of age, was buried on Wednesday in the family vault in the Old Independent Chapel, Farnworth, Bolton. Mrs Barnes's death will be felt very severely by her poorer neighbours near The Quinta and also at Farnworth, where Mr Barnes's large works are situated, in both of which places she was ever ready to do acts of Christian charity."

Ann Barnes's death was also reported in *The Bolton Journal* on 7 August with a simple announcement and a long article describing her funeral on the previous Wednesday. Her body had been taken from The Quinta to Manchester and from there by special train to Moses Gate station. The hearse, drawn by four horses, went first to Limefield, Thomas's house in Farnworth, where it joined the funeral cortege. This moved off from the house half an hour later at noon. The four mills belonging to the firm were closed from eleven o'clock until quarter past two and most of the workers and other residents of Farnworth lined the route. Nearly all the shopkeepers in Market Street either put up their shutters or pulled down their blinds during the funeral and for at least half an hour after it. Many people crowded into the chapel for the service.

There were ten carriages in the funeral cortege. The two ministers, Rev. W. Hewgill from Market Street Chapel in Farnworth, and Rev. Thomas Davison from The Quinta Chapel, drove in their carriage ahead of the hearse carrying the plain unpolished oak coffin with its simple inscription—"Annie Barnes, died 30 July, 1880, aged 76". Then came five family carriages. In the first were Thomas and his son James Richardson and daughter-in-law Ellen. The second contained Mrs Edward Richardson, Ann's sister-in-law, and Mr W. S. Holden of Little Hulton. Three younger members of the Richardson family, described as Ann's nephews and nieces, Mr and Mrs George Richardson and Mr Herbert Richardson, were in the third carriage. In the fourth carriage was another of her nieces, Mrs McMillan, with her husband Dr McMillan. Also in this carriage were Thomas's sister Jane Haslam and her husband James who had travelled to Farnworth from their home in Birkdale. The last of the family carriages contained Thomas's nephew Alfred Barnes and his son Harold Alfred, and James Richardson's parents-in-law, Mr and Mrs John Cheetham.

The last four carriages in the cortege were private carriages, only one of which was occupied. That was Mr Hinmer's carriage occupied by Mrs Hinmer. Alfred Barnes who was in one of the family carriages following the hearse had also sent his private carriage which followed the procession, closed, to represent him in his official capacity as a JP. Dr McMillan who was also in one of the earlier carriages as a family member had similarly sent his private carriage to represent him in his professional capacity. A third private carriage, also closed, represented Mr Blacklock.

The six coffin bearers were all men employed by the family firm—Samuel Winter, Thomas Ivers, William Green, John Collier, James Wilson and William Yates. The first three of these were all described as managers of cotton mills in the 1871 Census. The Chapel's minister Rev. W. Hewgill led the service and Rev. Davison from The Quinta Chapel gave the address. Many of the people in the chapel were visibly affected by what he said about the saintly and self-sacrificing life Ann had led and about the great suffering she had endured, especially in the last eleven years of her life. He knew that before she left Farnworth in the mid 1850s she had shown the same qualities of self-sacrifice and kindness which he had seen later in Shropshire. He said: "Her whole life was concentrated to the service of the Lord. [... ...] Her Christian character was distinguished by its benevolence. She was a true disciple of the Lord, and in this respect she had learnt to succour and help the needy and distressed. Those who knew her best knew it was her great delight to be able to render help to those who needed it—to the needy, the widow, and the fatherless, and he could assure them she had left behind her a great number of persons in his neighbourhood who had received of her great kindness, who had been helped in times of necessity, and who loved her the more." Even when she lived in Farnworth her health had been poor but for the last eleven years of her life she had been a real invalid. He had only known her in the last years of her life but had seen the comfort she gained from prayer. After the funeral address her coffin was taken to the burial ground at Halshaw Moor.

For several months after his wife's death there are no reports of any public appearances by Thomas, either in Shropshire or Lancashire. The first report of any public engagement which I have found was in December 1880 when Thomas attended the annual meeting of Lancashire Independent College in Manchester Town Hall and moved a resolution to appoint the Committee for the coming year. Thomas's links with this college went back a long way. He had been Treasurer to Blackburn Academy before it became Lancashire Independent College. Blackburn Academy was founded in 1815 for the education of Independent ministers. Around 1843 it moved to Manchester as the Lancashire Independent College. One of its chief founders was Thomas Raffles who was Chairman of the College from 1842 until his death in 1863. In November 1838 the Treasurer was George Hadfield. If Thomas Barnes was Treasurer of the college while it was still called Blackburn Academy, it must have been between 1838 and 1843. Newspaper articles written at the time of Thomas's death in 1897 reveal that he was then the last survivor of the original trustees of the Lancashire College and had served on its Committee for many years. His firm had been one of the largest donors to the building fund of the college. A report in *The Manchester Times* on 7 May 1842 included in a long list of donors the firm of Messrs J. R. Barnes & Sons who had contributed £200 towards the building fund for the new Lancashire College. When the new building was opened on 25 and 26 April 1843 Thomas was Trustee Number 30 in the list of the thirty Trustees. Rev. J. H. Gwyther who was Secretary in 1880 attended Thomas's funeral to represent the college as well as being a member of the family. In the memorial service at Francis Street Church reference was made to the generous contributions Thomas had made to the college. However, this was not all. "The help which he gave privately and anonymously to students unable to meet their own charges was munificent in its generosity."

Although Thomas chaired a meeting of the Provincial Assurance Company in Wrexham in February 1881, I have not traced him or his son James and his daughter-in-law Ellen in the 1881 Census taken on 3 April. They were not at home at The Quinta which was now supporting a large number of people—well over fifty. Even though there was no sign of the Barnes family, life was going on as normal at The Quinta. The Hall was being looked after by a housekeeper, a 55–year-old widow Eliza Milne from St Bees in Cumberland. There were also six servants—a waitress, a cook, a kitchen maid, two housemaids and a young pantry boy. A lady visitor, Mary M. Thompson, aged 36, born in Ardwick, near Manchester, was staying in the house. She was the daughter of John and Elizabeth Thompson who were living in Farnworth at the time of the 1851 Census in Spring Cottage, the house which Thomas and his first wife, Sarah, had lived in until her death. Mary Thompson who was born in 1844 was five or six years younger than James Richardson but the two probably knew one another from their childhood days. The waitress at The Quinta in 1881 was 49–year-old Sarah Hulme from Scotland who then moved to Farnworth some time during the next ten years and became housekeeper at Limefield after the death of Elizabeth Vickers. There were at least ten separate households living on the Quinta estate, including three large families. One was the family of William Lloyd, the blacksmith, with his five youngest children still living at home together with his 81–year-old father-in-law. Another was the family of the gamekeeper, John Hardy, with his ten children, and a third was the Louden family—James Louden, the head gardener and his five children. One of his daughters, Jane, aged 15, was described as a pupil teacher and was probably related to two more Louden women who lived nearby in Bronygarth— Marianne Louden, a certificated teacher and her niece Ellen, another 15–year-old pupil teacher, both teachers at the village school. Ellen Barnes was responsible for building a British School in Bronygarth in 1872. In 1887 it had been enlarged to take 140 pupils and had an average daily attendance of 128. Brookside, where James Richardson Barnes and his wife Ellen had been living in 1871 was occupied in 1881 by three unmarried female servants—a cook, a housemaid and a kitchen maid. Thomas Davison, the Congregational minister at Quinta Chapel, widowed since December 1875, was living in the Manse with his son Samuel, a sub-editor, and a young housekeeper.

In Farnworth Thomas's house, Limefield on Bolton Road, was still being looked after by his housekeeper, Elizabeth Vickers. She was now 53 years old and had the assistance of a housemaid, Fanny Vickers aged

27. As both women were born in Hanmer in Flintshire, they were probably related. There was also a kitchenmaid, Margaret Jones from North Wales. Their young visitor, Ernest Arrowsmith, was still with them and was now working as a warehouse boy. Rev. W. Hewgill, the minister at Market Street Congregational Church in Farnworth lived next door at No. 40 Bolton Road.

On 18 July 1881 Thomas was sworn in on the Grand Jury at the Denbighshire Summer Assizes at Ruthin. By August 1881 he was back doing his duties as Chairman of the Lancashire & Yorkshire Railway Company. In the same month *The Times* published on 5 August details of a new venture in which he was involved, the Assam Railways and Trading Company Ltd, a company with capital of £350,000 and offering preferred shares of £10 each. Under guarantee by the Secretary of State for India in Council, the company wanted to construct and run railways in Assam and at the same time exploit the coal, timber and petroleum there. Thomas was one of the seven Directors of the new company. As Chairman of the Lancashire & Yorkshire Railway he was joined on the Board by the Chairman of the London, Chatham & Dover Railway and a Director of the Alabama Great Southern Railway. This company was still in existence five years later when Thomas was due to retire by rotation as a Director.

In September 1881 he was in Moor Hall, Farnworth, to open a Bazaar and Fancy Fair to raise funds for the extension scheme proposed by the Congregational Church in Market Street, Farnworth, which had now grown so much that it needed yet another building and planned to build a new church in Francis Street. Soon after that, on Saturday 24 September 1881, Thomas laid a memorial stone at the new Congregational Church for Pendlebury and Swinton in Jane Lane and Pendlebury New Road, Swinton. He was now referred to as Thomas Barnes of Farnworth. His link with The Quinta was not mentioned in the Lancashire papers.

Thomas's name still appeared occasionally in reports about the Welsh Liberals. For example, in September 1881, his name was on the list of Vice-Presidents and people willing to act as stewards at a banquet for Sir Hugh Owen to be held in London on 18 November. When a meeting was held on 15 March 1882 at Westminster Palace Hotel after Hugh Owen's death to consider how best to commemorate his services, Thomas sent a letter of apology for absence. By July 1882 both Thomas and James Richardson had sent subscriptions to the Hugh Owen Memorial Fund. On 25 July 1884 both of them sent letters of apology for absence to a meeting of the Council of the Denbighshire Liberal

Association in the Association Rooms, Bank Street, Wrexham, to consider what action the association was to take now that the Franchise Bill had been rejected by the House of Lords. When James Richardson was invited to become President of the East Denbighshire Liberal Association at a meeting at the Reform Club in Wrexham on 10 November 1891, Thomas was re-elected as one of the Vice-Presidents. Three years later, on 13 February 1894, the First Annual Meeting of the Liberal Three Hundred for the Oswestry Division of Salop was held at the Granville Club in Shrewsbury. James Richardson, now Colonel Barnes, Chairman of the Oswestry Divisional Liberal Association, presided. Thomas was re-elected President and James Richardson Chairman. From then onwards any references to the Barnes family's links with the Liberals were in connection with James Richardson and his wife, Ellen.

At Christmas 1881 there was a fire at The Quinta which could have been disastrous. The report of the event was in *The Wrexham Weekly Advertiser* on 24 December:

"A fire, which from the nature of the outbreak, seemed as if it would have been very serious in its results, happened on Saturday night, at some private gas works at The Quinta, the residence of Mr Thomas Barnes. It seems that somewhere over the firehole was placed an old barrel for the purpose of catching the tar that was formed in the manufacture of gas. The barrel had been noticed to be somewhat leaky for some time past, but not to such an extent as to create any apprehension on the part of those who superintended. However, on Saturday night, it seems the tar had leaked sufficiently to form a kind of train from the barrel, and a hot cinder, it is supposed, dropping on to the train, caused the fire which ensued. It was discovered first by the coachman at ten minutes to nine and he raised the alarm. A messenger was at once dispatched to Oswestry to give information, and in the meantime everything possible was done by those on the premises, to subdue the flames, which, it will be obvious from the flammable nature of the material, threatened to spread to a considerable degree. The police having been apprised, quickly obtained a trap and proceeded to the spot, and the fire brigade followed them some time afterwards. With the aid of four "*extincteurs*", however, kept by Mr Barnes always in readiness, the conflagration was put out. The fire brigade which posted off with four horses, arrived too late in the spot, and therefore their prowess was only exhibited on the demolition of a sumptuous supper to which they were entertained at Mr Barnes's expense, and for which we need hardly say their exertions and the keenness of the night air gave them an appreciative appetite. After their spending a very pleasant Christmas Eve they returned home, their exploit displaying more of amusement than exciting danger."

In 1882 Thomas was one of the two executors for James Haslam's will which was proved in Liverpool on 16 February. Thomas was described as a cotton spinner and manufacturer and gave his address as Limefield, Farnworth, and not as The Quinta.

On 1 March 1882 Thomas sent a letter apologising for his absence at a public meeting called by the Mayor of Wrexham in the Public Hall in connection with the Wrexham, Mold & Connah's Quay Railway who were hoping to have a bill passed in Parliament for extensions to the line. He sent another letter of apology for absence on 18 July that year when there was another public meeting in the Public Hall in Wrexham, this time to present an address of thanks to the Duke of Westminster for the efforts he had made to obtain the re-committal of the bill.

Before her death Ann Barnes had begun to make plans to build a new Sunday School to replace the old Quinta Sunday School on the site of the assembly rooms [now demolished] in Weston Rhyn. After her death the family decided to erect a new school building in her memory near to The Quinta Chapel, on a much more lavish scale than anything she had ever envisaged. This new school was designed by T. Raffles Davison, now the editor of *The British Architect* and well-known in the architectural world. The brick chosen for the building was the fine Ruabon red brick made by the local firm of J. C. Edwards. Although dated 1882 it was not completed until 1884 at a cost of £4,000. One quarter of this was raised by funds from subscriptions to concerts and other events, and the remainder of the costs was met by the Barnes family. With its Victorian Gothic mixture of complex shapes and designs, its turrets and spires, it can truly be described as a "baroque fantasy in red brick".

On 1 April 1882 Thomas was in Oswestry together with his son James Richardson and his great-nephew Harold Alfred Barnes when they signed the Trust Deed for the new Quinta Schools.

One of the fund raising concerts for the New Quinta Schools was held in the evening of 23 January 1883. It was a concert of light music and song, opened by Thomas's son and his wife Ellen playing a piano duet. Mary Elizabeth Gwyther who went on to marry Thomas's great nephew Harold Alfred two years later sang two solos, "The River" by Hatton and the folk song "The Oak and the Ash". There were songs by the children's chorus and by the main chorus, part songs, violin and piano solos and two performances on the Fairy Bells by a Mr Beever. An eight-page booklet containing the words of five specially-chosen hymns was printed for The Devotional Service at the Opening of the Quinta New Congregational Schools on the morning of Tuesday 29 May 1883. In addition to being the Congregational Church's Sunday school, the building was also used for public functions and concerts. A printed syllabus for the six months from October 1925 to March 1926 lists the varied fortnightly programme. It included three social evenings, one of them a "United Social", a Members' Evening, a Musical Evening, a lecture by the Estate Agent at The Quinta, W. E. Frith, a talk on Negro Spirituals by George Le Maire Barnes, and another by his father, Harold Alfred Barnes, on the naturalist, Richard Jefferies. As both Barnes men were still based in Farnworth, they must have made a point of coming to The Quinta for these evenings. The talks were varied—a photographer from Llangollen, Mr Lettsome, gave a lantern lecture entitled "The Romance of the Dee and Ceiriog Valleys". Two ministers, Rev. F. Mackenzie and Rev. P. Buchan gave talks on Admiral Blake and "A Night on the Thames Embankment as a Tramp". The Headmaster from Weston Rhyn School, E. Wood, gave another lantern lecture, this one on Switzerland and North Italy, and the half-year ended with a talk by a local solicitor, G. W. Ferrington, on Shropshire folklore.

Until 1921 Quinta Church was the Barnes family's private property. After Ellen Barnes's death in 1921 it was administered as a trust. The Quinta School had been set up as a trust from the start with the Trustees acting only with Thomas Barnes's consent. In 1956 the Chapel Trust amalgamated with another trust, the Ellen Barnes's Charitable Trust, but the two trusts separated again around 1995. The Quinta Sunday School is still run as a trust separate from Quinta Church but they are closely related. Like the church, the Quinta Sunday School is now a Grade II listed building. I visited the Quinta Sunday School on a miserable morning in March 2006. The rain added to the air of desolation from the outside but inside, in spite of the emptiness of the building, it was still easy to appreciate the care and craftsmanship that had gone into the building of it. Everything is of the highest quality—the tiles on the floor of the entrance porch, the few items of original furniture such as a large table in the school room and a solid oak arm chair on the rostrum in the hall, all the door and window furniture such as knobs, hinges and brackets, the parquet floors, the enormous blue-tiled corner stove in the corner of the school room, to give just a few examples. The building had been very modern for its time. It once had its own gas supply piped from the Barnes private gas works at the Quinta Hall, gas lighting, a toilet off the school room, and a kitchen attached to the main hall. The kitchen was used by girls from Bronygarth

School for cookery lessons while the boys had gardening lessons in the garden provided at the school by Ellen Barnes. When I visited the building in 2006 the cosy library with its panelled walls and fireplace had no books, but was still furnished and obviously used on occasions for meetings. The impressive main hall is dominated by a semi-circular white-tiled panel with a quotation from Proverbs. Each tile is different, the whole pattern being of intertwining leaves. In fact, the fitting of the tiles must have been a complicated operation, so complicated, in fact, that one of the workmen managed to put a key tile in upside down—and so it has remained! All round the hall are small rooms, separated from the main room by wooden roller blinds—again, of superb quality and still in full working order. The stained glass by W. B. Simpson & Sons, mentioned by John Newman in his book *Shropshire* is still intact. The staircase is a spiral stone staircase of the sort found in medieval castles. It leads to an upstairs room, now used for storage of the schoolroom benches with their reversible backs, for the boxes of books from the school's library, and for boxes of archive material such as the original registers from the Sunday School. I noticed one for the Ladies' Class led by Ellen Barnes in, I think, 1897. The spiral staircase continues up one more floor to a small turret room with windows all round, some fitted with a swivelling hinge. The purpose of this room was not evident, but it fitted in to the over-all atmosphere of this unusual building.

The Manchester Times reported on 9 September 1882 that the firm of Thomas Barnes & Company, Limited, of Farnworth, had just lost a legal dispute with Mr John Richard Hutchinson of Daisyfield Mills, Bury, over an infringement of a patent awarded on 17 February 1880, Patent No. 686 for improvements in the manufacture of ribbed piled fabrics. The matter had been referred to the arbitration of Mr Joseph Bentley and Mr Silas Clarke, who appointed Mr John Robert Barlow of Messrs Barlow & Jones Ltd. as arbitrator. The hearing was held at the Albion Hotel in Manchester on 12 August with Mr J. T. Doyle, a Manchester solicitor, appearing for the Barnes Company. The verdict was that the Company had infringed Mr Hutchinson's patent and they had to pay him damages and costs.

On 1 November 1882 Thomas was one of four hundred men connected with the railways and docks of the United Kingdom who attended a banquet at the Mansion House in London as guests of the Lord Mayor.

At the end of 1882 the Barnes family was still raising funds for the new Quinta Schools. When a Grand Bazaar was advertised to be held at the new Quinta Schools from 23 to 25 November 1882, Thomas was expected to open the event. Special attractions were to be provided and special trains would bring visitors from other districts. I do not know whether Thomas did attend but on the evening before the Grand Bazaar he sent a letter to a committee meeting in Henblas Street Cocoa Rooms in Wrexham when a new venture, a Musical Festival in Wrexham, was being discussed. He wished the movement every success.

Quinta Schools

CHAPTER 16

1850–1883

The Lancashire & Yorkshire Railway Company

Shortly after his father's death in 1849 Thomas had been made a Director of the Lancashire & Yorkshire Railway, as his father had been. The Manchester & Leeds Railway was completed in 1840. It was at the Special 20th half-yearly meeting of the Manchester & Leeds Railway on Wednesday 9 September 1846 that the company absorbed eight smaller railway companies, including the Manchester, Bolton & Bury Canal Navigation & Railway Company of which James Rothwell Barnes had long been a Director. James Rothwell Barnes was one of the chief negotiators in the amalgamation process and was elected a

Thomas Barnes in middle-age

Director of the enlarged company, now re-named the Lancashire & Yorkshire Railway Company, at the meeting in September 1846. He was re-elected on 7 March 1849 at the 25th half-yearly General Meeting as one of the Directors retiring by rotation, less than a month before he died.

Reports in *The Manchester Times* trace Thomas's involvement in the early years. It was not until after the death of his father in March 1849 that Thomas's name first appeared in reports of the Company's meetings. On 25 July 1850 fifteen men from the Lancashire & Yorkshire Railway Company—six of its retiring Directors and nine representatives from the Proprietors—met at the Company's Offices at Hunt's Bank in Manchester to elect a new Board. This new Board was to consist of twenty Managing Directors—ten elected from the old Board and ten from the Proprietors. Thomas was one of the new Directors elected from the Proprietors. At the 28th quarterly meeting held in a room at the Manchester Exchange on 4 September 1850 Thomas was appointed on to one of the Committees. A month later the company held a special meeting, again in the Exchange Rooms, on Wednesday 2 October, which was adjourned to the following day. A motion was put forward to reduce the number of Directors to ten, not including those Directors who were entitled to seats on the Board as representatives of other Companies. Several amendments were proposed with various suggestions about the number required, each of which had to be debated and voted on. Finally an amendment was agreed on by which a quarter of the directors would regularly go out of office. I have not yet established whether Thomas survived this reshuffle.

There was no mention of Thomas at the half-yearly meeting on 3 March 1852. At the time the Chairman was Robert Gill. However, Thomas was soon elected as Chairman. On 7 May 1852 it was Thomas as Chairman of the Board of Directors who signed a notice announcing a special general meeting to be held at the Palatine Hotel on 25 May. He was Chairman at this very long meeting, called to confirm, or otherwise, two bills which were before Parliament. It was presumably business connected with these bills which meant that he spent most of the three months before the 1852 election in London. On 11 August 1852 the Directors issued a call on £19 10s shares, commonly called "Fifths", of £1 10s per share (making £15 per share called up), payable on 30 September 1852. Thomas was Chairman at the 32nd half-yearly meeting on 1 September 1852 and at the following one on 2 March 1853 when he was re-elected as a Director. In May 1853 the line started to be worked in two divisions, the Western and Eastern Divisions.

The Christian World reported that Thomas resigned his position as Chairman to enter Parliament. I have not yet found the date of his resignation but by 9 February 1854 notices for the Company were being signed by H. W. Wickham as Chairman. Thomas remained a Director of the company and one of its principal shareholders. He was listed as one of the twenty Directors in 1859 after the company had amalgamated with the East Lancashire Railway. By January 1860 the number of Directors had been reduced to fourteen and Thomas was still one of them.

As a Director of the company Thomas presided at the annual tea meeting of railway employees held in the Baths Assembly Rooms in Bolton in October 1863. When he replied to Robert Heywood's letter in March 1865 he was obviously referring to his influence in the railway company when he wrote, "If the man Peter Rothwell is under 25, he had better call on me. If he is above 25, he will not be eligible for any situation on the Railway." There was a meeting of the Directors of the Lancashire & Yorkshire Railway around 27 January 1866 to declare a dividend for the half year out of the next revenue at the rate of 6¼% per annum, less income tax. The railway eventually stretched across the country from the west coast at Liverpool, Southport, Blackpool and Fleetwood, to Goole on the east coast. At first it mainly transported cotton, wool, fish and coal. Then, with the development of seaside resorts such as Blackpool, it carried a growing number of passengers.

The system of divisional management was discontinued in 1871. By the time the new system of centralised management took effect on 1 May 1871 Thomas was already Deputy Chairman and Thomas Dugdale Chairman. It was reported in *The Wrexham Advertiser* on 17 April 1875 that Thomas had just become Chairman again after the death of Thomas Dugdale of Griffin Lodge, Witton, Blackburn: "The chairmanship of the Lancashire & Yorkshire Railway Company, rendered vacant by the death of Mr Thomas Dugdale of Blackburn, has devolved upon Mr Thomas Barnes of The Quinta, Chirk. Mr Barnes has long held a seat at the board, and from his commercial experience, coupled with his general urbanity, we have reason to think that the interests of the shareholders, and also of the travelling public will be carefully watched and considerably promoted."

It is not clear from Thomas Normington's *Account of the rise and progress of the Lancashire and Yorkshire Railway* written in 1898 whether Thomas's involvement with the company was a creditable one or not. The financial fortunes of the company were reflected in the dividends which varied from a minimum of 2% in 1850 to a maximum of 9⅛%

in the second half of 1872. From then onwards they fell to 3% in 1886 (after Thomas had resigned) and finally settled at about 4% to 4½% for the rest of the company's existence. The book is not very complimentary about the early years of the company. It attributed the rapid increase in the amount of the dividends to the "cheese-paring" methods used. Apparently the locomotives, the rolling stock and the "permanent way" were all run-down and only the bare minimum was spent on maintenance. According to this account the railway was run by "short-sighted, money-grabbing tycoons" who had an obstructive attitude towards Third Class passenger accommodation and the development of block signalling systems demanded by the Government. In February 1875 it was reported that the company was still extending the block system on the most crowded parts of the railway "at considerable expense and inconvenience". (The block system was a system worked by telegraph to ensure that there were never two trains in any one section at the same time.) Three years later block and interlocking systems had been completed on 312 miles of railway and had already cost nearly £500,000. Work was in progress on another 24 miles.

On Wednesday 26 February 1879 Thomas presided at a special meeting of the Lancashire & Yorkshire Railway Company at their offices at Hunt's Bank to consider a scheme prepared by the directors for the consolidation of ten of the guaranteed and preference stocks of the company. The directors believed that by reducing the number and simplifying the arrangement of the stocks "not only would considerable trouble be saved, but their marketable value would be improved". Thomas, as Chairman of the Company, presided, and proposed the scheme which was adopted unanimously. He presided again on Thursday 21 August 1879 at the half-yearly general meeting of shareholders of the company. As Company Chairman he was in Southport on Thursday 18 August 1879 as one of the invited guests at the inauguration of an extension to the promenade and the laying out of the town's new market. He was in one of the carriages for distinguished guests in the procession of 300 guests, local volunteers, members of trade and friendly societies who attended the ceremony performed by Lord Derby.

His position as Chairman of the Lancashire & Yorkshire Railway Company must have been a main cause of work and anxiety. At the half-yearly meeting of shareholders of the company on Wednesday 18 February 1880 he had to report that in this "year of great anxiety and distress" the company could only offer a dividend of 5¼% which was ¾% lower than in 1878 and was now at its lowest since 1872. Nevertheless, Thomas's proposal that the Company should contribute £200 towards the relief of the distress in Ireland was seconded by William Hinmers and agreed to by the meeting. By the time he chaired the half-yearly meeting on 24 August 1881, things were even worse. An even lower dividend, 4¼%, was offered and the meeting had to be reclassified as a special meeting to authorize the directors to borrow on mortgage sums of money not exceeding £449,000 which was the maximum amount the company was authorized to borrow under the powers of its Acts of Parliament. Thomas, as Chairman, had to move the resolution to do this. Things had improved by the time of the next half-yearly meeting on 22 February 1882 when Thomas was able to report that a 5¾% dividend was to be offered. He was again at the company's offices at Hunt's Bank in Manchester to preside at the next meeting on 23 August 1882.

On 21 February 1883 the company held one of its stormiest meetings. Thomas, then in his last month as Chairman, had to explain why the company was only able to declare a dividend of 5% for the previous half year when their rivals, the London & North Western Railway had declared one of 8%. He explained that the installation of the block system had now cost £581,000 with an additional annual cost of £80,000 for maintenance and wages. There was by then a block cabin at an average of every 1,700 yards. He did not mention its contribution to public safety but did blame it for the reduction in the dividends of over ½%. He said he believed there was "not another line like it in the country". Thomas Normington, the writer of the history, was not quite as impressed. He added: "If its complexity were considered, he was quite right."

At the same meeting Thomas had to face another source of criticism from many of the directors—the expenditure on some of the branch lines and the poor returns from them. He said that over the past ten years there had been an increase in capital expenditure of £12,550,988. Deducting stocks, the real increase was £10,847,420, or about 44% (which still sounds to me like an enormous amount for the time). Of this £4,400,000 had been spent on the construction of branch lines. He described these branch lines as mainly a form of defence, intended to fill gaps to keep out opposing companies who, if they had managed to build their own lines, would have caused a greater loss to the Lancashire & Yorkshire Railway than the branch lines themselves had done. When the branch lines had been built it was expected that many of them would result in an increase in trade. However, that had not happened and they were not producing more than 1% a year. He ended by saying that only seven of the directors who had been responsible for building the lines were still alive but he knew "that they were careful men". It does not sound to me as if he made out a very good case. I wonder if it is significant that the writer of the history added that after Thomas's retirement "the upward trend of LYR affairs, so far as they affected the travelling public, became established".

As well as chairing these meetings, Thomas was involved at this time with several schemes for extending the railway, and as Chairman, had to meet delegations from various places eager to have a line built through their towns. For example, on 27 September 1881 a deputation from Leigh Local Board and several coal proprietors, cotton spinners and tradesmen from Leigh and district met the directors to try to persuade them to build a new line from Pendleton through Worsley, Astley, and Leigh to Ince. Even in these circumstances, Thomas had not lost his sense of humour and managed to raise a laugh when he informed the deputation that the supporters of a scheme to take the route north of Leigh had written to the directors asking them to make no promises to the deputation. What they would promise, however, was that they would pay careful attention to the statements made by the deputation.

It was not long before another group from the Local Boards of Swinton and Pendlebury, Tyldesley, Atherton and Westhoughton and from the Corporation of Salford met the directors on 25 October 1881 to urge them to route the new line from Manchester to Southport through their towns. As before, Thomas said they would consider their request. "They had made out a very good case but they must remember that there was another side to the matter. They could not make a new railway without great expense, for every man owning land seemed to want about ten times its value, so that they were called on to pay an extravagant price for every bit they wanted. They did not look for an immediate profit in opening out a new line, and would be quite content if they could see they would lose nothing and could get a fair profit in the course of time."

In the second week of January 1882 pressure came from yet another direction. This time it was a deputation from Holmfirth, Stalybridge, Glossop, Mossley, Hollingworth and Clayton West who wanted an extension of their line from Haigh Station to Clayton West. Again, Thomas said diplomatically that the scheme would "receive their careful consideration".

Shortly before Thomas's final meeting as Chairman of the Board he had had to act as peace-maker after another stormy meeting on 30 January 1883 when an influential deputation from Blackburn met the directors of the Lancashire & Yorkshire Railway Company to ask for a reduction in the transit charges. At the end of the meeting one of the directors, Samuel Fielden, declared that he "regarded such an extensive deputation was so constituted only for the purpose of overawing by their numbers the directors of the company. They were, however, determined to carry on their line in their own way, and if Blackburn manufacturers could not make their business pay, they must close their mills".[1] The directors had to meet again on the following day to pass a motion of censure on Samuel Fielden and Thomas, as Chairman, wrote a letter of apology which was read out at a meeting of Blackburn Town Council. He expressed regret at the unfortunate incident, and hoped that the deputation would "acquit the directors of sharing the views expressed by one of their colleagues". He was to resign as Chairman less than two weeks later.

After Thomas's resignation the shareholders of the company held a special meeting on 21 March to discuss the situation. The directors had already held their own meeting in anticipation of this meeting of shareholders and because they were bound by the rules of their constitution to appoint a Chairman from their own Board at the first meeting after the February half-yearly meeting, they had already chosen Mr Pearson, a colliery owner, and invited him to accept the position. Thomas does not appear to have attended the meeting on 21 March which was chaired by Mr G. J. Armytage, Deputy Chairman of the Board of Directors. The shareholders were keen to appoint a Chairman who would also be the Managing Director and receive a proper salary for the job. The directors, however, reported that they had given careful consideration to the resolution passed by the shareholders at the quarter-yearly meeting in February, and had unanimously come to the decision that it was not desirable for the Chairman to also hold the position of Managing Director. They did think, though, that he should devote a large portion of his time to the business of the company, and that he should receive adequate remuneration. This does rather sound as though they were criticising the way Thomas had done the job of Chairman, and another comment reinforces this. Whilst criticizing the financial state of the company, and the choice of Mr Pearson, one shareholder said, "No doubt Mr Pearson was a good man of business, but so was Mr Barnes before him". The implication was that the company had not prospered under his chairmanship.

This shareholder was probably the same man who had made a scathing attack on the management at the meeting on 21 February. He said then "the only persons to blame for the decadence of the property were the present directors. They wanted experienced railwaymen, not amateurs to manage their line. He believed that the general manager of the company was not a gentleman who had been trained in the early stages of railway work. It seemed to him that there was too much of the amateur in connection with the line. Nothing was more needful than that there should be a first class general manager to guide the board of directors and on the Lancashire & Yorkshire system such a man seemed to be lacking. A gentleman possessed of railway experience [should] be invited to join the board as chairman, and such position should be offered to Sir Edward Walkin. (This man was the choice of the Yorkshire end of the company, and was not, in fact, offered the position.) It is not surprising that Thomas had announced at that February meeting that he intended to retire as Chairman. At the next meeting in July 1883 John Pearson was Chairman but Thomas was still listed as one of the directors.

In his book Thomas Normington leaves no doubt about his opinion of the management (and the chairman) after centralisation took place. "This change of management only took eighteen months to destroy the foundation laid for cultivating traffic by the divisional officers. After 1872 the Company's dividends gradually dwindled down in face of an increasing population and improved trade throughout the whole line. Up to the time of the changed management the directors were very sanguine, and I often heard them say that the line would eventually pay a 10 per cent dividend. I was of the same opinion, and I am sure it would have done had divisional management been adhered to similar to that of the London & North Western Railway Company. When divisional management was first adopted in 1853, dividends gradually went up to the time of centralisation, and since then the shareholders know best how they have had to suffer, which misfortune has led to so many stormy half-yearly meetings, all being eager for an explanation of the cause of the depreciation suffered by their stock. The meetings generally ended with a reply from the chairman that the directors had done the best they could."[2]

However, many positive moves were made during the years when Thomas was in office after he was elected Chairman of the Board for the second time in 1874. Under the Lancashire & Yorkshire Railway Act of 1871 a superannuation fund was established in 1873 to the benefit of the employees. After 1872, the year of the maximum dividend, the company undertook a series of huge projects. The block system was installed from 1874 onwards. From 1875 almost the entire locomotive stock was renewed. The wrought iron rails were replaced by steel ones.

Newton Heath carriage works was built and fitted out. Most of the coaching stock was replaced. Continuous brakes were fitted. (According to Thomas Normington, all passenger coaches had had Mr C. Fay's and Mr J. Newall's continuous brakes fitted in October 1860 after a serious accident in August that year when ten rear coaches broke loose on a steep hill between Accrington and Helmshore. Using the only brake provided, the one in the guard's van, the guard had been unable to prevent them from crashing into another train. There was another railway collision near Agecroft on 3 August 1872 when four people were killed and several seriously injured.) New lines were laid and stations rebuilt. All this obviously was a drain on finances and inevitably reduced the dividends. From the small amount of information I have on Thomas's involvement with the company it is therefore difficult to assess just what sort of impact he had. Was he one of the "short-sighted, money-grabbing tycoons" or was he the driving force behind all these innovations? When his son died in 1899 it was Thomas's role as a former Chairman of the Lancashire & Yorkshire Railway Company which was mentioned in James Richardson's Obituary in *The Manchester Times*, not the fact that he had been an MP.

Notes

1   *Manchester Times* [19th Century Newspapers online]
2   Thomas Normington *An account of the rise and progress of the Lancashire and Yorkshire Railway* (pub. 1898)

CHAPTER 17

1883–1887

A new start and a new marriage.
Tragedy and disappointment; illness and resignation.

On 23 January 1883, members of the Barnes family, but not Thomas, were involved in a fund-raising concert for the new Quinta Schools. On Tuesday 30 January 1883, the same day that Samuel Fielden upset the deputation from Blackburn at a meeting of the Lancashire & Yorkshire Railway Company, Thomas was one of the guests at a fashionable wedding at Marchwiel Church near Wrexham. Arabella Margaret Piercy, the daughter of the distinguished railway engineer, Benjamin Piercy of Marchwiel Hall, married. Thomas was described in the report as Chairman of the Lancashire & Yorkshire Railway Company but had probably first come into contact with Mr Piercy through his connections with the Wrexham, Mold & Connah's Quay Railway. Mr Piercy had recently completed the building of the Sardinian railway network with which Thomas had been involved.

Just over a week later on Thursday 8 February 1883 Thomas was on the Lancashire coast at his own wedding when he married Elizabeth Vickers, his third wife. They were married by licence at Cartmel Priory by the Vicar F. H. Paley. She was in her mid-fifties when they married and he was in his late sixties. It was an inscription on his tombstone at Halshaw Moor which first revealed that after Ann's death Thomas married again. The inscription gave his third wife's name as Elizabeth and added her date of birth—13 December 1827. The inscription also revealed that the marriage had been a short one as Elizabeth died on 20 October 1886, aged only 59. Thomas wrote his last Will in 1887 after his third wife's death and so the Will did not provide any information about her. However, I discovered in the Obituary Column in *The Bolton Chronicle* that on 20 October 1886 an Elizabeth Vickers, aged 58, died in Farnworth at Limefield, Thomas's house. Information on an In Memoriam card sent on the day of her burial revealed that she had been Thomas's "faithful and devoted housekeeper" for twenty-five years and so she must have begun to work for Thomas in 1861. She was recorded as the housekeeper at Limefield in the 1871 and 1881 censuses. On the marriage certificate Elizabeth Vickers was described as a spinster, of full age, the daughter of William Vickers, a gentleman, now deceased. She was living in Cartmel at the time of her marriage. Thomas described himself as a widower, a gentleman, the son of James Barnes, deceased, who had also been a gentleman. He did not give his father's full name—James Rothwell Barnes. He gave his own address as Weston Rhyn in the County of Salop and did not mention The Quinta. Nor did he mention as he did on other legal documents written around this time that he was a cotton manufacturer. The two witnesses at the marriage were William and Mary Ellen Lancaster. William Lancaster was a saddler who lived in Priory Cottage, Cartmel. He had been the Parish Clerk in Cartmel at least since the time of the 1871 Census. Mary Ellen was his 29–year-old unmarried daughter. The only possible link that I can find between Thomas and Cartmel is that the young headmaster of Cartmel Grammar School at the time of Thomas's marriage was a Joseph S. Cooper from Birmingham who had been a student at London University in 1871. The headmaster of Queen Street Seminary School in Farnworth from around 1860 to 1894 was a William Cooper. Up to now I have not found any link between the two men apart from their names and their occupation.

On Saturday 24 February 1883 Thomas presided at the half-yearly meeting of the Wrexham, Mold & Connah's Quay Railway Company at the company's offices in Wrexham and on the same day, 24 February 1883, resigned as Chairman of the Board of the Lancashire & Yorkshire Railway Company. When he returned to Halshaw Moor on 5 March 1883 to give a lecture on his impressions of America based on his trip in 1874, his successor, Mr Pearson, had been invited to become Chairman, but had not yet accepted the post.

When the new Quinta Schools were opened on 29 May 1883 Thomas was ill and unable to attend the ceremonies. His daughter-in-law Ellen stood in for him. His son was also unable to be there. However, Thomas had recovered by 18 August that year when he was back in Farnworth to lay a memorial stone at the new Congregational Church in Francis Street on the land which he had provided. In 1883 he also laid the foundation stone of the new Congregational Church in St George's Road in Bolton.

By the time Penybryn Sunday School went to spend a day at The Quinta in 1883 they were able to travel by train to Preesgweene station. From there they marched to Quinta Park for tea. The forty-one people who travelled from Oswestry in 1884 also travelled by train to Preesgweene on a special coach. They spent the afternoon in the grounds and the flower gardens. A party from Acrefair Wesleyan Sunday School arrived by boat on 13 July 1891, disembarking at Pontcysyllte Wharf and spent a "very enjoyable afternoon" at The Quinta. When the Sunday School from Wrexham went in July 1896 they travelled by train. By this time Thomas was in failing health and it was his son, Colonel Barnes, who had given the permission to use the park.

In December 1883 when the final bill for the building of the Quinta Schools was paid, Thomas was at The Quinta. On Monday 28 January 1884 he was on the Grand Jury at the Assizes in Ruthin, making his first appearance for many years. It also turned out to be his last. That evening he presided at a meeting at the English Congregational Church in Rhyl when recognition services were held to welcome the new pastor.

I have found very few references to Thomas's activities in 1884 and 1885 apart from his appearance at the Annual General Meetings of the Provincial Assurance Company in 1884 and 1885. In 1884 he did lay two more foundation stones in Shropshire, one at the new Independent Chapel at Ellesmere on 24 July when he donated £50, and another at Grimpo near West Felton on 3 November. When Sir Watkin Williams Wynn died on 9 May 1885 Thomas joined the funeral cortège for the 22–mile journey from Wynnstay Hall to the graveyard at Llangedwyn.

On 8 April 1886 he attended a bazaar at Church Stretton Congregational Church where he had laid the foundation stone twenty-one years earlier. Again he donated £50. Both Thomas and James Richardson (and presumably Ellen) were at Dukinfield Cemetery on Monday 24 May 1886 to attend the funeral of Ellen's father, John Cheetham. Thomas was still in Farnworth on 28 June 1886 to preside at an evening meeting in Moor Hall when R. Leake the Liberal MP addressed a meeting in support of his candidature.

I have not found any evidence that Elizabeth Vickers ever lived at The Quinta. She died on 20 October 1886. The marriage had lasted only three and a half years but there was no indication on her death certificate that she had ever married. According to information on the censuses she had been born in Hanmer in Flintshire and on her death certificate Elizabeth's father was said to be a wheelwright, not a gentleman as stated on her marriage certificate. In the 1841 Census a 54–year-old wheelwright, William Vickers, and Sarah, aged 53, presumably his wife, were living in the village of Hanmer in Flintshire. These were probably Elizabeth's parents. Elizabeth who would have been about 13 years old, was not at home but in the neighbouring village of Bronnington an Elizabeth Vickers of the correct age was working as a servant for a curate, Rev. Nathaniel Higgins. At home in Hanmer were four younger members of the family with ages ranging from 25 years to 11 months, presumably representing various generations. The head of the household was Joshua Vickers, aged 82, who had not been born in Flintshire. After that I have not been able to trace Elizabeth until she appeared in the 1871 Farnworth Census as Thomas's housekeeper.

When Elizabeth Vickers died the causes of death were certified by a surgeon, R. A. Clarke (not the same Farnworth doctor Dr J. C. Clarke who later attended Thomas's funeral in 1897). Around January 1886 she had been diagnosed with enlargement of the liver and when she died had been suffering from dropsy for eight months, that is, from around March of that year. The immediate cause of death was diarrhoea which she had been suffering from for two days. Both Thomas's second wife, Ann, and his son, James Richardson, had also had liver problems. The death was registered on 21 October 1886, the day following her death, by a William "Lindal Milomme"—or so the person at the Bolton Register Office who copied the entry on the death certificate interpreted the name. I think this must have been William Tindall Meldrum who was one of the two witnesses to Thomas's new Will made in the following May.

Amongst the Barnes family archives is an "In Memoriam Card" sent from Limefield on 23 October 1886 commemorating Elizabeth's burial at the Independent Chapel in Farnworth on that day. The left-hand page reads: "Interred this day at the Independent Chapel, Farnworth", and the right-hand page gives details:

In Memory of
Elizabeth Vickers
The faithful and devoted Housekeeper for
25 years of Thomas Barnes, Esq., J.P.
Born December 13 1827
Died October 20 1886.

There was no mention of her marriage. However, there is a brief pencil note below written by a later member of the Barnes family: "Subsequently, during her service to T.B. she married him. They had no issue."

In October 1886 William Tindall Meldrum gave his address as Limefield on the death certificate and stated that he had been present at Elizabeth Vickers' death. However, most unusually, no description was given of who he was. When he witnessed Thomas's Will in the following May he gave his address as The Quinta. I do not know what his role was either at Limefield or at The Quinta. William Tindall Meldrum had been a regular soldier serving with the 16th Lancers until he was seconded to the Denbighshire Hussars as a Sergeant Major with the Llangollen Troop on 23 June 1877. His service as a regular soldier ended on 8 July 1879 and according to his service papers he had been a model soldier, leaving with a Long Service and a Good Conduct Medal. He had spent 11 years in India and was in Bangalore in March 1865. He married for a second time in 1874 when the regiment was stationed at Secunderabad. He was living with this second wife, Harriet (née Kent) and three young children in Cefn near Llangollen in April 1881. One of their children had been born in St Martin's, Chirk, in 1878. It would appear that he lived near The Quinta when he first joined the Denbighshire Hussars in June 1877. As James Richardson was a Captain in the same troop in 1878 this would not be surprising. Three children were born while the family was in Cefn, Alice in 1880, Annie in 1883 and Charles in 1885. Why William Meldrum was at Limefield in Farnworth in October 1886 and at The Quinta in May 1887, I do not know. His last child, Frederick, was born in 1889 by which time his wife was back in Chirk. It appears that William Meldrum was in poor health. He died in September 1890 when he was only 49 years old. His funeral was reported in *The Wrexham Weekly Advertiser* on 13 September: "The remains of the late Sergeant Major Meldrum, formerly of 16th Lancers, and afterwards Sergeant Major of the Llangollen Troop, Denbighshire Hussars, were on Tuesday afternoon interred at the Lodge, near Chirk. Sergeant Major Meldrum, who had been in ill-health for some time, was only 49 years of age, and had been a general favourite in the regiment." Several members of the Denbighshire Hussars attended the funeral but I have not found any mention of the Barnes family being there.

After becoming a limited company the business in Farnworth had continued to prosper and make steady progress but in 1886 two separate fires at the Dixon Green Mill each caused five thousand pounds' worth of damage.

In 1886 it was reported in *The Times* that Thomas was still involved with the Assam Railways and Trading Company, now not only a Limited Company but a Reduced Company. At its Sixth Ordinary General Meeting which was to be held in London at the City Terminus Hotel in Cannon Street on 20 December, Thomas was one of the two Directors whose turn it was to retire. He had offered himself for re-election.

In February 1887 it was reported that Thomas was in the south of England and unable to attend a meeting. It must have been around this time that he began to suffer from a series of strokes. In 1887 Barton wrote that Thomas no longer took as prominent a part in the running of the Farnworth Mills which he had visited more or less daily before his health failed. It does sound as if he was based at Limefield during the time of his marriage to Elizabeth Vickers. However, the fact that she was still using her maiden name and was still described as a domestic servant at the time of her death would suggest that the marriage was not publicized. When Thomas died and *The Bolton Observer* printed incorrectly in his Obituary that he had married Elizabeth Howard Knowles in 1850, some reporter must have known of his third marriage to an Elizabeth and had found the best possible match for a marriage in the Bolton parish records.

In April 1887 there was a change of minister at the Quinta Church when Rev. Thomas Davison retired and was replaced by Rev. Edward W. Place BA from Lancashire College.

On 13 May 1887 Thomas wrote his last Will and Testament, revoking all previous wills. He left all his real estate and the residue of his personal estate after all his debts and funeral and testamentary expenses had been paid to his son, James Richardson, who was to be sole executor of the will. No other beneficiaries were mentioned. The main business in the Will was to set up a Trust Fund of £2,000 which was to be invested by James Richardson, the Trustee, as he saw fit. The interest from it was to be used to pay for the upkeep of the Quinta Church—Thomas described it as "the little church built by me at The Quinta". Any annual surplus was to be either given to the Minister for his own personal use or used to maintain divine worship in the church. Thomas stipulated that his son was not to be held liable for any losses he might make by investing the money badly on "insufficient, fluctuating or risky securities". Is this what had happened to Thomas himself? At Thomas's memorial service at Market Street Chapel on the Sunday after his death Rev. W. Hewgill referred to some heavy financial losses Thomas had incurred, for which he blamed himself for having a too easy-going trustfulness in other men. Very detailed instructions were given in the Will as to how the money should be invested if anyone other than James Richardson became Trustee. "Then I direct him or them to invest the same in or upon some of the Government stocks or funds of Great Britain or in the purchase of Preference stocks or shares or Debentures or Debenture bonds of any Railway or other Public Company in the United Kingdom which shall have for the last five years paid dividends on their ordinary share capital or at interest on the mortgage of any freehold copyhold or leasehold hereditaments in Great Britain such leaseholds being held for a term whereof not less than two hundred years shall be unexpired". Only two people witnessed the signing of this Will—Arthur Bailey, his solicitor from Bolton, and William Tindall Meldrum who gave his address as The Quinta. It was ten years before Thomas died and the arrangements made in the Will were implemented. Presumably during those years he continued to pay for the upkeep of the church himself.

At about half past six on the evening of Tuesday 5 July 1887, a fire broke out in one of the storerooms of the No. 1 mill at Farnworth and damage of at least £3,000 was caused. Fortunately it was covered by insurance.

On 26 August 1887 Thomas was in Llandudno where Christ Church, the English Congregational Church in Tudno Street, was holding a two-day Grand Bazaar in St George's Hall to raise funds for improvements to the inside of the church. On the first day, Friday, Thomas (described as Thomas Barnes JP) seconded the vote of thanks and made a short speech. I think this might have been one of his last, if not his very last, public appearance. His son opened the bazaar on the second day.

Thomas began his speech by thanking the ladies who had organized the bazaar. He was especially grateful to Mr McCulloch of Liverpool who had stepped in to replace the MP Mr Oulton who had been unable to attend. He continued: "A bazaar of that kind was a good opportunity for the different denominations to show sympathy for each other. The English Congregational Church was the first building erected in Llangollen and had a very interesting history. They had heard that even a band of music could attract visitors to their watering-place, and do much material good to the community; how much more should any building for the highest of all purposes be a means to attract to such a place as Llandudno? Llandudno had ever been celebrated for its beautiful scenery and life-giving breezes; but their church had a history in which some of the finest preachers of the day for thirty years had ministered to the spiritual comfort of the visitors to Llandudno. In supporting that bazaar they had an opportunity to help a Church that had done much good."

CHAPTER 18

1863–1884

The Wrexham, Mold & Connah's Quay Railway Company.

Thomas was also at one time a director of the Wrexham, Mold & Connah's Quay Railway, rescuing the company from difficulties, and building quays on the river. The First Ordinary Meeting of the shareholders of this company took place at the Wynnstay Arms Hotel, Wrexham, on 2 February 1863. At the time Thomas was Chairman of the company and presided at the meeting. Several influential shareholders were present together with the company's officers: Mr Thomas Minshall, Mr Edgworth and Mr Pugh, solicitors, Mr T. E. Minshall, the resident engineer, and Mr George Lewis, the secretary. The directors had succeeded in obtaining an act of Parliament for the section of their line north of Wrexham. Mr Savin was to construct the line. Thomas was not keen to keep the position of Chairman. He said he would be very glad indeed if they could find someone more suitable than himself to fill his place as director. To cries of "No, no", he was re-elected.

Four years later at the half-yearly meeting of shareholders held on 7 May 1867 at 19 Duke Street, Westminster, he was elected, again in his absence, as a director of the company in the place of Mr Rawlins, one of the retiring directors. The company was having difficulty raising enough capital to complete the work needed to get the line working. For example, they needed to build accommodation at Connah's Quay together with some short branches with additional sidings and accommodation amongst the works, and to convert the Buckley Railway into a passenger line. However they reported that "with assistance rendered by Mr Barnes, considerable progress has been made with the additional accommodation at Connah's Quay".

On 10 May 1867 a Select Committee in the House of Commons examined for the first time a bill for the Wrexham, Mold & Connah's Quay Railway Company. The bill was opposed by the London & North Western Railway. Thomas was called to appear before the

Committee. He said he had an estate "about seven miles from Wrexham", and he resided there. In 1861 he was asked by the leaders of that district to do his best to get a line from Wrexham to Connah's Quay and it was afterwards proposed to extend the line to Whitchurch. The London & North Western Railway gave evidence in favour of the scheme. He agreed to become Chairman of the company, and did so. Subsequently, owing to the state of his health and other engagements, he retired from the chairmanship of the company, though he took the same interest in the line as ever. Latterly there had been considerable difficulty in carrying on the line on account of the contractor failing to carry out his engagements in consequence of the financial crisis. Subsequently he was again asked to join the Board of Directors and he was now the Chairman again. He had been over the line himself two or three times and he was satisfied that when completed there would be a large amount of traffic upon it. He had advanced a large sum of money to complete the works at Connah's Quay, which were essential to the success of the line. Mr Merewether, speaking for the London & North Western Railway, asked the Committee to prevent Mr Barnes from going into this insane business as it had already ruined one or two people. The Committee decided to pass the preamble of the Bill, and the extension of time was granted.

At the half-yearly meeting of shareholders on 16 November 1867 Thomas had made an effort to get away from Parliament to chair the meeting in the company's office in Wrexham. The line was still suffering financially and they blamed the problems on the general commercial depression. The directors had felt it necessary to have a firm of eminent accountants, Chadwick & Co., look at the books and prepare the balance sheet. The meeting agreed that some plan was needed to raise more funds.

On Saturday 19 December 1868 *The Wrexham Weekly Advertiser* published details of the company:

Wrexham, Mold & Connah's Quay Railway

Chairman	Thomas Barnes, Esq., The Quinta
Consulting Engineer	G. Owen, Esq., Oswestry
General Manager and Secretary	John Broughton, Esq.
Goods Agent (Wrexham)	Mr C. Hughes
Bankers	North and South Wales Bank

On Saturday 11 March 1876 an annual meeting of shareholders was held at Wrexham. Thomas was again in the Chair and was able to report that this year the company was able to offer a dividend, not a very high one, but a dividend, of 4½% on the 5½% debenture stock, and of 5½% on the 6% debenture stock. The work at Connah's Quay had been completed and as a result there had been a considerable increase in the number of vessels using the port. By now James Richardson had joined his father as one of the directors. Both men retired as directors at this meeting and were re-elected.

When a bill came before Parliament in March 1882 to authorize an extension to the Wrexham, Mold & Connah's Quay Railway, the Mayor of Wrexham called a public meeting in the Public Hall on 1 March to consider how they could best support the bill. Thomas sent a letter of apology, expressing his approval of the projected extension of the railway. He hoped it would be warmly supported by the inhabitants of the town. One of the speakers at the meeting, Charles Hughes, said he would be delighted to find that Mr Barnes would live to see the present attempt successful and that this line would be one of those things which they all looked to for the success and prosperity of Wrexham. He mentioned that although Mr Barnes was connected with one of the largest railway companies in the kingdom—the Lancashire & Yorkshire—he came forward twenty-two years earlier and became the Chairman of Connah's Quay. On 18 July 1882 Thomas again sent a letter of apology for absence when the Mayor of Wrexham called another meeting in the Public Hall in Wrexham, this time to present an address of thanks to the Duke of Westminster for the part he had played in obtaining the re-committal of the bill to a Select Committee of the House of Lords.

When the company held an ordinary half-yearly meeting at the company's offices in Wrexham on 24 February 1883 Thomas presided at the meeting and was able to report that one of the branch lines authorized to be constructed in the previous session of Parliament for giving access to the colliery districts of North Wales was now half completed and opened for traffic. On 16 September 1884 there was a large meeting at Connah's Quay to celebrate the start of work to extend the port. *The Cheshire Observer* printed the name of J. Barnes, The Quinta, as one of the people attending. This must have been Thomas's son, James Richardson. A new wharf, about three-quarters of a mile long was to be built. The Manchester, Sheffield & Lincolnshire Railway had recently obtained an Act giving them permission to construct a line from Chester to Connah's Quay. They undertook to spend £50,000 on improvements to the port. Up to then, the railway connection between Wrexham and Connah's Quay had been just a single line for goods traffic but now that trade had increased, and more rail provision was needed, the Wrexham, Mold & Connah's Quay Railway Company had just completed a double line of track from Wrexham to Buckley. Passengers could now be carried between these two points. However, to travel further to reach Connah's Quay would require the construction of a loop line from Buckley through Hawarden to avoid a steep gradient. This loop line was only in its very early stages. Lunch for 150 guests at this celebration was provided in a tent next to the Connah's Quay Inn and was presided over by Benjamin Piercy. The first train to run on the new extension line into the centre of Wrexham was arranged for the day of Queen Victoria's Golden Jubilee, 21 June 1887, a day of celebrations in the town. I have not found any evidence that Thomas attended this event.

CHAPTER 19

1859–1888

The Provincial Assurance Company

After his resignation as Chairman of the Board of Directors of the Lancashire & Yorkshire Railway Company in February 1883 Thomas seems to have restricted his involvement in company matters to the Provincial Assurance Company and the Alliance Assurance Company both of which had offices in Wrexham.

The North Wales Chronicle provided details about Thomas's role in the Provincial Assurance Company. It had been established in Wales in 1852 as the Provincial Welsh Insurance Company with its headquarters in Wrexham. At its Sixth Annual General Meeting held in March 1859 there was no mention of Thomas but the Chairman of the Board, Mr W. Wright, was one of the directors due to retire by rotation and there was a movement afoot among the shareholders to "infuse new blood into the constitution of the Board" by electing a new director in place of Mr Wright. Thomas's name was not one of those brought before the meeting but an article in the paper on 18 June 1859 reported that Thomas Barnes was to be Chairman of the Company. At the Fifteenth Annual General meeting in March 1868 Thomas referred to the early years of the company. He said the first two years of the company's existence had been years of prosperity but they were followed by four years of losses. The decision to elect a new director would appear to have coincided with the end of this four-year period of losses. From 1859 to 1863 after Thomas's appointment, the business prospered. At the end of 1859 the company launched a scheme to build new offices on the High Street in Wrexham and on 3 January 1860 Thomas, as Chairman of the Board, presided at the grand ceremony to lay the chief stone at the new offices. It was a gala day for Wrexham, attended by a large number of important people, including nobility and gentry. The first names on the long list of guests were those of Mrs Barnes and Mr Barnes of The Quinta. Thomas presented Lady Wynn (the

wife of Sir Watkin Williams Wynn, one of the original trustees of the company) with a silver trowel for the stone-laying ceremony. At two o'clock a dinner was held at the Wynnstay Arms and Thomas made a speech, commenting that "his connection with the company was only of recent date". In that year (1860) an advertisement for the company listed its ten trustees together with an additional three trustees in Ireland. There were nine directors and Thomas was named as the Chairman. By the time of the Eighth Annual Meeting the company was called the Provincial (Welsh) Insurance Company. The newspaper report of the meeting included a large picture of the very impressive completed office building which apparently contained facilities for improving the education and well-being of the employees. By the time of the next Annual Meeting in 1862 the company's name had lost the "Welsh" and was now the Provincial Insurance Company. One interesting development was that around 1863 the company took on responsibility for the local fire brigade in Wrexham, presumably because a major part of its business concerned fire insurances. As a result of this, the fire engines belonging to the Wrexham Fire Brigade, the Prince of Wales Fire Brigade, underwent a complete transformation in the hands of the Provincial Insurance Company. Their large engine was renamed "The Quinta" after "the beautiful country residence of their Chairman, Thomas Barnes". By 1865 the company also had offices at 49 Moorgate Street, London, and 77 Buchanan Street, Glasgow, but in 1866 it was said that the company was still essentially a Welsh one even though its range of operations was not confined to Wales. Thomas continued to chair the annual meetings. At the Eleventh Annual meeting in February 1864 he was able to report: "The first time he had the privilege of addressing them in the position they had done him the honour to place him, he addressed them on the very satisfactory character of the Report, and each succeeding year it had been more satisfactory". The annual income was now £80,000 and they were able to offer a 10% dividend. Thomas admitted in 1868 that in 1863 the company had made what he believed at the time to be a mistake and had declared too large a dividend. The early years of prosperity were now to be followed by four years of losses. *The North Wales Chronicle* reported on 10 March 1866: "We are sorry to find from the Report of Directors that the previous uniform prosperity of the Provincial Insurance Company received a check during the past year, by reason of the very heavy losses by fire, and the unusual number of deaths so that in neither of the two departments [Fire and Life] was the profit very large. [...
...] We doubt not but that the next annual Report of the company

will be as cheering as the present one is disheartening. That it may be so is our sincere wish." The company also had a third department which offered annuities. It advertised regularly in the local paper, *The Wrexham Weekly Advertiser*. The following advertisement also appeared at three-monthly intervals in 1865 and 1866 in *The North Wales Chronicle*:

Established 1852

PROVINCIAL INSURANCE COMPANY

Fire—Life—Annuities

Chief Offices—High Street, Wrexham

49 Moorgate Street, London

77 Buchanan Street, Glasgow

Trustees

The Right Honourable Lord Boston

The Right Honourable Lord Tredegar

Sir Watkin Williams Wynn Bart., M.P.

Colonel Myddelton Biddulph M.P.

Townshend Mainwaring Esq., M.P.

Thomas Barnes, Esq., M.P.

The Very Rev. the Dean of St Asaph

Thomas Brassey, Esq., Westminster

Hugh Owen, Esq., Barnsbury, London

Chairman of the Board

Thomas Barnes, Esq. MP, Farnworth, and The Quinta, Salop.

All the usual descriptions of Fire and Life Insurances effected on the most moderate terms, and every attention given to the business with which the Company may be favoured.

Anthony Dillon, Secretary to the Company

Applications for Agencies are invited.

By the time of the Fourteenth Annual Meeting on 26 February 1867 James Richardson Barnes was also a shareholder and a director. Despite the fact that the year had been a disastrous one for commerce, marked by disasters and losses, Thomas was able to report that the company had "met with a greater amount of success than in any previous year".

Its income was now £107,000. However, the fire department had been badly affected by the large number of fires.

The situation had worsened by the Fifteenth Annual General meeting on 6 March 1868. For the first time in the company's fifteen years of existence they were unable to declare any dividend at all. Again, the fire department was chiefly to blame for this. There had been fires at cotton mills, including one in Bolton. Even weaving sheds which had never been considered a fire risk had caught fire. Thomas himself had never insured his weaving sheds in the forty years he had been in business, but he, too had had a loss from a fire in a weaving shed. However, the greatest risk from fires was in dwelling houses. The state of trade had also meant that many of the fires could have been the result of arson.

Thomas was unable to chair the meeting the following year on 27 February 1869 because of a sudden indisposition. It was two days after the big public ceremony in Bolton when he and Mr Pope as the defeated Liberal candidates at the General Election had been presented with tributes from the Bolton Liberals. His son did attend this Annual General Meeting in Wrexham but another missing face at this meeting was that of the company's secretary, Anthony Dillon, who appears to have left very suddenly. His name was still on company advertisements on 30 January and he attended public functions in Wrexham on 2 and 13 February. However, by 27 February he was said to be "residing in London" and was now referred to as the "late Secretary".

Both Thomas and his son were at the meeting on 27 February 1871 when James Richardson retired as a Director. Thomas and James Richardson were also present in February the following year, 1872, when the company's position had greatly improved. They had closed down the Scottish end of the business, something which their previous Secretary, Mr Dillon, had been very keen on keeping. They were now planning to build new offices in London near Mansion House. However, they were only offering a 2% dividend. Around this time advertisements for the company in *The Wrexham Weekly Advertiser* described Thomas, the Chairman, as of The Quinta and of Farnworth. Previously his address had been Farnworth followed by The Quinta. By March the following year, 1873, they had a fine stone building in London in Queen Victoria Street. In 1873 the Provincial was suffering, like many other insurance companies, from the suspension and collapse of two great insurance companies two years before. It did all it could to keep its running costs to a minimum but it was still agreed that the directors should receive £500 for their previous year's services. Gwynedd Council has in its archives a document dated 28 July 1874 (Reference XM/1457/5) which illustrates the financial problems. It is a mortgage of a property, Garreg Fawr in the parish of Llanbeblig, to secure £5,850 and the interest, with a reconveyance *en dorse*. The first party to the agreement consisted of Thomas Turner of Plas Brereton, Sir Llewelyn Turner of Parkia, and Morgan Lloyd of London, and the second party was Thomas Barnes of The Quinta, Co. Salop, and Hugh Owen of 21 Richmond Crescent, Barnsbury, Co. Middlesex, Trustees of the Provincial Insurance Company. However, in spite of these efforts, the company decided to sell off its fire department business and become a life assurance company only. On Saturday 3 October 1874 the following two advertisements appeared in *The Wrexham Weekly Advertiser* showing how the division had been made. Thomas was a director of both companies.

Provincial (Life) Insurance Company

Established 1852

Capital £200,000

Life claims paid 30 days after production of proofs of death

The Company has, since its establishment, paid to the Widows and other representatives of deceased Life Assurers nearly £200,000

Accumulated Life Fund in 1865 £89,865; in 1873 £192,612

Chairman Thomas Barnes Esq., of Farnworth near Bolton and The Quinta, Salop

Robert Williams, Secretary

Chief Offices: Wrexham and London

Provincial Fire Office

United with Alliance Assurance Company

Established 1824

Subscribed Capital £5,000,000 (of which £550,000 is paid up)

Fire Reserve Funds upwards of £200,000

Chief Offices: Bartholomew Lane, London

Chairman Sir Moses Montefiore Bart. FRS

Secretary Robert Lewis Esq.,

Welsh Branch: High Street, Wrexham

Chairman Thomas Barnes, Esq.

Fire Insurances of every description transacted on moderate terms.

For Prospectuses and other information apply at the above Office,
or to any of the Agents of the Company

Robert Williams, Secretary;
E. Llewelyn Lloyd Assistant Secretary (Wrexham)

A year later at the 1876 meeting all Thomas could say was that "business had been satisfactory, although very far from being what we should like it to be". However, the new offices in London had proved to be a satisfactory investment and they were able to report that all the premises in the building were now let.

The Provincial Fire Office was soon absorbed into the Alliance Assurance Company and on 31 May 1879 an advertisement appeared in *The North Wales Chronicle* for the Alliance Assurance Company naming Thomas as Chairman of its Welsh Branch in Wrexham. The company under its new name specialised in fire insurance and was based in London at Bartholomew Lane with Sir Moses Montefiore as its Chairman. Thomas was still Chairman of the Welsh Branch of the Alliance Assurance Company in 1886 and 1887 when the Chairman of the main company was Lord Rothschild. There do not appear to be any advertisements for the company after this which include Thomas's name as Chairman of the Welsh Branch.

I have not traced any reports for the Provincial Insurance Company in *The North Wales Chronicle* from 1877 to 1880 but Thomas chaired the annual meeting on Monday 28 February 1881 and made very similar comments to those he made in 1876. Circumstances were more favourable than in the previous year but, he said, "the same thing which has been affecting trade generally has also affected most businesses. In looking back on a quinquennium which has been marked by the severest commercial depression known in modern times [... ...] we can very hopefully look to a better time coming". A comment was made by another director which would suggest that Thomas had not been able to attend some of the previous years' meetings. "They were always glad to see him amongst them and deeply regretted when he was unable to be present. They looked upon Mr Barnes's annual visit in connection with the Provincial Insurance Company as one of the pleasant days they had of listening to a gentleman who could so well describe the contents of a report and balance sheet and who could temper it with so much judgement and courtesy. They were glad to see him there that day and hoped he might long be spared to preside over their deliberations."

Even if Thomas's health was beginning to cause him problems, he was obviously still managing to fulfil his duties. He chaired the Twenty-ninth Annual General Meeting in Wrexham on Friday 24 February 1882, two days after chairing a meeting of the Lancashire & Yorkshire Railway Company, presumably at its headquarters in Manchester. He did make a comment that he was getting older and explained why he had taken out a life insurance policy: "I should never have insured my own life simply from seeing printed papers and forms, but it was the personal interference of one wise and judicious man that led me to do what I did." He chaired the next Annual Meeting on Friday 23 February 1883. By now he had resigned as Chairman of the Lancashire & Yorkshire Railway Company. He was at the 1884 Annual General Meeting and was re-elected as Chairman of the Board in February 1885. He was now 72 years old. However, at the Quinquennial Valuation Annual General meeting in February 1887 he was in the South of England and unable to take the meeting. It was only a few months after the death of his third wife and it was around this time that his health began to fail.

On Wednesday 22 February 1888 the Thirty-fifth Annual General Meeting of shareholders of the Provincial Insurance Company was held at the company's offices in Wrexham. Richard Venables Kyrke, the Chairman of the Company, presided. Amongst those present was James Richardson Barnes, now Colonel Barnes. The Chairman of the meeting read his report: "Mr Thomas Barnes, the Chairman of the Board, whose failing health has, for a considerable time, prevented his taking an active part in the company's affairs, has lately felt compelled to retire altogether. The directors desire to record here their deep appreciation of the valuable services rendered by Mr Barnes during his long connection with the company."

James Richardson first moved a resolution that Sir R. A. Cunliffe and Dr Edward Davies be re-elected as directors, and that a vote of thanks of the shareholders be given to the Board for their services during the past year. He then said that on behalf of his father he wanted to thank the Chairman, his fellow directors and the shareholders for the kind things they had said about him. He was very sorry that his father had been forced to give up his business affairs. The decision to do this had taken a great deal of serious consideration but it had been thought necessary, not only where the Provincial Company was concerned, but also with every other company with which his father was involved. The family was very gratified to feel that what his father had done for the Provincial and other companies had been appreciated and recognized. He would be pleased to pass on to his father that they felt very keenly the loss caused by his retirement.

At the Thirty-sixth Annual General Meeting on Friday 8 March 1889 the Chairman of the Company was still Sir Richard Venables Kyrke. James Richardson again spoke at the meeting and referred briefly to his father's many years with the company. Thomas had served as Chairman of the Company for nearly forty years and they always seemed very pleased with their choice of Chairman. In the early years, in 1864, for example, they commented that he "had in his usually clear, satisfactory and able manner, shown the good points that belonged to the company and the stability upon which their prospects rested", and that he was a man with a "high commercial position, and well-known integrity, who had amassed a fortune through the successful management of his own affairs". They obviously had continued to be satisfied with him over the next twenty or so years.

CHAPTER 20

1887–April 1897

The final years.

During the last ten years of Thomas's life his health began to fail and he suffered from a complicated set of ailments following a series of debilitating strokes. He was in the south of England in February 1887, apparently unwell, and by the following February was in such

Thomas Barnes in old age

poor health that he had to resign as Chairman of the Provincial Assurance Company. The onset of all this would appear to have coincided with the death of his third wife. After that he was no longer able to visit his home in Farnworth and could only leave the house for short drives during the finest weather in summer. However, he had a very strong constitution and received round-the-clock nursing care and frequent visits from his doctor, Dr Hughes of Oswestry.

On Thursday 17 April 1890 he was fit enough to attend the evening Recognition Service for the new minister at the Quinta Church, Rev. W. E. Hughes. The minister before him, Rev. Edward Place, had resigned the previous November. Thomas's son and daughter-in-law and his great-nephew Harold Barnes and his wife were also present and played their parts in the service.

On 7 June 1890 a public notice appeared in *The Wrexham Advertiser* announcing the names of subscribers to a testimonial to John Francis, the secretary of the Provincial Insurance Company. Thomas and James Richardson had both promised to subscribe £5.

On the afternoon of Thursday 14 August 1890 Thomas allowed the Lodge and Bronygarth Cottagers' Flower Show to be held in Quinta Park. He and James Richardson and Ellen were amongst the many visitors.

When the Census was taken on 5 April 1891 Thomas was at home at The Quinta. It was now four years after he made his Will, eleven years after his second wife Ann died and four and a half years after his third wife's death. He was 78 years old and described in the Census as a JP and cotton spinner. Limefield House in Farnworth was still being run by a housekeeper, a housemaid and a cook. They were no longer the same women who had had charge of the house in 1881. The housekeeper was 59–year-old Sarah Hume from Scotland who had worked for Thomas at The Quinta at least since 1871. The housemaid, Wilhelmina Brown, also came from Scotland. The cook, Jane Fletcher, was from Wigan. I wonder how often members of the family used the house?

His son James Richardson and his daughter-in-law Ellen were living with him in Quinta Hall. James Richardson, now Lieutenant-Colonel Barnes, was described as a JP and cotton spinner. There were two visitors staying in the house at the time who reflected the family's love of music—35–year-old Mrs Mary Elizabeth Davies, a vocalist, and her 23–year-old unmarried relative, Gwen Ellen Davies, a teacher of singing. Both women were born in London. The Hall was full of servants: Elizabeth Siddel, a nurse for Thomas, Margaret Pears, a lady's help, a cook, a waitress, two housemaids, a kitchen maid and a pantry boy. Edward Hughes, the estate bailiff, an elderly widower aged 80, lived with his unmarried daughter in a small four-roomed cottage, Quinta Lodge. James Louden, the Head Gardener, still lived with his wife and five children in Gardener's House. He was already 60 years old, his wife 58, and his children's ages ranged from 29 to 11. All five children, including the youngest son, Alexander, who was listed as an imbecile, appeared to be employed as assistant road surveyors. There were also two younger gardeners living in separate accommodation. Two grooms lived in the Quinta stables. A 45–year-old man who lived with his widowed sister-in-law in Quinta Cottage also worked as a groom and gardener. His sister-in-law, Martha Lloyd, was the head of the household and described herself as a blacksmith. Her eldest son, Frederick William, aged 19, was also a blacksmith. There were also three unmarried daughters aged 19, 15 and 13, the youngest still a scholar. In and around Quinta Hall Thomas was, therefore, providing work and accommodation for at least twenty-six people. The minister of the Quinta Church, William E. Hughes, lived in the Manse. The Church was flourishing. The original small band of nine Church members now numbered around fifty-four. Not only that, but because the congregation did not have to pay the minister's salary or the cost of running the church building, in 1891 the Quinta Church was able to fund its own missionary, Mr W. E. McFarlane, to go out to Mongolia. When he had to return to England for health reasons he was replaced at the mission in Mongolia by Rev. T. Cochrane.

An entry in Worrall's 1891 *Directory of Cotton Spinners* reveals how big the business in Farnworth with its four mills now was:

Thomas Barnes & Co., Limited, Farnworth Cotton Mills

56,674 spindles, 168/308 weft and twist; 1,800 looms, cords, swansdown, moleskin, grey and white twills, etc.

Pay day at the Manchester warehouse, 21 Marsden Square, on the last Friday, and at Gladstone Road Mill, Farnworth, on the following day.

Telegrams "Barnes, Farnworth" "Cords, Manchester".

Edwin Whittaker, Secretary

In May 1892 electric lights were installed at Quinta Hall by the firm of Verity and Co. of London. The event was of such interest that it was reported in the local paper.

Thomas was still linked to Liberal politics but whether he took an active part in the local Liberal association, I do not know. He was re-elected as one of the Vice-Presidents at the Annual Meeting of the East Denbighshire Liberal Association held on the evening of Tuesday 10 November 1891 at the Reform Club in Wrexham.

When the Second Ceiriog Vale Industrial, Art and Loan Exhibition was held at the Quinta on 22 August 1892 the items on loan in the art and museum sections were displayed in Quinta Hall. Thomas, described as "the Squire of The Quinta", was the main contributor of paintings and had also lent various items including a coat which once belonged to the Emperor of China.

I happened to find an item on the internet about a sideboard belonging to Thomas Barnes at The Quinta. It went up for auction in the USA in 1993 and was described as Lot 246: A large oak sideboard 1852, the design attributed to A. W. N. Pugin. Further details were given: "Superstructure with crocketed finials above linenfold panelling carved with the initials EB flanked by pierced vine and grape above three drawers and two cupboards with canted sides. 160cm high, 274cm wide, 84cm deep (5'5" x 9' x 2'9"). Provenance: Thomas Barnes, Quinta Hall, Weston Rhyn, Oswestry, Shropshire 1852. By descent until 1927. (Purchased from Quinta Hall by a relative of the present owner.) The maker of the Quinta cupboard is unrecorded, but it is likely to have been either Gillow of Lancaster or J. G. Crace, both of whom worked for Pugin on the Palace of Westminster commission, and continued to produce furniture to his designs following his death in 1852. Gillow would have been an obvious choice for a patron of Lancastrian origin, but the Pugin-designed furnishings and decorations at nearby Leighton Hall, which include polychrome plaster ceilings of virtually identical design to those at The Quinta, were executed by J. G. Crace." Some biographical details about Thomas were included which added information about the building of Quinta Hall: "Thomas Barnes was a wealthy cotton manufacturer from Bolton in Lancashire who represented the city as Liberal member from 1852–7 and again from 1861–8. In 1852 he purchased and demolished the old Quinta Hall, ancestral seat of the West family, and raised a new house on the same site in the fashionable Gothic style, doubtless inspired by A. W. N. Pugin's Palace of Westminster which Barnes first entered that year. Indeed Pugin had designed the interiors of two houses adjacent to Quinta Hall, namely Chirk Castle (1845–8) and Leighton Hall (1850–6) and so in his choice of the Gothic style it would appear that Barnes was conforming to a local precedent." The sideboard had been dated in this sale as 1852. Presumably this date was correct unless it was based on the interpretation of the initials EB. This was wrong. It confused Thomas's wife, Ann, with his son's wife

Ellen, and also must have been based on the incorrect obituary in the Bolton newspaper which named Thomas's second wife as Elizabeth Knowles. "The sideboard incorporates the initials EB, which also appear on the plaster ceiling in the dining room at Quinta Hall, and are likely to be those of Ellen Barnes, (née Knowles), whom Thomas Barnes married as his second wife in 1850." In fact, the initials are more likely to be those of Ellen Barnes (née Cheetham), the wife of Thomas's son, James Richardson, who inherited The Quinta after her husband's death. The sideboard probably moved with the couple into The Quinta from Brookside when they went to live there.

On Tuesday 3 April 1893 the firm in Lancashire suffered another serious fire, this time at their warehouse in Marsden Square, Manchester. There was a report of the fire in *The Manchester Times* on the following Saturday: "Shortly after six pm on Tuesday, smoke was discovered emanating from the windows of the warehouses of Messrs T. Barnes & Co, Ltd (Farnworth), Marsden Square, in this city, and Messrs Walter Albrecht & Co. (Leeds) in Cannon Street. The two buildings form part of the same block and between them are premises occupied by Mr Abraham Barlow and others. All the firms are connected with the Manchester cloth trade. The fire brigade were quickly on the spot, and soon gained entrance to the premises of Messrs T. Barnes & Co, while, by the use of the fire escape, firemen speedily smashed a number of windows to let out the blinding, suffocating smoke. Marsden Square and the portion of Cannon Street adjacent were in a short time thronged by vast crowds of onlookers, who watched the operations of the firemen with much interest. The man on duty at the Piccadilly station was the first to be informed of the outbreak. This part of the premises extends into an adjoining street opening into Market Street. The firemen, having gained access to the building, got a jet to work. Shortly afterwards Mr Savage and the brigade arrived from the chief fire station with a steamer, a hand engine, and three tenders. Owing to the dense smoke the firemen had a difficult task, but they conquered in a manner which calls for special commendation. At one time it was feared that a serious conflagration would be the result. By dint of undaunted perseverance in getting at the locale of the fire, and after working about half an hour, the flames were subdued. It was then found that considerable damage had been done by fire and water to the back part of the two lower floors and their contents, and also to the floor above by heat and smoke. The articles burnt were chiefly fustians and cords. The origin of the outbreak has not been ascertained."

In 1893 Farnworth Council bought from Thomas Barnes and others over an acre of land and property known as Birch Hall and Gladstone Villa for £3,500 with a view to extending the Park at some future date.

On 13 June 1895 Thomas did not go to Farnworth for the unveiling of the monument to him in the Park. He was represented by his son. However, he did appear in the garden at The Quinta in August that year when the Weston Rhyn and Bronygarth Flower Show was held there.

Thomas died peacefully at The Quinta at quarter to ten on Saturday night, April 24 1897, in his 85th year, after having been unconscious for most of the day. A week before his death he contracted influenza which a number of the residents at The Quinta, including his valet and a nurse, had been suffering from. On the night before his funeral Rev. W. E. Hughes preached at a memorial service at the Quinta Congregational Church. The following account of Thomas's funeral is based on two newspaper reports, one from *The Border Counties Advertiser* and the other from an unknown source, probably a Farnworth or Bolton paper. His death was also reported in the Obituary Columns of *The Liverpool Mercury* and *The Daily News* in London.

The funeral was held on the Wednesday following his death, 28 April 1897. His body was taken in the morning from Chirk to Bolton by train. His daughter-in-law Ellen Barnes and other mourners travelled on the same train. His son, James Richardson, was too ill to attend the funeral and had been ordered by his doctor to stay at home. (In fact, he only survived his father by two years.) The train arrived at Moses Gate Station at half past twelve and the mourners made their way to Limefield, Thomas's house in Farnworth, where his great-nephew Harold Alfred Barnes now lived. Thomas's body continued in the train to Trinity Street Station in Bolton where the undertaker who had been in charge up to that point handed over to a Bolton undertaker. The body was transferred to a hearse and taken back to Farnworth by road. The family had asked that the funeral should be "of a quiet and simple character". It was anything but.

Long before the service in the afternoon, Bolton Road and Market Street, the main streets in Farnworth, were crowded with people, many of them employees from the firm's four mills and warehouses which had stopped work for the day at noon. Almost all the residents along the route had drawn their blinds and the shutters at all the shops and businesses were closed. Irrespective of politics, creed or anything else, flags were flying at half-mast on the public buildings, at the Park which

Thomas had given to the town, on the firm's mills, the political clubs, the Sunday Schools and many other places. The police were there to keep order, as they also did later when the cortege reached the Old Independent Chapel and burial ground.

The long cortege left Limefield and went past one of the mills belonging to the business still named after him, and of which he had been the head, and past the Park which he had donated to the people of Farnworth for ever. The coffin was covered with some of the wreaths and tributes and an open landau was needed to carry all the rest of them. Eleven carriages formed the main procession—the three in front of the hearse carrying the representatives of the clergy, the law, the medical profession, politics and education. The three clergymen were the Rev. W. Hewgill, pastor of Market Street Congregational Church, who, together with the Rev. J. H. Gwyther, also represented the Lancashire Independent College, the Rev. J. F. Munro, pastor of Francis Street Congregational Church, and the Rev. W. E. Hughes, pastor of the Quinta Congregational Church. Then came the Rev. J. H. Gwyther, of Liscard, who was representing Lancashire Independent College but was there in a dual capacity as he was also the father of Mrs Harold Alfred Barnes, Thomas's great-nephew. The third carriage contained Thomas's solicitor Colonel Bailey, and Dr J. C. Clarke, his medical advisor in Farnworth, who also represented the Farnworth Liberal Association and Reform Club.

The mourners followed in eight carriages. Mrs Ellen Barnes, his son's wife, and Mrs Georgiana Barnes, the widow of his late nephew Alfred, travelled together immediately behind the hearse. Then came Alfred's son, Harold Alfred, and his wife Mary Elizabeth (née Gwyther) and their 11–year-old son, George Le Maire Barnes. The third of these carriages contained Ellen's brother, F. H. Cheetham, Alderman Alfred Topp, William Hinmers and H. Blacklock, four important family and business connections. The next carriage contained three representatives from the firm of Messrs T. Barnes & Co, Ltd: C. Young, S. Rogers and Newman. Then came representatives from The Quinta: T. Frith, W. E. Frith who was the agent at The Quinta, and James Richardson and John Jones of Orsedd Wen, two old tenants on the Quinta estate. In the fifth carriage were Messrs Kenyon, Ivers, Crossley and J. W. Watkinson; in the sixth Mrs Crompton and Miss Hume, and in the last carriage were Mr Louden, the Head Gardener at The Quinta, and Mr Jenkins, Thomas's valet.

At the end of the cortege were the private closed carriages of Mr W. Hinmers of Eccles, Mrs Alfred Barnes, Alderman Topp and Colonel Bailey, all of whom were amongst the mourners in the previous carriages.

Six of the most able-bodied of the oldest employees of the firm had been chosen to act as coffin-bearers at the chapel: S. Cooper, T. Blower, A. Whittaker, Wolfendale, W. Brooks and one other.

The procession left Limefield just before half past two and a service was conducted in the Old Independent Chapel which had been draped in black for the occasion. The three ministers conducted the service at the Chapel where Thomas had worshipped for many years, and at the graveside. He was buried in the family vault adjoining the Old Chapel. Only the mourners were allowed in the Chapel for the service apart from a few other people who were admitted by ticket. After the burial party had left again for Limefield, large numbers of people went to inspect the vault and the flowers.

The floral tributes reflected the many sides of Thomas's life. They came from family and friends: from his son and his wife, from his great-nephew H. A. Barnes and his wife, from Mr and Mrs F. Cheetham of Eastwood, and from Miss Cheetham who was living at Brookside on the Quinta estate; from friends such as Mrs Blacklock of "Sea View" in Southport, Mr and Mrs F Andrews in Ashton-under-Lyne, Mr and Mrs T. Ivers, and Mr and Mrs S. Rogers. In addition, flowers had been sent from all the departments of the firm: from the Secretary, Mr Charles H. Young, from the Counting House in Farnworth and the employees at the Manchester Warehouse, from the No. 1 Mill's weavers and mechanics and employees in the weaving, spinning and finishing departments, from No. 2 Mill's employees and those in its spinning department, from the card room and throstle room at No. 3 Mill, and from the employees in the weaving and spinning departments at No. 4 Mill. Tributes had been sent from the two Farnworth churches: from Market Street Congregational Church and from the Deacons at that church, and from the Minister and Deacons of Francis Street Congregational Church, its sister church. Another came from Rev. T. Davison who had been pastor at the Quinta Chapel for twenty years until his retirement. Flowers had been sent by the servants at Limefield, at The Quinta, and at Brookside. Many floral tributes had been sent from their neighbours at The Quinta—from Mrs G. Horsfall of Sodylt Hall, from Dr and Mrs Lloyd of Chirk, from Mr and Mrs John Evans of Brookside, from Mr Sidell at The Quinta, from Mr R and Mrs Jenkins of Rhos Cottage, from Mrs Thomas of Celyn House, from Mr Darlington of Chirk, from Mrs Lloyd and Mr and Mrs Cush. There were also flowers from Bronygarth School. And according to the report, these were just some of the many tributes received. It must have been quite a sight.

Memorial services were held on the Sunday following his death. In the morning two were taking place at the same time, one at Market Street Congregational Church in Farnworth, and the other at the Congregational Church in Ruabon in the neighbouring parish to the Quinta Chapel. Both preached from Genesis 25:8: "Abraham breathed his last and died a good old age, an old man and full of years, and was gathered to his people". The church in Ruabon was another church which Thomas had supported financially for the forty years of its existence. He had been one of the highest contributors to the building fund in the late 1850s at a time when he was also building the Quinta Chapel. In the evening the other Farnworth Church in Francis Street held their memorial service. Their Biblical text was the text which appeared on Thomas's funeral cards: "And even to your old age I am here, and even to hoar hairs will I carry you: I have made and I will bear; even I will carry and deliver you."—Isaiah 46:4.

When Thomas's Will was proved at Shrewsbury on 1 January 1898 his son, James Richardson, was the executor. His effects were valued at £11,780 14s. In December that year the Will was resworn and his effects revalued at £12,848 1s. When his son died two years later he left effects valued at over £210,333. I cannot explain this discrepancy but there is a hint in a legal document held in Oswestry Library that around 1887 when Thomas had started to be ill he was also in some sort of financial difficulty, barely solvent, and possibly bankrupt. Paragraph 3 of a document relating to some property sold by Thomas, dated 24 March 1893, reads: "The deed of 20 July 1887 being Voluntary is voidable as against a Trustee in Bankruptcy, the purchaser will therefore require to be satisfied that at the time of its execution, Mr Thomas Barnes was possessed of sufficient assets for the payment of his debts irrespective of the property comprised in the settlement." A couple of weeks later the same solicitor had more questions: "The fact that the present sale is for value would appear not to affect the question. [... ...] Can the Vendor's Solicitors assure us that Mr Thomas Barnes was solvent at the date of settlement? [... ...] Have the Trustees mortgaged the land in question for the purpose of raising money for the payment of Mr Thomas Barnes's debts?"

Barton was writing in about 1887 when he said about Thomas: "Although he does not now take as very prominent a part in the working of the mills as formerly, which he visited more or less daily, his interest, counsel, and advice at the meetings of the directors of the limited company, into which the concern a few years ago merged, are highly valued, and he may still be said to be the 'guiding star' of the extensive works." At about the same time Ernest Elliot wrote that since Thomas's health had failed his son James Richardson Barnes and Thomas Frith had been elected as deacons of the Quinta Chapel. He added: "All his friends will earnestly pray that now he is laid aside by great physical inability and entire incapacity for any active work, he may have a peaceful and happy waiting for his heavenly reward." This reminded me of Thomas's own words about Mrs Lord: "What a blessing that she has such a bright hope of the future.

> 'Like a fine setting sun
> She wakes richer in grace.'

These things tell us how *our* sands are running. When I think of the departed worthies, I sigh and feel sad."

Ernest Elliot just had time to include in his book before it went to publication: "Mr Barnes passed to his rest on 24 April 1897." Perhaps Thomas's comment on Mrs Lord is an appropriate one to end on for Thomas himself. It seems to say much more about this man's rich life than the epitaph by Nightingale in his *History of Farnworth*: "His strong personality marked him out as one of the leaders in the life of the county. He did much for the district owing to his keen interest in the welfare of the people". That is true but as I have discovered it is by no means the whole story.

Tributes paid to him at the time of his death sum up much of what I have learnt about him through a study of his life. "He was one of the most distinguished townsmen Farnworth has produced." Writing in *The Independent*, the journal of the Lancashire Independent College, Dr Rogers said: "He was one of the last survivors of a noble band of givers and workers who made Lancashire Congregationalism a power in the country." He had many qualities: a fund of good sense, wide experience, energy, devotion, and integrity, but it is nice to think he was best remembered for another quality. Rev. Munro referred to it as the affection many people in Farnworth had for him, especially those with whom he had come into contact in the early days. He said when he had heard men and women talk of those early days, what he had envied him most was not his mills, or estate, or wealth, but the place he had won in the hearts and affections of others, through faithful work in Sunday school and elsewhere. "A quality very prominent in Mr Barnes was his homeliness and approachableness. There was no stiffness about him, nor the least suspicion of affectation. He and his workpeople knew one another; there was a real link between him and those he employed." Rev. Hewgill echoed this: "His relations with his workpeople were always of a most simple and friendly character. As a citizen and neighbour he was ever ready to do what lay in his power to promote the comfort, welfare, and happiness of those among whom he lived." This also applied to his relations with his tenants on the Quinta estate. At his son's coming of age celebrations at The Quinta in December 1860 Mr R. S. Perkins, a neighbour and friend, referred to the dinner provided by Thomas on the occasion of the annual rent audit. He said: "It was my lot only a week or two ago, to receive an invitation from Mr Barnes to be present at a rent dinner, when I saw him preside at a table, with all his tenants around it. I must say that I never saw a more contented scene, and one that gave me more pleasure. A good, kindly feeling seemed to exist between landlord and tenant. I only wish that Mr Barnes's example was more generally followed,— and that their tenants could on such occasions always sit down with their landlord and enjoy a hearty meal." When Gladstone made his long speech at the opening of Farnworth Park in 1864 he, too, was referring to the same qualities when he called Thomas's gift a "wise, liberal, enlightened, and Christian act". He said: "In this busy, stirring, critical, industrious, enterprising, money-making, money-accumulating age, [... ...] it should not be forgotten that there are other wants and other interests; and, in particular, I call Mr Barnes on this occasion the representative of the deep and growing conviction with respect to the relations which ought to prevail, and that happily now do to a very great extent prevail, between the employers of labour and the labouring population of the land. [He] has not only been ministering in the act that he has done to his own benevolent instincts, and to his sense of justice to his workpeople, but he has been taking share in a great and gigantic process which aims at producing social improvements of inestimable importance to mankind." Maybe Gladstone's rhetoric was a little too effusive but there is no doubt that Thomas did make an impact on many aspects of public life, both locally and nationally.

Another tribute paid to Thomas during his lifetime was in 1865 when an article from *The Christian World* was reprinted in *The North Wales Chronicle* on 2 December 1865. He was classed as one of the "Manchester men", a term defined as "those who are engaged in the cotton trade, though very few of them are found residing in Manchester itself. They are for the most part men who have risen, and therefore without pedigree. Few of them have had a grandfather, and most of them are proud of their humble antecedents." Thomas was described as "an advanced politician". He was a close friend of Cobden and one of the active members of the Anti-Corn Law League, an advocate of voluntary education, a member of the Liberation Society, was in favour of manhood suffrage, and voted for the introduction of the Permissive Bill. "And all these," it added, "what some would designate '*ultra*' sentiments, he holds with such honesty and sincerity, and advocates with such Christian courtesy, that he secures the respect of all political parties". It continued: "May the race of such men be greatly augmented— high in station, but deep in humility; at home equally among the great and the lowly, associating with nobles, but loving to the people from whom they sprung, true to their principles, though unfashionable; not buying themselves off from active labours by lavish contributions; diligent in business, but also fervent in spirit and serving the Lord; patrons of art, science, and literature; zealous in all healthy political movements, but feeling that, above all things, "righteousness exalteth a nation, sin is the reproach of any people".

The family's cotton mills in Farnworth have vanished. In Bolton archives is a photograph taken in 1949 of the site of the demolished Barnes Mill with Francis Street Chapel in the background. Only a few piles of rubble remain. Many of the graves in the old burial ground of Halshaw Moor Chapel were moved in the 1960s when Club Monaco (later Blighty's) was built. In 1992 when Howard Lambert transcribed the monumental inscriptions in it, Quiet Walk, a narrow strip of land behind Market Street, between Church Street and Chapel Street directly opposite the Police Station, still contained thirty-one gravestones of Farnworth benefactors, moved there when the churchyard was demolished. An old people's home was built on the site of the burial ground around 2003. Few traces of the Barnes family are left in Farnworth. However, the Park which Thomas Barnes gave for the use of the people of the town "for ever" is still there. So, too, on a mound at the high end of the Park, is the Barnes Monument which was erected by Farnworth Corporation in 1895, two years before Thomas's death, to commemorate his gift of the Park. One evening, on 13 June 1895 after a meeting of the Local Board, the monument with its bronze inscribed plaque was unveiled by Alfred Topp. It was designed by Bolton architects Bradshaw & Gass and built out of York stone and red Ruabon brick. Its three tiers provided areas for planting. A London sculptor, William Charles May, modelled the bronze bas relief based on pictures supplied by the Barnes family depicting Thomas at around the time he donated the Park.

In 1953 the Town Clerk of Bolton Corporation wrote to Messrs Hulton, Bailey & Co, the family solicitors in Bolton, hoping to make contact with the Barnes family to discuss what was to be done about Farnworth Park and the memorial statue of Thomas Barnes which, they said, were "in a very neglected state". James Freeland Barnes, Thomas's great great great-nephew, was contacted and he approved the Corporation's proposals subject to one condition that the statue and the Park were put into presentable condition. In 1999 Farnworth celebrated its Sixtieth Anniversary as a Municipal Borough and plans were made to erect a memorial stone. However, a report in *The Bolton Evening News* on Saturday 26 January 2002 would indicate that nothing had happened by then: "A memorial to one of Farnworth's most famous benefactors is to take pride of place in the park he created. For years the gravestone of Thomas Barnes has been forgotten in a litter-strewn and overgrown alleyway called Quiet Walk. Councillors now plan to restore and move it to Farnworth Central Park, which was one of the nineteenth century MP's gifts to the area." A message on a more recent website reported that Thomas's gravestone had been removed by Bolton Council a few years before to protect it from vandalism as promised in 2002 and had now been repaired. However, when I contacted the Council in 2007 no site for it had been found. In August 2011 I checked again with Bolton Council but have not been able to discover what has happened to the gravestone in the intervening years. The other gravestones belonging to the Barnes family are still in the tree-lined plot of land called Quiet Alley, covered in leaf-mould and half-hidden by long grass and foliage, but Thomas's gravestone is not there. Searches are still being made for it.

However, the monument in the Park still looks down over the lawns and the trees as it has always done even if it is no longer crowned with its original globe and topped by a cross. In 2005 the condition of the monument was poor. The surface was crumbling, the bricks splitting and parts were loose. Vandals had added their graffiti. Since then, it has been repaired and it is now enclosed in sturdy iron railings. Nevertheless, there are signs even now that vandals have managed to remove some of the flagstones surrounding the base in spite of the railings. There are still some street-names in the area—Barnes Street, Limefield Avenue, Darley Street, Darley Avenue and Darley Grove in Farnworth and Summerfield Road in Great Lever—which mark the family's presence, but that is all. This once very influential family has not yet been quite forgotten, but the traces that it left are fading rapidly.

In Memoriam*
THOMAS BARNES
Died 24th April, 1897

Few be our words, but heartfelt and sincere,
For him who claims the public meed of praise,
Glad if our sons shall learn from his career
Some useful lesson for their future days.

The lowlier place he filled with mind intent,
And proved the ancient proverb's truth again,
"Seest thou a man in business diligent,
He before kings shall stand and not mean men."

Alike within his country's senate hall,
And in our busy industry's domain,
His heart was ever stirred at duty's call,
And kept in touch with human joy and pain.

Peace, honoured townsman! We this tribute pay,
Who knew thy worth, and mourn our loss today.

WILLIAM CRYER

* Composed by a local poet and printed at the end of one of the newspaper reports of his funeral.[1]

Note

1. *The Bolton Evening News,* 8.4.1897

Select Bibliography

BARNES, H. A.   *The Story of Halshaw Moor Chapel* (1908)

BARTON B. T.   *History of Farnworth and Kersley* (1887)

BARTON B. T.   *Historical Gleanings of Bolton and District* (1881)

BARTON B. T.   *History of Bury* (1874)

BEEVERS, Ken   *Farnworth* (Chalford Press, 1997)

BURTON, Anthony   *The Rise and Fall of King Cotton* (Andre Deutsch, 1984)

CLEGG, James   *Annals of Bolton* (1888)

DYSON, Simeon   *Rural Congregationalism* (1881)

ELLIOT, Ernest   *Shropshire Congregationalism* (1897)

HOWE, Anthony   *The Cotton Masters 1830–1860* (Oxford: Clarendon Press, 1984)

HURDSMAN, C. Neville   *History of the Parishes of St Martin's and Weston Rhyn* (Wrexham: Bridge Books, 2003)

LONGMATE, Norman   *The Hungry Mills—The Story of the Lancashire Cotton Famine* (London: Maurice Temple Smith Ltd, 1978)

NORMINGTON, Thomas   *An account of the rise and progress of the Lancashire and Yorkshire Railway* (Manchester: John Heywood, 1898)

RICHARDSON, H. M.   *Reminiscences of Forty Years in Bolton* (1885)

WHITTLE, Peter Armstrong   *Bolton-Le-Moors and the Townships in the Parish: An Historical, Statistical, Civil, and Moral Account of the Borough of Bolton Including a Curious Description of the Parish of Deane, Etc.* (Bolton: 1875)

Photographs and Pictures

Opening of Farnworth Park   *The Illustrated London News,* 22 October 1864, page 422

Farnworth Mills ca 1840   © Bolton Council from the Bolton Museum & Archive Collection

Thomas and Ann Barnes   © Bolton Council from the Bolton Museum & Archive Collection

James R. and Ellen Barnes   © Bolton Council from the Bolton Museum & Archive Collection

Thomas Barnes (old age)   Quinta Press

View of Quinta Church   From E. Elliot *Shropshire Congregationalism*

View of Quinta Schools   From E. Elliot *Shropshire Congregationalism*

Thomas Barnes (middle age)   From E. Elliot *Shropshire Congregationalism*

View of The Quinta   Postcard by J. Maclardy, Oswestry

Index

C

G